Ho! For Wonderland

HO! FOR WONDERLAND

TRAVELERS' ACCOUNTS OF YELLOWSTONE, 1872–1914

Edited and Annotated by
LEE H. WHITTLESEY
and
ELIZABETH A. WATRY

Foreword by
Paul Schullery

UNIVERSITY OF NEW MEXICO PRESS | ALBUQUERQUE

© 2009 by the University of New Mexico Press

All rights reserved. Published 2009

Printed in the United States of America

14   13   12   11   10   09   1   2   3   4   5   6

Library of Congress Cataloging-in-Publication Data

Ho! for wonderland : travelers' accounts of Yellowstone, 1872–1914 /

edited and annotated by Lee H. Whittlesey and Elizabeth A. Watry.

    p. cm.

Includes index.

ISBN 978-0-8263-4616-2 (hardcover : alk. paper)

1. Yellowstone National Park—Description and travel.

2. Travelers—Yellowstone National Park—History.

I. Whittlesey, Lee H., 1950–

II. Watry, Elizabeth A.

F722.H6 2009

917.87´52042—dc22

2008053299

Book design and type composition by Melissa Tandysh

Composed in 11.25/14 Dante MT Std   •   Display type is ITC Zapf Chancery Std

The world will journey to this spot more and more. The mighty pilgrimage has but just begun. It will keep moving through all ages, and each visitor will never cease to tell of the magnificent geysers, the beautiful lakes, the lovely wildwood, the sheltered nook[s], and all the countless glories of this grand spot.
—Bozeman *Avant Courier*, September 30, 1880, 1

That indescribable mountain-locked gem of the entire world!
—A Chicago, Burlington, and Quincy Railroad
writer, about Yellowstone, in *Landscape Wonders*
of the Western World (Chicago: Rand McNally, 1883)

CONTENTS

FOREWORD

PAUL SCHULLERY

ONE OF THE MANY FASCINATING THINGS ABOUT YELLOWSTONE IS that the very word has magical abilities. No matter how far you may be from the park, if you drop the word into almost any conversation with almost any group of people, it's virtually guaranteed that people will—involuntarily, it seems—say, "I went to Yellowstone once, and. . . ." From that invariable opening line, they will immediately launch into their personal Yellowstone story. Maybe it will be from the old days of roadside bears, or the newer days of charismatic wolves, or just from any day when this or that Yellowstone thing, whatever it was, happened to them. It may not even be an especially interesting story, but that doesn't matter to them because it's their own personal Yellowstone story.

An even more wonderful thing about Yellowstone is that after a hundred-million-plus visitors, all of us can still have an experience there that really is ours alone. Going there, doing whatever we do there, and turning our memories loose to frame the experience into a tale constitute a highly personal, deeply compelling thing we do. We seem to have no choice in the matter. Yellowstone is so powerful a presence that our visit is incomplete until we tell the tale.

And perhaps the most wonderful thing of all is that these millions of distinct, personal stories we tell somehow bring us together. Each of our Yellowstone stories is in fact authentically unique; there are as many Yellowstone stories as there are Yellowstone visitors. And yet having a Yellowstone story of our own gives us common ground with all those other Yellowstone story tellers. We all feel the Yellowstone magic, and we all need to share what it meant to us—to compare notes, as it were, on what this amazing place is all about.

It is this extraordinary power of the park—Yellowstone's way of becoming everyone's personal story—that makes this wonderful new book of early Yellowstone tales so engrossing and so much fun. Lee Whittlesey and Betsy Watry, thanks to their unparalleled depth of familiarity with the huge literature of the park experience, have selected just the kinds of Yellowstone tales that we can best compare with our own tales and that will cause us to dream of other tales we might hope to tell after future visits.

These are wonderful stories. From Lee's lifelong winnowing of literally thousands of firsthand accounts of Yellowstone and Betsy's lifetime passion to research Yellowstone's cultural history that became the vision for this project, the editors have chosen those narratives that not only will entertain and engage us but will also challenge us. For it is another trait of Yellowstone aficionados that we are all bearers of mighty opinions—about park policy, about management, about the service at the hotel, about the visitor in the car (or on the horse) in front of us, about the weather . . . in short, about pretty much everything we encounter.

I suppose it's because we know, on some deep level, that Yellowstone is hugely important to the world that we feel compelled to have equally important (in our minds, at least) opinions about it all. We feel obligated to react to everything we see and hear, and in this we are only honoring the great tradition of equally forceful reactions from all the generations before us. So as you read these stories, I would be most surprised if you don't find yourself reflexively jumping to agree, or argue, or otherwise continue the conversation. It all seems, after all, so important.

In real life, Lee Whittlesey has himself long been a great guide to the park, with a vast experience of the place and a formidable gift for explaining its marvels. Betsy Watry has likewise added splendidly to the book by selecting accounts for readability and eloquence and by doing further research into who these writers were. Lee and Betsy display those skills here in another way, by unobtrusively providing a wealth of helpful background information in the book's references and notes. It's easy to get a little lost in narratives from so long ago, but they see to it that in this book, at least, you will always find your way.

Enough of invitations. Turn the page, button up your duster, and embark with these tourist pioneers on the great enterprise of making the Yellowstone story your own. I envy you the journey.

Bozeman, Montana

PREFACE

WHAT DO WE MEAN BY "HO"? "HO!" WAS A NINETEENTH-CENTURY interjection commonly used in everyday speech to signify triumph, as in "Let's go!" Earlier it had been used to draw triumphant attention to something specified, as in the seafarer's phrase "Land, ho!" The Old Testament used the triumphant phrase "Ho, everyone that thirsteth, come ye to the waters" (Isa. 55:1). Later, Oregon Trail journals used the phrase in a triumphant fashion. "Ho, for California! At last we are on the way!" wrote traveler Helen Carpenter in 1857. And our phrase "Ho! for Wonderland" as an exclamation drew triumphant attention to its own specification in the 1870s—namely, Yellowstone National Park.

In these cases, "Ho!" was a term of triumph. But the term also evolved to express surprise, admiration, and even derision. Shakespeare used it in *The Merchant of Venice* to illustrate surprise when he allowed Lorenzo to say, "Ho! who's within?" Alfred Lord Tennyson used it to illustrate admiration when his character exclaimed, "Ho! for England." And the phrase "Ho! I'll show you!" illustrated taunting or derision.

The interjection "Ho!" probably became most well known when it referred to points west. Shakespeare's 1602 play *Twelfth Night* seems to have originated the phrase "Westward, ho!" to refer to a journey "west" toward death, as analogized to the sun setting in the west. In the play Olivia says to Viola, "There lies your way, due west." "Then westward-ho!" replies Viola. "Grace and good disposition attend your ladyship." In 1604, writer John Webster used "Westward, ho!" as the title of his play. In that production, boatmen on the Thames River shout the phrase to refer to the direction of travel on the river. Metaphorically, the reference was to London's evolving journey toward a more democratic and

Ho for Wonderland!

AND THE

Mammoth Hot Springs.

I am now prepared to carry INVALIDS and PLEASURE PARTIES to the celebrated Mammoth Hot Springs of Horr & McCartney, and othe points in the

NATIONAL PARK.

G. W. A. FRAZIER'S four-horse conveyance will leave Bozeman weekly, or oftener if necessary, connecting with my trains at the Yellowstone Canyon.

For terms apply to Gov. Williams, Exchange, Saloon, Bozeman, M. T.   JOHN WERKS.
31tf

Ho! for the Great

WONDERLAND

——THE——

Yellowstone National Park,

——OR THE——

Great American Wonderland,

A New, Complete and Accurate Description of the

NATIONAL PARK AND ALL ITS WONDERS,

Written in the Order of a Tour by

⇒W. W. WYLIE, B. S., A. M.⇐

Who has Made Three Complete Tours of

WONDERLAND

FOR THE EXPRESS PURPOSE OF PREPARING A RELIABLE BOOK.

Ho!. For The Yellowstone Park.

All you people that want to go and see the Wonderland of the World can save time and money by calling on AL. BRUNDAGE & CO. for your transportation in the Park. We will furnish you any kind of an outfit you want. We have tents, cots and bedding, saddles, packs and cooking outfits. Buy your own provisions and camp where you please, this is the only proper way to see the Park. Now the Transportation Company will tell you that there is no Outside or Private Conveyance. Now don't you let them rob you by paying their prices.

We will let you have a four-horse team for $10 per day and a two-horse surry for $8 per day. We carry five persons in the four-horse teams and three in the two-horse wagons. Our wagons are not handsome to look at but they are comfortable and easy and if you go with us we will guarantee you a pleasant trip.

We have been guiding tourists for nine years and think we know the Park. Give us a call and save your time and money.

AL. BRUNDAGE & CO.,

CINNABAR, MONTANA.

HO FOR THE PARK!

I Am Prepared

—TO FURNISH—

GOOD TURN OUTS

—AND—

EXCELLENT GUIDES

To those who contemplate making a tour of the National Park during the summer of 1891.

References, National Park Bank. · : · Correspondence Solicited.

Wm. A. HALL, Gardiner, Mont.

FIGURE P.I.

Authors of these early advertisements proclaimed to the world that they were ready to take tourists to Yellowstone National Park. They were John Werks in Harry Norton's *Wonderland-Illustrated* (1873), W. W. Wylie in *The Yellowstone National Park or the Great American Wonderland* (1882), Al Brundage in a handbill "Ho! For the Yellowstone Park" (archive document 672, n.d. [probably 1893]), and William A. Hall in a broadside marked "summer of 1891." (Dean Larsen collection, Brigham Young University, Provo.)

equitable state. The west side of the city was apparently a newer and wilder place and, hence, more egalitarian.

Travelers carried Shakespeare's phrase "Westward, ho!" from England to points farther west. Writer Charles Kingsley used it in his 1855 novel *Westward, Ho!* to refer to the trip from Britain to the New World ("the heaven-prospered cry of Westward-Ho!"), and James K. Paulding used it in his 1832 book of the same title to characterize the trip west from the U.S. East Coast to the Ohio Country.

We are tempted of course to believe that uses of our Yellowstone phrase "Ho! for Wonderland" contained a grain of the same philosophy that John Webster and his London boatmen trumpeted, namely, the idea that Yellowstone and the American West could give Mr. Traveler Everyman a new, independent, egalitarian "lease on life" in what some saw as an inherently more democratic place. In the West, it seemed that everyone was more equal, as the rigors of travel seemed to reduce social boundaries among travelers. As a phrase, "Ho! for Wonderland" cried out to everyone an invitation to revel in the western escapade, transcending boundaries of class, gender, and race.

For us, the phrase "Ho! for Wonderland" thus signifies not only triumph but also equality along the way. And to be sure, the phrase resonates with more than just the journey; it beckons the adventurer to consciously savor the essence of Yellowstone.

Authors' disclaimer: The visitors in these accounts traveled through Yellowstone National Park at a very different time in history. Feeding animals, walking on formations, cutting trees, picking flowers, collecting specimens, throwing objects into geysers and hot springs, destroying natural or cultural objects, and washing clothes in, cooking in, and swimming in hot springs are all today strictly prohibited by the National Park Service.

Introduction

Travel and America's First National Park

—∞∞∞—

YELLOWSTONE BECAME THE WORLD'S FIRST NATIONAL PARK IN 1872 and, remarkably, achieved nationwide fame almost immediately, primarily because journalists and other writers reported on the discoveries of the 1870 Washburn party and the 1871 Hayden survey. Reporters and exploration party members told the nation about those discoveries in major U.S. newspapers like the *New York Times, Chicago Evening Journal,* and *Frank Leslie's Illustrated* and in then-popular magazines like *Scribner's Monthly* and *Overland Monthly.* Soon after, newspapers all over the country picked up these exciting chronicles of exploration. In the West, the *Daily Oregonian* and the *Deseret Evening News* were only two of the newspapers that carried early information. Some intrepid travelers made the difficult horse trip to the new Yellowstone place and wrote of their accounts in books like Harry Norton's *Wonderland-Illustrated* (1872), James Richardson's *Wonders of the Yellowstone* (1873), and Edwin Stanley's *Rambles in Wonderland* (1878). Even as early 1872, the editor of a Wisconsin newspaper was proclaiming that a long-distance trip was the new requirement for esteem and learning in America and was listing Yellowstone first in a series of desirable places to go. "Now it is the Yellowstone, the Yosemite, or Europe, Paris, Venice, Florence, Naples or Rome," wrote this editor, instead of "baptism [as] the thing most needed to make a person respectable."[1] As early as March 12, 1873, the *New York Times* declared that "it is only necessary to render the Park easily accessible to make it the most popular summer resort in the country."

It did not take long for photographers and lecturers to take their turns at spreading the word about the strange and wondrous Yellowstone. America's new park quickly became world famous as well as nationally famous. Books like the Earl of Dunraven's *The Great Divide* and American reports republished by the newspapers of Europe such as *The Times* and the *Illustrated London Times* spread the word. By the time a railroad arrived at Yellowstone in 1883, the place was already legendary. In sum, it is amazing how quickly Yellowstone became famous.

Travelers to Yellowstone at this early time faced a 5 ¼-day stagecoach trip that was hot, dusty, and tiring at six miles per hour. They stayed in relatively primitive hotels and tent camps or camped out along the way, an even more challenging endeavor. Some visitors, such as British writer Rudyard Kipling, did not like anything about the new American wonderland, but most found at least a bit of it enjoyable.

Nineteenth-century readers devoured these travelers' newspaper and magazine articles about trips to Yellowstone, and those accounts appeared in the newspapers of all fifty states and other countries. Long forgotten, many of these stories have been gradually rediscovered as historians find them hidden in archives, in family papers, and most recently in digitized newspapers now available on the Internet.

FIGURE INTRO.1.

This 1898 map shows the towns along the Northern Pacific's route and both Cinnabar and Gardiner as well as "Mammoth Hot Springs Hotel," "Norris Hotel," "Fountain Hotel," and a hotel at Old Faithful. Strangely, Shoshone Point and Lake View are shown with hotel blocks, even though there were no hotels at those places. "Lake Hotel," "Canon Hotel," and a "Lunch Station" at West Thumb are also shown, along with "Yancey's Camp." The west and south entrance roads had appeared, along with the late-coming P. W. Norris's plateau road to Lower Basin, but no east entrance road was present at this time. (Northern Pacific Railroad, *Wonderland '98,* Yellowstone National Park Library, Yellowstone National Park.)

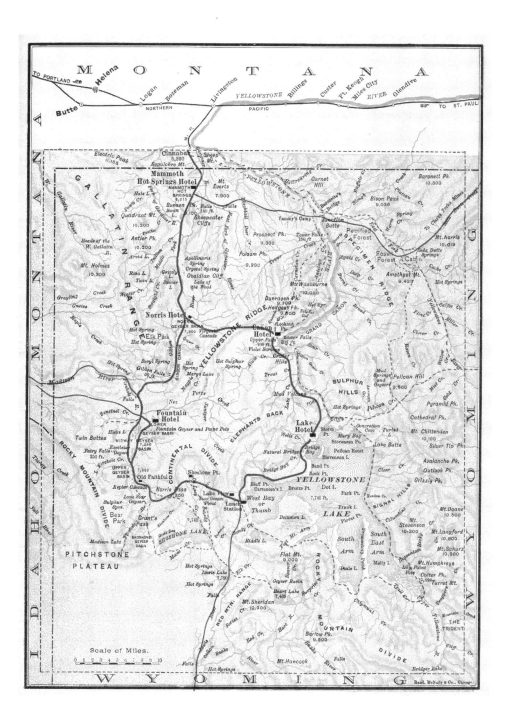

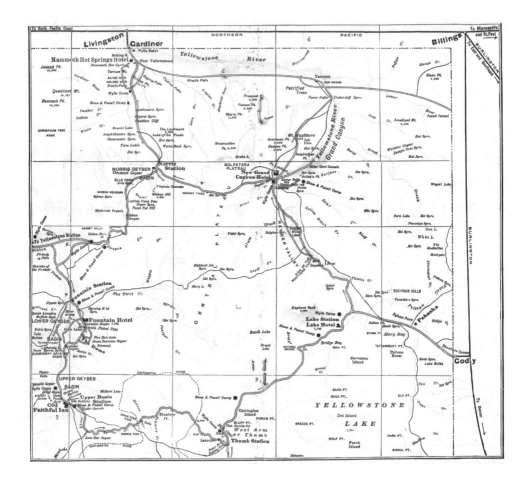

FIGURE INTRO.2.

This 1916 map represents the culmination of Yellowstone's stagecoach-era facilities. Hotels are shown at Mammoth, Fountain, Old Faithful, Lake, and Canyon but strangely not at Norris. In addition to the "Wylie Hotel" at Gardiner, Wylie camps are shown at Swan Lake Flats, Sleepy Hollow, Riverside, Old Faithful, West Thumb, Lake, and Canyon, with Shaw/Powell camps at Willow Park, Gibbon Falls, Nez Perce Creek, Old Faithful Lodge site, Little Thumb Creek, Bridge Bay, and Canyon Lodge site. Yancey's is shown even though it had long been closed, along with Pahaska on the east entrance road. (Chicago, Burlington, and Quincy Railroad, *The Cody Road to Yellowstone Park 1916*, University of Wyoming, Laramie.)

Such is the case with the nineteen accounts we present here. Intended for casual readers and general wilderness aficionados as well as certified Yellowstone experts, these accounts range in time from very early (1873) to near the end of Yellowstone's stagecoach era (1914). We selected these from literally thousands of known Yellowstone accounts for their readability, eloquence, unusualness, and appeal to general readers. We chose accounts written by persons of varying social backgrounds who traveled using various stagecoach companies with various touring arrangements through varying park entrances and in both small and large groups. As we found these, we discovered that the writers were often persons of education and even some renown in their day. While they were not famous people, such as those saluted by Paul Schullery in his 1972 book, *Old Yellowstone Days*, these authors were the next best thing. Most of these accounts have never before been cited by historians, let alone studied by them, and this fact alone—that the accounts represent "new" history—makes them worthy of study as examples of early Yellowstone tours.

So what is and was a typical Yellowstone tour? Although some historians have tried to make the case that every (or most) Yellowstone tours were the same or similar, we disagree. Anyone who has ever served as a tour guide in the park knows better. Every tour is different in features seen, stops made, method of conveyance used, entrances entered and exited, hotels stayed in, campgrounds utilized, direction of travel experienced, comrades traveled with, and interesting characters encountered.

Did the accounts published here help to make Yellowstone more famous? Undoubtedly even the ones published in obscure newspapers did, especially when their authors were estimable persons of reputation. And even Yellowstone's most lowly visitors, if they left a published account, must have influenced a few (or even many) newspaper buyers who read their accounts. All of those (and these!) writers spread the word so widely about Yellowstone that by 1897, the park was a grand, tourist success with more than ten thousand visitors passing through its "gates." "Would Yellowstone equal its reputation?" wondered visitor Elizabeth Rowell in 1907, but based solely on the Mammoth Hot Springs alone, her party soon "no longer questioned" the park's "right to fame." Her account agreed with an early assessment that has been reproduced in this book: "About 8 o'clock A.M. we went close up to THE

FAMOUS OLD FAITHFUL."[2] Indeed, to that 1873 writer, Old Faithful was *already famous!*

Come with us now and experience a bit of life during America's horse-and-buggy era and learn why and how these early visitors reacted to an already famous place. Learn about Yellowstone when its visitors numbered in the hundreds and thousands, rather than in the millions. Read about these early visitors' impressions of a place that welcomed tourists from all corners of the globe. Discover why they and many others decided that Yellowstone was in fact deserving of recognition, thus joining legions of other Yellowstone visitors who ultimately made it a "pilgrimage" site and made "Wonderland" one of the most famous places in the world.

Notes

1. *Janesville (WI) Gazette*, March 28, 1872, 1.
2. Elizabeth Rowell, "Ten Days in the Yellowstone," *Alaska-Yukon Magazine*, August 1907, 475; "One of the Scramblers" [Granville Stuart?], "Scrambles in Wonderland," 1873, this volume, emphasis added.

ONE

Scrambles in Wonderland

"One of the Scramblers"

[GRANVILLE STUART?]

1873

THIS 1873 ACCOUNT REPRESENTS ONE OF THE EARLIEST recorded trips to the new Yellowstone National Park, and it is unusual for being a very long and detailed account. The author was probably Granville Stuart, one of Montana Territory's most famous citizens. His party included other well-known pioneers who traveled together to Yellowstone early in its history—only one year after the new national park was established. The writer stated that the final party was made up of twenty persons, and he named sixteen of them. While at one point he mentioned that "Granville Stuart, C. A. McCabe, and W. W. Dixon, were ahead of me," we believe that he included himself there as merely a way of telling us who the party members were while possibly keeping his own identity secret (although for what reason we do not know). At later places in his text, the writer conveniently eliminated others as potential authors by listing them as accompanying him on side trips, although his use of his own name admittedly complicated our attempt at author identification. Stuart was living in Deer Lodge in 1873 and so was in place to have given this written account to the Deer Lodge newspaper.

Granville Stuart (1834–1918) was one of Montana's earliest and most famous citizens. Sometimes called "Mr. Montana," he claimed to have

FIGURE I.I.
Granville Stuart was one of Montana Territory's earliest settlers. This photo
was taken later in his life, long after he made one of the state's earliest gold
strikes in 1858 and traveled to Yellowstone in 1873. (www.mtbeef.org/.)

been descended from Mary Stuart, Queen of Scots. Arriving in the territory in the late 1850s, he prospected near present Deer Lodge and was
present during Virginia City's famous "vigilante days and ways." He
stayed in Montana for the rest of his life, producing in 1865 one of the territory's earliest books, *Montana As It Is*, and the important two-volume
set about his life entitled *Forty Years on the Frontier* (1925). Interestingly, at
the time of his Yellowstone trip Montanans were suffering through an
economic downtown known as the "Panic of 1873," and Granville Stuart

had just experienced the death of his brother, James Stuart. So perhaps the trip to the park was therapeutic for him.

The party traveled from Deer Lodge, Montana, to Virginia City to Yellowstone via the west entrance. Its sixteen members were Granville Stuart; Wilbur Fiske Sanders; (Judge) Hiram Knowles; W. H. Todd; C. A. McCabe; W. W. Dixon; Robert Miller; D. P. Newcomer; T. T. Frazier; Mr. Robbins, a journalist, "late of New York City"; Charles Asphing; the Rev. Edwin J. Stanley; Miss Mary Clark; Dick Dickenson; Pat Ryan; and a Mrs. Birdseye of Blackfoot City, Montana.

We thought originally that the writer of this unauthored piece might have been Stuart's friend Hiram Knowles, a Montana judge who lived in Deer Lodge like Stuart, but discussions with two other Montana historians convinced us that Knowles did not have the poeticism in his nature to write this account. They believe that this account was authored by Stuart, and so do we.

In November, after Stuart returned from the park, he wrote to the Department of the Interior asking for permission for a lease to erect a hotel in the park and noting that from his hotel he could help "prevent visitors from mutilating or despoiling the objects of interest there."[1] Unfortunately, interior officials and Superintendent N. P. Langford treated Sanders's request in the same manner as many others. No one was given a hotel lease until 1880 in the park, although James McCartney operated his crude hotel at Mammoth by simply squatting there.

The writer of this account stated near the end of the piece that his motivation for writing was simply "to portray a glimpse of Wonderland"—that Yellowstone place that even by 1873 was becoming famous.

Number I

New Northwest, Deer Lodge, Montana, October 4, 1873

GETTING UNDER WAY.

The fourth day out from Deer Lodge, we rode into Virginia City. The day was hot, the road dusty. A few of the party had gone forward in advance of the train to purchase supplies, not expecting the rest to reach the city that evening. But finding grass scant, it was decided by the vanguard about 4 P.M. to drive briskly for the city, twelve miles distant. Then followed some lively whooping up.

ALDER GULCH

Echoed and re-echoed to such names as "Sunflower," "Bucephalus," "Toby," "Samantha," &c, calling up a scene we imagined must have often occurred in the palmy days of Alder. Of former prosperity, many vestiges remain in this famous gulch. Now, however, deserted habitations, with a few scattered squads of "Celestials," render it desolate, indeed, though still eloquent of a "day that is dead."[2]

THE CAPITAL CITY,

At first sight, seemed to share in the decay so prominently depicted in the gulch below. Unsightly hovels, dilapidated and tenantless, are grouped without order in ravines and over ridges. Suddenly reaching Wallace street, the aspect changed, and as we rode up the sloping thoroughfare, many fine, commodious business houses were seen grouped on either side, while on the higher ground above, tasteful residences bespoke of that refinement and liberality which prosperity eliminates. Here we met Judge [Hiram] Knowles of Deer Lodge, Col. [Wilbur Fiske] Sanders and W. H. Todd, Esq. of Helena, Mr. Robbins, late of New York City, and others, who became members of the excursion party, which on starting again numbered twenty.[3]

The next morning, Friday, Aug. 22d, was rainy. Having good accommodations and square meals at the "Crescent," the boys found agreeable companionship in old time friends, among whom Harry Norton, Esq., of the *Montanian*, evinced conspicuous courtesy.[4] After dinner, the clouds being rifted with sunshine, we started

OFF FOR THE MADISON [RIVER],

And, after scrambling over some pretty steep hills, were overtaken on the divide by a [rain] shower. Here we beheld a vision of peerless beauty. It was one of those chance scenes which nature often presents among lofty mountains through a happy combination of her ever-shifting elements, but which man seldom sees, owing to the fortuitous relation of the observer and the thing observed. In this instance, the sharp, serrated, inaccessible peaks and ridges of the Madison range east of the river, burst suddenly into view; while around and above, earth and sky were shadowed in gloom by lowering rain clouds, riven, ever and anon, by the flame-eyed messengers of Jove. Thus drearily surrounded, the low western sun blazed full on the distant picturesque mountain, lending it a more than earthly radiance. It was a scene that could be felt. We thought of

BUNYAN'S DELECTABLE MOUNTAINS,[5]

While we gazed with a silent satisfaction such as thirsty souls would feel, we fancy, in quaffing the Elixir of Life. In a few moments the glory of the vision had departed—the mellow-tinted sunlight had vanished, leaving the castellated mountain range grim, somber, [and] sullenly inglorious.

Just before us in the valley, on a small stream called Spring Creek, stood a log cabin, which attracted our attention, because the weather signs indicated an unpropitious night. Approaching, we discovered that some party had possession in advance of us, but being beckoned forward by friendly gestures, we soon recognized Col. [W. F.] Sanders and others, who had started earlier in the day.

A BUSY CAMP

Scene followed. The wood pile with abundance of chips favoring our wishes, fires soon blazed cheerfully athwart the gathering darkness; while cabin, milk house, wood-shed, stable—in fact, every available roof-tree was appropriated. Though there were fresh evidences of an owner somewhere, no one seemed to care particularly who had furnished the hut or planted the fields—we had unmolested possession. A sheet iron stove and various kitchen utensils were put in service in preparing supper, though someone with acute olfactory perception declared there was an ill-favored, caninal odor about the premises. No matter, "out of the rain" was realized; blankets were spread on the dirt floor; song and jest and laughter went around; when abruptly as

THE APPARITION OF POE'S RAVEN,

There came a form to the door, dark as Erebus, and, for a moment, stood [as] silent and ominous as that portentous bird of yore.[6] It was the dumb struck owner of the premises—"struck with establishment" at our impertinent intrusion, as was observed with true Partingtonian speech by "our Ike."[7] On recovering speech, this descendent of Ham[8] hesitatingly exclaimed: "Why, gracious sakes, gemmen, I didn't 'spect so much company no how!" Explanations followed, and we were indebted to the hospitality of Mr. Roberts (colored) for lodging.

Up the Madison, which at this section has a remarkably straight and even current, and [our trip]

OVER TO HENRY LAKE

Occupied two days. The lake, for scenic attractions, is hardly worth the deflection made to reach it. Its sedgy shores, however, afford a covert for numerous flocks of aquatic fowls, while the waters abound in large mountain trout, which may be speared by torchlight with abundant success, as proved by the young man at Sawtelle's,[9] who, in an hour or so of the evening we spent there, speared more fish than our whole party cared to eat or carry away.

IN THE CANYON OF THE MADISON

We enjoyed some rugged scenery. The upper canyon, especially, is diversified by precipitous cliffs, densely-wooded slopes, darkly green with fine foliage, and rocky chasms through which the river rushes with foaming impetuosity. One feature at the upper end of the canyon is worthy of especial mention. Passing around an abrupt curve, the attention of the whole party was drawn to a rocky prominence to our right across the river, upon which stood out in bold relief against the horizon a sculpturesque bust, having a profile so strikingly perfect that all agreed no elaborate work of art could more justly represent the features of man at such an elevation. Looking at this rocky projection down the river, after passing it, the illusion was dispelled. Just above, we crossed the East Fork of the Madison, and after climbing a rough trail through thick timber many miles, following up the Fire Hole Fork, entered upon the Lower Geyser Basin. Some ludicrous scenes occurred here while [we were]

HUNTING A CAMP.

Two of our titled and more adventurous comrades, pressing too hastily upon pastures fair but all untried, found in dismay they were swiftly sinking in the soft clay deposits of a recent formation. Suddenly unhorsed, there was some animated scrambling to get away from their plunging steeds, which came out in the struggle painted with delicate tints of pink and yellow, yet all unharmed. Retreating to more firm founda-tions, [we noticed that] packs were released from the inexorable grip of the "diamond hitch," and all rushed forth to the hot spring and gey-ser mounds, where rose, from earth to sky, innumerable white steamy pillars, whose Gothic, Ionic and Composite capitals, in this imaginary architecture, were the fleecy clouds of heaven.

Number II

New Northwest, October 11, 1873

THE GEYSER BASINS

A grassy valley, averaging one to two miles in width, between hills thickly wooded with small pine trees, and drained by the Fire Hole River, is presented. Clumps of small timber intersperse the grass plats on every side. Between the Upper and Lower Basins there intervenes eight miles of wooded valley, quite free from Hot Springs or Geysers. The Fire Hole fork of the Madison is clear, cold and rapid, average[s] thirty to forty feet in width, and bears northward. These are general characteristics. The special feature of the Lower Basin is the

HOT SPRINGS

Which abound in such variety that a full description would require a volume. Some groups are marked by white silicious mounds covering several acres of ground; others occur in the most unlooked for places—skirting a patch of timber, on the brink of the river, in the nook of the forest—everywhere they present features of weird novelty. Columns of dense steam arise from many whirled off by the fearful commotion of boiling waters, while others, less hot, look as serene as a placid lake. The hot springs, almost universally, are like ponds, margined with delicate silicate formations.

FINELY BLENDING [sic—BLENDED] TINTS AND HUES

Adorn their cavernous depths in which spongiform masses of rare elegance are revealed, extending into fathomless leagues of ethereal water. Their outflow is usually a small channel encased with pearly silicate, but some overflow their rims almost uniformly, thus spreading the drainage thinly over much surface. As the water cools, a growth of exceedingly delicate diatoms [bacteria] takes place which fascinate the beholder with an indescribably beautiful glow of brilliant colors. Liquid fire could not exceed these shimmering corruscations. Indeed, it seemed to me, with favorable relations of sunshine, these lustrous colors were the most fascinating sights presented by hot springs.

Rambling alone on the west side of the river, to which, several of us, finding a favorable place had waded, I saw at mid day visions of surpassing beauty in the clear, deep,

FAIRY LIKE CHAMBERS

Of many large springs a few rods distant from the river. In one were seen all the varieties of blue, from the darkest shades of indigo to the lightest tints of sky-blue. The rock on the vaulted cavities seem checkered with geometric cleavage which fairly scintillates with dazzling brightness as the spring's surface ripples to the light breeze. In another spring yellow tints and shades present the same enchanting appearance of radiant cross lines inclosing squares of intense depth of coloring. Springs of variegated green and other colors show a similar fantastic arrangement. In most deep springs, however, the prevalent color is blue.

The most noticeable group in the Lower Basin is situated on

A WHITE MOUND

East of the river and about a mile distant from it.[10] Here are several geysers of moderate power, and numerous boiling springs. Fifty or more acres, quite destitute of vegetation, are thus occupied, being covered with a white silicious incrustation which is constantly receiving fresh additions from the mineral-laden waters overflowing it. In some places there seems to have been a mossy growth which is now superbly dressed with a frosty deposit, rendering it exceedingly fragile. F[a]rther up, and across a point of timber, is the Fountain Geyser; also one that amused us by its regular spasmodic action, having convulsions and intervals of one minute each.

Near these geysers is a surprising novelty in the way of

LAKES OF BOILING CLAY.[11]

Their substance, of the consistence of mortar, is apparently the finest quality of porcelain clay. A constant puffing and blubbering by ebullition makes them resemble huge mush pots. They differ in consistency and color. Some are white, others pink, others yellow. In some the clay is stiff enough to stand up in little cone shaped chimneys out of which issued steam and mud flakes.

THESE PAINT POTS

As they have been designated, have around them extensive deposits of clay and chalky substances which may sometime be utilized. A boiling clay vat near our camp elicited such remark from its unique contour, being shaped like a huge funnel, at the smaller end of which an enormous bubble arose, and broke with a thud that sent the mud several feet up against the sloping embankment.

On the verge of the river are many wonderful exciting hot springs. One is encased to the height of five or six feet in a tub like formation which is constantly sprinkled by the furious sputter of hot water, boiling with prodigious intensity.[12]

Many of our party, including myself, visited

THE TWIN BUTTES

Situated on the west side of the river. The trip was made on horseback, though it was rather rough scrambling through the thick set pines on the intervening hillside. The rocky eminence once attained commands a comprehensive view of the Lower Basin. N. P. Langford's fanciful idea of numerous "manufacturing villages" where groups of springs send up curling clouds of vapor, is best appreciated from this elevated, distant position.

A charming cascade, described in Hayden's report, is near the [Twin] Buttes, and was plainly seen, leaping in foamy spray over the gloomy precipice.[13]

At the extreme upper verge of the Lower Basin, on the west side of the river are

TWO MONSTROUS HOT SPRINGS

Which, from the immense volumes of steam ascending, early attracted the attention of Messrs. Stuart, McCabe and Frazer who visited them immediately after camping. On our way to the Upper Basin most of our party crossed the river to examine these gigantic Springs, pronounced by Dr. Hayden to be the largest in the world; though he evidently mistakes in stating the uppermost to be one hundred and fifty feet in diameter, since it is almost as many yards.[14] Picture in imagination, two hundred acres of elevated land, sloping on three sides toward the river, and

ENVELOPED WITH A SNOWY CRUST

Of silicious substance. On the side f[a]rthest from the river the timber approaches the bigger spring which appears [to be] a steamy lake, circular in form, comparatively shallow near the margin, and fringed with a pearly border, superbly rich in golden sheen. On its southern side from which the water overflows, there seems a broad highway leading down, vivid and glowing with effulgent hues of vermillion. A few rods nearer the river on the hill slope is

A YAWNING CAULDRON

About fifty feet wide by one hundred and fifty feet long,[15] in which the water is seen [to be] boiling and raging with terrific agitation twenty to thirty feet below the general surface. The sides of this chasm are rough and irregular having apparently broken down from the undermining process of the furious water underneath. Dense volumes of steam issue from this awe inspiring pit, frequently filling the orifices and indicating the intensity of its action. Much water flows from this enormous spring, beautifying as it goes, the hillside with elegant designs and resplendent coloring.

Few visitors, perhaps, care to encounter the drifting steam in order to view the gorgeous spectacle presented in the shallow water channels leading to the river. Let me assure the lovers of exquisite art that in them are displayed the tracings of a Master's hand.

Number III

New Northwest, October 18, 1873

GEYSERS

Among the many curious and wonder-exciting objects that have rendered the National Park a veritable "Wonderland," none have arrested more attention than geysers. Curiosity is universal; a love of the marvelous is inherent in the most ordinary mind, while ideas of the sublime and aesthetic, in Art or Nature, depend upon liberal endowment and culture.

The geysers of the Upper Basin present attractions for all minds.

Fear and joy are awakened, while a sense of beauty and grandeur combined, pervades the mind during the exhibition of a first-class geyser.

Here is an extract of first impressions from my diary "Saturday, 30th Aug., 1873, camp near Castle Geyser—sunrise—awakened by roaring and rumbling sounds. Some of the boys shouted: 'Grand Geyser is spouting!' [I] Rose half bewildered by the strange situation. [I] Ran, after a moment's preparation, toward the noise, guided by a prodigious column of steam across the river, northwest from camp. Granville Stuart, C. A. McCabe, and W. W. Dixon, were ahead of me. We found dire commotion, but not the real geyser action anticipated. All sat down on the adjacent rock, and for several minutes watched the frantic water hiss, and heave, and leap in foamy spray from an elliptical basin some 3 ft. high and 20 ft. long. We had hardly noticed a smaller orifice fifteen or twenty feet distant, when, with terrific force there burst from it a volume of steam and hot water, rising rapidly higher and higher, until it seemed with its steamy envelope to reach the clouds. We sprang to our feet—we shouted and swung our hats in wild enthusiasm. It was majestic. The huge sparkling pearls of hot water came whirling back in radiant cascades. The sun rose as we stood spellbound with the fascinating scene. Its rays gleamed in prismatic splendor against the massive fountain.

THIS WAS THE GRAND GEYSER.

In less than ten minutes its action had ceased. The fallen water lay spread out in a circular, shallow pool around the orifice, and now began to run back with a gurgling rumble. In a moment the yellow-tinted cauliflower masses of silicate lay bare and glistening under our precipitate feet."[16]

A DAY OF WONDERS

Was thus inaugurated. Surprise and astonishment fed our high wrought appetites. We strode recklessly through hot water and peered with wondering eyes into craters whose seething spray would frequently send us scrambling off with false alarm.

About 8 o'clock A.M. we went close up to

THE FAMOUS OLD FAITHFUL,[17]

Situated on the upper edge of the Basin, nearly a mile from camp. This geyser stands on an easy incline about two hundred yards from the river.

It erupts regularly every hour. Duration of eruption [is] four to five minutes. Its crater is twenty-five [feet] high, somewhat irregular in outline, but covered with symmetrical masses of bead-like silica, hard as flint. A succession of little pools of water in delicate rimmed porcelain vases are attached like marten's nests around the turret of a castle, forming an elegant series of terraces which serve the tourist to ascend as steps around a tower. Passing up we look into an orifice six feet in diameter.

WE HEAR THE MUFFLED DASHING

Of sullen waves below. The angry surge grows louder—nearer—splash! The lucid spray leaps over the crater. "Time!" We rush off pell mell. See the big silvery drops ascend! Circling out in graceful curves they quickly fall at our feet. The next impulse makes a higher sweep—higher yet—look!

A SPLENDID PYRAMIDAL FOUNTAIN

Of snowy whiteness stands one hundred and fifty vertical feet skyward; while above columnar masses of steam rise up to kiss the fleecy clouds. The crater we stood upon a moment since is hid by a tear-dropping mantle—which the Eastern Day-King paints with the many colored dyes of his wardrobe.[18] Listen to the stern music of its roar! Power—resistless, overwhelming power is the solemn undertone it sings. As you gaze in mute astonishment it drops to a lower altitude. In another moment all is quiet, save the myriad purling rivulets that rush through alabaster channels to the river.

The first day among the big geysers was spent in excited scrambling within a radius of two or three miles from camp—sometimes wading the river—splashing through hot water—finding here and there

UNIQUE SPECIMENS

Of silicified wood, some hard and some translucent, others newly coated with calcareous or silicious incrustations, giving them the appearance of plaster [of] paris or pearl, agreeing with the substance of the coating. Twigs and grasses thus dressed in enamel lay in the scalloped pools around the small geysers and small springs like toys on the shelves of a curiosity shop.[19]

Just here let me protest against the vandalism that with axe and hammer despoils that fantastic tracery which adorns the cones and craters of geysers already historical. This barbarism is the more reprehensible on account of the abundance of detached specimens and the equally beautiful though less conspicuous variety found in the water channels in the background.[20]

CASTLE GEYSER,

Standing like a monument on a snow-clad hill, frequently dashes out jets of spray, fifteen to twenty feet above its crater. Once during our stay it sent up a beautiful fountain, similar to those already described, of about ten minutes duration.[21] Near it is a[nother] most beautiful, circular hot spring, twenty-five feet across. Its deep, cavernous chambers, decorated with fungiform embroidery, [are] revealed as in a mirror. Looking down full sixty feet into its depths the spectacle is enchanting. The whole concave is radiant with rainbow tints more pleasing and fitful than those of the kaleidoscope.[22]

Toward evening, when all had gathered into camp

A TUMULT OF DISCORDANT SOUNDS

Arose from the high mound across the river, northeast from Castle. Earlier in the day we had examined this gray, encrusted mound and found it studded with geysers and hot springs, among which The Bath Tub, The Dental Cup, Bee Hive and Giantess [geysers] are prominent.[23] *Then*, the latter appeared a hot spring with an elliptical orifice eighteen by twenty-five feet, brimful of placid water. *Now*, it was violently agitated, heaving and dashing with terrible uproar. A shout rose from camp. We had watched with almost feverish anticipation for an exhibition from

THE GIANTESS [GEYSER].

Many rushed across the river and clambered up the steep embankment. The action was sustained, massive and beautiful, but instead of the 250 feet projectile force observed by Langford in 1860 [*sic*—1870], we saw but twenty or [at] most forty feet elevation. Presently there came a strange reaction. The boiling ceased. The water quickly sank with a reverberating gurgle into the vast abyss, more awful now than ever before. One after another of our company stepped up to the orifice and looked down its almost vertical side. The water had disappeared, but could be heard surging and dashing hundreds of feet below. "Our Ike" said he could see clear down out of sight.

Presently the water rose again

FIGURE 1.2. This woodcut illustration and others like it were promoting the new Yellowstone National Park at the time of Granville Stuart's trip in 1873. Images like this one represented the first visual exposures the American public received to the "new Wonderland." (*Harper's Weekly*, April 5, 1873.)

WITH FITFUL PAROXYSMS.

It would leap frantically upward and then for a few minutes rest. Peering into the transparent water we saw huge, blue bubbles rising, like submarine balloons, from unknown subterranean depths and bursting at the water's surface with stormy impetuosity. Rising with successive spasms the water approached the orifice. The whole mound adjacent now shook and trembled as if in the grasp of an earthquake, while a jarring report like the thunder of heavy artillery was heard for several minutes, suggesting what "our Poet" expressed, thusly:

"It makes one think of an 'engineer'
With a big machine, below."

During this fearful quaking, as the waters vaulted again over its barrier, we all rushed back, much to the amusement of those who had kept at what they thought a safer distance. In outward show, as before, this eruption disappointed us. Presently, with murmur and groan, the water sank back to its Plutonian caverns, but directly rose again with all the accompaniments above related. About an hour was observed to be the period from one eruption and subsidence to the next. After dark, Mr. Chas. Asphing and myself built a fire at the orifice of Giantess, and witnessed two more repetitions of the same character. Uniformly, the detonation commence[d] when the water had nearly reached the surface, and the whole mound quaked at each report as if it were a mere crust over a battle rent cavern. Awful as it seemed in the gloom of a dark night, we had learned to regard these menacing demonstrations as a mere trick of the old Giantess to frighten us away, so we stubbornly remained until after ten o'clock. Since many other tourists have been disappointed with the behavior of Giantess, its latest observed actions seem worthy of the lengthy note I have here made. It is deserving of mention that while we were watching by bonfire the Giantess, what had seemed an unpretending hot spring near it suddenly shot up a fountain high enough to rank as a second class geyser at least. The glare of our blazing pile against the crystal spray and pillars of steam, lent new and magical effects to the sight.[24]

From one to two miles below Castle [Geyser], on the same side of the river, is a remarkable group of geysers.

THE GIANT AND THE GROTTO [GEYSERS]

Are most prominent. Nearly opposite on the margin of the river are the Fan and the Riverside [geysers]. The action of these various geysers is so similar that it would be much like repetition to describe them. The Fan is peculiar as having five vents all playing at once in different directions. The Grotto [Geyser] will always excite remark on account of its beautiful and grotesque exterior. Its name is appropriate and suggestive. The Giant [Geyser] is notable for sustained action. It has a crater 12 to 15 feet high, shaped like the stump of a broken horn. [Its] Orifice [is] . . . 5 to 6 feet diameter. About half past twelve, Sunday, Aug. 31st, this geyser burst forth with enormous power and continued for an hour and forty minutes to sustain a magnificent fountain varying from 200 to 90 feet in altitude—highest at first and gradually diminishing with occasional impulses at the end of an hour even, reaching nearly the highest altitude reached at first. This was truly

AN IMPOSING SPECTACLE

And gave better satisfaction than most others on account of its duration.[25] More than thirty spectators witnessed this grand display, among them Mrs. Mary Clark, lately from Chicago, who with her aunt, Mrs. Birdseye of Blackfoot City, M.T.,[26] and a military escort from Camp Baker, met us here. We have a special reason to remember Miss Clark for the sweet songs she sang that Sabbath evening.[27] The

RICH CADENCES OF A CULTIVATED VOICE

Had doubtless never before resounded in "our" old Castle's tumultuous halls. Maj. Freeman of Camp Baker, also, sang "The Last Leaf," in a deep baritone, with excellent taste, while others of the circle, less gifted in the arts of melody, recited a story, scriptural or otherwise. "Our Ike" was too much excited to sing, but he was reminded by the passing exercises of more stories that happened in Walla Walla than the oldest inhabitant could possibly substantiate. At any rate, the other boys (jealous, of course) said they were extracts from Æsop's Fables.

Reverting from this digression, let us take a hasty leave of geysers.

THE BEE HIVE [GEYSER]

Was situated just above our camp on the opposite side of the river. After the exhibition by Giant we had gathered into camp pretty well satisfied; but since we intended to strike camp in the morning and hie to the Yellowstone, there lingered a regretful thought that we had not seen the Bee Hive in action. As if willing to satisfy us, at half-past four o'clock, it gaily shot forth a clean, sheer column, like that from the nozzle of a hose, three feet in diameter. Its vertical height, as measured by others,[28] is two hundred and nineteen feet. Running to the river bank, we sat down and quietly enjoyed

A ROYAL PANORAMA.

A gentle breeze turned the misty spray northward, like a suspended curtain, at right angles to our line of vision. To crown the picture with supernal beauty, the setting sun spanned the arching crystals with the most brilliant rainbow I ever beheld. It was so near—so vivid—so superbly set in glittering pearls, that, like "a thing of beauty," it haunts my fancy still, and will remain "a joy forever."

Number IV

New Northwest, October 25, 1873

THE VALLEY OF THE YELLOWSTONE

A forest covered mountain, quite steep on the western declivity, separates the Geysers of the Fire Hole from the upper waters of the Yellowstone. It is an easy day's ride across. On the summit of the dividing range are some huge mounds of sulfur deposits from which issue numerous steam vents. By breaking through the outside crust about these vents, beautiful crystallizations of sulfur are found, delicate as frost work, and rich in lustrous tints of yellow. Near by are a group of large hot springs. In some of these the water is yellow with sulfur; in others it is a saturated solution of alum. I dipped a cup of the latter, boiling hot, and found its taste exceedingly astringent.[29]

Six miles below the [Yellowstone] lake, near some villainous looking pits of hot, turbid liquids,[30] we made out first camp on the Yellowstone [River]. Notwithstanding the horrible boiling cauldrons near us, our tents were pitched in a pine grove of a most lovely valley. I am not saying this with an eye to agriculture, though grass and flowers were then abundant; but, as a picture, the Yellowstone valley, throughout, is a rare masterpiece.

We rode from camp [south] up to

YELLOWSTONE LAKE

On the morning of September 3d. The trail following the river, leads through groves of pine with open vistas of sward, stream and islets variegated by herbage, rich in autumnal leaves. The [Yellowstone] Lake, from our point of view, was an idealization of serenest beauty. Its shape is very irregular, having on its southern boundary several long, finger-like projections, which give it an extreme length of 22 miles. In width it ranges from 5 to 15 miles. The clear, emerald-tinted river issues from the lake northward with a fine sweep of waters two hundred feet wide. In the dim distance southward was seen steep mountain slopes, dark with evergreen foliage, and, nearer, Steven's Island,[31] but slightly elevated, and covered with intermingling groves and lawns. By the aid of an opera glass we could see white capped waves rolling in the distance. An elevation, called Elephant's Back, west of our position, doubtless affords a grander view of the lake and high peaks to the east and southeast than we witnessed. Some of our party commences angling for the big trout wondering whether the reports of vermicular infection by ichthyologists were true. It took but a few minutes to verify their statements. Below the Falls, however, the fish are healthy.

The high econiums written by Dr. Hayden in the U.S. Geological Report for 1871, on this beautiful lake, elevated 7,427 feet above the sea,[32] have been often quoted; and since our enthusiasm did not reach its climax here, we pass back to note a few of the

STRANGE SIGHTS

Near our camp below. Nearest was a mud geyser thirty feet in diameter. A casual observer might mistake it for a quiet pool of thin mud. Hearing a succession of dull reports, accompanied by the hiss of steam which now rose in dense, black clouds, we hurried forth to find the geyser heaving up its muddy contents 20 to 30 feet. When it ceased this action, twenty minutes after, the turbid liquid sank until its basin was almost empty.[33] Only a few rods distant in the side of a steep embankment was

THE GIANT'S CAULDRON,

The most infernal pit I ever peeped into.[34] Its mouth is forty feet across, tapering down to twenty feet at the bottom, where, at a depth of fifty feet, rushes darkly a turbulent river, more fearful, because more real, than the Stygian shades of the ancients. From the seething abyss issues dense clouds of steam visible for many miles. All around are evidences of late ejections of mud; trees thirty feet high being covered with it. The eruptions are probably caused by the caving of the adjacent sides which must occasionally occur.

Two hundred yards beyond this is a cavern in a hillside with an opening sufficiently large for a small person to walk in without stooping; but, so far as heard from, visitors have preferred to stay outside. The angry dash of rock-bound waves roar within, while a continual jarring report similar to that made by a powerful engine and heavy machinery is heard accompanied by a rush of scalding hot steam from the portal. A small stream of perfectly clear water flows from this dismal, subterranean cell.[35]

SULFUR MOUNTAIN,

Conspicuous on account of its white and yellow escarpments, is situated two miles below. "Seven Hills" and "Crater Hills" are other names given to the same locality.[36] Many of our party following closely the river, passed this remarkable group of alum and sulfur hot springs—some clear, some turbid, some thick as boiling mush—in fact, most of the kinds already described, with variations in size, temperature and consistency innumerable. One of the tributaries of Alum Creek has its source in this group. Seeing we had passed, D. P. Newcomer, T. T. Frazier, and myself rode back, finding ample reward for the delay it cost. One sulfur spring here is especially noteworthy. Situated at the front of the hills, it occupies a circular area fully twenty-five feet across, and is partly covered by a thin rim which extends over the water like a margin of ice around a pond. It constantly boils with violent agitation, lifting the water several feet.[37] The rim and adjacent formation is strikingly beautiful, surpassing any seen in the Geyser Basin. The finest porcelain is not more delicate than the fanciful embroidery here displayed, glistening in hues of yellow, pink and purple. We scraped from the scalding hot water a few round, smooth pebbles, which, on being broken, showed concentric layers of sulfur and silica throughout. Evidently these pebbles grow by deposition from the mineral waters.

Turning our faces northward, we again passed down the Yellowstone with glowing anticipation of the near approach to

THE GRAND CANYON,

Now less than ten miles distant. Our train being ahead we rode briskly down the trail amid scenes of woodland, copse and lea which

"Nice fingered art must emulate in vain."[38]

The roar of the Falls gave note of their proximity, but we had no glimpse of the Falls or Canyon until after crossing Cascade Creek, when we suddenly approached the mighty chasm. At the first partial view I stood fast in mute surprise, and admiration. There was present an overpowering sense of the possibilities a few steps further would reveal, and yet I hesitated to take them. All my high-wrought fancy had pictured, paled before the ineffable impressions of this first sight. Tying my horse to a small tree, I stepped out on one of the beetling rocks, that stand like giddy parapets on Gibraltar, and instinctively uncovered my head. The scene was

A REVELATION OF VAST SUBLIMITY.

Bewildering splendor, incomparable grandeur, here meet and mingle in the superb garniture of these gay-colored, colossal walls; thrilling the beholder and begging description. "My Father, I thank Thee," welled up from my heart in grateful praise to the Master—Nature's Great Artificer. But the Falls? Come stand with me. Look down beneath us a thousand perpendicular feet and see the foaming water arch out of sight. From our position we can see only the top of the Lower Falls, making a magnificent cataract of 140 feet. But your eyes will not linger in that direction. These Falls, grand as they are of themselves, here seem mere side fixtures to adorn the marvelous concavity beneath and before us.

"He who observes it, ere he passes on
Gazes his fill, and comes and comes again.
That he may call it up when far away."[39]

My first impressions as recorded in my pocket diary are here introduced:

"THURSDAY, SEPT. 4TH, 1873.

About 10 o'clock I reached the Grand Canyon and Falls of the Yellowstone. No words can express the awful beauty Nature here displays. Astonishment, wonder, glad surprises met me on every hand. I moved excitedly from cliff to cliff, and caught glimpses of

THE BOLD RIVER LEAPING DOWN

A precipice several hundred feet in height, forming a mighty cataract; but in the wondrous Canyon, it seemed a little cascade a thousand feet below me. The river, though 200 feet wide and 20 feet deep, seemed a frothing brook a child might step over, as it sped away from the snowy spume at the bottom of the Canyon. Some energetic scrambling soon commenced in an effort to reach the rocky verge of the Lower Falls. Down, still down, I struggled and slid—lingering on each basaltic rampart to sweep with eager vision the spheroidal concave, stretching to distant miles of

SAFFRON MOTTLED PALISADES AND STRIATED GORGES,

Whose every cliff and every escarpment was flushed with [lumin-] escent sheen—until, at last, the shelving buttress was reached. Then I stood where a few moments since I thought I might dip the water in my hand. Delusive thought—it was still thirty feet below. Grasping the branch of a friendly pine that grew from a cleft in the rock, I leaned over the dizzy ledge and breathless watched the crystalline deluge curve and plunge so grandly into the misty depths beneath; then, under the ambiant maze again gathering its scattered molecular legions leap out, as from a cloud, to scurry, and whirl, and eddy in virescent foam down the gorgeous canyon. The whole vast survey was magical—intoxicating.

A BEAUTIFIC ENCHANTMENT

Held me spellbound. Beneath and around me was arranged a mighty amphitheatre, studded with castles, domes and towers; and palaces of sculptured ruby; and moss grown cathedrals; and galleries of titanic statues; and fortresses, carnage stained; and gilded adamantine walls; and over all was spread a many-hued, gauzy veil, concealing only little things I did not care to see. Did I dream? Turning myself and seeking reassurance by reflection, again I looked and again saw all before me in reality, more astonishingly fair than words can tell. Oh, can there be, thought I, in Nature's whole realm a sight compatible for this? If so, let Nature's devotee see it and die.

All conceptions of the Grand Canyon must be feeble. If we could take man's loftiest structures—our capitol at Washington, St. Paul's, St. Peter's—and set them in the niches of this vast amphitheatre, they would appear as a childish trick, like that to adorn the starry firmament with a jeweled trinket. The name—Grand Canyon—misleads. You think at once of a precipitate gorge between two high mountains ranges—gloomy at mid day, even. No so. This is a stupendous chasm, washed out from an undulating, grassy plateau. Instead of dusky shades, its architectural sides are

BRIGHT AND GLOWING WITH COLORS,

White, yellow, red, pink, maroon, blue, green, orange—all these and more; not stunted and dimly seen, but more copiously sp[r]ead out than art has ever conceived. The undertone or ground work of color throughout this grand *chef d'oeuere*,[40] are tints and shades of yellow. But, whether its walls rise in gothic columns, or slope up on slides of variegated sands and clays, the coloring is everywhere present, unique in character and without a parallel in the world."

Number V

New Northwest, November 1, 1873

THE YELLOWSTONE FALLS

Dr. [Ferdinand] Hayden's theory that the region embracing the falls of the Yellowstone was once a lake-bed, of which the site of the present lake is but a remnant, and that by hot spring deposits around peaks and in fissures of volcanic origin, together with sedimentary accretions from the lake, there was accumulated from 1,000 to 2,000 feet of deposition, is doubtless correct. When the lake rim gave way at the northern extremity, the impetuous waters cut an immense channel out of the deposited material, leaving the basalt standing in cones and crumbling walls, or weathered into fantastic forms, with occasional transverse precipices over which the waters can now plunge.

He says: "While the canyon has somewhat the appearance of a great cleft or canyon, it is simply a channel carved by the river out of pre-deposited materials after the drainage of the old lake basin." This accounts for the almost incredible display of colors, which are the effects of mineral decomposition and percolation. Thus the rock and earth is permeated with colors like fresco, instead of being superficial like paint.

The average elevation at the falls is about 8,000 feet above the sea, while the primary basin rim ranges from 10,000 to 11,000 feet. After the rim gave way, wherever in the direction of drainage there happened vertical transverse sections of the unyielding basalt, falls in the river would be inevitable. The river above

THE UPPER FALLS

Is very rapid, with occasional cascades and the whole volume (500,000 inches miner's measurement)[41] is hurled off with prodigious velocity, making a grand cataract one hundred and forty feet in altitude.[42] These falls are visible from all points about the canyon and may be approached without much difficulty, thus affording the tourist the advantage of looking up, as well as down, at them. From a rocky projection half way down, there is a splendid view, so near that what seemed in the distance fleecy foam, here appears a shower of pearls, in which some of the beady, white globules can be distinctly seen skipping swiftly through the others as if shot forth with a superior impulse from the emerald arch above. As this booming cataract impinges on the rocky basin below, it darts like a flight of white plumed arrows through a radius of 200 feet. [With] This tremendous rebound, it dictates the immense cumulative force that is gathered in the rapids above. There is a music in the dash and roar of this surging flood that well accords with the awe-inspiring scene. Between the Upper and Lower Falls, Cascade creek comes in from the west. As the name indicates, it reaches the river by

A SERIES OF PICTURESQUE CASCADES,

Which of themselves constitutes a scene of romantic interest.[43] The basaltic columns interrelated with breccia, between it[s] rushes and leaps in foamy spray, are full of "volcanic walnuts," or geodes, varying in size from a buckshot to a cannon ball. They stick in the fractured surface of the rock like shot in a plank, and when broken open are seen to be somewhat hollow and lined with crystals of quartz.

THE LOWER FALLS

Are quite inaccessible except at the topmost verge, as already mentioned. Possibly they could be approached from the east side of the canyon—a position we could not well occupy. One fourth of a mile below the falls, however, the canyon may be entered from the west side and the descent made with moderate difficulty, down as far as a cone-shaped hillock of ferruginated basalt. This cone or butte is situated half way down the canyon's side and by its maroon color contrasting strongly with the light colors around it, soon arrests the attention of an observer.[44] From a position near its base are obtained magnificent views of the canyon and of the Lower Falls. Still, it does not afford a near view.

A PERILOUS ADVENTURE.

Urged by an enthusiastic desire to get a close view of the Lower Falls from the bottom of the canyon, several of us essayed to go down from our position at the red butte to the bottom of the canyon and thence, if possible, move up the bed of the stream to the falls. Sallying out in the order named, C. A. McCabe, myself, D. P. Newcomer and Robert Miller, each leaning on a pine staff, commenced a wide roof-like slide of sand on a substratum of shale. Near the farther side of this was a rivulet in which the sand had been washed down, making the footing perilous. McCabe and I finally secured a foothold and crossed, but our companions went back—not trusting the strength of their staves. After getting around some shelving ledges and over some precipitous ridges, we overtook Rev. [Edwin J.] Stanley and W. H. Todd, who, by a more circuitous route, were moving down a rocky ravine on the talus.[45] When we found ourselves all on the same slide, a little rivalry seemed to spring up as to who should be first[;] Rev. Stanley leading, furnish[ed] an apt illustration of the poet's thought— "On, Stanley, on!" Alas! this heroic phase was brief. We saw with dismay the reverend gentlemen with his staff projecting in the treacherous debris at an angle of 45 deg., glide suddenly forward as if he had struck ice or "ile." Fortunately as he approached the brink of a precipice, he lodged in the narrow passage—lodged and sat—and nothing more.[46]

HERE WAS A QUANDARY.

With commendable presence of mind, Mr. Stanley sat quite still. His hold was so frail it was dangerous to move. Standing ten rods above, we dared not go forward to his assistance for fear of crowding upon him the talus under our feet. He felt around him cautiously right and left, but no friendly niche was near—nothing but the sliding fragments, and under it the hard smooth rock. We called: "Do you want help?" "Yes." How could we give it? The crisis demanded a man of muscle and of will, and the demand was promptly met. He climbed out around the adjacent cliffs and presently approached the imperiled Stanley. Getting near enough, he reached his staff, and directly both stood on the rocks above. What now? The gorge was impracticable on account of the precipice so narrowly escaped. Could we go further? McCabe said we could. From his position with Stanley he saw the way and led us on; over a sharp ridge; around a shelving abutment where the shattered rock, yielding to hand and foot, went chattering into the abrupt chasm; down an inclined plane; and we again had a footing of coarse talus, on which we slid to the water's edge. Here we felt the exultation of first explorers. We swung our hats and shouted to the boys who had watched our progress from above. The foaming river ran exceedingly swift in its rock girt channel, and we saw at a glance we could not proceed up stream a single rod. Bold abutments, on which there was no foothold, rose defiantly at the very outset. Still our labor had not been quite in vain. The cyclopean escarpments sloping in 2,000 feet above us, with their scattering trees, deep fissures, serrated ridges and overhanging cliffs reflecting the varied hues of a butterfly's wing, [were] glory enough. We rested, left our cards, took a drink and a pebble from the river, and glancing upward commenced

THE HARDEST SCRAMBLING

Our journey had yet called forth. When on the talus it was "getting up one step and sliding back two"; when crawling around the ritted rocks,[47] whence the fragments had fallen, it was a "tooth and toe-nail" struggle for dear life. After much tribulation, toil and sweat, we emerged safely from our hazardous adventure.[48]

I shall not detail the mishaps of the next day when we lost the trail and followed down the gorge of Tower Creek. There was some fretting, some cursing, of course; but jolly Dick Dickinson, never whining at trifling discomforts, led gallantly forward; while our peerless in *cuisine*—Pat Ryan—attentive as a lover to his "Kitty," brought up the rear.[49] That evening we camped near the confluence of Tower Creek and the Yellowstone.

The next morning the train left early, but several remained behind to view more intently the fine scenery at this point.

THE TOWER FALLS

Are so hedged in by nature's minarets and towers that it is quite difficult to get near them from above. By entering the gorge below, near the mouth of the Creek, and traveling up the rugged banks of the stream, we got close to the foot of these beautiful falls. The scene here is as romantic as a dream of fairy land. The great, weather-worn towers stand like sculptured domes on a massive temple from which the stream leaps down 156 feet.[50] Columnar buttresses of weathered breccia, weird as the portals of some gothic fane, rise far up into the fanciful pinnacles, hundreds of feet above their bases. The hills around and above are wooded and grassy, but precipitous and charmingly picturesque.

Here, too, in close proximity, is seen the lower extremity of the Grand Canyon more than twenty miles below its inception, and still a marvel in contour and coloring. More regular than above, it here slopes up in three distinct terraces, each terrace being capped by an adamant palisade showing a jointage closely resembling massive masonry. This entire locality is destined to become famous for its varied and impressive, natural scenery. No admirer of Nature in her wild caprices and sublimest aspects can go away disappointed. As we rode again on our journey toward Gardiner River, we had constant occasion to admire and wonder at and praise the munificent liberality with which she is endowed in the valley of the Yellowstone.

MAMMOTH HOT SPRINGS

Or White Mountain Springs, on Gardiner River, eighteen miles below Tower Falls, were reached about 3 p.m. September 6th. After our experience, there would seem to be some reason for the opinion of one of our party who, on his arrival home, being interrogated as to the character of the scenes he had witnessed, would invariably reply, "Too much— entirely too much hot water."

I did not expect anything new, but must confess that here was the most singular and imposing hot spring formation yet seen. These springs have new features and characteristics combined with those already described. The deposit here is mainly calcareous, while in the Geyser Basin it is silicious. *There* the deposits are great; *here* they are gigantic; rising by terraces to the aggregate height of 1,000 feet, and covering an area two miles square. The principal active springs now occupy a middle terrace, in shape a circular, snow-white mound 200 feet high with a flat top like the trustrum of a cone.[51] Hayden says of this mound, "It had the appearance of

A FROZEN CASCADE.

If a group of springs near the summit of a mountain were to distribute their waters down the irregular declivities, and they were slowly congealed, the picture would bear some resemblance in form." Add to this idea the decoration of exquisite alabaster water-vases with gold and silver linings, arranged like spiral steps around a tower, and adorned with the multiform tracery and brilliant coloring already faintly described and still the picture is incomplete. To see is the only way to know the mystical witchery that nature has here so cunningly devised.

Though the half has not been told, I here lay down my pen deeply conscious of its impotence to portray, even as, "through a glass darkly," a glimpse of Wonderland.[52] What may have seemed to some readers the foolish exaggeration of a florid style, has been written with a conscientious regard for truth; but, since we all see through colored glasses, if a false impression has been conveyed let it be an impeachment of my "goggles."

Notes

1. W. F. Sanders to Columbus Delano, November 28, 1873, Record Group 48, letters received 1872–82, roll 1, Yellowstone National Park Archives, Yellowstone National Park.

2. *Palmy* means "prosperous," and he refers here to the prosperous old days of Virginia City (1863–70). "Celestials" refers to Chinese, who were common at that time, and the names in quotes are probably the names of various prospectors' claims during bygone days. See Richard Lionello, "John Chinaman the Forgotten Pioneer," in *Nuggets of History from Virginia City*, ed. Richard Lee (Virginia City, MT: Virginia City Alliance, n.d. [2005?]), 18–19.

3. All of these people were prominent citizens of Montana Territory who were accompanying the Reverend E. J. Stanley on his trip to the park. Stanley authored *Rambles in Wonderland*, a famous early Yellowstone trip account, and on this trip they named Mary Lake for another member of their party, Mary Clark. See Lee H. Whittlesey, *Yellowstone Place Names* (Gardiner, MT: Wonderland Publishing Company, 2006), 166. Judge Hiram Knowles was known for serving three terms in Montana territorial courts. Wilbur Fiske Sanders (1834–1905) founded the Montana Historical Society and served as a U.S. senator. The Montana Historical Society holds personal papers for both men.

4. Harry J. Norton was a Virginia City newspaper editor who traveled to Yellowstone the previous year (1872) and who was in the process at this time of producing the first guidebook to the park. Entitled *Wonderland Illustrated; Or Horseback Rides Through the Yellowstone National Park*, Norton published it in 1873.

5. The reference here was to John Bunyan's classic book *Pilgrim's Progress* (1678).

6. In Greek mythology, Erebus or Érebos was a netherworld god, the personification of darkness. Erebus was often used as a synonym for Hades, the Greek god of the underworld. Also, Erebus was the name of the gloomy space through which souls pass on their way to Hades. The "portentous bird of yore" refers to the title character in Edgar Allen Poe's poem "The Raven."

7. Mrs. Partington was the name of a scatterbrained character created by U.S. humorist Benjamin P. Shillaber (1814–90) for a short sketch that he published in the *Boston Post* in 1847. The popularity of the character, who was often

described as an American Mrs. Malaprop because of her humorous misuse of words, led Shillaber to feature her in several books, notably *The Life and Sayings of Mrs. Partington and Others of the Family* (1854), *Partingtonian Patchwork* (1873), and *Ike and His Friends* (1879)—hence the reference to "our Ike."

8. The reference is to a black man. Traditionally, it was held that Ham was one of the sons of Noah who moved southwest into Africa and parts of the near Middle East and was the forefather of the nations there. Scholars around the sixth century A.D. introduced the idea that the sons of Ham were marked by dark skin. In the Middle Ages European scholars of the Bible picked up on the Jewish idea of viewing the "sons of Ham" or Hamites as cursed, meaning "blackened" by their sins.

9. Gilman Sawtell (1836–98) homesteaded his ranch in the Henry's Lake area in 1867, and in 1868 he built a rough road from his ranch to Virginia City. Five years later he was instrumental in completing an early road into Yellowstone through the west entrance. He ran a fish-selling business from his ranch on Henry's Lake and served as one of the area's earliest guides for travelers into Yellowstone. Sawtelle Peak, misspelled on current maps and located west of Yellowstone National Park, is today named for him. Aubrey L. Haines, *The Yellowstone Story* (1977; rev., Boulder: University of Colorado Press, 1996), I, 80, 195.

10. This was probably the Fountain Group of hot springs in Lower Geyser Basin.

11. This was today's Fountain Paint Pot. Whittlesey, *Yellowstone Place Names*, 108–9.

12. This was probably Fortress Geyser, also known as Conch Spring.

13. This was Fairy Falls, 197 feet high, on Fairy Creek. The report is F. V. Hayden, *Fifth Annual Report of the U.S. Geological and Geographical Survey of the Territories* (Washington, DC: Government Printing Office, 1872), 112.

14. These were Excelsior Geyser and Grand Prismatic Spring. Excelsior is measured today at 276 feet by 328 feet, while Grand Prismatic is 250 feet by 350 feet in size. For Excelsior, see generally Lee Whittlesey, "Monarch of All These Mighty Wonders: Tourists and Yellowstone's Excelsior Geyser, 1881–1890," *Montana Magazine of Western History* 40 (Spring 1990): 2–15.

15. Excelsior Geyser is actually much larger in diameter than his estimate. See Whittlesey, "Monarch of All These Mighty Wonders."

16. These men, impressive and important in Montana history, had just seen one of Yellowstone's most impressive and important geysers. In 1873, Grand Geyser was erupting often to heights of at least 150 feet, for the Reverend E. J. Stanley was probably present at this same eruption and noted that Grand Geyser erupted that high for fifteen–twenty minutes. He thought that it erupted about every twenty-four hours that year (*Rambles in Wonderland: Or, Up the Yellowstone . . .* , [New York: D. Appleton and Company, 1878], 109–10). Another simultaneous traveler, William Gaddis, recorded that there were thirty-two people camped at Upper Basin at this time

("Leaves from My Diary of the Yellowstone Trip—1873," unpublished copy of manuscript, Washington State University, Pullman, August 30 entry).

17. It is fascinating to learn that even this early, only one year after the park became a park and only three years after its discovery by white people, these men considered Old Faithful Geyser to already be "famous." This is a testimonial to just how quickly Yellowstone and its wonders became famous. For elaboration, see Lee Whittlesey, *Storytelling in Yellowstone: Horse and Buggy Tour Guides* (Albuquerque: University of New Mexico Press, 2007), 2–3.

18. He referred here to the sun, illuminating the sky in early morning.

19. Unfortunately, most of these specimens were carried away by early souvenir collectors.

. 20. This documents that as early as 1873, visitors were vandalizing the park's hot springs and geysers. In 1875, Captain William Ludlow lamented the damage done "by the rude hand of man" with names written on thermal features and specimens detached from them. "Miracles of art," he fumed, "can be ruined in five minutes by a vandal armed with an ax" (*Report of a Reconnaissance from Carroll, Montana, to the Yellowstone National Park, Made in the Summer of 1875, Annual Report of the Chief of Engineers for 1876*, Appendix NN [Washington, DC: Government Printing Office, 1876], 29). As late as 1886, Captain Moses Harris noted that "not one of the notable geyser formations in the Park has escaped mutilation or defacement in some form" (*Report of the Superintendent of the Yellowstone National Park to the Secretary of the Interior 1886* [Washington, DC: Government Printing Office, 1886], 8). Until 1886, when the U.S. Army arrived with its men and money, there was no protection for the geysers.

21. In 1873, Castle Geyser was fitful in its eruptions. Theodore Comstock saw it erupt to only thirty feet, and the Rev. E. J. Stanley did not see it erupt, although he was told that it would erupt fifty feet high. Lee Whittlesey, *Wonderland Nomenclature*, 1988, unpublished manuscript, Yellowstone National Park Library, Yellowstone National Park, Castle Geyser entry.

22. He spoke here of present Crested Pool, a fabulously beautiful, superheated spring that was mentioned by nearly all early visitors. It was variously known as "Fire Basin," "Castle Well," "Diana's Bath," "Beautiful Blue Crested Spring," and "Circe's Boudoir." Whittlesey, *Wonderland Nomenclature*, Crested Pool entry.

23. The Bath Tub was probably Vault Spring, named because of its resemblance to a burial vault. It has sporadic periods of geyser activity. The Dental Cup was so named by Dr. F. V. Hayden but by 1883 became known as Sponge Geyser. Hayden, *Fifth Annual Report of the U.S. Geological and Geographical Survey of the Territories*, 119.

24. Giantess Geyser was known in early days for the sounds it made, described here as like "the thunder of heavy artillery." During the long periods (twelve–forty-three hours) that it erupts, water phases and steam phases

will occur in unpredictable combinations, and the geyser will do different things at different times, sometimes erupting up to two hundred feet in height and other times simply bursting to less than sixty feet. Whittlesey, *Wonderland Nomenclature*, Giantess Geyser entry. From this observer's description, it was behaving similarly in 1873. The Reverend E. J. Stanley, who probably saw parts of this same eruption, thought that "its glory is departing" as at that moment Giantess erupted only fifty feet high, but he admitted that the geyser made "repeated sounds like claps of thunder, and heavy concussions like the firing of a cannon underground" (*Rambles in Wonderland*, 102–4).

25. In 1873, Giant Geyser erupted 200–250 feet high at times with durations of (like today) up to an hour and a half. In fact, the Reverend E. J. Stanley, whose party probably saw the very same eruption as our "scramblers," stated that it lasted for ninety minutes and was 250 feet high. Stanley thought that Giant Geyser erupted every twenty-four–twenty-nine hours, and he spent three pages describing it. Stanley, *Rambles in Wonderland*, 113–16; Whittlesey, *Wonderland Nomenclature*, Giant Geyser entry.

26. Montana Territory. Montana did not become a state until 1889.

27. This was Miss Mary Clark, for whom E. J. Stanley's party had earlier named Mary Lake. See Stanley, *Rambles in Wonderland*, 123.

28. This measurement of Beehive Geyser was made by the 1870 Washburn party. See Nathaniel Pitt Langford, *The Discovery of Yellowstone Park* (Lincoln: University of Nebraska Press, 1972), 111.

29. These were and are the Highland Hot Springs east of Mary Mountain.

30. Mud Volcano, Mud Geyser, and other springs.

31. This was Stevenson Island, named for Hayden survey manager James Stevenson. Aubrey L. Haines, *Yellowstone Place Names: Mirrors of History* (Boulder: University Press of Colorado, 1996), 91–92.

32. Yellowstone Lake is currently measured at twenty miles by fourteen miles. It has 110 miles of shoreline and is 136 square miles in area. Its elevation is 7,731 feet above sea level.

33. This was the Mud Geyser, which erupted muddy water from 1870 to around 1905 to heights of thirty–fifty feet and was considered a great wonder by early travelers. Whittlesey, *Wonderland Nomenclature*, Mud Geyser entry.

34. This was the Mud Volcano. For several years (1870–73), it threw mud into the tops of trees, but it later settled down into quiet bubbling. Whittlesey, *Wonderland Nomenclature*, Mud Volcano entry.

35. This was the Dragon's Mouth Spring, a spring of acid water with a tonguelike lashing action that often is 185 degrees Fahrenheit. Whittlesey, *Yellowstone Place Names*, 90.

36. Confusion between Sulphur Mountain and Crater Hills existed for many years, until in 1930 mappers incorrectly moved the name Sulphur Mountain to an innocuous single hill just south of the Crater Hills. The two names

originally referred to the same feature(s), namely, the two Crater Hills. Whittlesey, *Yellowstone Place Names*, 75, 242.

37. This was Sulphur Spring, also known as Crater Hills Geyser, which was seen and admired by so many early visitors. It is unusual in that it is a gas-driven geyser rather than a heat-driven one. Whittlesey, *Wonderland Nomenclature*, Sulphur Spring entry.

38. This line is from *The Task and Other Poems* by William Cowper (1784).

39. The passage is from Samuel Rogers's (1763–1855) "Ginevra."

40. The words are French—*chef d'œuvre* means a masterpiece, especially in literature or art.

41. A miner's inch, in hydraulic mining, is the amount of water flowing under a given pressure in a given time through a hole one inch in diameter. It is a unit for measuring the quantity of water supplied to a mining claim.

42. The cataract is 109 feet in altitude.

43. This is Crystal Falls, 129 feet in height.

44. Today this is known as Red Rock.

45. Talus is merely loose rock. W. H. Todd was the source of information that a photograph was taken of his 1873 party while they were encamped at Old Faithful. Todd recalled that the photographer was from Bozeman, but he could not remember his name and wondered whether it was "White Calfee." This photographer was Joshua Crissman, known to have been in the park that summer, as evidenced by mention of him in the account of a contemporaneous traveler, William Gaddis. The photo mentioned by Todd and Gaddis is probably one or both of two photos taken by Crissman showing seven people (including two women) on the Mammoth terraces, available on the Library of Congress Web site as photo number LC-DIG-stereo-1s01154. The five men are probably Gaddis's party, and the two women are probably Mary Clarke and her companion, Mrs. Birdseye. W. H. Todd to Hiram Knowles, July 26, 1909, Knowles papers, MC 2, box 1, folder 6, Montana Historical Society, Helena; Gaddis, "Leaves from My Diary of the Yellowstone Trip," August 24 entry.

46. "Lodged and sat—and nothing more" is a reference to Edgar Allen Poe's "The Raven"—"perched and sat and nothing more." The "ile" reference is obscure.

47. He probably means *retted*—moistened or soaked.

48. The Rev. Edwin J. Stanley also mentioned this descent in his 1878 book but said considerably less about it. He described descending "the fearful gorge down to the water's edge a few hundred yards below the falls" with his friend W. H. Todd. Remembering that our author stated there were at least four other gentlemen on this hiking trip, perhaps Stanley was overcome by the beauty of the trip or did not know the other men well, for he mentioned only "my friend W. H. Todd and two other gentlemen." Nor did Stanley mention being helped by Mr. McCabe, instead claiming that he found the way down from his dangerous perch by himself. But like our author, he

mentioned the feeling of being "first explorers" in this region and then launched into a religious sermon (*Rambles in Wonderland*, 75–77).

49. Patrick Ryan served in the Montana legislature in 1864–65. Tom Stout, *Montana: Its Story and Biography* (Chicago: American Historical Society, 1921), I, 282.

50. Tower Fall is 132 feet tall.

51. Surely he means *frustum*—the portion of a solid, normally a cone or pyramid, that lies between two parallel planes cutting the solid.

52. To see "through a glass"—a mirror—"darkly" is to have an obscure or imperfect vision of reality. The expression comes from the Bible—the writings of the Apostle Paul, who explained that we do not now see clearly, but at the end of time, we will do so.

Across the Continent

II.—The National Park

THOMAS E. SHERMAN

1877

❧

THOMAS EWING SHERMAN (1856–1933) WAS BORN THE SECOND
son of the hugely famous army general William Tecumseh Sherman
but gained public fame on his own as an orator and Catholic priest.
Nevertheless he was sobered by his father's accomplishments and
remained amazed by them for the rest of his life. Although he learned
early to love the military, he elected to join the Jesuit priesthood after
being raised in a life of privilege.

Young Sherman "sang loud, enjoyed stimulating conversation and
had a great sense of humor," wrote a biographer, and he seemed to be
good at nearly everything he did. Attending college at Yale, he transferred to the University of Law in St. Louis and graduated at the top of
his class. When he announced his decision to be a priest, his father took
it hard and refused to speak to him for a long time, but eventually they
made up. He became nationally famous 1900–1905 as an honored guest
of President Theodore Roosevelt and as a traveler and religious lecturer
who drew huge crowds to hear his talks on Catholicism.

Late in life, Thomas Sherman's circumstances grew dim. He suffered
a nervous breakdown, and that foreshadowed even worse fortunes.
Rallying for a few years, he suffered a complete mental breakdown in
1911, and relatives placed him in a sanitarium. Attempting suicide, he

FIGURE **2.1.**

Thomas Ewing Sherman was a recent law student at the time of his Yellowstone trip. The photo here was taken in late 1877, only a short time after he returned from the park. A year later he decided to enter the ministry. (www.soysite.com./newsletter/Sepo1.html.)

moved through a string of insane asylums and was finally released, only to begin causing trouble for his old Jesuit order. He finally retired to a quiet life and ended his life again institutionalized in 1933.[1]

But in 1877, Thomas Sherman was only twenty years old and a college student—seemingly invulnerable and on the threshold of a successful life and career. In Yellowstone he saw religion and the glories of the Creator, and those things no doubt influenced him into the religious journey that he was to take for his life's work as a priest.

⁂

In my last letter I tried to give you some idea of the Yellowstone [River] from its mouth to the point where it issues from the Mountains; if now we glance at its course still higher up, we shall find that our journey hitherto has been tame and dull in comparison with the more mountainous district on which we are now entering. The Yellowstone rises in the land of wonders known as the *National Park*, which has been set aside by an Act of Congress "as a public park or pleasuring ground for the benefit and enjoyment of the people," and which "is reserved and withdrawn from settlement, occupancy, or sale under the laws of the United States" [Revised Stat. 2474].[2]

We have rolled over eighty miles of passable wagon road, and reached the mouth of Gardner's River.[3] Here vehicles must be left behind, for there is no highway into Wonderland,[4] and the visitor who dares to trespass on Dame Nature's secret fastnesses, must bear the fatigues of rough riding, and trust his baggage to the mercy of a pack animal.[5]

At the mouth of Gardner's River, [near] the northern extremity of the Park, rises a wall of volcanic rock, as if to bar all entrance.[6] Our guide leads us safely by a winding valley between the rugged hills on to the rolling uplands, where our eyes are cheered by rich wildflowers, our path shaded by groves of stately pines, and where even our beasts of burden find delight in tall waving grasses, at which they nibble eagerly, as we pause to rest from time to time. We have passed the forbidden portal, and entered the charmed region. Out of the pine woods, the trail leads across open undulating country, until after some miles it [leads to?] the edge of a marked ridge, and descends a thousand feet or more into Pleasant Valley. Next day, in the early morning, we pass Tower Falls, a handsome cascade in the midst of beetling [overhanging] crags and lofty pines, and then begin to ascend one long hill after another, until I become aware that we are on the slope of a mountain. So gradual and gentle are [our] approaches of Mount Washburne [*sic*] from the north, that the traveler is not fully conscious of its character or elevation until the summit is fairly reached. Almost the whole ascent can readily be made on horseback. The top once gained, so grand a prospect bursts upon the gaze that we realize to what an elevation we have risen, and how favorably this isolated spur is situated to command a view of the whole surrounding country. To the east lay the Big Horn Mountains,[7] distant but clear and bold, their summits glistening with snow, and stretching sharp and cold up into the soft blue summer sky. To the south, in the middle distance, gleamed the Yellowstone Lake, brilliant in the sunshine, a gem in the dark setting of the surrounding mountains. F[a]rther on, Mounts Sheridan and Hancock, and many other peaks towered among the clouds; whilst to the west, range after range rolled one beyond the other, until the sight grew dim and confused by heaps of mountains piled beyond, and failed to distinguish further. From the lake, the [Yellowstone] river winds towards us, a silver thread, and in the dark mass of foliage, where it is lost to view, we know that it takes a fearful leap. Somewhere in the midst of that ocean of green, by which we are surrounded, lie sulphur mountains, mud volcanoes, geysers, hot springs, cascades and wonders innumerable completely hidden from us now by intervening ridges and dense forests, but soon to disclose themselves on a nearer approach. The prospect from Mount Washburne [*sic*] fills the eye with seeing, but the imagination increases the interest of the panorama a hundred-fold. Near those peaks, to the south of us, lie the headwaters of the Snake River, the great southern branch of the Columbia. From mountains west and north flow the Gallatin, Madison and Jefferson [rivers],[8] branches of the Missouri, and at our feet, deep down in its grand cañon is the Yellowstone. So the imagination spreads the continent out before us, follows the Snake River through all its windings across lava deserts, through mountain ranges, down to the Pacific Slope,—sees the great sweep of the Father of Waters, north, then east, then south, till he has traversed a continent and reached the Gulf,— pictures the Rocky Mountains before us, not one ridge or two, but a huge uplift, hundreds of miles in width and thousands in length, forming the backbone of the continent,[9] vast stores of mineral wealth, not gold and silver merely, these are but tokens, but solid rocks of fertile substances that are gradually to be loosened by frost and avalanche, carried down, broken and ground by torrent and cataract, transported by ever-flowing streams, and deposited to supply the wants of future generations. A thousand thoughts come crowding to the mind, and reason, aiding the imagination, looks back over countless ages, then forward to the distant future, and makes us creatures of a day bow before Him to Whom past, present, and future are as one, Who lives on in the never-ending present of his limitless and unchanging being. Awe and admiration fill the heart, and one's soul conscious of that higher unseen Presence [to] which the wonders of nature so plainly testify, shrinks abashed in nothingness before Him, is dazzled by the brightness of His beauty, overwhelmed by His power and majesty, and stunned by the fearful thought that it is so easy to offend one so grand and terrible, so beautiful and loving.[10] Within a few feet of the summit, wild flowers were growing, every leaf and petal witnessing to the tender care of One, Who seems to delight to smile in the flower, rather than to frown in the storm. Which is most admirable, the delicate finish of each portion of grand painting, or the striking effect produced by the whole? While I am reveling in the enjoyment of the panorama before me, and of the emotion it awakens; the millions of crowded cities of the East are trembling [before?] the railroad strikers and socialists should lay waste [to] their firesides,[11] while not far to the West a column of troops is hotly pursuing a band of hostile Nez Perces,[12] whom they will soon encounter in [a] brave but disastrous fight. One of our party has found under a loose stone a small tin box containing the names of many visitors who have climbed the peak, among others, of General Belknap and party.[13] At the bottom of the list containing the names of those who accompanied him are scribbled the words: "We drink to the next travelers in Chaunay." Time was, when such a scene as this would have awakened in men's minds only reverence and awe, but now "pleasure in the mountains is never mingled with fear, or tempered by a spirit of mediation, as with the mediaeval; but it is always free of fearless, bright exhilarating and wholly unreflective, so that the painter feels that his mountain foreground may be more consistently animated by a sportsman than a hermit, and our modern society in general goes to the mountains, not to fast, but the feast, and leaves their glaciers covered with chicken bones and egg shells."

Our trail skirts the heavily-wooded sides of Mount Washburne [sic] on the west, and gradually descends to the valley of Cascade Creek.

Passing by the Cañon and Falls of the Yellowstone, for the present, we emerge upon open park country, through which the river winds broad and shallow, full of beautiful trout and bordered by grassy meadows, desolate, barren of vegetation, blighting the trees and shrubs about it.[14] Near its base is a huge caldron of irregular shape, filled with boiling water, emitting a strange sulphurous smell, and surrounded by smaller vents, sending forth steam and sulphur vapor. Minute yellow crystals line the vents, but they are too delicate to bear transportation. This hill or mountain has evidently been formed by the deposit from fountains or vents such as those now in action near its base.[15]

Some miles [farther] on we reached Mud Volcano situated among pine trees near the banks of the river. The principle mud volcano resembles when tranquil, an ordinary pond filled with water of a light green color. But as it is usually in a state of agitation, the calcareous mud at its sides and bottom being stirred up by steam jets from below, the whole bears the appearance of a huge boiling mud-puddle. The ebullition was most violent near the centre, and once the muddy water was thrown up several feet in the form of a fountain. Round about this pond, in the bare hardened mud, there are many curious funnel-shaped apertures, at the bottom of which the mud is soft and plastic, dull *thud*-like sounds issuing occasionally with sulphurous steam. Passing by many such openings, our attention was attracted by a tall column of steam rising from the side of a hill, and by a dull splashing sound that seemed to come from the same direction. Approaching the spot, we ascended a steep conical slope some thirty feet high, composed of mud and sand, and from the summit gazed down a still steeper slope into a huge caldron beneath. The sight was a horrible one. Twenty feet below great volumes of muddy water boiled, fumed and dashed about, roaring and bellowing as if demons were torturing the bodies of their victims, under its turbid waves. Puffs of steams obscured the view, but the clashing and crashing of the agitated waters sounded ceaselessly on the ear. This curious spring issuing from the side of a hill has built about itself a volcano-like cone, at the bottom of which, it groans, and roars, and seems to struggle, belching forth slimy showers that coat the surrounding trees with dirty grey mud. Not far off is the Devil's Den,[16] a cave in the hill side, from which, clear as crystal, breaks a spring of boiling water, ejected from some cavern further under the hill, with regular beats like those of a force pump, accompanied by the sound of a huge bellows. Startled by our approach, a small snake darted into the water near the spring; the next moment he coiled up, quivered and sank dead upon the pebbly bottom, boiled alive before our eyes. Where was the wisdom of the serpent? It had passed into our cook, perhaps, for he prudently availed himself of the spring to prepare a ham for us, putting it into the water that evening, and taking it out[?] at daybreak thoroughly boiled.

Against a great tree near our camp a huntsman had left a proof of his marksmanship. A huge swan, delicate in plumage, hung with outstretched wings nailed to the rough bark. What a mass of down on its swelling breast, what power in those long, tapering wings, what a silky gloss on the neck once proudly arched, now drooping like a bruised reed. It must have been a beautiful creature as it glided over the ripples of the river, or sailed through the clear air, and precisely because it was go goodly to the eye, it was laid low by a bullet, its whiteness sullied by its own blood, those wings stretched round the tree. God sends us a creature pure and white and spotless; man welcomes it with a bullet and three nails.[17]

The Great Geysers, thc main object of interest in the Park, lie along the Fire Hole River, a branch of the Madison. Between the waters of this stream, and the Yellowstone [River] is a steep, thickly-wooded divide, which is crossed with considerable difficulty, but the traveler soon forgets the toil of the journey when he has pitched his tent in the midst of the Great Geyser Basin.[18] The trail from the Mud Volcano to the Geysers leads westward through meadows thickly clad in waving grasses, the gentle slope on both sides being covered with pine trees.[19] Here and there the somber woods are brightened by a streak of sunlight, or by a glade that stretches the light green of the valley far up among the dark shadows of the pines. Several small tributaries of the Yellowstone lay across our path, forming ugly, steep ditches, which we were obliged to jump, testing our horsemanship, and the agility of our animals, as little accustomed as their riders to such exercise. We soon passed beyond this park-like region, and began to mount the divide.[20] Here the trail became dim and uncertain, the standing timber was dark and dense, fallen trees large, and numerous, rendering our march very toilsome. It was amusing to watch the pack mules wriggling to and fro, sometimes choosing the narrowest passages, sometimes increasing their gait when they came to two trees very close together, evidently with the intention of damaging their loads, if not entirely freeing themselves of the burden. The brutes are sagacious enough to measure with the eye the distance between two trees for their broad packs, so that, though often obliged to scrape and scratch through, they seldom or never have to turn back and seek another passage. Passing the summit, and descending to waters that flow into the Madison, we found ourselves involved in a morass that compelled us to make a long detour northward.[21] We then turned West along a branch of the East fork [Nez Perce Creek], which [joins] the Fire Hole River, some distance on. Our route then lay [south] along the valley of the Fire Hole River, until we reached the Geysers.

The Fire Hole River flows through a region in which for many miles on both sides of the stream hot springs, geysers, and boiling lakes occur, the principle ones lying in a tract known as the Fire Hole Basin.[22] The upper or southern portion of this basin contains the Great Geysers; the lower part, distant seven or eight miles, is filled with less active jets, while, in the long interval between, varied wonders attract the traveler at almost every turn.

Our camp is at the head of the Great Geyser Basin. A tent fly is stretched between two trees, so as to afford shade, but not to prevent the breeze from entering on every side. In front of us lie saddles, bridles, and guns; a few yards f[a]rther on, the camp-fire is crackling and blazing; the coffee-pot is doing its best already to vie with the hot springs about us, and our cook is busy with frying-pan and Dutch-oven. We are on a little knoll covered with verdure, but standing in the midst of what seems like a snow-clad valley. The green boughs of the trees that shelter us, and the dark fringe of fir and cedar round the valley, and are in marked contrast with the dazzling white of its surface. Curious cone-shaped structures [geyser mounds] rise here and there, from which jets of steam are issuing. Occasionally one of them splutters and spurts, casting out a few gallons of water, and seeming by its convulsive effort to be in pain, anxious, perhaps, to be rid of a weightier burden. The basin is not more than a few hundred yards in width, and three quarters of a mile in length, so that we can without difficulty command a view of the whole. The Geysers are situated on both sides of the stream; all are surrounded by a hard white siliceous deposit, though not all have formed cones above the surface immediately around their orifices. As we are gazing about a cry is raised, and the cook drops his frying-pan and runs towards us with the intelligence that "Old Faithful is going to spout."

Old Faithful is the name given to one of the Geysers most regular in its discharges, and we have chosen this particular spot for camp in order to be near Old Faithful. All eyes are at once turned in the direction of its cone, distant about three hundred yards. A puff of steam is rolling away from the orifice; a second puff curls upward, and then a jet of water is dashed a few feet into the air, falling back at once into the opening with a loud splash. A few moments of suspense follow, when suddenly a stately column of dark blue water rises before us, towering up towards the clouds. Higher and higher it mounts, until it has reached its limit. Straight it stands as an arrow, massive as marble, graceful as the slender jet from a fountain. The top spreads delicately outward, and then curving down, casts showers of glistening spray in all directions, whilst from the summit clouds of steam roll lightly up into the sky. For some minutes it stands steady and unbroken; a noise like the rolling of thunder, mingled with the roar of a cataract, telling what power is being exerted to sustain that vast weight of water in mid air; then, gradually, it sinks into its cavern. Every hour in the day and night, Old Faithful sings his roaring song of praise. Every hour, winter and summer, he seems to strive like the giants of old to mount the skies, and each time sends a cloud to join the rack that hangs over peaks higher than Olympus. The eruptions occur at intervals of from sixty-two to eighty minutes. The jet rises from one hundred to two hundred feet, our party estimating the height at one hundred and thirty feet, though the column of steam rose much higher. Trees are dwarfed in comparison with the stately crystal tower, men seem the merest pigmies, a feeling of awe creeps to the very marrow of one's bones. When the eruption is over, the monster has sunk back into the cavernous bosom of the earth, and all that remains of it is seen trickling in rills down to the Fire Hole River close by, leaving a deposit of white incrustations as it cools. The dead stillness and calm of nature make us feel the absence of the geyser, and a sense of oppression and listlessness succeeds the former feeling of dread and wonder.

Crossing by a narrow rustic bridge the pretty river that winds among these springs,[23] and is largely fed by their hot waters, we roam down the opposite bank. Here and there is a geyser, its opening surrounded by delicate incrustations, sometimes pearl white, sometimes softly tinted in yellow and brown. The tiny rills by which it sends its waters to join the river are fringed too with lace-like borders, colored in parts by the deposit from the water, in parts by a fungous growth such as I have never seen elsewhere.[24] Fresh wonders meet us at every step. There is a rushing sound ahead, and hastening on we find the Fan Geyser in full play. Issuing from a number of small openings close together, it spreads its waters in a graceful semicircle not unlike a huge fan. For many minutes the brilliant sheet of water stood before us, and scarcely had it subsided when we had the good fortune to see the beautiful display of the Riverside Geyser. It stands close to the right bank of the Fire Hole, its cone touching the water's edge. The orifice is small, probably eighteen inches in diameter, and inclined at an angle of 65 or 70 [degrees]. The column of water bending over the river falls more than midway in the running stream. As we approach, the sunlight struck the liquid arch in such a manner as to form two glorious rainbows one within the other. These nearly coincided in curvature with the fountain. For twenty minutes we stood spell-bound. Imagine the picture. Firs and cedars round the valley, in the centre a clear stream flowing between banks white but not with snow, and right in front of you a bridge, one pier of which is like a mound of ice covered with hoar-frost, its causeway of limpid crystal guarded by a double rainbow, its further pier, lost in clouds of steam ending mysteriously in the river, floods of light streaming around and through the whole fairy fabric. Suddenly it is gone like a dream, the river flows on, the branches sigh, the twilight plays across the valley, which seems now as if wrapped in a winding sheet, cold, white, and dead. Queen Mab and her fairy train have floated down the stream, the goblin army has passed from their cavern below the valley to the their barges of foam on the brook, destroying the valley to the bridge behind them, and leaving only one elf to teaze me with the thought that I never again shall see that vision of light and beauty.[25] Re-crossing the river we examine the many wonders that meet us on the other bank. The Castle Geyser stands up prominently, its huge jagged cone seemingly like some old ruined tower, near it yawns the great open mouth of a pool, the azure depths and snowy sides of which carry my imagination away to fairy-land again. The Grotto Geyser not far off with narrow passages and curving fissures, all lined with the same gleaming pearly deposit, tempts me to a closer examination of its wonders, but puffs of scalding steam or spurts of hot water check this curiosity, and remind me that my elfin friends will not bear to have their abodes too narrowly inspected.

Each of the Great Geysers is surrounded by a sloping mound [that] its waters have built up, and immediately about the aperture which is the centre of this mound, are series of basins, formed by the falling waters and beautifully fringed with colored incrustation. Where the Geyser has formed a cone about its orifice the interior of the cone is sometimes as smooth as glass with the luster of chalcedony.[26] In other places it is partly crystalline in structure, but here are no large distinct crystals. Many of the geysers have no such cones, but are merely marked by the gentle slopes which surround them. The Giantess, for instance, presented a great circular opening like a well, full of boiling water to the very brim. Gazing into its transparent depths of light blue, there was not the slightest sign of disturbance. The white rocks that line its crater could be seen far down, sharply defined as if looked at through the medium of air, and it was not till I had scalded my finger in the pool, that I succeeded in banishing the desire to plunge into what seemed to be a delicious bath. I can only touch upon a few of the wonders of this weird valley, but I must not leave the basin without mentioning the sense of insecurity the traveler feels in moving about. The incrusting layer is crisp and brittle; in places the foot sinks several inches, sometimes a hollow sound echoes the tread, a jet of steam spurts up from the tiny opening, a boiling caldron is sunken in your path, so that one feels prepared at any moment to have the earth give way, and to be dashed into a steaming lake below. What would have been Tom Thumb's sensations had he found himself rambling on a huge pie crust that had been rolled thin, made very short, and baked thoroughly. Not very different, I am sure, from those we felt while strolling about the Fire Hole. No wonder the Indians avoid the region in superstitious dread; its hollow caverns, sulphurous vapors, and startling discharges of boiling water, are all too suggestive of hell and its demons.

As we were breaking camp, and about to move out of the Geyser Basin, the Beehive saluted us with a handsome discharge. Its orifice is much smaller than that of Old Faithful, and the jet, slender in proportion, rises to a vast height. So superheated was the water it ejected, and so intermingled with steam, that the whole mass, spreading after it had reached a great elevation, floated away in a beautiful glowing cloud, and but little spray fell back about the Geyser. Not a word was spoken by our party, as they stood with eyes fixed upon the Geyser. Doubtless, the older members knew too well that words are poor, weak things in the presence of such a marvelous display of power, grace and beauty; one, however, less experienced than the rest, could hardly restrain such

FIGURE **2.2.**
Sometimes erupting to heights of over two hundred feet, Beehive Geyser
was a spectacular attraction from the earliest days. Our traveler Thomas
Sherman saw it in 1877 and proclaimed, "Words are poor, weak things in
the presence of such a marvelous display of power." (Wade Warren Thayer,
Marvels of the New West [Norwich, CT: Henry Bill Publishing, 1888].)

exclamations as "Grand! superb! magnificent! sublime!" but the words died upon his lips. "Mirabilis Deus in operibus suis."[27]

Passing the great Basin, and treading our way amid boiling springs and extinct geysers, we entered the pine woods [heading north], emerging some few miles f[a]rther down, near Hot Spring Lake. This is a great pond, the water if which is boiling hot and continually overflowing. With its gently sloping shores, dark blue ripples, and pretty outlet into the river, it seems like an ordinary pond. Near by it is a second pool, not so well disguised. Its shores are precipitous, the water extends back into great caverns under the hill, and slabs of stone thrown in all directions show plainly enough that it is simply an immense geyser.[28]

The most novel features in the lower Geyser Basin are the mud-pots or flower-pots.[29] Fancy an enormous tank of plaster or clay in a state of finest comminution and most perfectly plasticity. Color it pink or yellow, and then let bubbles of steam from below pass through the viscid mass, breaking over the surface in a thousand spots. The steam, of course, in escaping, throws the mud slightly up, then it sinks back in a circular wave, and for one moment a convolvulus, or a tulip, or rather a new species of flower, is blooming before you. These artificial plaster casts of flowers are forming every instant: the eye is distracted by the number and rapidity of the changes, so your glance wanders around and across, then back, to and fro once more, while the ceaseless blooming and decaying continues. Such a sight is very amusing and inviting to the eye, but I cannot imagine it possible that a man should build a hut on the edge of that pool, and set his heart upon those mud flowers. No more can I understand how a being with a soul can enjoy contentment, or cajole himself with the idea that he finds complete happiness in any creature of earth's mould, however highly colored or delicately shaped be the clay.

I could linger for hours about the lower Geyser Basin, but the sun is high, and many a weary mile over mountain and through forest must be passed to-day. So away we ride, with a last look back at the valley steaming and smoking behind us, a great manufactory or laboratory, rather a spot where at the Author of Nature, Workman as He is, has left things as though his task were not quite completed, and something remained to be done in fitting together the rocks of which earth's crust is composed, or in adjusting the relations between the chemical constituents of the rocks.

Back we ride across the steep divide, [east] through the dense forest, past Mary Lake,[30] over bog and moor, until we reach our former camping ground near the Falls of the Yellowstone. To understand the cañons and falls of the great Western rivers, it must be borne in the mind that the park regions, between different ranges of the Rocky Mountains, are very elevated, so that in finding their way from these districts to their valleys in the plains outside the mountains, the rivers must make somewhere a very rapid descent. The effect of such a descent is, of course, to form a deep gorge, which is gradually extended f[a]rther and f[a]rther back into the mountains, as the water wears away the rocks over which it has been tumbling during the ages. The largest cataracts are not found, then, at the point where streams emerge into the prairies, but in the very midst of the mountain chain. Following the Yellowstone from its broad outlet at the lake, we find it a smooth, quiet sheet of water, flowing between open prairies. Twenty miles down, it encounters rough opposing hills, and, contracting and deepening its channel, leaps a hundred and twenty-five feet down between rocky walls, then foaming, eddying and lashing against rocks, half a mile on it plunges three hundred and fifty feet f[a]rther into its cañon below.[31] Scrambling through brushwood and over logs and rocks, directed by the roar of the falls, I reached the upper cascade, and, lying at full length on a jutting crag, leaned out over the seething water. When fully sated with the grand sight, I scrambled through a steep ravine and up the opposite slope, little imagining that a scene awaited me more superb than the beautiful plunge at which I had just been looking. The sun was fast sinking, so I hurried to a rock some distance beyond the lower falls, and out upon the steep slope of the cañon. As if preparing for its second leap, the river comes surging and tumbling in waves and eddies towards the brink,

> Advancing, and prancing, and glancing, and dancing,
> Recoiling, turmoiling, and toiling, and boiling,

Until, almost at the edge, it unites into one glassy mass curved upwards at the sides, and then leaps forward and downward, soon separating into spray, and ending in a light vapor that floats down the valley, clothing the rocks with a soft green moss. The sides of the cañon, precipitous slopes of a thousand feet, are gorgeous in red, yellow and brown tints that light up the scene with their varied hues. Down below, the river winds away, a mere thread, as if utterly broken and almost annihilated by the fall, so slight and slender it is between its mountainous banks. Such is the magnificence of the scene that the cataract with all its sublimity is but a small feature in the picture. A vast shrine in nature's bosom—curtains of gold and scarlet made of crumbling rock—fringed at the base with the silver of the stream, bordered at the top with the green of the forest, canopied by Heaven's blue—the waterfall, a cascade of delicate spray streaming down into the shrine like white-winged spirits descending in vain held back by dark masses of opposing rock, the great chasm filled and glowing with sunlight, and spreading eastward toward the prairie country—a temple, in which resides the angel of the stream, to receive honor and reverence for the work done by the river, and to carry heavenward the cries of praise and wonder of poor humanity, admiring in nature's beauty the magnificence of nature's God.

The width of the cañon is little more than half a mile, its depth, as has been said, a sheer thousand feet, the descent on both sides being too precipitous to be attempted at this point. The falls are half way down the cañon and though extremely beautiful, seem dwarfed by the immense proportions of the surrounding scene.

Twilight begins to draw a veil over the picture. The slanting rays of the sun that pierced through the gloomy woods, and shooting like arrows against the opposing bank, drew out, as if by magic, the colors locked in its rocky breast, now no longer dart across the cañon; the tints mingle and fade, and gloomy precipices stand in place of superb curtains; the column of mist and spray at the foot of the cataract, that rivaled the Great Geysers a few moments ago in airy, cloud-like splendor, no longer is seen, but the deep sullen roar of the waters seems to grow louder and louder, and as the eye loses, the ear gains, distinguishing in the deep tones rolling up from the cañon, the echo of the voice that speaks to us in the roar of the ocean and the crash of thunder.

Those who have not witnessed such scenes will find it hard to realize the complicated nature of the impressions they produce. The soul, aroused as if from a slumber, is stirred to its depths. Enchanted, yet appalled, admiring, but fearful, exhilarated, and at the same time humiliated and depressed, she longs to break forth in praise and exultation, but is restrained and hampered by a sense of the weakness, meanness, sinfulness of poor human nature. We know that God is everywhere, we fancy perhaps that we enjoy a lively sense of His Omnipresence, but let

Him lift the veil that hides His power and splendor for a moment, as He did of old on Tabor, or let Him shine through the cloud with unusual brightness in some vast landscape, and we cower and crouch to something like our true proportions, as if before one whom we had never known before.

At the northern end of the Park, a few miles above the Gardner's River, are situated the Mammoth Springs, which travelers usually visit on entering Wonderland, but which we had reserved for our return trip.[32]

The largest of these springs gushes out on the summit of a hill some two hundred feet above the valley, and overflowing along the face of the hill, its bright blue water, saturated with salts held in solution, forms in its descent tier after tier of basins, varying in size and shape, but all of singular beauty. These basins are only a few inches in depth; the material of which they are composed is soft and friable while moist, and still more so on drying. The edges are fringed with the most delicate and beautiful masses of crystal, the bright rosy tints of which contrast strikingly with the blue liquid they encircle. But the colors fade and the forms crumble when they are removed from the water which has deposited them. The whole hill seems to have been built by the action of the spring, the portion now visible being the outside coating that covers millions of basins, which were successively formed, left dry by the waters, destroyed by the air, their material building up the hill itself, and a new overflow spreading fresh terraces above them. The process can be seen going on at this moment; many basins are empty, faded, fast efflorescing and crumbling to dust, and here and there the foot sinks two or three inches in the soft plaster-like surface of the hill. On a plateau above the first huge mound I have been describing, rises another, seemingly older, and similar in structure. Beyond this second elevation extend a number of small ridges of very curious character. They lie parallel with one another, running from northeast to southwest, in height varying from thirty to fifty feet, their breadth at the base being about the same as their height. These ridges are cleft along the summit, the division being sometimes several inches wide, and marked in places by a row of hot springs, bubbling and spurting. So rapid has been the deposit from these springs, that growing trees are buried as they stand. Great caverns are formed at the sides of the ridges, and the waters, trickling into these dark recesses, line them with pretty incrustations, and petrify pine cones and branches that happen to fall in.

The baths are considered very fine. My own experience was too nearly that of being scalded to allow of my giving of fair judgment, and others of our party complained of feeling partially petrified on emerging.

An enterprising frontiersman, McCartney by name, has built a number of bath houses to facilitate the use of the water, by patients who come here to avail themselves of its salutary properties. A log house of good size serves as an inn, or "hotel" as it is called, and wonderful cures are said to have been wrought by the giant fountain.[33] Doubtless, before long the Mammoth Springs will be a common resort, perhaps a fashionable watering-place,[34] where the old will go to hobble and croak, and the young to dance and chirp, introducing scenes from the farce of life to mare [mar] the plot of nature's stately drama.

In a brief sketch, such as this, I cannot give you a detailed account of our journey from day to day, nor of the thousand little things that go to make up the charm of camp life. For the city-bred man there is a novelty, not only at every turn of the road or trail, in the varying landscape, but in rising, eating, sleeping and all the commonplaces of life. Crawling from between your buffalo robes, you dress hastily, and run to wash in the brook that flows near by. The water is cold as ice, so it drives sleep from your tired eyes, and gazing about, you see that nature, too, has washed her face in hoar-frost,[35] which the sun, just now lighting up the east, will soon wipe away. The camp-fire is already crackling, and the cook—how like a gnome he looks in that peaked hat and grizzled beard, stooping over the fire at his work in the grey light of dawn—is busy preparing your coffee and bacon.

Breakfast now finished, the animals are led up, shivering with cold. Now the beds are rolled up neatly, and strapped in their canvas covers, the tent-fly is struck and folded, the camp equipage is stowed in bags, and the pack animals are brought forward. How meek and unoffending is the expression of that mule "Patsy"['s] injured innocence over again, but beware of her heels; she has been known to knock a man down with a soft tap of her left hind leg, and then to turn quietly, as if to ask what caused his fall? The other day, just as our guide, Anderson, was adjusting her pack-saddle, she turned and darted down a steep hill-side, dragging him and two others, who had quickly seized her picket-rope. The loose shingle of the hill-side afforded find anchorage for Anderson's heels, as he moved, in a sitting posture, like a small avalanche or an inverted snow-plow, gathering the debris in his descent. When Patsy was finally brought to bay, nothing could exceed the tranquil, modest air with which she received her burden. The last embers of the campfire have been carefully extinguished, to prevent any danger of its spreading, the mules have all been loaded, saddles, adjusted, and we are off just as the sun peeps over the hill, driving away the cloud of mist that hung about us, and converting the hoar-frost into brilliants, with [which?] it soon gathers like a harvest. Now we are traveling indeed, even Ruskin would admit it,[36] two or three miles an hour, and plenty of time to enjoy all the details of scenery as they are unfolded. As the track is very narrow, in places steep and difficult, you are nearly always alone, left to your own quiet enjoyment of nature, to meditate on yesterday's experience, or to picture the wonders you are still in search of. The panorama, viewed quietly and slowly from day to day, is like a revelation; the dark mountains and rugged ravines, the prairies and streams, "trees and flowers seem all, in a sort, children of God, and we ourselves their fellows, made out of the same dust, and greater than they in having a greater portion of the divine power exerted on our frames, and all the common uses and palpably visible form of things become subordinate in our minds to their inner glory, to the mysterious voices in which they talk to us about God, and the changeful, and typical aspects, by which they witness to us of holy truth, and fill us with obedient, joyful, and thankful emotion." In the evening a place for camp is being chosen, some spot where wood and water are at hand, and where there is good grazing for the mules and horses. As the poor brutes are unloaded, they roll and tumble on the ground, rejoicing to be free from the galling weights that have pressed upon them for these long hours, then scamper away to their pasture. Wood is at once gathered for the camp-fire, boughs are cut for tent-poles; soon you are provided with food and shelter, and you feel you are at home. The sun sinks behind the mountain, twilight soon fades, the stars shine out with wonderful brilliancy in the rare atmosphere, dead stillness reigns, and with a lingering look at the shadowy scene about, your back is turned to the camp-fire til tomorrow. T[HOMAS].E[WING].S[HERMAN].

Notes

The account was originally published as T.E.S., "Across the Continent. II.—The National Park," *Woodstock Letters* 11 (1882): 25–42.

1. Biographical information is from Joseph T. Durkin, *General Sherman's Son* (New York: Farrar, Straus, and Cudahy, 1959).

2. The Organic Act of 1872 (*U.S. Statutes at Large*, vol. 17, chap. 24, 32–33) established Yellowstone as the world's first national park.

3. Today this is called Gardner River, although in Sherman's day it was Gardner's or Gardiner's River.

4. Even before Yellowstone was a national park, journalists seized upon the name Wonderland because of the many curiosities there. By the 1880s, the term was so entrenched that guidebooks were published using the name. Aubrey L. Haines, *Yellowstone Place Names: Mirrors of History* (Boulder: University Press of Colorado, 1996), 48.

5. Except for crude tracks that were not much more than bridle paths from near Gardiner, Montana, to Mammoth Hot Springs to Cooke City, Montana, and from the west entrance to Lower Geyser Basin, there were no roads in Yellowstone until 1878, when P. W. Norris built the first road from Mammoth to Old Faithful. Aubrey L. Haines, *The Yellowstone Story* (1977; rev., Boulder: University of Colorado Press, 1996), I, 242.

6. Sherman referred here to the Black Canyon of the Yellowstone on the east and the Gardner Canyon on the south, imposing drainages that blocked the way into the new park. Because his party was headed east to Pleasant Valley, they probably took the "Turkey Pen Road" down Rescue Creek and up Blacktail Deer Creek to reach the Cooke City road.

7. Actually, Sherman was looking at peaks of the Absaroka Range, which form the park's east boundary. The Bighorn range is much farther east and not visible from the Washburn summit.

8. These rivers were so named by Lewis and Clark in 1805, when their party reached Three Forks, Montana.

9. Sherman probably refers here to the Continental Divide, which snakes through Yellowstone Park to the southwest of his vantage point.

10. The more religious of many early park visitors, like Sherman, poured forth such sentiments as they beheld the beauties of the park. See, generally, Joel Daehnke, *In the Work of Their Hands Is Their Prayer: Cultural Narrative and Redemption on the American Frontiers, 1830–1930* (Athens: Ohio University Press, 2003).

11. Sherman referred here to "the Great Railroad Strike of 1877," which was the first major railroad strike in the United States. The strike spread from Pittsburgh to San Francisco and involved hundreds of cities across the United States. It resulted in nearly one hundred deaths and property damage that reached into the millions of dollars. George Brown Tindall and David Emory Shi, *America: A Narrative History* (New York: W. W. Norton and Company, 1999), 910–12.

12. He referred here to the Nez Percé War of 1877. For background, see Jerome Greene, *Nez Perce Summer 1877: The U.S. Army and the Nee-Me-Poo Crisis* (Helena: Montana Historical Society Press, 2000).

13. This mustard tin was mentioned by many early travelers as being on the summit of Mount Washburn and containing many pieces of paper with the signatures of those who had ascended. For example, see the account in this very book by Mrs. L. D. Wickes, who noted: "On its rock ribboned peak was a mustard tin box containing the autographs of some fifty persons who among the many tourists since 1871 were the only ones that had sufficient time and patience to climb to the very top." Unfortunately, this mustard tin containing many interesting signatures has long since disappeared.

14. This was the Crater Hills (Sulphur Mountain) area in Hayden Valley, through which the main tourist road eventually ran until it was removed in the 1920s.

15. This was Sulphur Spring, also known as Crater Hills Geyser, at the base of one of the Crater Hills. Lee Whittlesey, *Wonderland Nomenclature*, 1988, unpublished manuscript, Yellowstone National Park Library, Yellowstone National Park, Sulphur Spring entry.

16. This was Dragon's Mouth Spring, six miles north of Lake Village. Lee H. Whittlesey, *Yellowstone Place Names* (Gardiner, MT: Wonderland Publishing Company, 2006), 90.

17. Hunting was technically legal in Yellowstone until January 1883. Haines, *The Yellowstone Story*, I, 304, 364n31.

18. The proper name, then and now, is Upper Geyser Basin, of which Old Faithful Geyser is a primary feature.

19. The trail they took west across Hayden Valley to Lower Geyser Basin was probably the Mary Mountain road, which in 1877 was just being developed and marked by eastbound soldiers under Lt. Spurgin who were pursuing the fleeing Nez Percé Indians. Greene, *Nez Perce Summer 1877*, 197.

20. While not the Continental Divide proper, this is the divide between the waters of the Firehole River and the Yellowstone River. Both of those streams flow to the Atlantic Ocean.

21. A morass is a marshy or boggy area. This was undoubtedly one of the large marshes at the head of Nez Perce Creek, which stream they were following west.

22. This general name referred early to both the Lower and Upper Geyser Basins.

23. This was one of the earliest bridges in Yellowstone National Park and perhaps the earliest human-built structure at that location. It was present before the first wagon road was built to the Upper Geyser Basin in 1878 and was apparently a footbridge in Upper Basin that went undocumented in official reports but appeared in anecdotal accounts like this one.

24. This "fungus growth" is actually cyanobacteria, a hot water life-form that grows in various colors according to the temperature of its environment.

Though it was formerly thought to be algae, its bacterial origin was finally understood in the 1980s. See generally, Thomas Brock, *Life in the Geyser Basins* (Yellowstone National Park: Yellowstone Library and Museum Association, [1971]).

25. In English folklore, Queen Mab was a fairy. She is memorably described in a famous speech by Mercutio in *Romeo and Juliet*, in which she is a miniature creature who drives her chariot across the faces of sleeping people and compels them to dream dreams of wish fulfillment.

26. Chalcedony is a microcrystalline translucent variety of quartz, often milky or grayish. It is celebrated in the park today by the place-name Chalcedony Creek. Whittlesey, *Yellowstone Place Names*, 65.

27. The phrase is Latin for "God of miracles in his own works."

28. They were traveling north to Midway Geyser Basin, and thus "Hot Spring Lake" was probably today's Grand Prismatic Spring, while the "second pool" was Excelsior Geyser. Four years later, Excelsior would become one of the world's tallest and widest geysers.

29. The reference here was to Fountain Paint Pot at Lower Geyser Basin, eight miles north of Old Faithful.

30. They were returning via the route they had come, today's Mary Mountain trail.

31. This first plunge is actually 109 feet; the second, 308 feet.

32. The north entrance served as the primary starting point for thousands of visitors due to the Northern Pacific Railroad and its promotional efforts that began with its arrival in 1883. It served north entrance visitors through 1948 and continued to carry freight to Yellowstone through 1975. Craig Reese, "The Gardiner Gateway to Yellowstone," *The Mainstreeter* 15 (Spring 1996): 5–18.

33. James McCartney (1835–1908) built his primitive hotel in Clematis Gulch and erected bathhouses on nearby Hymen Terrace in 1871. Park authorities evicted him around 1879, and he wandered down to Gardiner, Montana, to found that town in 1880. Haines, *The Yellowstone Story*, I, 254, 266.

34. Hot spring spas were popular at the time on the East Coast, and persons who frequented them were referred to as "taking the waters" for medicinal and drinking purposes. See Thomas A. Chambers, *Drinking the Waters: Creating an American Leisure Class at Nineteenth-Century Mineral Springs* (Washington, DC: Smithsonian Institution Press, 2002), esp. 4, 27, 225; and John Sears, *Sacred Places: American Tourist Attractions in the Nineteenth Century* (New York: Oxford University Press, 1989).

35. Hoarfrost is frozen dew that forms a white coating on a surface.

36. He probably referred here to John Ruskin (1819–1900), who was an English author, poet, and artist, although more famous for his work as an art critic and social critic. Ruskin's thinking on art and architecture became the thinking of the Victorian and Edwardian eras. The long quote a bit later is from John Ruskin, *Modern Painters*, 5 vols. (New York: Wiley and Halstead, 1857; copy at Yale Beinecke Library, New Haven), n.p.

THREE

Camping Out in the Great Yellowstone Valley, Montana Territory

MRS. L. D. WICKES

1880

⌘

BORN ABOUT 1848, MRS. L. D. WICKES (1848?–1944) APPARENTLY used her maiden initials "L. D.," and that was unusual for women of her day. The 1930 Census gave her name as Elizabeth D. Wickes, so perhaps she called herself Liz D. Wickes. Mrs. Wickes came to Montana with her husband, the Rev. Thomas A. Wickes, in 1879, making the final stages of the journey up the Missouri River by steamboat. Both natives of Marietta, Ohio, Mr. and Mrs. Wickes previously lived in Joplin, Missouri, where they both taught school following their marriage. After his arrival in Montana, Thomas held the Presbyterian pulpit in the town of Boulder. Retiring from his pulpit after a few years, he went into business in the town of Wickes with Montana pioneer Samuel Hauser.

Wickes is today a mining ghost town south of Helena. Thomas Wickes appears to have given the name to the mining community after a relative (probably his father), W. W. Wickes, an engineer and promoter for the Alta Mining Company. Later, Thomas and L. D. lived in Helena and Missoula. They were enthusiastic skaters all of their lives and led skating parties on the river at Missoula at age seventy-eight (the two were the same age). Their final move was to Kalispell around 1924. Following Thomas's death in 1934, L. D. continued her church activities until just before her death at age ninety-five. Her last few years were spent with her daughter, Mrs. W. W. Taylor. She was also survived by a son, W. W. Wickes, eleven grandchildren, and nineteen great-grandchildren. At the time of her death on March 11, 1944, Mrs. L. D. Wickes had been a Montana resident for sixty-four years.[1]

Other than for her viewings of many of the park's large geysers, perhaps the most fascinating portions of Mrs. Wickes's account detailed her party's meetings with numerous early Yellowstone personalities: Superintendent P. W. Norris, toll road keeper James "Yankee Jim" George, photographer Henry Bird Calfee, and bridge builder and guide C. J. "Jack" Baronett. Baronett was then owner of the toll bridge over Yellowstone River, and Mrs. Wickes transposed his Scottish brogue into actual sounds for modern readers. She stated that her reason for writing was to stimulate others to make the Yellowstone trip, and she left us an important record of the park before real roads and genuine stagecoach tours appeared on the scene.

—∞—

In 1879 less than 50 people passed through our "National Wonderland," while last summer the number was swelled to several hundred, and it is with the hope of stimulating your readers to take their summer vacation here, among the great numbers whose coming is anticipated and provided for by stage lines and hotels, that the following record of our last summer's six weeks' expedition is given.[2]

Over smooth and even roads, bordered with bunch grass and wild flowers, went a gay party from Wickes, Montana territory, numbering 13 persons—eight gentlemen and five ladies—with complete appointments for the expedition.[3]

Two heavy wagons, a light express, 16 horses and the dog, "Nigger,"[4] completed the company. Provisions for the entire journey, the supply regulated to supply mountain appetites, quantities of robes, bedding, tent, hammock, kitchen utensils, together with all the valises, shawl straps and bundles, [and] containing all the innumerable necessities for the toilet, which even pioneer women find indispensable, were packed in the two heavy wagons.

The express wagon was for the sick or weary, and furnished with a small but ample medicine catchel, which was continually getting lost.

FIGURE 3.1.

Like Mrs. Wickes's party, these unidentified tourists visited the park
in their own wagons rather than patronizing the commercial stage
lines and hotels. Campers, such as the group pictured here (1874–81),
were commonly referred to as "sage brushers." (YELL 127319,
Yellowstone National Park Archives, Yellowstone National Park.)

The horses were available as pack animals, draught horses, and for
use under the saddle; no feed for them being required, on account of the
fine pasture lands [that we passed through].

The first few days were especially trying. [Because we were] Unused
to riding, the 30 miles of travel each day brought fatigue to the ladies, and
the express was extensively patronized. The packing and unpacking of
so much baggage proved an arduous undertaking also to men who could
travel indefinitely with their extra clothing tied in [only] a handkerchief.

Very shortly systematic work prevailed and when the sun, casting
long shadows from the mountain peaks, gave the signal for camping
for the night, the horses were picketed,[5] cooking utensils produced, oil-
cloth laid in a smooth spot, and set with tin dishes, fire roaring, kettle
boiling, supper steaming, tent erected and bedding arranged by many
and willing hands, long before darkness settled on the busy picture and
made us pile up the crackling pine logs to shed a ruddy light on the

happy company circling around the fire while, with songs and laughter, we recounted jokes and incidents of the day.

Each lady had her forte in the culinary line, preparing trout, grouse, venison, antelope, tomatoes, potatoes or beans, while the bread-making fell upon the experienced and ever willing frontiersmen of the party. And such bread!

Not considering our brief stopping at Bozeman, nor our passing glimpse at the cavalry post, Camp Ellis,[6] our first objective point was the Mammoth Springs.

Taking the only route to that point, we passed through Rocky canyon, with its crags, caves, and evergreen clad mountains on either side; refreshed ourselves with gooseberries, raspberries, service and choke berries, while our bulky team hesitated about ascending the mountain on the f[a]rther side.[7]

Occasionally we met a returning party from the springs, but oftener we spent the entire day without sight of any other living creatures, save jackrabbit or ground squirrel, until in the Yellowstone valley we overtook a charming party from Deer Lodge, who had passed us near Camp Ellis, the distinguished member of which was Mr. [Horace] Claggit [sic—Claggett], well known as territorial representative in 1875.[8]

Our first view of the Yellowstone was after a snowy, stormy night, when the gentlemen of the party, tired of swallowing the snowflakes as they inhaled the oxygen of the night air, took refuge in the tent, where we also breakfasted in close quarters, while we looked out on a landscape white with snow. Towards noon, however, the snow disappeared, leaving the valley fresh and beautiful; as, in a slight mist, we climbed the Point of Rocks, a cliff above us 60 feet high, seemingly one rock, and another below us of at least 160 feet, we looked down upon the yellow fields of pasture and a green, waving, ribbon-like river, the Yellowstone, with dark, undulating mountain sides beyond, and a brilliant rainbow below us, thrown by the struggling sunlight upon God's meadows, bringing pots of gold to our very feet.[9]

Up the cañon, on roads where heads turn dizzy, we followed the river towards its source, listening to its wonderful music as impetuously it tears its way among the rocks, deepening its narrow bed until the channel is often hidden from the roadside.

Our energies being for the time overcome, we camped at sunset near the tollgate of "Yankee Jim."

Here the Deer Lodge party sent us salmon trout for supper, and Yankee Jim the same for breakfast; joining us to tell us of his squaw wife, who is a preacher, and of his road through the mountains, now valued at $35,000, although the building of the same, when begun in 1871, had seemed the commencement of a foolish enterprise.[10]

With the ever-varying and exquisite scenery, our artist [name unknown] made frequent and characteristic sketches of the mountains, labeling each important feature, to assist recognition.

Making slow progress, on account of the team, whose natural propensity was to camp at the foot of each elevation, we at last succeeded, after ascending a three mile grade, in obtaining a first glimpse and commanding view of the Mammoth Springs.

[The place is] A white plateau, steam floating over the painfully quiet surface, surrounded by mountains, save on the northern side, where extends, some fifty feet below a plain of white, dried mud, dotted with small, cavernous openings, some of which are enlarged below the surface into large rooms, sixty feet deep and forty feet in diameter, still below which are unfathomable wells. These are undoubtedly very ancient, extinct [hot] springs, the calcareous deposit of which, having effectually obstructed the passage of the waters, the latter have forced comparative recent openings in the plateau above.

Passing [a] Geyser cone, "Liberty Cap," we climbed the wet, slippery semi-petrified sides of the plateau, walked on hollow sounding, heated earth, resembling bone-dust, which emitted a strong sulphurous smell; balanced ourselves on the firm, rapidly forming, raised, scalloped borders of pools containing clear, transparent boiling water; peeped into the huge, shell-like reservoirs; followed in chalky tracks of now dried surface streams; listened to the bursting bubbles of hot water, suggestive of mud-turtles in the hidden depths, and passed many hours of interesting investigation, exclaiming often, as did our German friend, "It is a wonderful formation, it is indeed."[11]

Here, in the "Grotto of the Glen," from whose dome, with a dull roar, rises a stream of hot water, flowing over its sides in innumerable, gentle streams, we collected for our home cabinets, exquisite stalactite specimens, resembling white coral, tinted with green, blue, rose and cream colors.[12]

Strange sea green mouths, two feet in height, rise to the surface in some of the pools, like plants, whose buds spout water from their crimson centers. And in the edge of the cliff, to be subjected to the falling water, we left, during our absence of ten days, small demijohns to be found on our return coated white as snow.[13]

The demijohns we had found empty by the wayside, although our statement to that effect would have been discredited perhaps, had we been seen carrying them on horseback, with sunburnt faces, disheveled hair and disarranged toilets.

The baths at this place are invigorating although not equaling in medicinal qualities and softness of the water of the hot springs at Boulder [Montana], near Wickes. The latter have a temperature of 160 degrees Fahrenheit, and have been utilized by the construction of bath-houses, swimming pools, and kept in most excellent condition; [whereas] we were not tempted to indulge freely in bathing in the strong lime-water, lest we make "hardened sinners" of ourselves.

Leaving the wagons, and proceeding to the great canyon of the Yellowstone, with pack-horses and a limited supply of provisions and bedding, we followed the trail forty miles to the falls, passing on the way Tower Falls, where the river drops into a secluded glen one hundred and thirty-five feet below,[14] from between five turrets of granite, like cathedral spires, pointing upward to the speck of blue sky visible between the pine foliage, overshadowing the evergreen ferns and delicate mosses below.

Climbing down the cliffs, clinging to fallen logs, stones and roots, we resembled a party of kangaroos; one of the gentlemen using, unfortunately, his nose as a plow, before he reached the bottom, where we were covered with spray from the divided stream above, breaking on a huge rock at the base.

The next day's sun found us well on our way to Mount Washburn, where we met the line of perpetual snow—it was very dirty, the snow, not the line, and we played snowball while we picked bluebells to press in our notebooks. Mount Washburn being ten thousand feet above the sea level is a station in the primary and secondary triangulation.[15]

On its rock-riven peak was a tin mustard box containing the autographs of some fifty persons, who, among the many tourists since 1871, were the only ones who had sufficient time and patience to climb to the very top.[16]

If we were not with distinguished persons, our autographs were [nevertheless] placed above those of Belknap, Marcy, Schurz, Sherman, John Boyd, Principal of Hertford College, England, and others.

The written statements of these gentlemen were quite interesting. One told of his horse falling down the cliff, resulting in his death; one found the road impassable in July; and was compelled to turn back; another, on a clear day, saw a geyser "go off," one hundred miles away; while we, looking down on boiling mountain tops, in every direction recognized the Big Horns of Wyoming and the Tetons of Idaho.[17] Donning our zeph[y]r rubber coats, we hurried down the steep mountain sides in a brisk thunderstorm. A few miles beyond, after following a bear trail, we saw the shaggy, black fellow, but left him unmolested, as one will frequently cause a stampede among horses, and some used by the ladies being easily terrified.

Going directly to the Yellowstone falls, we met the Superintendent of the park, Mr. P. W. Norris, who sent us elk meat for our dinner, and with it much valuable information.[18]

We spent an entire day amid curious and wonderfully beautiful scenery, unmolested here, as everywhere in the park, by guides or specimen peddlers.

Without regulations, exorbitant charges or policemen, we climbed from point to point, trying to realize the magnitude of the canyon, with its picturesque walls of shaded yellow and red, down whose precipitous and shelving sides five persons have dared to go, and have returned safely, although taking their lives in their hands as well as their pick-axes. Niagara's height faded into insignificance, as we rested and sketched, while we gazed, peering over the edge of the lower falls, three hundred and ninety feet, and then climbing through the underbrush and woods to the side of the upper falls, one hundred and ninety feet in height,[19] casting a vast, tumultuous body of water below. We culled ferns for pressing, and red huckleberries, together with wild September strawberries, for present consumption, and then spent the only anxious hours of our journey until midnight, when the return of the missing horses was announced. "Cached" is the mountain expression, learned from the Indians, signifying "stolen and hidden, perhaps in hope of reward," and the peculiar circumstances of the disappearance of the horses, together with the fact that we had but a limited supply of provisions in an unpopulated country, without available means of transportation, gave us much uneasiness until the animals were found.

Retracing our steps, for a day, we turned eastward, toward Specimen mountain. This promontory is one of a chain containing remarkable petrifications. In the present undeveloped condition of the park, every discoverer of remarkable things hides his researches until an opportunity arrives for converting his knowledge into dollars and cents. We contented ourselves with the oft culled-over specimens of amethyst chrystals lying on the surface of the mountain, leaving to more earnest seekers the huge crystallized trunks of trees, almost wholly embedded in the earth, which require arduous toil to unearth, although amply rewarding to the curiosity hunter.

From this mountain hundreds of dollars' worth of curious specimens have been shipped to the states. As we watched the many-hued tints in the spread of the sun, as it sunk to rest, a wild wind-storm gathered blackness behind us, and when we hurriedly turned our thought from the most exquisite bit of sky-coloring we had ever beheld, to the descent of the mountain, we suffered much anxiety. We led our horses by the bridle reins, scarcely able to keep our footing. The dead pines creake[d], threatening to fall on us every moment, and the darkness dropped upon us like a mantle.

It was with difficulty we found our way to camp, and the near proximity of a mountain lion, whose voice could occasionally be heard, did not increase our comfort.

Over one of the forks of the Yellowstone, near this mountain, "Scotty" has built a bridge.[20] He is his own toll-keeper, and spends his long summer fishing, meditating and collecting a dollar poll-tax on every horse that crosses.

Learning the low state of our larder he gave, unasked, of his own tea, bacon, fish, and bread, for which we gladly paid him out of our store of sugar. He eagerly courted our society and begged for songs. Some one suggested "Gospel Hymns," but although the backwoodsman had never heard of Moody and Sankey,[21] he expressed a strong dislike to sacred music, claiming that he was brought up on Scotch psalms in the old country. But we insisted on singing the "Ninety and Nine," and at its close the poor Scotsman dropped his head on his hands, exclaiming, "I'm that sheep, I am; can ye gie me the buk, and I'll tak one day for the Lord a reading it, the first for mony a year."

He seemed surprised to learn we had entered the month of September, and then looking pensive again he urged, "sing it again, won't ye? And do ye coll thot church music?"

From Scotty's camp we took a forced march on a very warm

Sabbath, not even stopping in the heat of noon, our provisions being completely exhausted.

After reaching the springs and the wagons, we spent a few days cooking, hunting stray horses and doing a "family washing," and then "resuming the march," had stereoscopic views taken of the party by one of the traveling photographers who are collecting the remarkable views of Montana for stereopticon entertainments.[22]

Passing a day in camping in Geyser Meadow, a huge plateau, surrounded by high peaks, and waiting for the cessation of a snow-storm, we found an opportunity to examine the paint-pots or pools of gurgling muddy water and clay, in many brilliant colors.[23]

We also climbed Mt. Schurz, 8,500 feet high, and heavily wooded, on the top of which, surrounded by pines cut off from all sight of the rest of the world.

It would be difficult to depict the excited anticipation of every member of the party, which now, after witnessing most curious freaks of nature, were about to enter the Lower Geyser Basin. The travelers we met urged our leaving it unexamined and using all haste to reach the Upper Geyser Basin, to witness the "going off" of the Giantess geyser, which explodes but once in 16 days, and that time having almost expired since an eruption.[24]

On entering the basin, which is simply a vast and regular depression amid mountains, we found some 50 people in camp, most of them waiting for the troubling of the water of the Giantess geyser, before leaving the park.

After a hurried repast we climbed the slope of the Giantess, on whose flat summit extended a huge pool of boiling water, whose rocky walls were uncomfortably warm, and whose throbs, as from pent-up emotions, almost terrified us. That night we slept in our clothing, boots buttoned and hats within reach; but notwithstanding the firm belief that the display, accompanied by loud reports, as from a cannonade, would take place before morning, not a soul in all the basin awoke until the subsiding of the waters, about 5 o'clock a.m. Such is the heavy sleep caused by breathing the cold, out-door mountain air.

Such a sleepy, unwashed, disappointed concorse of people as assembled in the dull mist of the morning around the subsiding geyser, it has never been our misfortune to behold, and only the sense of the ludicrous enabled many of us to keep our temper.

As we went back to our various encampments and watched the rising, individual vapors from 50 different [geysers that] covered the basin, the hush which covered the basin, the hush of nature fell upon us, and not until the strong sunlight and a cup of coffee were announced, did we rally to our accustomed hilarity. The oatmeal we had for breakfast had been cooked slowly all night over a fissure in a small mound, through which rushed hot steam continually. The beans, which were cooking in a flour-sack in a geyser pool, held in place by a pile of small stones, "went off" with the geyser, and were lost.[25]

The "Beehive," with its symmetrical cone, five feet high, sends with tremendous force an upright column of water four feet in diameter, to the height of 100 feet.[26] It gave us daily exhibitions of great beauty.

"Old Faithful," beloved by every visitor, unsurpassed in beauty, stands at the upper end of the basin, and every hour, both day and night, shoots the boiling water over 200 feet high,[27] which then falls back into rocky pockets on [its] sloping sides, affording unrivalled wash-house facilities; beautifully corrugated white tubs, hold, some of them, over a barrel of clear, soft water of varying temperature, as selected near the top or bottom of the slope, and with wash-board surfaces, which are most convenient.

Occasionally garments are thrown into the mouth of "Old Faithful," and in an hour the clever laundress sends them up again unrivalled in whiteness, but often torn to tatters, from her furious under-ground machinery.

"The Lioness" and her two "Cubs" stand together; the mother growling while the water gurgles beneath the surface of the little ones as if they were at play.[28]

"The Castle," quite a large, picturesque structure of the same curious white formation as the rest, keeps up a light but steady cannonade, with insignificant water discharges.[29] The "Riverside" stands on the banks of the Fire Hole river, which latter runs through the entire basin, and when playing sends steam through one orifice, and a vast amount of spray and water through another, the whole with a sound bearing close resemblance to a large, ordinary steam fire-engine.[30]

The "Fan" sends coquettish streams that resemble the article from which it is named; the wind flinging it in many directions like the fan of a gay coquette.[31]

The "Saw Mill" and "Tea Kettle" are quite small, taking their names, respectively, from the cross motion of the water stream, and the noticeable spout, from an otherwise demoralized looking tea kettle, just partially revealed above ground.[32]

The "Giant" followed the example of the "Giantess" in manifesting himself in the dead of night. His usual coming is heralded with loud thunder and moanings, followed by a terrific burst of water, which raises the Fire Hole river two or three feet, and all this about once in four days.[33]

Our camp was three-quarters of a mile from the rascally fellow, and after sitting up all of one night for him, and spending a long day at his side, he waited until we had gone back to camp for this noisy demonstration. This time, however, we had left a watchman on the spot, and at the terrific thunders he sped his horse to the camp, shouting as he neared us.

Our horses stood harnessed, and springing from our blankets we tumbled promiscuously into the wagon and were rattled in ten minutes to the scene of action.

The height of the water thrown must have been nearly 300 feet; the whole heavens were obscured from our sight by clouds of steam.

We were at breakfast quite late the following morning, under the cluster of firs and pine trees. Damp towels hung on the branches; the open flaps of our tent fluttered in the breeze and swung the suspended looking-glass until it reflected the glory of the morning sunlight. The yesterday's washing of many colored flannels festooned the cedars, looking like poor people's Christmas trees. Nature's tea-kettles around us were all steaming and boiling.

Our tea-kettle had done its duty, and we were spilling hot coffee on each other, while trying to balance our tin plates of hot biscuit and pork gravy. The boss had raised the bake-oven cover with a crooked stick to examine the last batch of biscuit, when, rubbing his smoke-filled eyes, he discovered that "Geyser, the Grand" was in eruption.[34]

Instantly, we played a game resembling "fruitbasket" for we rose, dropped everything, knives and forks flying into the bushes and in the ashes, forgot the kettle of beans, which boiled on, unnoticed, to a burnt consummation, and with a whoop worthy of the occasion, we filled the light express with a freight of eight precious souls, while the rest, catching the riding horses near at hand, made them gallop, carrying double, over the sandy road to the scene of action.

The "Reservoir" is a large, nearly square opening in the ground,

FIGURE 3.2.

Photographer Henry Bird Calfee took this stereo view of tourists "lunching in the Geyser Basin" near Old Faithful during the period 1874-81. Stereo views like this one were double-image photo cards that could be looked at through a special viewer to give the observer a three-dimensional effect. The unknown persons pictured here could indeed be members of the Wickes party, because Mrs. Wickes noted that her party was photographed "by one of the traveling photographers who are collecting the remarkable views of Montana for stereopticon entertainments." (YELL 129272, Yellowstone National Park Archives, Yellowstone National Park.)

with natural walls one foot in height, and the same in thickness; never having any grand eruption of its own, it stands as a sentinel to herald the display of "Geyser the Grand," by sending the water it holds, in gushes over its walls for a few hours previous to the more important display.[35] "Geyser the Grand," is an unpretentious circular pool, 30 feet in diameter (close by the "Reservoir"), the bowl of which is in the shape of an inverted, hollow cone, with an irregular hole, about one foot in diameter at its apex. If a porcelain fruit dish could be sunk in the ground, up to its rim, and filled with hot and slightly tinted indigo water (some chunks of cream candy thrown in to represent rocks), and then a part of the bottom knocked out by a subterranean hand, we could have at no great expense, a model of a miniature geyser like the "grand," in a state of repose. By the time we reached a spot, the waters burst with a roar from their cavernous home, as if released from the power of a demon; they hissed and rushed, pushing their way through dense steam, rose 300 feet in the still air, against the cloudiness blue of the autumnal skies, and then breaking into spray, fell gentle back to earth. The vapor spreading out like the foliage of a gigantic, spectral elm, rested above all, while spout after spout of water revealing themselves at intervals amid the vapor. Silently we watched for 15 minutes, and then exclamations of delight rose to every lip, and were responded to by shouts from parties beyond the river, who, with us, had seen the most beautiful display given during ten days in Wonderland.

In half an hour all the waters had disappeared from both geyser bowls, the water on the plain ran in tiny, wandering streams to the river, and then we knew nature had gone to work again. Twenty-four hours would elapse ere she could pump and fill again with water those wonderful reservoirs which she had so ruthlessly emptied.

Our only sad thoughts in the basin were caused by seeing the autographs of those who were murdered in the Nez Perces' unavoidable raid in the park, a few years since.[36] The party had dipped out the hot water from one of "Old Faithful's pockets," and penciled their names in the soft white interior.

Although constantly washed by the falling hot water, every line is as distinct as on the days it was written; but the precious lives of some of the writers were blotted out in a few short days.

No Indians were in the park this season; their superstitious natures make them avoid, if possible, the scenes of geyser action.[37]

The "Fire Hole Falls" and surrounding scenery were strikingly suggestive of Adirondack views; after leaving which, we followed the course of the river, passing through the basin the "Devils Half Acre" and on towards home.[38]

This plain is so bleak that it supports no vegetation on its wet, heated surface, retains no trails, the path between the unfathomable pools of hot water only indicated by dead evergreens placed as guide posts, at irregular distances.

Shallow red stream beds conduct tiny creeks of water here and there, and the sunlight reflected fiery hues in the steam and spray that everywhere prevailed.

As our startled horses pranced on the hot ground, we grew in haste to leave the long, extended plain and realized that the devil had cheated the government in its purchase, as only a half-acre.

The salmon trout in Henry's Lake have large mouths and were very hard to catch with our ordinary fish-hooks, while from the Madison river we extracted 200 white trout in less than two hours, which we salted and gladly used on our homeward journey. The scenery in Madison canyon was quite fine and we enjoyed it in spite of our ragged clothing and dilapidated shoes.

Virginia City and Whitehall passed, we soon entered our own little village in triumphal procession notwithstanding our unprepossessing exterior.[39]

The increase of hotel facilities near the park, of extended stage lines and mail stations, at reasonable prices, camp outfits and cooks, for four weeks' service, will make such a trip as the one herein described much more enjoyable and feasible to the ordinary traveler during the coming season, and no lover of nature could fail to enjoy it intensely.

[MRS.] L. D. WICKES
WICKES, MONTANA

Notes

Originally published in an eastern newspaper during winter 1880, this account was republished as "Aged Clipping Gives Account of Camping Trip of Tourists in Yellowstone Park in 1880," *Livingston (MT) Enterprise*, July 19, 1927.

1. "Funeral Services Are Held in Whitefish for Mrs. Wickes, Widow of Man Who Gave Name to Jefferson County Town," *Helena Independent Record*, March 14, 1944; Roberta Carkeek Cheney, *Names on the Face of Montana* (Missoula: Mountain Press Publishing Company, 1996), 289.

2. She was not correct. According to historian Aubrey L. Haines, park visitation in 1879 was about 1,030 and about 1,000 in 1880 (*The Yellowstone Story* [1977; rev., Boulder: University of Colorado Press, 1996], II, 478).

3. From Wickes, Montana, located about twenty miles north of Boulder, Montana, the party traveled to Bozeman and entered the park from the north probably via the Trail Creek road. This was the standard route to Yellowstone in 1880.

4. Black animals, including dogs and horses, were typically named using this uncomplimentary epithet in nineteenth-century America, a time of rampant racism.

5. Picketing was the practice of tying the horses to deeply set stakes to prevent them from running off during the night.

6. Fort Ellis, at Bozeman, Montana, was established in 1867 to protect settlers in Gallatin Valley from Indians. Robert W. Frazer, *Forts of the West* (Norman: University of Oklahoma Press, 1965), 80.

7. Rock Canyon is today located south of Livingston, Montana. But that town did not exist in 1880. She was probably talking about the Trail Creek route that left Bear Canyon and headed southeast to Paradise Valley and Yellowstone River.

8. Horace Claggett was territorial delegate to Congress from Montana Territory in 1872 when the bill was passed that made Yellowstone the world's first national park. He introduced the bill into the House of Representatives, even though, being territorial, he was a nonvoting member. Haines, *The Yellowstone Story*, I, 168–70.

9. Point of Rocks was so known as early as 1871, when the Henderson brothers built the first road through Paradise Valley to Yankee Jim Canyon. Located at the twenty-mile marker north of Gardiner, Montana, it was a barrier to travel from the earliest days because the rocks on the west side of Yellowstone River dipped sharply to the water here and blocked southbound travelers. The Northern Pacific Railroad utilized explosives in 1883 to blast away rock so that the new tracks could be laid. Newly blasted rock obstructed the tracks for eighteen days. Haines, *The Yellowstone Story*, I, 179; Aubrey L. Haines, "Notes for an Excursion from Livingston, Montana to and Through Yellowstone National Park, August 10, 1979," unpublished manuscript in possession of author (copy at Yellowstone National Park Library, Yellowstone National Park), 4.

10. James "Yankee Jim" George, the man for whom this canyon was named, squatted there for nearly fifty years, 1873–1920, manning the toll road that he was involved with as early as 1873. Doris Whithorn, *Yankee Jim's National Park Toll Road and the Yellowstone Trail* (no place [Livingston, MT]: no publisher [Livingston Enterprise], April 1989), 6–7, 49.

11. Liberty Cap is a thirty-seven-foot-high extinct hot spring cone that was never a geyser.

12. "Grotto of the Glen" was a name given by the 1871 Hayden survey to present Orange Spring Mound, an active hot spring some fifteen feet high. Lee H. Whittlesey, *Yellowstone Place Names* (Gardiner, MT: Wonderland Publishing Company, 2006), 195.

13. Demijohns were glass bottles, used for storage or transport of liquids. Wickes's party left them so that they could be coated by the Mammoth Hot Springs with travertine. Entrepreneurs later sold these coated specimens in a business that catered to tourists. Lee. H. Whittlesey and Elizabeth A. Watry, *Images of America Yellowstone* (Chicago: Arcadia Publishing, 2008), 25–26.

14. Tower Fall, located near present Overhanging Cliff, is 132 feet in height.
15. Mount Washburn's elevation is 10,243 feet.
16. With regard to this mustard tin that contained the names of ascenders for many years, see this volume, chap. 2, n. 14.
17. The geyser the man saw erupting had to have been closer than one hundred miles away. "Boiling mountain tops" must refer to boiling springs rather than mountains. The Grand Tetons, visible from the top of Mount Washburn, are actually in Wyoming, although they are close to the Idaho boundary. The Bighorns to the east cannot be seen from here; she was looking at the Absaroka and Beartooth ranges.
18. P. W. Norris served as second superintendent of Yellowstone National Park from 1877 through early 1882. He was noted for giving information to early tourists and in that respect was one of the park's first interpreters. Lee Whittlesey's *Storytelling in Yellowstone: Horse and Buggy Tour Guides* (Albuquerque: University of New Mexico Press, 2007) contains an entire chapter about Norris's "valuable information."
19. The height of Lower Falls is actually 308 feet; and of Upper Falls, 109 feet.
20. "Scotty" undoubtedly referred to C. J. "Jack" Baronett (1829–1906), a Scotsman who built the first bridge over the Yellowstone River in spring 1871. It subsequently became known as Baronett's Bridge. Remarkably, Mrs. Wickes here proceeded to phoneticize Jack's Scottish way of talking, giving us an insight into the way he must have sounded. Haines, *The Yellowstone Story*, I, 144–46, 243.
21. Moody and Sankey were traveling, musical evangelists in the 1860s. During that period primitive photos and prints circulated in America bearing their likenesses. Dwight L. Moody (1837–99) was a well-known Evangelist, originally from Massachusetts but largely active in Chicago from 1856 on. In 1871, Moody met Ira D. Sankey (1840–1908), a gospel singer, and the two worked together, with Moody preaching and Sankey singing. Our thanks go to Dr. James Brust for bringing these men to our attention.
22. Although this photographer could have been Thomas Rutter, the best candidate is Henry Bird Calfee, who is known to have been in the park that summer photographing with an eye toward producing stereos for entertainment. Several of Calfee's photos show tourist parties in camp, traveling, or posed at park features. Such a photo is shown in Lee Whittlesey, *A Yellowstone Album* (Boulder: Roberts Rinehart, 1997), 24. Another is #222, the one we reproduce in this book. See generally, Lee H. Whittlesey, "'Everyone Can Understand a Picture!': Photographers and the Promotion of Early Yellowstone," *Montana the Magazine of Western History* 49 (Summer 1999): 6–7.
23. Her "Geyser Meadow" is today's Gibbon Meadows, and the "paint-pots" are today's Artists' Paint Pots.

24. In 1880, Giantess Geyser erupted 50 to 250 feet high, lasting sometimes five–six hours, at intervals of around fourteen days. Lee Whittlesey, *Wonderland Nomenclature*, 1988, unpublished manuscript, Yellowstone National Park Library, Yellowstone National Park, Giantess Geyser entry.

25. Use of hot springs to cook food was a common practice by tourists at this early time.

26. Actually Beehive Geyser has generally erupted to much greater heights than one hundred feet. In its history it has often attained heights of 150 to 219 feet. Travelers Carrie and Robert Strahorn saw it erupt in October 1880 to two hundred feet. Carrie Adell Strahorn, *Fifteen Thousand Miles by Stage* (New York: G. P. Putnam's Sons, 1915), 265.

27. She has Old Faithful Geyser's height as too tall. Its average height has been 130 feet, and its gamut, 106 to 184 feet, since its white discovery in 1870. George D. Marler, *The Story of Old Faithful* (Yellowstone National Park: Yellowstone Library and Museum Association, 1969), 27–29.

28. Mrs. Wickes's mention of "Lioness and Cubs" could refer instead to Lion Geyser and Little Cub Geyser, as Lioness and Big Cub have histories of erupting much less frequently. Whittlesey, *Wonderland Nomenclature*, Lion Geyser, Little Cub Geyser, and Lioness and Big Cub Geyser entries. (The next seven notes all utilize Whittlesey, *Wonderland Nomenclature*, for information.)

29. At least two other 1880 observers saw Castle erupt to around one hundred feet high and lasting an hour to an hour and a half.

30. Mrs. Wickes's mention of two orifices for "Riverside Geyser" and the absence of observed eruptions for Riverside Geyser during the period 1872–82 would ordinarily make us believe that what she saw were Fan and Mortar geysers, except that she mentioned Fan Geyser separately. So if she truly saw Riverside Geyser in eruption in 1880, then she is the only known observer to do so for that year.

31. Records of observed eruptions for Fan Geyser for 1880 are difficult to find. Wickes's account is one of the few.

32. Like several other geysers, Sawmill Geyser has no known observers of its eruptions for 1880, except for Mrs. Wickes ("cross motion of the water stream"). Her "Tea Kettle" was probably the Deleted Teakettle Geyser of today. Its activity history is obscure.

33. While numerous parties must have seen Giant Geyser erupt in 1880, only Melvina Lott and Mrs. Wickes are known recorders. Lott's account stated that Giant's eruption was "all we had anticipated."

34. As for Giant, accounts of eruptions of Grand Geyser in 1880 are relatively rare.

35. This feature was probably today's Turban Geyser, a stone reservoir of sorts.

36. Only two white persons were killed in the 1877 Nez Percé foray, and one of those was at Mammoth Hot Springs rather than here at Old Faithful. Mrs. Wickes may thus be referring to the Helena party of tourists that

included Charles Kenck, killed by Nez Percé Indians at the forks of Otter Creek. See generally Jerome Greene, *Nez Perce Summer 1877: The U.S. Army and the Nee-Me-Poo Crisis* (Helena: Montana Historical Society Press, 2000), chap. 8; and Lee Whittlesey, *Death in Yellowstone: Accidents and Foolhardiness in the First National Park* (Boulder: Roberts Rinehart, 1995), 132–34.

37. This statement, although pushed as truth by Superintendent P. W. Norris and others in that day in order that tourists would believe themselves safe in the park, is not correct. While many tribes of Indians revered Yellowstone and its geyser basins as a sacred place, most did *not* fear it. See Peter Nabokov and Larry Loendorf, *Restoring a Presence: American Indians and Yellowstone National Park* (Norman: University of Oklahoma Press, 2004), 274–81.

38. Firehole Falls in Firehole Canyon is forty feet tall. "Devil's Half Acre" referred to the present Midway Geyser Basin. Whittlesey, *Yellowstone Place Names*, 105, 170.

39. Wickes, Montana, is located twenty miles north of Boulder, Montana. Although largely a "ghost" town today, it remains on state maps.

FOUR

A Trip to America

WILLIAM HARDMAN
1883

SIR WILLIAM HARDMAN (1825?–90), OF LONDON, ENGLAND, WAS a mayor, lawyer, judge, writer, reporter, editor, and English aristocrat. One biographer has called him "a kind of Pepys of Victorian times" because of his detailed diaries that described London life at that time. Said this writer,

> From 1872 until he died in 1890 he was Editor of the *Morning Post*, an ultra Tory Journal, and [was] Mayor of Kingston-on-Thames for a period. He surveyed the London scene with a critical eye and as the Editor of a national paper he had insights into affairs usually withheld from others. His eagle eye missed very little in the social and political life of London.[1]

In 1878, newspapers reported that not one of Hardman's four thousand decisions against prisoners as recorder at Kingston, England, was ever reversed.[2]

Later Hardman became a journalist, one of the many who were invited by Yellowstone entrepreneur Rufus Hatch to visit Yellowstone National Park in 1883. Hatch hoped that Hardman and others like him would promote Hatch's enterprise positively. A fellow newspaperman

FIGURE 4.1.

William Hardman as shown in his memoirs, published in 1925. A London newspaperman, he traveled to Yellowstone in 1883, the first year that railroad tracks reached the already-famous national park. (*The Letters and Memoirs of Sir William Hardman* [New York: George H. Doran Company, 1925].)

called him "Mr. Hardeman [sic], the rubicund editor of the London *Morning Post*" and went to some lengths to describe his physical appearance at Mammoth Hot Springs Hotel that summer:

> Another type of Englishman is Mr. Hardman, who is entitled by virtue of this office as Judge of Quarter Sessions in the country of Surrey, to be addressed "Your Lordship." Tall erect, clean shaven features, fresh complexion, gold-rimmed spectacles, he looks, as he steps along in a sort of olive-green check suit, canvas shoes, and trousers turned over, a very dignified, but at the same time, good-natured traveler, as he proves to be, conservative in politics, ready and anxious, to see and hear all he can while here, and willing to humor everybody's weakness of insisting upon a comparison of everything noticeable in America with something presumably less note worthy in Europe. As the proprietor in part of the London *Morning Post*, he is everywhere published as a newspaper man, but he appears to regard his judicial honors above those won in the editorial sanctum.[3]

Hardman attracted some attention when he came to America that year. A fellow journalist stated that he "might be taken for a British country squire": "He is, in appearance, the personification of the British Tory of the old school. He is tall, portly in figure, broad-shouldered, and of florid complexion. His age is about sixty. His face is smooth-shaven and his hair is white." Asked why he was traveling to the American West, Hardman replied: "It will at least enable our people at home to get a clearer idea of your vast country than it has hitherto done. That is my reason for coming out here."[4]

Cecil Palmer of London published a portion of Hardman's diaries in 1926 under the title *The Letters and Memoirs of Sir William Hardman*. Hardman wrote the account reproduced here for his book *A Trip to America*.[5] Although Hardman was thrilled by Rufus Hatch's lavish arrangements to celebrate his company's new enterprises in Yellowstone, Hatch would later suffer bankruptcy and dishonor when his business failed.

We were confessedly a party of pioneers, and expected to have to "rough it." But I must say that our "roughing" was, even here, greatly softened by the admixture of the "smooth." The hotel at the Mammoth Hot Springs erected by the Yellowstone Park Improvement Company, of which Mr. Rufus Hatch is president, was simply the most remarkable product of civilization in my experience.[6] I don't think that any of us appreciated it at its true value until after we had quitted it.

A plateau of the vast formations of sulphur and magnesia, deposited by the Hot Springs, has been selected for its site. A level area of many acres surrounds it, with mountain and forest on every side, except where, far away in the valley beneath, the Gardiner River rushes along to its junction with the Yellowstone.

The hotel is throughout of wood, except the chimneys, which are of red brick. Only a third of it has been completed at present. [It is a] very picturesque structure, with gaily painted red roof and deep verandahs, capable of accommodating a couple of hundred guests. The very trees of which it is built were growing in the adjoining woods in March; the foundations were laid in June, and in August it was crowded with travellers. The rooms and corridors are very spacious, and the latter are illuminated by the electric light. There are two excellent billiard-tables, and Steinway has presented the Yellowstone Park [Improvement] Company with one of his finest grand pianos.[7] I should like to have that grand piano's opinion of the journey from the end of the railway track. It has come much farther in a waggon than I had, for the railway had advanced [only] ten miles since its arrival.[8]

The novelty of having anything approaching civilization in their midst, attracted all the hunters, drivers, settlers, and "cowboys" for miles around, and they congregated in the great hall of the hotel until it resembled a stage filled with the "supers" in "Fra Diavolo."[9]

Somb[r?]ero hats, high leather boots and leggings, belts of cartridges, and revolvers abounded especially at night. It was rather an alarming spectacle to some of the ladies, especially when they were told that Mr. [Carroll] Hobart, the able but impulsive manager of the hotel, had found it necessary to pitch one of these gentlemen off the verandah some days previously, and it was rumoured that a "shooting" was possible at any moment. However, "use is second nature," and we were soon all accustomed to our melo-dramatic or operatic surroundings, and

CHARACTERS IN HALL OF MAMMOTH HOT SPRINGS HOTEL

YELLOWSTONE PARK, ILLUSTRATED—I.

FIGURE 4.2.
Traveler Thomas Henry Thomas drew this sketch of the
cosmopolitan assemblage of visitors at Mammoth Hot Springs
Hotel in 1884. Our chronicler William Hardman saw similar colorful
tourists there the previous year. (*The Graphic*, August 11, 1888.)

should probably have accepted a little revolver practice as an ordinary incidents [*sic*—incidence] of everyday life.[10]

It was really a mistake to imagine that our visitors were so dangerous as they looked. Several of them were gentlemen by birth, and had received university or public school education. These were the "failures" of society, come here to seek their fortunes amid the rough life of the frontier. I soon came to know several of the rough fellows well, and to feel quite at home with them. But there was one peculiarity which was an insuperable drawback to the pleasures of their society, and that was their habit of chewing tobacco and spitting—no, splashing great floods of yellow juice all over the place.

When the distance from the outer world was considered—we were 2,000 miles from Chicago, and 3,000 miles from any Eastern city—the accommodation at the Hot Springs was wonderful. Certainly we had not the luxurious carpets and frescoed rooms of the Fifth Avenue Hotel at New York. But we had very good and clean beds, an excellent table, the best champagne, and plenty of Lager beer also. The beer, by the bye, did fail for one day, and the next waggon load was eagerly watched for its progress over the hillside, and its arrival was duly cheered.

At every meal the French cook used to give us that great luxury in such a climate—American ice cream. I say "American" ice cream advisedly, for you must cross the Atlantic to taste ice cream in perfection. It is a staple article of food with them in the hot weather. A propos of the French cook, who was an importation from New York, having arrived only a day or two before our party, he bore the journey pretty well, until he came to the descent of the last hill before reaching the hotel, and then he exclaimed, "Do you mean to tell me that any one will come here for pleasure?"[11]

Facing the verandah of the hotel we saw a picturesque range of mountains, in the middle distance were wooded hills, and in the near foreground was the most remarkable object in the Park—a vast white and yellow mass, resembling nothing so much as the Rhone Glacier, but of greater dimensions, protruding from the side of the mountains. This was the more recent deposit of the Mammoth Hot Springs. By "recent" I mean since the geological period known as the glacial epoch; for these springs were active long before that date, and the actual area of their deposits is many square miles in extent.

I devoted such spare time as I had to a careful examination of the country round this formation, and I discovered distinct traces in two instances of lofty craters which must have been active in remote ages before they were partially buried beneath the moraine which now surrounds them. Our time in the Park was far too limited for anything more than the most cursory investigation of a portion only of its natural wonders.

In the plateau on which the hotel stands are numerous extinct craters, baby geysers, small boiling lakes, and bottomless caves. The whole of the drainage of the hotel is carried into one of these extinct geysers, and it was a matter of speculation as to what effect, irritating or otherwise, it might have upon the hidden machinery and the unseen workers in the regions below![12]

The soil, if so it can be called, is an incrustation of brimstone, but save for the sense of insecurity, not unpleasant to walk upon.

A lovely wood of pines, yew, and juniper, carpeted by sage brush and cactus, tempted me to wander to the blue sparkling waters of the Gardiner River.[13] There I found several anglers. I was, unfortunately, not provided with a fishing rod, but one of tour party, Mr. Thomas Mack, of Boston, had gone to the river for the express purpose of doing what has been so contemptuously discredited in England, but which is a common feat in the Park, namely, to catch a fish in one stream, and cook it immediately in another without shifting your position. The Water of the geysers is boiled at grea[te]r pressure, and certainly for some reason retains its heat much longer than ordinary boiling water. A stream of this boiling water comes out of the earth and runs for some distance by the side of the Gardiner [*sic*] River before joining it.[14] The Gardiner abounds with small and not very healthy trout, which are easily caught. Mr. Mack was not long in hooking a fish, and he dropped it, still hanging to the hook, into the geyser water, which, being hotter than he expected, cooked the trout so quickly that it almost fell to pieces. A second attempt was more successful, and in a few minutes a second fish was caught and cooked, several of us partaking of morsels of it, for the sake of saying that we had done so. The earlier as well as the later travellers to the Yellowstone Park have had their stories discredited. But I can assure my readers that this fish catching and cooking holds a very unimportant place amoung the wonderful curiosities of the region. The whole Park, or rather series of Parks, is or has been more or less given up to this geyser action, and I can well understand how the Indians avoided it as a place inhabited by evil spirits.[15]

To the artist, the scene at Mammoth Hot Springs is at once an allurement and a cause of despair. Who shall give the most remote reproduction of that deep blue sky, that cloud-less dome of cobalt? The hills reflect the yellows of the glorious sunshine, and at my feet is the Hot Spring Lake,[16] a dazzling surface of brightest orange and burnt sienna. The bubbling water in the centre is of blue, so delicately brilliant that no artificial colour could convey any idea of it.

There is but one step from the sublime to the ridiculous, and in the midst of one of nature's grandest scenes, I am compelled to compare the Hot Spring Lake to a huge cauldron, perhaps a quarter of a mile in diameter, resembling nothing so much as poaching eggs on a gigantic scale. The deepest of froths seethe and bubble around them while at the edge of the cauldron lies quiet clear blue water, looking so innocent, but at boiling heat.

From the terrace where I am standing, the successive terraces of this sulphurous deposit extend for more than 1,000 feet down to the river, clothed at their base with fir, cedar, and junipers, which have thrived in the alkaline formation until they have become forest trees. Looking upward to the horizon of the mountain ridge, 2,000 feet above me, I see the same formation clothed with mighty forest trees to the summit. The terrace whereon I stand, with its giant egg-poaching establishment, is only the modern living example of the vast formation.[17]

The ground beneath is full of rumblings and murmurings. A slight crack of a few inches wide reveals a fissure of unknown depth, from which issues a noise as of big steam-engines bubbling and hissing, while the smell I encounter beggars description. That smell of sulphuretted hydrogen pervades the park. Wherever you may go you can scarcely ever escape from it.

How dry the air is! The thermometer stands at from 90 degs. to 100 degs.—and yet the skin shows no moisture. The perspiration evaporates as quickly as it is given forth, the results being that you never feel [hot]. For days and weeks clouds may threaten overhead towards sunset, but there is not rain. The next morning the sky is as blue as ever.

Twenty-seven miles of hard riding or fatiguing waggon driving had to be undergone before we reached the nearest geyser basin, named, after one of the commandants of the park, the Norris Geyser Basin.[18]

The first business was to climb the mountain side for about 3,000 feet. The road lay through a dense forest, and was the steepest, dustiest, and hottest I ever remember.[19]

After two hours' hard struggle we got our waggon and its contents safely to the plateau at the top. I did not know at the time, but I found out afterwards, that we had to return down this terrible hill. On the way back one of the wagons, team and all, turned over and tumbled down the mountain side. Fortunately the occupants had wisely taken to their feet just before the accident, and the only result was the loss of a lady's dressing bag, for the horses recovered their feet, and did not seem to trouble much about their sudden descent.

When once we were on the summit we found a long level elevated valley, with a pretty lake, called Swan Lake, but I saw no swans, for the reason that there are not any.[20]

Passing beneath the lofty cliffs of obsidian,[21] or volcanic glass, along the shores of Beaver Lake—with obvious traces of the dams and houses of these quaint animals, all of whom have long since been trapped,—we left a poisonous green coppery stream on our right,[22] and mounted another terrible hill chiefly of sulphur and magnesia, and catching a glimpse only of the Lake of the Woods, entered another level valley, partly prairie,[23] partly forest, and arrive at our first night's camp at 4 p.m.

One of the greatest drawbacks of travelling in the park is the difficulty of obtaining water that is fit to drink. On the route we had just passed there were two springs deliciously cold and pure, but all other streams small or great, were more or less poisonous, from the coppery stream I have just mentioned, which was simply and obviously deadly, to the river by which we were now encamped, and which was highly impregnated with alkali, and sulphur, although difficult to detect by the taste. When the park has been more thoroughly explored not doubt many valuable springs will be found, which will refresh the traveller of the future. About a mile from the Hot Spring Hotel their [*sic*— there] was a delicious spring very fully charged with carbonic acid gas, and which was actually an Apollinaris spring.[24] There is much of this gas escaping on all sides, but it generally finds its way to the open air through a hot medicated water. No doubt this Apollinaris spring will yet be turned to profitable account, with many other valuable Brunnen at present unknown.[25]

Our camp made a good deal of show externally, but it was not well provided. The ravenous tourist was difficult to satisfy. Our cook and his wife lost their tempers and their civility. The accommodation was not equal to the demand, and I was not sorry, when darkness closed round us, to wrap myself in a rough grey blanket, put my overcoat under my head for a pillow, and sleep on the bare ground the sleep of the just.

The Norris Geyser Basin was about half-a-mile beyond our camp, and was on our route to the Lower Geyser, Midway Geyser, and Upper Geyser Basins, the first of which is about twenty and the last about thirty miles distant. The Norris Geyser Basin is doubtless the oldest and highest in the Park, being about 7,400 feet above sea level.[26] Its geysers are not so large as some at the Upper Basin, notable those known as "Old Faithful," "The Castle," "The Giant," "The Giantess," "The Beehive," and others. But the Norris Basin has this great advantage over the others, that it is the first "fire-hole" that greets the astonished eyes of the visitor who enters the park from the Mammoth Hot Springs side. It is of vast extent, and jets of steam rise from the white surface as far as the eye can reach up to the low fir-clad hills that are its boundary.

Beyond, in the extreme distance, rise the bare, parched mountains of the Gallatin Range. The whole basin is a collection of hot springs and pools, varying greatly in colour. "Frying-pans," as the guides call them, sputter and hiss violently; "paint-pots" boil and bubble; and geysers, little and big, throw up their columns of water at long or short intervals. The earth rumbles and shakes, and the air is hot and stinks abominably. Where the water does not boil over, it seethes and gurgles underneath and great caution is necessary in selecting your path where the surface is so treacherous.

The chief geyser in this basin is known as "The Monarch."[27] He is said to spout once in twenty-four hours, throwing up an immense volume of boiling water through three capacious orifices to a height of over one hundred feet. The eruption lasts for about twenty minutes. When I was there, of course, it was not his time for showing off his powers, but he was very busy getting ready his forces for another display. We did our best to provoke him, by pitching great lumps of rock down his throat so as to destroy the equilibrium below. But he contended himself with grumbling severely for a short time, and then returned to his normal condition of active preparation. However, there were plenty of less important geysers to exhibit the working of the machinery. There is a most useful little model geyser called the "Minute Man,"[28] which punctually once every sixty seconds spouts a bold stream to the height of twenty-five feet or thirty feet from an orifice about six inches in diameter. I should add that "Monarch" had cleared the ground for his operations by blowing out a large gap in the side of the mountain.

Surrounded by fir trees whitened by the steam and spray, is "The Workshop."[29] And certainly is well named, for the varied sounds given forth by this "fumarole" exactly resemble the noise of a busy establishment with much machinery hard at work. In fact it is difficult to believe that there is not some place of the kind among the trees. Another very striking effect is produced by a "blow-hole" in the rocks by the side of the road. The name of "Steamboat Vent" has been given to this evident safety valve.[30] You feel instinctively that if the safety valve were screwed down, the appalling force of the steam must necessarily lift the neighborhood far and near into the air. The steam escaping from "Steamboat Vent" is so super-heated, that it is not visible in the form of steam for some distance after it leaves the ground. Its roar is awful, and branches of trees laid across the aperture shrivel up in a few moments.

In these various basins, besides many others less important, the apertures whence steam, water, or coloured mud are discharged have never been counted. I should say there must be hundreds, if not thousands. Some geysers discharge their contents in such a manner that a deposit is formed round the aperture, which assumes in many instances fantastic shapes. Thus you have the Monument, the Castle, the Beehive, the Orange, the Liberty Cap (an extinct geyser), &c.[31]

"Old Faithful" in the Upper Basin is the tourist's pet geyser, because of the frequency and regularity with which his magnificent eruptions occur, this affording excellent opportunities for observation. Its crater, an oblong opening, two feet by six feet, is situated on a mound of geyserite about twelve feet in height. This mound is composed of layers of deposit formed in the manner referred to above. "Old Faithful" "operates" as the Americans say, every hour or thereabouts, throwing a large column of water for four or five minutes to a height of 100 feet or 150 feet. This geyser affords amusement to the tourist by kindly acting as a laundry on occasion. Pocket-handkerchiefs placed in the crater during the period of quiescence are punctually restored, thoroughly washed, to their owners when the eruption takes place. I was told that it was made to take in washing on a larger scale sometimes, by the surveying expeditions[,] which have camped for a long time in the Park. General Sheridan's men, in 1882, found that linen and cotton fabrics were uninjured by the action of the water, but woollen clothes were torn to shreds. The whole scene is very wonderful, very unlike anything else, very well worth seeing, extremely uncanny, and very difficult to get at. And no one can say it does not repay him.

A third hard ride brings the traveler to the climax of his journey, after which all are agreed that the majesty and beauty of the scenery of the Rockies can no farther go. It ends at the Falls of the Yellowstone River and the Grand Canyon. The Upper and Lower Falls are about half-a-mile apart. The Upper is not so grand as the Lower, but it is more picturesque. The clear height of the Falls has been accurately measured, and is 112 feet. The Lower Falls is about 310 feet in height.[32] After quitting the pool at the foot of the Upper Fall the river turns somewhat abruptly to the left, rushing [past] Cascade Creek until its sea-green water leaps from the brink of the Great Fall into the Grand Canyon.

The Grand Canyon is supposed to be unique and one of the wonders of scenery. It is of the nature of a Swiss defile, and yet so totally different that the recollection of any well known pass in no way helps the description. But try to imagine a huge mountain, with two jagged summits and a "col" of the brightest coloured rock—no dull greys of slate or granite, but yellow and orange tinted strata, to which the rocks at Alum Bay may be compared as pigmies to giants;[33] then imagine this bright coloured mountain cloven in two at its very base, and in the fissure, flowing at an immense depth, sometimes visible, sometimes quite hidden, the Yellowstone River. It is a scene never to be forgotten.

A bridle-path goes for ten miles on the summit of the fissure on the left bank of the river. Above the path rise lofty "dents" and "aiguilles."[34] On the opposite side are displayed the dazzling sides of the huge mountain, on which the brightest hues alternate with each other, from the most brilliant canary, orange, and bronze, to the mossy green of the river's bed. The burning rays of the sun play on these colours, shining in full force down the gully. This gorgeous scene lasts throughout a ride of ten miles, leaving an impression that can never be effaced. "Of its kind," said one of our party who gave me this description, "there is assuredly nothing finer in the whole world!"

Several of our party found their way back over Mount Washburn to the Mammoth Hot Springs Hotel, but the inadequacy of the means of transport, the want of horses, and the general breakdown of the commissariat department, added to the illness of more than one, interfered greatly with the plans as originally projected. [In] Another summer matters will be very different and much better arranged. As it was, the majority of us retraced our steps. At one place on the road back the crust in the vicinity of a crater gave way, and the contents of one of the waggons were precipitated into it. The occupants of the vehicle, among whom were two ladies, had fortunately got out a few minutes before, otherwise the accident might have been more serious than the laughter which it aroused. Among the articles turned out into the geyser was a basket containing fresh eggs, and the negro servants from the railway train, who had accompanied us, grinned with delight when they finally fished out the eggs and found they were boiled hard!

The Great Yellowstone Lake in the south-eastern quarter of the Park was not included in our hurried tour. In itself alone are the materials to occupy the explorer for a much longer period than we had at our disposal. Up to the present it is known only to much more hardy travellers than we were. No attempt even has been made to accommodate travellers, and the hut of a trapper here and there is all the shelter its banks afford. The lake is reported to be full of curiosities, sub-aqueous boiling springs, geysers like cauldrons on its shores, and the enterprising but cautious traveler can take a hot or cold bath in its waters, as he may prefer. Strange to say, it abounds with trout, but they are unhealthy and "wormy."

The Park generally has but little game. I saw a dead bear, a tame elk, and an abundance of wild ducks. Possibly the bears, buffalo, elk, and other large game go elsewhere during the summer months. Elk is plentiful somewhere in the vicinity, because we had it as food at the hotel. But the sportsman—and we had a good many in our party— will assuredly be disappointed if he goes to the Yellowstone Park in the hope of securing a great bag. Our sporting friends had gone prepared to find bears and wolves as plentiful as blackberries, and were provided with such an arsenal of weapons and ammunition as to be objects of apprehension to their more peaceful fellow-travellers. But they never killed anything or (happily) anybody. One of the party went away with a hunter into the mountains for ten days, but he only killed one elk and some ducks, catching, however, an abundance of fine trout.[35]

In addition to the wrong impression which has gone abroad with regard to the abundance of game, there is another very prevalent in the United States, and that is that there are glaciers among the mountains. As an old and very unworthy member of the Alpine Club, I may be allowed, at any rate, to say that I know a glacier when I see one. In this part of the range of the Rocky Mountains, I saw some detached patches of snow remaining unmelted from last winter and lodged in deep hollows and crevices. But here was not a trace of a glacier. The limit of perpetual snow in Switzerland is about 9,500 feet. The mountains of the Yellowstone rise to 10,000 feet or 12,000 feet, and the Park is considerably south of Switzerland, and in a country under very different climatic conditions. There is an abundance of beauty and interest in the Yellowstone Park, but it is not, and never can be Switzerland.

The roads, which are now unworthy of the name, are being rapidly improved by the United States Government. President Arthur, accompanied by General Sheridan, Mr. Secretary Lincoln, Mr. [Schuyler] Crosby, Governor of Montana, Captain Clark, and others made the tour of the Park this season, with mounted military escort, baggage mules, and relays of horses.[36] Even with so many advantages the task was not an easy one. There are difficulties of climate, the sulphurous soil and smells, the heat, and the sometimes sudden changes of temperature to frost at night. Moreover, the supply of water has to be chosen with great care, or the traveler may be prostrated. Warnings are to be put up at the poisonous springs, rivers, and lakes, and notice given also to travellers when they may freely drink of the roadside springs, or bathe in wholesome water. The uncertainty of procuring fresh food, wine, or spirits, makes it advisable for each party to provide themselves to a great extent with their own supplies, and not to depend upon the chance of what they may find at the "Hotel Tents" in the interior. The supply of horses, too, is at present quite inadequate to the demand of the travellers, when their numbers, the badness of the paths, and the length of the stages—twenty, thirty, or forty miles—are considered. But we, pioneers, cheerfully submitted to these disadvantages, feeling that the energetic Americans will have many improvements by next summer and in every succeeding summer.

So new is the Yellowstone Park to the people in the Eastern States of the Union, that no photographs of its geysers could be obtained in New York,[37] when we were there. But the State Department at Washington is causing large maps, drawings and the photographs to be made. Their *employees* were engaged on this work last summer, and any art publisher can now be furnished with copies on application. Dr. Oskar Beggruen, of Vienna, who was one of my companions, is about to reproduce them in his forthcoming book on the Yellowstone Park, which will be translated into French and English, and will be one of the most valuable additions to the literature of the Yellowstone yet given to the public.[38]

On the return journey to the Hot Springs Hotel we suffered terribly from heat, especially when, on the open prairie near Swan Lake, where there was not a particle of shade, our team, which had been a great trouble, and anxiety to us all day, finally gave out. One of our horses fell as if dying, and the other declined to struggle on any farther. The heat was awful. Our driver, [a] particularly pleasant young fellow, appealed, and happily not in vain, to a "freighter," who was ahead of us with two waggons and two teams, to spare us one team. With that desire to help one another in difficulty, which is a marked characteristic of the rough denizens of the frontier, this man immediately hitched one of his waggons on behind the other, and taking the teams this set at liberty put the horses to our waggon and drove us to the end of our journey down the terrible hill, which I have already described.

We found Judge Pierrepoint quitting his carriage in order to make this dangerous descent,[39] which he thought it safer to do on foot. The Judge, who was formerly American Minister in London, had been furnished

FIGURE 4.3.

This rare 1883 photograph depicts the Mammoth village as our traveler
William Hardman would have seen it. At bottom is Hymen Terrace
with one of the James McCartney bathhouses standing on it. The largest
building is the Mammoth Hot Springs Hotel, which Mr. Hardman
called "the most remarkable product of civilization in my experience,"
probably because it had electric lights even at that early date. (YELL
114950, Yellowstone National Park Archives, Yellowstone National Park.)

with mules and a military escort by the United States Government, and
was trav[el?]ing, so to speak, in grand style. I had afterwards, the pleasure of having him as my partner in many a friendly game of whist,[40]
during our stay at the Mammoth Hot Springs Hotel, and a very good
"hand" he played. In America they have a species of whist which is neither "long" nor "short" but between the two. Seven points are "game,"
and "honours" are not counted.

Several days passed before the whole of our scattered party was once
more collected under the roof of the Hot Springs Hotel.[41] It was a happy
result when all had got back without injury beyond that arising from
heat, bad food and water, and fatigue. Each detachment as it arrived had

its own special story of difficulty, danger, or disappointment. The negro servants shook their heads earnestly, and told me they did not like it at all. But, then, who expected they would? For myself, I suffered up to the time I left the district from a mild but unpleasant attack of fever of an intermittent character.

One day the President of the United States [Chester A. Arthur] arrived with all his party at the superintendent's house, the most conspicuous object on the mound in front of the hotel.[42] It gave us a new sensation to see the "Stars and Stripes" flying like the Royal Standard to inform our small world that the Head of the State was in our neighborhood.

After dinner that evening we went in a body to serenade the President, who received us by his campfire. It was a sight never to be forgotten, so wild and so strange was it. Later in the evening President Arthur returned our visit, bringing with him General [Philip] Sheridan, Secretary [Robert] Lincoln, and the other members of his party. We were especially interested in making the acquaintance of General Sheridan, who is not only a remarkable man, but [also] a remarkable looking man, being very short and stout, in fact, almost as broad as he is long. He has grown much stouter since the first time when he made his celebrated "Ride" of twenty miles to the fight.[43]

I was especially favored by being placed on the President's right hand when we adjourned for a cigar to a private room. I found him a most courteous and agreeable man, ready to speak of public matters with less reserve than I should have anticipated. He had much to tell me of his travels in Alaska and Oregon. He was also good enough to give me his views on Ireland, Protection, and Fair Trade. I found from him that his grandfather had fought at Waterloo, and that he still preserved as a valued heirloom a decoration which had been bestowed upon his ancestor by the Duke of Kent.

The President and I had both been "roughing it," but he had undergone much more of it than I had. We had both been out of the vicinity of washerwomen for some weeks; but I flattered myself that he looked shabbier and dirtier of the two as we sat side by side; besides, the skin hung in strips on his nose; which did not improve his appearance.

However, I enjoyed a very pleasant chat with him for three-quarters of an hour, and I doubt if any other Englishman ever before had an interview under similar circumstances with any of the chiefs of the Great Republic across the Atlantic.

The next morning, soon after sunrise, he broke up his camp, and making for the nearest point of the railway, returned to Washington.

—∞—

Editors' note: Hardman left Mammoth soon after this, pausing to listen to melodies being played on the large Steinway piano that then graced the Mammoth Hot Springs Hotel. He entrained north and then east to Washington, D.C., and New York. In Washington, he searched resolutely for the famous U.S. "Declaration of Independence," being bound and determined to see it, and then went to the White House to again see President Arthur, but alas, Arthur was traveling. In New York, Hardman again met up with his host, Rufus Hatch, and ended his book with the following: "Here ends my long story, and I have only to record with a sad pleasure the genial parting from my American host, 'Uncle Rufus,' who, with many other friends, came to the landing-stage and wished us God-speed as the *Brittanic* turned her bows down the Hudson, and so eastward to England."

Notes

1. J. F. Burns, "From Whoredom to Evangelism: The Story of Mrs. Thistle-thwayte (nee Laura Bell, who was a native of Glenavy)," Lisburn Historical Society, available at www.lisburn.com/books/historical_society/volume2/volume2_2.html.
2. "Variety Columns," *Chester (PA) Daily Times*, April 1, 1878, 1.
3. E. G. D., "Uncle Rufus's Guests," *New York Times*, August 30, 1883, 3.
4. "English Press Lords," *Fort Wayne (IN) Gazette*, August 29, 1883, 2. See also "Editor Hardman Dead," *Chicago Tribune*, September 13, 1890; "Editor Hardman's American Experience," *Chicago Tribune*, September 15, 1890, 5.
5. William Hardman, *A Trip to America* (London: T. Vickers Wood, 1884).
6. Originally named the National Hotel because it was in the national park, by 1885 this hotel was also called Mammoth Hot Springs Hotel. Rufus Hatch's company, the Yellowstone Park Improvement Company, built it in 1883, and at the time of Hardman's visit the hotel was still under construction. See the 1883 Carleton Watkins photo reproduced in Lee H. Whittlesey, *Yellowstone Place Names* (Gardiner, MT: Wonderland Publishing Company, 2006), 290.
7. With regard to the Steinway piano at Mammoth Hotel, see the letter from Maurice Hodgen of Riverside, California, and Lee Whittlesey's letter

back to him for additional information. Hodgen to Whittlesey, July 9, 2003 (a second letter to Whittlesey), says that the piano was moved from Mammoth Hot Springs Hotel to Glenwood Hotel (now the Mission Inn) in Riverside. Historian's files, "H" boxes, Yellowstone National Park Archives, Yellowstone National Park.

8. The Northern Pacific Railway at this time was building a spur line in Montana from Livingston to Cinnabar during summer 1883 that had not yet reached Cinnabar.

9. Fra Diavolo (frä dēä′ vōlō; Ital., Friar Devil; 1771–1806) was an Italian bandit and soldier whose real name was Michele Pezza. He entered the service of the king of Naples in 1798 and with Cardinal Ruffo resisted the French invasion (1799) of the kingdom. He was captured (1806) and hanged by the French. The plot of Auber's opera *Fra Diavolo* (libretto by Scribe) is in no respect historical.

10. The Carroll Hobart Papers at Yale University make it clear that Hardman was not exaggerating here. The hotel company had trouble paying its carpenters, and there was much disgruntlement over that. The following winter, the unpaid carpenters seized possession of the hotel by force.

11. Hardman's quote here was probably the source of the title of historian Richard Bartlett's article about early Yellowstone concessionaires: "Will Anyone Come Here for Pleasure?" *American West* 6 (September 1969): 10–16. "Descent of the last hill" and, earlier, "its progress over the hillside" indicate that the "old Gardiner road" from the town of Gardiner was in use for travel to Mammoth Hot Springs.

12. Early maps of the Mammoth area show this cavity marked "geyser hole" near the site of the present Juniper Dormitory, and the hotel's sewage was unapologetically dumped down it, where it found its disgusting way to the Gardner River. That fact resulted in periodic outbreaks of disease. See, for example, William Hallett Phillips, "Letter from the Acting Secretary of the Interior, Transmitting, In Response to Senate Resolution, January 12, 1886, Report of W. H. Phillips on the Yellowstone Park," 49th Congress, 1st Session, Sen. Ex. Doc. 51, January 29, 1886, 11.

13. The yew is not present in Yellowstone National Park, but all of the other trees he mentioned are.

14. This was the Boiling River, a discharging hot spring near Mammoth and one of two places in the park where this catching-fish-and-cooking-them-on-the-hook feat was practiced, the other one being at Fishing Cone at West Thumb.

15. This was a common misconception that was routinely passed on by Euro-Americans of that day. Most Indians were not afraid of Yellowstone's hot springs and geysers but, rather, revered them. Peter Nabokov and Larry Loendorf, *Restoring a Presence: American Indians and Yellowstone National Park* (Norman: University of Oklahoma Press, 2004), 274–81.

16. This was probably either Blue Spring or Main Spring on the Main Terrace of Mammoth Hot Springs.

17. "Giant egg-poaching establishment" probably referred to the smell of the hot springs at Mammoth, akin to eggs being cooked. Hardman appears to have been impressed by the odor of the hydrogen sulfide gas, which was commonly called "sulphuretted hydrogen" in that day, as below.

18. Norris Geyser Basin was named by park superintendent P. W. Norris for himself in 1878. Aubrey L. Haines, *Yellowstone Place Names: Mirrors of History* (Boulder: University Press of Colorado, 1996), 131.

19. The first few miles south of Mammoth were horribly difficult until 1885, when a road rerouting moved the road to its present alignment through the Golden Gate. Hardman's route ran over this difficult route—Snow Pass via Orange Spring Mound, Soda Spring, and Jeweled Cave. Parts of it are a foot trail today.

20. Trumpeter swans, then as now, occupied the park but were and are not commonly seen.

21. This was Obsidian Cliff, near Beaver Lake.

22. Because the stream was on their right (west), this stream must have been present Obsidian Creek. However, Lemonade Creek, a much smaller stream, is the creek in the area that is thermally poisoned to an acidic green. It flows down the hill that they traveled up to reach Lake of the Woods.

23. South of Lake of the Woods, they entered a long valley situated on Solfatara Creek, which was known as Miller's Valley.

24. This was probably today's Soda Spring at Mammoth. Apollinaris Spring, some eight miles farther south, was so named by 1890 due to references by travelers like Hardman. Whittlesey, *Yellowstone Place Names*, 37.

25. *Brunnen* in "high German" means "fountain" or "well" or, colloquially, "spring."

26. Geologists debate whether Norris Geyser Basin is the "oldest" in the park, with some believing that it is. At 7,484 feet, it is not the highest of the geyser basins. West Thumb Geyser Basin reposes at an elevation of 7,731 feet.

27. Monarch Geyser erupted 125 feet high in 1883 and was considered a "must-see" by tourists.

28. This is today's Constant Geyser, which in 1883 erupted twenty-five to thirty feet high every minute.

29. "The Workshop" is unknown today, but the name may have referred to Black Growler Steam Vent.

30. Steamboat Vent was not the present Steamboat Geyser but, rather, a fumarole in a location (unknown today) convenient for all to see, as documented by T. W. Ingersoll's 1887 stereo photograph number 1171B.

31. Like many tourists, Hardman became confused as to which geysers and hot springs were located where. Monument is in a basin south of Norris, Castle and Beehive are in the Old Faithful area, and Orange and Liberty Cap are at Mammoth.

32. Hardman's heights are very close to today's: Upper Falls is 109 feet; Lower Falls, 308 feet.

33. Alum Bay is a sandy bay near the westernmost point of the Isle of Wight, England, within sight of the Needles. The bay is noted for its multicolored sand cliffs.

34. An aiguille is a sharp-pointed mountain peak, while a dent is a more rounded one.

35. The idea that there was little or no game in the park was a common misconception to 1880s travelers, because of a massive slaughter of park animals that had occurred from 1871 to 1880. But just because they did not see many animals does not mean that the animals had not formerly been there in great numbers. See, generally, Paul Schullery and Lee Whittlesey, "Documentary Record of Wolves and Related Wildlife Species in the Yellowstone National Park Area Prior to 1882," in *Wolves for Yellowstone?* vol. 4, ed. John D. Varley and Wayne G. Brewster (Yellowstone National Park: National Park Service, 1992), 1–173. Hardman's party's eating of elk at the hotel confirms that hotel company hunters were shooting animals in the park in clear violation of the recent "no hunting" decree by the Department of the Interior.

36. For the Arthur trip to Yellowstone, see the nation's major newspapers during August and September 1883, such as "The President's Trip," *New York Times*, August 27, 1883, 5. A recent study of the trip is Robert E. Hartley, *Saving Yellowstone: The President Arthur Expedition of 1883* (Westminster, CO: Sniktau Publications), 2007.

37. This is unlikely, but apparently they could find none there.

38. If this book was ever published, it is obscure today.

39. This was Edward W. Pierrepont, who published a book about his trip that summer entitled *Fifth Avenue to Alaska* (New York: G. P. Putnam's Sons, 1884).

40. The game of whist was an early form of bridge but without bidding.

41. References and usage like this one by Hardman ultimately changed the hotel's name to Mammoth Hot Springs Hotel from National Hotel.

42. The "mound" refers to Capitol Hill, on top of which stood the home of the park superintendent that had been built in 1879 by Superintendent P. W. Norris and which was styled the "Norris Blockhouse." It resembled a fort. Aubrey L. Haines, *The Yellowstone Story* (1977; rev., Boulder: University of Colorado Press, 1996), I, 246–48.

43. This referred to General Philip Sheridan's famous Civil War ride of October 18–19, 1864, in which Sheridan rode twenty miles to "save the day" in the Battle of Cedar Creek, Virginia. The story was so well known to virtually everyone in 1883 that no other explanation was thought necessary, and poems and songs were written to celebrate it. The story was featured on the cover of *Harper's Weekly*, November 5, 1864.

FIVE

Mount Washburn

The Folly of Three Persons in Yellowstone Park.
A Fifty Mile Walk in the Wilderness by Pedestrians
Who Did Not Count Well the Cost—Heavy Packs and
a Poor Supply of Provisions—Climbing Steep Mountains
in High Altitudes—A Dangerous Ascent at Lower Falls—
A Haven of Rest for the Weary Travelers

H.F.G.

1883

⸻

"H.F.G.," THE AUTHOR OF THIS LITTLE-KNOWN ACCOUNT, WAS presumably a staffer on the *Brooklyn Eagle* newspaper, but we do not know his name. Whoever he was, he was a member of the first known backpacking party ever to hike in Yellowstone National Park. Nor do we know who the persons were that accompanied H.F.G. and to whom he referred as "the Dominie" and "the Dude." This account appeared as chapter 4 of a four-part newspaper account about their trip around the park, and the other parts of that trip are not reproduced here.

Regardless of the author's anonymity, the account is noteworthy for being the first known backpacking trip in Yellowstone history. It also documented the existence of a heretofore-unknown cabin apparently built by prospectors sometime before 1883, the year that H.F.G., whoever he was, went backpacking across Mount Washburn with his two friends.

⸻

From the Upper Falls of the Yellowstone Park, by a trail over Mount Washburn to the Mammoth Hot Springs, it is about fifty miles. At present there is no carriage road, and teams are obliged to return to the springs the same way in which they came, requiring about three days to make the journey. The Dominie, who has had considerable experience in climbing mountains, the Dude, who had rather walk any day than ride, and, myself concluded that rather than return by the same route we would take our packs and foot it over the mountains, and meet our wagons at the hot springs. We could have taken two horses with us, but thought that they would be in the way and we would have trouble and bother with them at night, so on foot we poor fools started out for what we, in our ignorance, thought would be a very pleasant little tramp. We did not even have sense enough to find out how much or what kind of provisions we should need but each one of us going to the commissary department took out what food we wanted. The [D]ominie secured two cans of baked beans. The Dude took a can of beans and a can of oysters, and I followed suit. Besides this, we took a little sugar, some tea, and each one a few crackers. Any one can readily see that in this stock of provisions there was not much opportunity to vary the menu three times a day for two days. Had we been wise we would, of course, have selected our provisions together, and then divided them into three lots. Had such been the case, beans would not have found so prominent a place among our supplies. We each took a pair of blankets, and the Dominie to protect himself from the cold packed an extra one. Then we had our overcoats and rubber coats and numerous other articles, so that when our bundles were strapped on our backs they were of no small proportions and must have tipped the scales at twenty pounds each. When we were ready, Tute suggested that we had better take a pack horse, but we spurned the idea, and replied that we guessed we were pack horses enough for what bundles we had, and so with merry hearts we struck out into the wilderness. The charm of the grand cañon was still upon us, and so hiding our packs in the bushes we again visited that wonderful gorge, and for miles walked along its edge, and saw by the morning light beauties that we had not noticed the day before. Several hours spent in this way, and we returned to the mountain trail, and with our packs on our backs start on. We walk on at a rapid pace, and for awhile all goes well, but soon the noonday sun appears, with much warmth, and our bundles somehow grow heavy, and we are constantly shifting them from one side to the other, but by no means begin to lose courage. We come to a cold mountain stream, and here we stop for

Our First Meal.

It was then for the first time that we began to comprehend the state of our edibles; we had neither salt nor pepper or seasoning of any kind. We had neither cup nor plate nor spoons and forks. But these trifles did not bother us. We built a fire and warmed a can of beans. With our pocket knives we whittled out rough spoons. We then opened the can of beans and seating ourselves around it began to eat. They tasted well and we were hungry and so we made a very good meal of crackers and beans. The tea we attempted to make was a failure. Resting for some time, we again took up our burdens and began a somewhat steep ascent over a range of mountain to Mount Washburn, the highest in the group, about seven miles distant. It was a beautiful afternoon and we really enjoyed our walk. I never before saw wildflowers in such profusion and of such variety. For acres the ground was covered with choicest blossoms, giving off most fragrant odors. It was like walking through cultivated garden beds. Then, too, now views of scenery engaged our attention, but at least, notwithstanding these beauties of nature, we could not rid ourselves of the fact that we were constantly going uphill and that twenty pounds of good avoirdupois were pulling at our backs. We would occasionally stop and rest, only to find that when we again shouldered our bundles they were heavier than ever. We labored on until at last we reached what we supposed to be Mount Washburn. We were told that the trail would take us to the top of the mountain; but here we were at its base as we thought, but the trail continued on down into a valley and apparently away from the mountain. We thought the matter over. The Dominie said he had climbed every prominent peak in the White Mountains and thought he was good for the trip. The Dude had no fears but what he could amble up the mountain in awhile, and so we decided to leave the trail and go up Mount Washburn the nearest way. As we were to go down the mountain on the other side it necessitated our keeping by our baggage else we would have very willingly parted company at the foot of the hill. We plodded on for about an hour, and at last drew our weary limbs to the summit of the mountain to find our surprise that Mount Washburn was beyond us and in height far above us. There was but one course for us to pursue. Our conscience would not let us remain where we were and say to our friend that we had been on top of Mount Washburn and so down the mountain we went and again started up among the clouds, but this time it was

Up Mount Washburn.

Mount Washburn is 10,340 feet high,[1] over 4,000 feet higher than Mount Washington in New Hampshire. Had we surveyed the mountain and taken its altitude and slopes we could not probably have suggested a more difficult side on which to make the ascent than the one we chose. It was straight up like the side of a barn. But from the bottom, of course, we could not judge very well the lay of the land[.] Our trip over one mountain puts us in not very good condition for a tussle with old Washburn, but we grasped firmly our alpenstocks and with new courage started on. In the morning when we talked lightly of our day's journey we were judging of such a trip by our experiences in the White Mountains, and did not take into consideration the fact that we were in an altitude where air was a scarcity, and it was very difficult to get a good supply of oxygen, and especially so when gravity was working with all its might to pull off our packs. But we very soon discovered those natural laws to which before we had paid little heed. About every twenty steps up Washburn's rugged face we had to stop and catch breath. We soon found that there was not so much pleasure in the business after all. It was not long in dawning upon our sluggish minds that we were a set of fools. We frankly confessed that we were idiots, and threatened to shoot the man who said we were not. The Dominie was anxious to see for a few moments the man who suggested the trip, but as there was no looking glass in the party he was unable to wreak vengeance upon the unfortunate person. "We are not exiles," the Dominie would exclaim, "sent here by a cruel tyrant. We are not compelled by stern edicts of law to climb this mountain. No, my comrades, we are here for pleasure and we call this fun." The Dude would give a sickly smile in response to these expressions of the parson, but could utter not a syllable, for his breathing apparatus was taxed to its utmost capacity and gave him no chance to vociferate. I was willing to admit that we were engaged in a piece of voluntary foolishness, but that we must go to the top or perish in the attempt. Well it was excruciatingly tedious. The rarity of the atmosphere, our heavy packs, [and] the steep incline altogether made the ascent difficult in the extreme. But after hours of labor we crawled to the summit and throwing ourselves on our packs took a good long breathing spell. We were not in very good condition for sightseeing, but from that magnificent height we gazed upon the picture stretched out before us with liveliest interest. I can hardly say whether the view paid for our trouble. But I do know it was a grand sight. The mountain comes to a sharp peak of rocks, and from this point we looked upon the surrounding country for miles and miles around. In the south we had a magnificent view of the Yellowstone Lake, where we had been two days before. We saw its outlines perfectly and formed a good idea of its size. We saw the deep gorge of the Yellowstone River and followed its windings the entire length. Snow clad mountains of the Rockies were all about us, and we saw mountain scenery as we had never before. But the sun was dropping behind the hills and we were cautioned to see the valley before nightfall, and buckling on the blankets and beans, started

Down The Mountain.

It is no easy matter to go down a steep mountain. Again I call attention to the matter of a few pounds on our backs. Down several hundred feet and the trail which we found at the top of the mountain leads over a series of high ridges. We might have camped in several good places and melted snow for water, but we thought best to hurry on till we found a good supply of water. So we pushed as fast as possible, the twilight rapidly turning into darkness. We slide on our feet down long banks of snow and pelt snow at each other, an amusement we imagined many Brooklynites would have liked at this time of year. Here were immense snow banks almost attaining the dignity of small glaciers. But we spend little time in sport and hurry on. We keep on over ridge after ridge and gradually descend, but no signs of water, and we cannot camp without it. The coming darkness admonishes us that something must be done. We halt. On either side of us is a valley where we know there must be water and we can see plenty of wood. We start down on the right side. It seems as if we will never reach the bottom. At last we strike the woods. It is low, marshy ground filled with underbrush and fallen trees. We grope our way over huge logs, falling into bogs and covering our feet with mud. We hunt for the stream which we know must be fed by the mountain snows. At last we hear running water. We go on and on, stumbling and falling, and at last we reach a small brook. Near its bank we find a spot of high land suitable for camping. A quantity of cotton-wood is found on the ground and we soon have a rousing fire. By this time it is pitch dark, and we have to carry a torch to get water from the brook. Our evening meal consists of canned oysters with a few crumbs of crackers. We collect a large supply of wood and with our feet toward the fire and wrapped up in our blankets go to sleep.

Beans For Breakfast.

It was nearly 9 o'clock the next morning when we arose. We thought a can of Boston baked beans would be about the thing to stand by us on our long tramp. But while beans are very good occasionally they are not just the thing for a steady diet. With nothing but beans the inner man would not be satisfied and so after worrying down a few mouthfuls we strapped on our packs and start on. About noon we arrive at the famous Tower Falls. Leaving our bundles on the ground, we walk some little distance from the main trail and have a fine view from the top of the falls. But we are anxious to go down to the bottom of the deep cañon and see the falls from below. To do this we have to go about a mile and then walk up the river. Rather than return like sensible men the way we came, it occurred to us that the quickest way would be to shin up the side of the gorge. It is perhaps 800 feet deep and near the top the sides are almost perpendicular. We each selected what appeared to us to be the most favorable position and began our ascent. It was easy enough at first but for the last two or three hundred feet it was simply terrible. The rocks were of a soft crumbling kind and we were every moment in danger of losing our foothold. Once started it was more dangerous to go down than to keep on. So, for over an hour we clung to that wall for dear life, several times finding our pluck and strength almost gone. But, finally, with bleeding hands and limbs we crawl to the top and though almost exhausted were once more safe on terra firma. No language was too strong to upbraid ourselves for this new folly.

Our First Square Meal.

We continue on our walk without stopping to eat and about 3 o'clock reach a log cabin. We were tired and ravenously hungry and the hut seemed like an oasis in a desert. There were two young men in the house and when we told them we were nearly starved they rustled about in great haste to get us something to eat. They cooked antelope meat, fried potatoes, made pancakes, and [brewed] a good cup of tea. With a hearty relish we soon disposed of the food set before us. We felt like new beings, but when told we had a walk of four miles before us up a very steep hill we were not exceedingly elated over the prospect. But we soon found relief. There were two horses on the ranch.[2] These were engaged to go with us for six miles, one to carry our packs and the other the Dominie. In this way we got along very nicely. Leaving the horses we walked on about six miles and camped on the banks of a creek, it being nearly 9 o'clock when we arrived there. For some reason we did not sleep very well that night, but the next morning we were up bright and early and started on our last seven miles' walk. A miner's wagon carried our baggage that distance. Arriving at the hot springs, we waited about an hour when our team came up and we started on for Bozeman. Thus ended the journey of three as big fools as ever entered the park. But somehow, notwithstanding our supreme folly, after we had rested sufficiently and the bruises had healed, and sore feet were better, we were on the whole rather pleased that we had taken the journey but no money would have tempted us to repeat it. . . . H.F.G.

Notes

This account was originally published in the *Brooklyn Eagle*, August 17, 1883, 1, by a "Special Correspondence of the Eagle."

1. Mount Washburn is 10,243 feet high.
2. Apparently this was John Yancey's crude stage stop that predated the hotel he built in 1884.

SIX

A Lady's Trip
to the Yellowstone Park

O. S. T. DRAKE

1885

O. S. T. DRAKE WAS A FEMALE ENGLISH WRITER ABOUT WHOM little is so far known. She had interests in folklore and religion, for in 1876, she wrote "Stray Notes on Folk-lore" in which she recounted poems of children who caught ladybugs and blew them from their wrists. And in 1887, she wrote "Old Roman Catholic Legends" for *The Antiquary* magazine. She also had an interest in history, as her story of Sir Francis Drake (perhaps her ancestor) attested in *Tinsley's Magazine* and her article "A Strange People and a Strange Language" bore witness to in the obscure *Churchman's Schilling Magazine*.[1]

It is not known why Ms. Drake journeyed to America and Yellowstone in 1885, but her account is delightful. Among other stories that it tells, it fills voids about the park's Norris tent hotel (1883–86) and the Marshall's Hotel (1880–91). No doubt she used her initials instead of a first name in order to play down the fact that she was a woman, and this was considered fashionable and proper for women writers to do in her day. She gave her account to the obscure (yearly) magazine *Every Girl's Annual*, where it was published in the 1887 edition of that magazine. Strangely Ms. Drake's party traveled only from Mammoth to Old Faithful and then back to Mammoth without visiting the canyon.

The glowing accounts which have from time to time appeared in the papers and journals as to the marvels of the National Park of America, set apart in 1872 by a notable Act of Congress for the use and enjoyment of the American people for ever, determined us upon a visit to this the eighth wonder of the world, on our route homewards for the north-western provinces of Canada.

It is not perhaps universally known where this region of wonders is situated; it will therefore be desirable to premise that this land of geysers and volcanic activities lies in the most elevated part of the Rocky Mountains. Here rise the springs of the great Missouri and Mississippi rivers. Speaking generally, it is included in north-western Wyoming, and comprises a strip of Montana, famous for its cowboys. The area is said to be 65 miles in length by 55 broad, or about 3575 square miles.[2] The mountains range from 10,000 to 12,000 feet above the sea-level. Indeed, the whole region [is] 6000 or 8000 feet in elevation. It was first revealed to the American public by Captain de Lacy in 1863.[3] Previous to that trappers and hunters had roamed over the plains and forests, and strange tales were told and disbelieved of the wonders they had encountered. Tales of petrified forests, bearing fruits of diamond and emeralds; of animals turned to stone in the attitudes of life, were, as an American writer tersely puts it, "manufactured from whole cloth."

In 1871 Dr. Hayden mapped and explored the country, and recommended to Congress the retention of it as a national collection of wonders, a measure which, as we have said, was promptly carried out.[4] No settlers may settle upon it, nor are its surprising natural wonders to be turned to base utilitarian purposes, or its abounding fish and game to be wantonly destroyed for trade or profit; while hotels, on ten years' leases only, are to be erected for the accommodation of travellers. Such are the wise and enlightened provisions of the Yellowstone Act of Reservation, which deserved to be placed on honourable record. Livingstone [sic— Livingston, Montana], on the Northern Pacific Line, is the station whence we took our departure for the National Park, by a short line 57 miles in length, which deposited us at Cinnabar, ten miles from the Mammoth Springs.[5] The line ran through a picturesque valley with the Yellowstone river foaming below. Farms of the rough border character were scattered along the valley for the first few miles;[6] but as the road rose to higher altitudes, corn-fields gave place to the monotonous sage brush and mats of prickly pear and blazing sunflowers.[7] Cinnabar, where the line terminated, consisted of a wayside saloon and a few huts. From here we drove to the Mammoth Springs; the road, a bed of the thickest dust, wound upwards for some ten miles, the mountains towering grandly overhead. Below us we saw the first hot spring pouring into the river, sufficiently near for the fish to be caught in one stream to be cooked in the other—a not uncommon performance in these regions.[8]

Our driver, who combined the independence of America with the civility of Europe, gave us sketches of his personal history, and sought by dint of many questions to arrive at ours. We ended by engaging him and his carriage and pair of good wiry horses for the sum of forty shillings a day, and had no reason to regret our bargain; for the carriage proved to be an exceedingly comfortable one. The Mammoth Springs Hotel turned out to be a huge wooden structure, with an imposing exterior, which the unfinished bare walls, unplastered ceilings, and air of general discomfort did not carry out within. As to the cookery and attendance, the less said the better.

The wonderful hot springs fall over a lofty hill of snowy whiteness, piled in a series of circular terraces, [and] formed by the calcareous deposits of the different springs. They resemble nothing so much as frozen cascades of dazzling whiteness; while again some of the water is of the blue of turquoise, trickling over ledges of rock of every conceivable colour, caused by the different precipitates of iron, sulphur, lime, and alkalies in varied proportions.[9] The water bubbles up through the crust at a temperature of 150 to 170 Fahrenheit; a steaming mist rises over [this] extraordinary freak of nature's handiwork; one lovely spring fell gently over a rose-pink rock; another showed a pool of transparent green, framed in a fairy setting of pink and white. No straight lines, no sharp angles are seen anywhere, but a series of graceful curves, with the water flowing quietly over the rock in a perpetual cascade. The splendid sky and luminous atmosphere made the surrounding mountains (some covered with pines, others snow-clad) appear almost within reach. In the moonlight the strange character of the scene was even more striking. The snowy mass of the hill, the broken and lofty pillars formed by the cones of extinct geysers, composed a picture of extraordinary beauty, which for strangeness and singularity must surely stand unrivalled in the whole world.

At nine o'clock next day our carriage arrived, and we heard the driver inquiring if his "crowd was ready?" We proceeded to our first halting place at Norris Geysers, over a track ablaze with sunflowers, lupin[e]s, larkspurs, columbines, and hollyhocks.[10] The road followed the course of the river up a narrow cañon, the narrowest part of which is called the Golden Gates [sic—Gate], from the dazzling colour of the rocks, yellow and red. Then we came upon some dreary tracts of burnt forest, the dead pines standing withered and stark against the vivid and deep blue sky. This part of the road was sufficiently well engineered, but beyond it became execrable and a long space of what our driver called "Sidleing" made our bones ache, for at times a staircase of huge rocks formed the sole road. Down drop the wheels until the horses become invisible, and the consequent jolts may be more easily imagined than described.

The ascent is a gradual one of about 2000 feet from the Mammoth Springs. Snow clad mountains range majestically around, with hot springs rising at frequent intervals, and geysers spouting slate-colored water and boiling mud, until we reached a place named, with startling distinctness, "Hell's Half-acre," and again beheld a boiling spring of blue water surging over a platform of whitish line, streaked with every shade of orange and blood-red.[11]

We arrived at Norris'[s] Camp, where we lunched on a cold potato and a morsel of bread, for which one dollar was exacted, baited the horses, and proceeded by a road over long stretches of prairies, varied by pine forests, until 7 p.m., when we reached Firehole, and had a delicious hot-spring bath. The hotel was primitive, being an unfinished log-hut, the daylight peering through every plank. My room was about six feet square sufficiently filled with two beds. It boasted neither drawers nor table, and a door that declined to shut. The walls were stretched over with canvas. It could not be described as luxurious, and every snore was audible.[12]

Next morning we started at 8 a.m., and arrived at the Lower Geyser [Upper Geyser Basin] at noon. The air was so bright and exhilarating that we did not dream of fatigue, the excessive dryness of the atmosphere preventing all feeling of lassitude. After dinner at the hotel, a mere log-house, we found ourselves literally in the midst of Geyser Land.[13]

Picture a huge column of water 150 feet in height, and a steaming cloud rising twice that altitude. Such was a geyser of irregular habits

FIGURE **6.1.**
George Marshall's second hotel, built and shown here in 1884 at Lower
Geyser Basin, provided shelter but little else in the way of comfort
for our park chronicler Ms. O. S. T. Drake in 1885. (YELL 32045,
Yellowstone National Park Archives, Yellowstone National Park.)

which thought fit to play as we were driving by. The surrounding
cone is a wall of white deposit; the ground is everywhere snowy in
whiteness, diversified with bubbling hot-springs or spouting geysers
of every size. One is known as Old Faithful, from the regularity with
which his enormous jet spouts into the air every hour for a duration of
five to seven minutes. Some of the precipitates are iron, and tinge the

cones with beautiful shades of orange and deep red. Everywhere the overflow of these springs pours into the river which runs through this wonder-land, and the waters of which are consequently milkwarm. I saw a nice little cone at hand, and sat down upon it to watch a geyser in a state of turmoil. Finding it very hot, I sprang up and found I was sitting upon an infant geyser which was beginning to roar and boil. The geysers exercise a strange fascination. We stayed at least three hours watching one of them, and all the afternoon was spent in wandering from one to another lost in wonder and speculation. The everlasting Celestial has utilized one of the smaller geysers and turned it into a wash-tub, placing the clothes in the springs and stirring them up with a stick; and after a few minutes boiling he hooked them out, passed them through a wringer, and the work was done.[14] On our way back we made a detour to see the so-called Paint-pots; geysers,[15] that is, filled to near the brim with coloured gypsum, some white, shading into rose colour and other tints. The gypsum resembles oil-paint in consistency, and boils up incessantly. Close at hand too, is a beautiful geyser spouting to an immense height, and pouring torrents of water over the cone. That night we slept in tents at Norris'[s] Camp,[16] breakfasted early and departed, reaching the Mammoth Springs again at noon; then on to Cinnabar; the scenery very lovely. High on a sharp rock above the Yellowstone river we spied the eyrie of an eagle, which resembled a mass of sticks on the edge of a perfectly inaccessible rock.[17] There sat the eagle, showing her white throat, sunning herself in her majestic solitude. The hotel at Cinnabar turned out to be a little timber house, consisting of a bar and back parlour, and two or three bedrooms above.[18] A married couple kept the house; the wife said she had never had a lady under her roof before. They gave me a very clean bed-room, provided with the only jug and basin in the house. There was no door, but she nailed a sheet over the door-way and unnailed it in the morning; the food was excellent, and the good woman waxed quite pathetic in her regrets over the fact that we were hardly likely again to meet in this world. Next morning we took the train at Livingstone [*sic*—Livingston], and pursued our journey to New York. . . .[19]

Many more are the wonders of the Yellowstone Park; much that we did not see; the lake itself, wooded and beautiful; the famous Obsidian cliffs,[20] made of volcanic glass; Kessler's [*sic*—Kepler's] cascades, and

FIGURE **6.2.**

"Chinaman Spring" (today known as Chinese Spring), so discussed by Ms. O. S. T. Drake, was photographed in 1885 with the Chinese laundryman's tent erected nearby and the tent's wooden extension actually stretched over the spring. (Doris Whithorn collection, Yellowstone Gateway Museum, Livingston, MT.)

those of the Yellowstone river; the Painted Cliffs,[21] of every shade of colour, due to sulphur and oxidized iron; the Fossil Forest with trees standing petrified—as once they grew—into blocks of solid, clear, white agate; the decayed and prostrate trunks filled with crystals of shining quartz and calcite. Then [come] the Hoodoo, or Goblin Mountains,[22] where the rocks take every curious shape of bird or beast, gigantic in proportions. Such are some of the less explored wonders of this enchanted land, where it seems almost as if nature were at play, and had given the wildest scope to here power the grotesque or fantastic, far exceeding the limits of human imagination. Here at least it cannot be said that "Expectation fails where most it promises," for it is well-nigh as impossible to exhaust as it is to describe the wonders and surprises of the Yellowstone.

O. S. T. DRAKE

A Lady's Trip to the Yellowstone Park   III

Notes

This account originally appeared as O. S. T. Drake, "A Lady's Trip to the Yellowstone Park," *Every Girl's Annual*, 1887: 346–49.

1. O. S. T. Drake, "Stray Notes on Folk-lore," *Churchman's Schilling Magazine*, December 1876; "Old Roman Catholic Legends," *The Antiquary* 15 (January–June 1887): 214–16; in *Tinsley's Magazine*, as mentioned by W. H. K. Wright, *The Western Antiquary; or Devon and Cornmall Notebook*, vol. 8 (Plymouth, England: W. H. Luke, 1889), 134; and "A Strange People and a Strange Language," as cited in David Mayall, *Gypsy Identities 1500–2000* (Oxford: Routledge, 2003), 144n24.

2. Today the park's size is sixty-three miles by fifty-four miles or 3,472 square miles.

3. It is not quite correct to say that De Lacy was first to "reveal" Yellowstone. Walter W. De Lacy (1819–92) traveled through Yellowstone with a party of around forty prospectors searching for gold in 1863. Although he saw present Shoshone Lake and geysers at Lower Basin, he failed to publish his discoveries until 1876 and thus did not receive credit for discovering the Yellowstone area. Instead, the 1870 Washburn party received the credit. Aubrey L. Haines, *The Yellowstone Story* (1977; rev., Boulder: University of Colorado Press, 1996), I, 64–67.

4. President U. S. Grant signed the Organic Act to make Yellowstone America's first national park on March 1, 1872. Haines, *The Yellowstone Story*, I, chap. 6, "The New Creation."

5. Cinnabar, located three miles west of Gardiner, Montana, on the "Old Yellowstone Trail," was the terminus for the Northern Pacific Railroad from 1883 to 1903. Only cellar holes, nails, glass, bricks, and pieces of metal mark the site today.

6. These farms were largely crude one-story log buildings with barns and corrals.

7. Probably prickly pear cactus (*Opuntia* sp.) and one or more of many yellow composites such as arrowleaf balsamroot (*Balsamorrhiza sagittata*).

8. This is Boiling River, on Gardner River below the present campground at Mammoth Hot Springs. This place was so used to cook fish on the hook, but the more famous such place was and is Fishing Cone at West Thumb.

9. Actually the colors are caused largely by hot-water bacteria, called cyanobacteria, rather than by minerals, although the deposits of deep white color are calcium carbonate.

10. While all of the other mentioned flowers occur today near Norris, the hollyhock (*Illiamna rivularis*) is difficult to find. It occurs today mainly on the park's east entrance road.

11. This was Midway Geyser Basin.

12. "Norris's Camp" was the tent lunch station at Norris, operated by the Yellowstone National Park Improvement Company. The hotel she mentioned

was Marshall's Hotel (1880–91), later called the Firehole Hotel. See Lee H. Whittlesey, "Marshall's Hotel in the National Park," *Montana Magazine of Western History* 30 (Fall 1980): 42–51.

13. The existence of the Upper Basin Hotel (Shack Hotel) in the Old Faithful area and the presence of the Chinese laundry, mentioned below, date Ms. Drake's trip to summer 1885.

14. Chinese at this time were referred to as "Celestials," and this was the inaugural summer (1885) for the Chinese laundry at Old Faithful. A Chinese or Japanese man erected a tent just north of Old Faithful Geyser next to a hot spring that is today known as Chinese Spring. According only to legend and subject to no documentation so far, the boiling spring erupted as a geyser one day, possibly because of the soap used by the Chinese, thus throwing the man and his tent into disarray. Until 1990–91, the spring was known as "Chinaman Spring." Lee H. Whittlesey, *Yellowstone Place Names* (Gardiner, MT: Wonderland Publishing Company, 2006), 67.

15. She was incorrect. This was the feature later called Fountain Paint Pot, and it is a mud pot not a geyser. Her party went to Old Faithful and then turned around and traveled back to Mammoth over the same route, staying the second night at Norris.

16. The Yellowstone National Park Improvement Company tent camp at Norris was in place for the summers of 1883–86. In late 1886, officials built a large hotel there that burned to the ground in spring 1887. The cone geyser that she spoke of may have been Jet Geyser. Lee H. Whittlesey, "A Post-1872 History of the Norris Area: Cultural Sites Past and Present," September 30, 2005, unpublished manuscript, Yellowstone National Park Library, Yellowstone National Park, 13.

17. This was Eagle Nest Rock in Gardner Canyon, inhabited historically by ospreys rather than eagles.

18. This hotel was probably the one owned by E. J. Keeney, which others were running that summer. Lee Whittlesey, "'They're Going to Build a Railroad!': Cinnabar, Stephens Creek, and the Game Ranch Addition to Yellowstone National Park," 1997–2005, unpublished manuscript, Yellowstone National Park Library, Yellowstone National Park, 16.

19. Omitted here is a paragraph that does not relate to Yellowstone.

20. Her party drove past Obsidian Cliff twice, but her stage driver apparently did not point it out to them.

21. To see the Painted Cliffs requires a hiking trip to Seven Mile Hole in the park's Grand Canyon of the Yellowstone. Whittlesey, *Yellowstone Place Names*, 196.

22. She referred here to Hoodoo Basin, located in the backcountry of eastern Yellowstone and formerly known as the "Goblin Land," a place of strangely eroded pinnacles that requires a fifteen- to thirty-mile hike or horseback ride, depending upon the route taken, to reach. Lee Whittlesey, *Wonderland Nomenclature*, 1988, unpublished manuscript, Yellowstone National Park Library, Yellowstone National Park, Hoodoo Basin entry.

SEVEN

Yellowstone

How the National Park Appears in Midwinter. Monuments in Ice and Snow—A Scene of Cold Grandeur without a Parallel

CORRESPONDENT, *PHILADELPHIA TIMES*

1886

IN 1873, HENRY N. MAGUIRE MADE ONE OF THE EARLIEST known winter trips to Yellowstone and briefly wrote about it in his book *The Coming Empire* (1878). As early as 1903, President Theodore Roosevelt stated that "sometime people will surely awake to the fact that the Park has special beauties to be seen in winter; and any hardy man who can go through it in that season on skis will enjoy himself as he scarcely could elsewhere."[1] But winter as a real season in Yellowstone did not really "take off" until the winter of 1971–72, when continuous, overnight, winter lodging was first offered.

We do not know the identity of the writer of this fascinating account. Regardless, he (it was probably a *he*) left us the earliest known extended account of a trip to Yellowstone *in winter*. It occurred during the winter of 1885–86.

The Yellowstone National Park, the greatest of wonderlands, has been ably written up each year by tourists and newspapers correspondents, all of whom have visited it during the Summertime. But which of all these writers has seen the Park in dead of winter? The geysers spout

FIGURE 7.1.

This rare T. W. Ingersoll photo depicts an unknown skier in Yellowstone, between 1884 and 1887. Mysteries surround this photo, because Ingersoll is not known to have traveled to Yellowstone in winter. So who was this man, and what were the circumstances of his and Ingersoll's early ski trip? Could this be our midwinter traveler, the *Philadelphia Times* correspondent? (Yale Beinecke Library, New Haven.)

with their usual regularity, the snowfall is the same as upon the surrounding country and the cold streams freeze up just about the same as they would elsewhere. But place the geyser basins in the midst of snow white valleys, with their thousands of steam vents spouting and sputtering as they always do, and the picture is far grander than when beheld in midsummer and one seldom witnessed except by the Indians and the few hunters who pass through it and the employes who patrol the Park the year round. At Mammoth Hot Springs I found the whole basin boiling and bubbling as usual, except that the odor of sulfurous gases appeared to be stronger and more unpleasant than in the Summer time. There are no frogs near the Mammoth Hot Springs, as has been stated. The sulfurous fumes overcome all birds, beetles, butterflies and even the humming birds, when they venture too near.[2] I found, however, great numbers of the salamander fly and a few gallinip[p]er mosquitoes.[3] These two insects are about the only living creatures that dare venture with impunity within the space occupied by this deadly, torrid abyss.

From the Mammoth Hot Springs I rode up an old trail over the top of Summit Mountain,[4] and here I must say the scene spread out before me upon miles and miles of nature's canvas was simply sublime. Close by on my right towered the majestic Electric Peak, which is the loftiest eminence within the confines of the park.[5] The mountain was clothed from its dome to its base in a soft, snowy covering of white, which lent to it a picture of such sublimity that would be difficult to describe in words. Continuing along the trail, I descended first into a valley and then rode along the edge of a piece of timber[,] which finally brought me to the first crossing of [a branch of] the Gibbon River. I kn[e]w this stream was fed by hot springs and I was somewhat curious what effect the severe temperature of Montana, 6,000 feet in the air, would have upon this stream. There it was rushing along pell mell, as usual its surface uncongealed, but at a very low depth. The stream was not more than two feet deep at any place. In the summer time, when the snow melts, this branch of Gibbon River is from eight to ten feet in depth.[6] On each side the banks were lined with snow, which rose up like a white wall of solid material, between which rushed the waters of the river.

Traveling on for some miles I crossed another mountain, upon the summit of which is situated the beautiful "Lake of the Woods."[7] The surface of this beautiful body of water was frozen from shore to shore in one glassy sheet. It appeared that there had been a heavy snowfall on this mountain recently, but that the winds had blown the flaky substance entirely from the surface of the lake [so that the ice showed]. Along the edge of this mountain I skirted for some distance and looked with becoming awe down the awful chasms, where the snow must have been at least two hundred feet deep. It was in one of those unhealthy looking ravines that not long since a traveler on mule back was carried down with a snow slide at railroad speed, which covered him and his mule completely out of sight. He spent the night in the drift, but somehow succeeded in getting both himself and animal out next day, not much hurt either of them, but both very much frightened.[8] At the Norris Geyser Basin I again crossed the Gibbon River, also unfrozen at this point, and climbed the trail which brought me out near the [M]inute geyser and [S]teamboat [V]ent. The former was still going off with its usual regularity, while the latter also puffed and snorted away like a steamboat letting off steam. The princip[al] geysers in this basin are the Constant, throwing up a column of water every thirty seconds; the Fountain, [T]wins and [T]riplets; Black Geyser, Opal Spring, Mound Geyser, Mud Geyser, hurling mass of paint-like mud, ten feet high every twenty minutes; Minute Man Geyser, sputtering out steam and hot water thirty odd feet high every minute; Monarch Geyser, largest in the basin; New Crater Geyser and the Vixen.[9]

This whole basin was overflowing with scalding hot water, which not even the sixty odd degrees below freezing point was able to cool. When I came in sight of Lower Geyser Basin the sight was one I will never forget. I was standing on a lofty precipice, the country before me spread out like a panorama on a gigantic scale. In the distance was the main divide of the Rocky Mountain, the backbone of America, sending the headwaters of the Columbia River down one side and the springs of the Missouri system down the other. The ridge stood out bold and white in the distance. While standing and admiring the beauties of nature in this wonderful region I was surprised and delighted to see in the valley below and almost at my feet a band of elk that must have numbered at least 500. The noble animals saw me at about the same time I first espied them, and taking alarm at once they went trooping off down through the timber and out of sight. It is, indeed, a blessing that there are a few regulations now being enforced to spare what few game animals we yet have left in the Yellowstone National Park. I descended the valley and followed for some miles in the beaten trail made by the band of elk. In a little while I discerned far ahead what appeared to be jets of steam rising from the factories of a manufacturing town. It was steam, but it came from the hot springs and fountains of the Lower Geyser Basin. Directly over this basin hung a cloud of frost or mist, which was caused by the hot steam rising and coming in contact with the cold air above. The geysers in the basin are not clustered, but are scattered indiscriminately over an area of about thirty square miles. Within this area are nearly 700 hot springs constantly sputtering and bubbling and seventeen geysers in active operation.[10]

This basin was covered with snow to depth of from two to six feet. Here and there could be seen great bare places, where the hot springs and geysers were busily at work. I observed especially a new wonder, which had never been named or noticed until quite recently. This was the Chemical Basin,[11] of which there are three divisions, containing vast bowls or basins of decomposed rock, pulverized and in liquid form, of every shade and color, and so hot even then, that it would be instant death to any thing which had the misfortune to slip down the oily wall into one of these seething abyssess. On the banks of Firehole River, near the Chemical Basin, is a cabin which is a station for some of the employes of the park.[12] I remained overnight at this cabin and next morning resumed my journey to the upper basin. Nothing can be more lovely on a cold, frosty morning than the sight of the white steam jets tinged by the rays of the rising sun ascending against the background of dark pine woods and the clear sky above. This was the sight I had all the way to the upper basin. For the distance of six miles the roadway is lined with active and extinct geysers, also hot bubbling springs and others, which I remembered to have seen before, but was sure had been dead for many years. I observed that many of these former quiet geysers and dead springs had sprung into action again. Could it be that these craters, like the volcanos of the world remain idle for a long period and then come to life again? It must be so, for while many of the geysers in the park are evidently on the decline, on the other hand, many old fellows that have possibly been silent for ages are renewing operations and going to work again. Former tourists will mark that many of their old friends have ceased to spout with their accustomed regularity, while others which they will remember gave no sign of life have broken out into active eruption.[13]

The upper basin is at all times the most attractive spot in the park. Here are gathered the most remarkable collection of geysers on the face of the earth. Winter and Summer, day and night, the world famous Splendid, Castle, Giant and Giantess, Beehive, Fan, Old Faithful, Grotto, Saw Mill, Fountain, Comet, Spray, Pyramid and hundreds of others do their duty without fail. Now, it must be remembered that nearly all these geysers have regular stated periods at which to come into action. Some go off every hour or less; others in from two, three, four to five hours, or more, and others again at intervals of a day or two. With one or two exceptions all the geysers in this basin spout water that varies from moderately warm to scalding hot. Some guide books say that the Fan Geyser sends forth only hot water; but [this] Times correspondent has stood near the Fan when in eruption and being deluged with a shower of as cold water as ever gushed from mountain spring or rivulet. This geyser must have been spouting cold water lately, for from the apex or cone was built up a most beautiful chimney of pure ice, which had been coated by the water freezing as it gushed over the sides of the crater.[14]

On the opposite bank of the Firehole River is the Castle geyser, which, as I saw it on this frosty morning, was spouting from its yellow coated throat a column of water five feet thick and one hundred feet high, accompanied by the most awful rumblings and groanings imaginable. The effect was gorgeous. Millions of brilliant spangles reflecting the sun's rays fell back over the chimney of the crater, encircling that magnificent natural tower with a prismatic halo of great beauty. I have seen the Castle in eruption in midsummer, but it certainly never had in Summer the grand, beautiful appearance that it possessed on this Wintry morning, caused by the steam of hot water and steam coming in contact with the cold atmosphere of the outer world.

The road from the upper basin to Yellowstone Lake was in reality no road at all. It was simply a beaten trail over the snow, made by hunters, Indians, and employes of the park.[15] I found Yellowstone Lake also frozen over, at least this was true of the central parts of that body of water. The shores of this lake are lined with hot springs, but the great body of the lake itself, even in midsummer, is delightfully cool and contains great numbers of large sized trout. I have caught as fine speckled trout from this lake as the North American continent can boast of, but it may not be generally known that they are wormy and not fit to eat. The Indians, however, eat them, and appear to relish the fish, but as an Indian will eat anything, no matter what, from a sick dog to the putrid carcass of a decayed beef, their judgement in regard to the

FIGURE 7.2.
Early photographs of winter scenes in Yellowstone are rare. This image of
Billy Hofer, an early tour guide and winter skier, was photographed at Red
Rock near Lower Falls in February 1887 by then official park photographer
F. Jay Haynes. (Montana Historical Society, Helena.)

wormy Yellowstone lake trout as an article of food should be taken with
a good many grains of allowance. The ice of the lake appeared to be
solid enough, even a short distance from the land; but the hot springs
seemed to form, as it were, a complete circle of water around it, like the
tire around a wheel, which kept the icy center detached from the land.

The grandest sight in the park is beyond question the lower falls
of the Yellowstone. I have never seen but have frequently read of the
beautiful sight presented by the Falls of Niagara in Winter and of the
wonderful ice bridge formed at their base by the freezing of the waters,
but I cannot imagine how Niagara can compare, even considering
the tremendous volume of water, with the sublime lower falls of the
Yellowstone River in midwinter. Here was the ice bridge, too, or rather

an ice mountain which rose to a height almost equal to the descent of the falls. A feeling of awe creeps over one beholding in this wilderness such desolate granduer [sic—desolate grandeur] as cannot be seen elsewhere on earth. I stood on Lookout Terrace a short distance from the falls and saw a great sheet of water shoot out from the land and with a mighty roar plunge fully 395 feet into the abyss beneath.[16] Nothing could freeze in the basin that received this deluge, for the force of the descending river must have broken anything that came in its way; but the spray that shot far out beyond the solid stream froze as it fell and formed the beautiful ice bridge or ice mountain I have mentioned. The walls of the great canyon of the Yellowstone certainly are the most awe inspiring, majestic, sublimest spectacle on God's earth.

Nowhere in this wonderful Park nor elsewhere on the globe can there be found such an extensive view of combination of stupendous natural scenery and gorgeous coloring. On this Wintry day, far in the depths of the Park, away from humanity and alone with nature, I cannot describe the feeling that came over me. I hurried out of the canyon and after a long, cold journey made my way back to Mammoth Hot Springs and thence to Cinnabar, where I am penning these lines. There are a few mountain buffalos still left in the park and great numbers of deer and elk, which are now being protected by saving statutes rigidly enforced.

Black bear and grizzlies are also said to be among the canyons and on the Park mountains, but I caught sight of no wild animals on my trip, save the band of elk I encountered soon after leaving the Gibbon Geyser Basin.

CORRESPONDENCE *PHILADELPHIA TIMES*.

Notes

Reproduced from the *Brooklyn Daily Eagle*, April 30, 1886.

1. *Gardiner (MT) Wonderland*, April 30, 1903.
2. It is not the sulfur from these springs that kills small animals, insects, and birds but, rather, the carbon dioxide. See, for example, Poison Spring in Lee H. Whittlesey, *Yellowstone Place Names* (Gardiner, MT: Wonderland Publishing Company, 2006), 205–6.
3. It was not mosquitoes that this observer saw, as they cannot live in Yellowstone in winter. Instead, he probably observed brine flies (ephydrid flies) that live on bacterial mats in hot springs. See, generally, Thomas

Brock, *Life in the Geyser Basins* (Yellowstone National Park: Yellowstone Library and Museum Association, [1971]).

4. He probably referred here to present Snow Pass, as there is a Summit Lake there. Lee Whittlesey, *Wonderland Nomenclature*, 1988, unpublished manuscript, Yellowstone National Park Library, Yellowstone National Park, 1794–95.

5. At 10,922 feet, Electric Peak is actually the sixth highest peak in the park. Eagle Peak on the east boundary of the park is highest at 11,358 feet. Thomas Turiano, *Select Peaks of Greater Yellowstone: A Mountaineering History and Guide* (Jackson, WY: Indomitus Books, 2003), 259–60.

6. This was not Gibbon River but probably Obsidian Creek, as nearby Lake of the Woods was called "Gibbon Lake" by the Hayden party because it seemed in the drainage of Gibbon River. Whittlesey, *Yellowstone Place Names*, 146.

7. He was traveling on Superintendent P. W. Norris's original road (today a trail), which ran south from Solfatara trailhead past Amphitheater Springs and down Solfatara Creek to the present Norris Campground. See generally, Lee H. Whittlesey, "A Post-1872 History of the Norris Area: Cultural Sites Past and Present," September 30, 2005, unpublished manuscript, Yellowstone National Park Library, Yellowstone National Park.

8. This event is so far unmentioned in other known Yellowstone literature.

9. Of these, the "Fountain," "Twins," and "Triplets," although mentioned often in early accounts, referred to features that are unknown today; "Black Geyser" referred to Black Growler steam vent; "Minute Geyser" and "Minute Man Geyser" referred respectively to Constant Geyser and Minute Geyser; and New Crater Geyser referred to present Steamboat Geyser. "Steamboat Vent" did not refer to present Steamboat Geyser but, rather, to a steam vent of uncertain location, as shown in T. W. Ingersoll's 1887(?) photograph, number 1171B, "Steam Boat Vent, Norris G.B.," purchased in 2007 for the Yellowstone National Park Museum collection.

10. These numbers probably came from the 1878 Hayden report, although today it is known that there are many more than seventeen geysers and seven hundred hot springs in Lower Geyser Basin.

11. This was probably today's Pocket Basin or Microcosm Basin. The latter contains some of the park's largest mud pots. Whittlesey, *Wonderland Nomenclature*, 1064, 1421.

12. What was this cabin at Lower Geyser Basin? It was probably one of the ones built in 1882–83 by Superintendent Pat Conger on the south bank of Nez Perce Creek. Finding information on the buildings here has been difficult, but researcher Bob Flather has recently filled in some of the answers, and a photo of the buildings at a ford on Nez Perce Creek has also been found in the collections of Park County Museum. One of the buildings was a jail, mentioned by George Wingate in 1885 (*Through the Yellowstone Park on*

Horseback [New York: O. Judd Company, 1886], 97), and it was probably in existence in 1883, for Carl Schmidt stated:

> Shortly after leaving the Captain [Lindsay at the Nez Perce Creek soldier's camp] we forded Nez Perces [*sic*] Creek, on the f[a]rther bank of which stood a rude log house which Fitz [Selleck Fitzgerald] had built years ago for the state of Wyoming and which was the first prison in that section, proving that even twenty years ago civilization had found its way into this country of solitude. (*A Western Trip* [Detroit: Herald Press, 1910], 1901 trip, 26.)

A photo of this building is H-25063, at the Montana Historical Society, Helena.

13. Like this observer, many early park visitors incorrectly surmised that the geysers and hot springs were dying, simply because some had dried up and ceased to spout. See, for example, Dr. Roland Dwight Grant, "Changes in the Yellowstone Park," *American Geographical Society, Bulletin,* 1908: 277–83.

14. Again, the observer was incorrect. Geyser water cools very quickly as it falls from an eruption, even though it emerges from the earth boiling hot. As a result, ice cones form easily in winter around many geysers.

15. This was the Mary Mountain road, today a trail, which was used as the main route to Yellowstone Lake and the canyon prior to completion of the Old Faithful–West Thumb road in late 1891. It is a bit remarkable that this traveler was able to find the road in the snow-covered winter, as it was only vestigial even during summers. See Lee H. Whittlesey, "A History of the Old Faithful Area with Chronology, Maps, and Executive Summary," September 14, 2006, manuscript prepared for the National Park Service, Yellowstone National Park Library, Yellowstone National Park, 7–8.

16. He was apparently standing at present Lookout Point on the canyon's north rim. Lower Falls of the Yellowstone is 308 feet tall.

EIGHT

A Midsummer Ramble

Being a Descriptive Sketch
of the Yellowstone National Park

H. Z. OSBORNE

1888

HENRY ZENAS OSBORNE (1848–1923) WAS A PRINTER, REPORTER, editor, newspaper publisher, and U.S. congressman from California. In 1888, at the time of his trip to Yellowstone, he was the owner and editor of the *Los Angeles Evening Express*, a newspaper that remained influential until it ceased publication in 1962 as one of the oldest daily newspapers published in Southern California. Osborne purchased it in 1884 and published it until 1897, using it as a vehicle to make himself well known. He later became Los Angeles collector of customs, U.S. marshal for the southern district of California, commissioner of the L.A. Board of Public Works, and finally U.S. congressman from the tenth district of California, 1916–23, in which office he was serving at the time of his death. A veteran of the Civil War, Osborne spent much time in Congress and on his own in improving the harbor at Los Angeles. He was an important citizen in Southern California and left personal papers at the University of California at Los Angeles, Stanford University, the Huntington Library, and the University of California at Berkeley.[1]

At the time of his trip to Yellowstone, he was thirty-nine years old. His 1888 account, published here, is long and detailed and gives us many insights into what was going on in the park that summer. His mention of obtaining "an extension of my leave of absence" was modest, because he was, after all, one of the owners of the newspaper. Osborne admitted that "Park fever" took possession of him before he even reached Livingston, Montana, and he rode around Yellowstone on the high outside seat next to his driver, "Red-Headed Hank."

Although Osborne loved Yellowstone, he also loved civilization, for at the end of his trip he noted that he could not wait to get a bath, shave, and change of clothes. "The road from here to the *Evening Express* office and 22 West Pico street," he exclaimed, "cannot be short enough, nor can the railroad trains run too fast [for] my pleasure."

Livingston, Montana, July 13, 1888.—

Having obtained an extension of my leave of absence, and determined upon a tour through the Yellowstone National Park, I find myself this evening at the starting point from the main line of the Northern Pacific Railroad. Livingston is a typical frontier town of 1500 inhabitants, situated on the Yellowston[e] river, which is a clear, rushing mountain stream of large volume, surrounded on all sides by lofty mountains. It is 1032 miles west of St. Paul and 881 miles east of Portland. The Northern Pacific Railroad Company[,] which advertises the Yellowstone Park very extensively throughout the East, runs a Pullman sleeping car daily from St. Paul to this point. It was my fortune to be located in this car for Portland, and as all my fellow-travelers were prospective tourists in the Park, that circumstance may have been the cause for the Park fever which took possession of me before reaching Livingston. At all events, there I am, at the Albemarle Hotel,[2] which is well filled with people who will go into the Park to-morrow, and those who have returned to-day, and who are here await the trains for the East and West. I have taken a stroll about Livingston, and I find that it has a bank, a newspaper office, two or three churches, a well-built brick schoolhouse, no end of saloons, a gospel tent and a dance house in full operation, and that it costs two bits for shave. The female portion of the population [is] well dressed, and the mountain climate appears to agree with them.

A prominent object on the open ground in front of the hotel is a mountain lion, secured by a lariat about twenty feet long to a stake. He moves about restlessly, and my tourist friends are careful to give him all the room he wants, although the town dogs seem to be on a pleasant speaking acquaintance with him and treat him with canine familiarity. About the hotel returned tourists tell big stories about what they have seen for the benefit of myself and the other "tenderfeet" about to enter. They divide the time with an elderly person of great eloquence and marvelous loquacity, who runs a sort of opposition to the Yellowstone Park Association. Mr. Henderson is an old-timer in the Park,[3] and a veritable encyclopedia of information upon all matters in connection with it; but he is something like the Encyclopedia Britannica, which is so voluminous that I have never been able to find anything in it that I wanted. Mr. Henderson has given names to many objects in the Park;[4] and in their nomenclature there is ample evidence of his classical education; but if he could in some way repress in part the tide of his voluble enthusiasm fewer tourists would go into the Park with a headache.

How The Tour Is Made.

The Northern Pacific Railroad Company sells tickets from St. Paul, Minneapolis and other eastern termini, and from Portland, Oregon, and Tacoma, W.T. [Washington Territory], to and through the Park and return for $110. This includes railroad fares, one berth in Pullman car, meals in dining cars, stage transportation through the Park, and accommodations for five days in Park Association hotels. At Livingston book tickets are sold at $10, $30 and $40. [T]he first is for a single day's trip to Mammoth Hot Springs, the first station in the Park; the second embraces four day's accommodations in the Park, including railroad and stage fares from Livingston to Mammoth Hot Springs, Norris, and Lower and Upper Geyser Basins, and the $40 ticket includes also a day's detour from Norris to the Yellowstone Grand Canyon and Falls. These tickets are good from June 15th to September 30th inclusive. At Livingston people must pay their own hotel bills; but from the time of taking the cars at Livingston for the Park these book tickets cover all absolutely necessary expenses. If tourists indulge in wine at dinner, and have guides to show them the sights at the various stations, they of course must pay extra for such luxuries.

The evening has been enlivened by the professional antics of a cowboy on a jamboree and a vicious broncho. They have been capering about in the vicinity of the mountain lion sometimes with the horse on top and sometimes the man. My sympathies were strongly in favor of the horse, and I waited anxiously in the hope of seeing the lion take a bite out of the cowboy's leg or the horse break his neck. I am disappointed. He has now gone into a convenient saloon to take another drink, and I will go to bed.

Mammoth Hot Springs

Mammoth Hot Springs Hotel
National Park, Wyoming Ty.,
July 14, 1888

This morning at 8 o'clock the expectant tourists were gathered in the single car at Livingston in which they were to be transported south over the 51 miles of branch road to Cinnabar.[5] They were about thirty in number. Among them were all the pleasant people who had come on the same cars as I from Minneapolis, excepting a delightful Minneapolis family, who had gone to Hunter's Hot Springs for a few days.[6] There was a party of four—two gentlemen and their wives—from Milwaukee, and a lady teacher from the Illinois Normal School on a summer tour. From the west there were a party of four, whose homes are at Cincinnati, just returning from a trip to Alaska; a Minneapolis gentleman and his wife, accompanied by a San Francisco lady, who had been making the tour of California, including the Yosemite Valley; a young German gentleman who is visiting the United States for pleasure, and from whose neck is suspended a small amateur camera with which he has photographed hundreds of historical and interesting objects in this country and Europe.[7] He is accompanied by two German friends from Chicago. There are a good many others, not the least among whom are two Chicago gentlemen, connected with large commercial establishments of that city, who have been on a trip over the coast for their houses, and now on their way home, are relaxing and having a pretty good time.

From Livingston To Cinnabar

In its westward course the Northern Pacific railroad runs up the Yellowstone river for 550 miles, and the branch from Livingston, where the river takes an abrupt turn to the south, still follows that wonderful stream. The scenery from one end to the other of this branch road is picturesque, and at some points it is grand. Paradise Valley extends thirty miles in length along the river, and is twelve miles wide. It is all good land, and is divided up into extensive ranches. To the east a range called the Snow Mountains,[8] rising 3000 or 4000 feet above the adjacent country, gird[s] the valley, and on the west are other mountains less pretentious. Emigrant Peak is the most conspicuous mountain along the road, and it reaches an elevation of 10,629 feet above the sea.[9] What is known as the Middle canyon is a narrow pass where the river is confined within walls about 100 feet apart.[10] This canyon is about three miles in length, and at some points the road is compelled to encroach upon the already narrow boundaries of the rushing stream. The walls are very abrupt and rise to a height of several hundred feet.

The most notable natural feature along the railroad is Cinnabar mountain, about seven miles south of Middle canyon. It lies on the west side of the valley and takes its name from certain brilliant vermillion streaks that run from its summit to its base. It is also ribbed at one point like an umbrella, with remarkably regular and high ledges of rock, gently converging. These ledges from a distance present the appearance of huge walls, that might well have been constructed by the mason's art, so even and regular they are. They do not look either so high or so broad, but they are said to be 200 feet high and 50 feet wide. The spaces between are called "The Devil's Slides."[11] The formation and general appearance is much like that in Weber canyon, Utah, where the same name is given that peculiarity of nature. It has always seemed to me singularly inappropriate that so many of the most striking and remarkable of the works of God should be used to familiarize humanity with the name of the incarnation of evil. There are the Devil's Punch Bowl, the Devil's Nose, the Devil's Thumb, the Devil's this and the Devil's that all over the Pacific Coast. It suggests a degree of superstition more compatible with the character of the Chinese than of the American people. I am afraid that some of the clerical readers of the EXPRESS do not think that I am as deeply prejudiced against the Devil as I ought to be; but I am free to say all this honoring of the Devil by attaching his name to the marvelous handiwork of the Creator is most disgusting to me.[12] But to return to Cinnabar Mountain, it may be said that its name is a misnomer, as no cinnabar has even been found there. Its color is produced by some other agency.

The little town of Cinnabar, three or four miles f[a]rther south, is the end of the railroad line.[13] Here the passengers were all taken on stages, a sufficient number of which are always at hand when the train arrives, and transported eight miles over hill and valley, to the Mammoth Hot Springs Hotel. This hotel is three or four miles within the northern boundary of the Park.

The Yellowstone National Park

It should be recollected, takes in a narrow strip of the eastern portion of Idaho and of the southwestern portion of Montana, but is for the most part in the northwestern portion of Wyoming. It is sixty-five miles from north to south, and fifty-five miles from east to west, and numbers within its boundaries the headwaters of the great river systems of the United States. The Gallatin, Madison (or Firehole) and Jefferson, here rise and combine to make the Missouri, with its outlet in the Gulf of Mexico. The Snake here has its head, and its waters find their way to the Pacific, while the headwaters of the Colorado lead eventually to the Gulf of California. The Park is a vast elevated table land, and cut up into a series of valleys by great mountain ranges, or spurs of the one great mother range—the Rockies. The valleys range from 6000 to 8000 feet above the level of the sea, while the summits of the mountains, which are to be seen in every direction, are from 10,000 to 12,000 feet above sea level. By act of Congress this immense and interesting tract, somewhat larger than Rhode Island and Delaware combined, has been set aside perpetually as a park and breathing place for the American people.

Mammoth Hot Springs

The stage ride from the Cinnabar station to the springs involves a tolerably stiff climb. The road branches to the right from the Yellowstone river to the West Gardiner. At a distance of a mile or so from the hotel a stream of hot water runs into the river, and here it is said that one may catch trout in the cold water, and turning the pole over to the hot stream, cook the fish in the latter.[14] Upon driving up to the hotel we found a building 300 or 400 feet long, with a broad piazza the full length, and a number of people lounging about to take a look at the new arrivals, among them a brace of English tourists, an army officer or two, in uniform, and a pretty, black-eyed girl who sells Haynes'[s] photographs of the park when the band does not play dancing tunes.[15] The view from this piazza is particularly fine. Mountains covered with pines, and others tipped with eternal snows, are to be seen in all directions; but what most immediately attracts the attention of the stranger is a small mountain to [the] right, the base of which is not more than a hundred yards from the hotel. Which at first glance looks like ice, or as I should imagine the lower end of a glacier might appear. Under closer investigation it proved to be a sedimentary formation from the hot springs which give this locality its name, composed principally of magnesia, lime, sulphur, and silica. From the base of this white mountain it presents the appearance of a succession of steps, terraces, and plateaus, of irregular height and breadth.[16] The almost perfect right angle upon which these steps are formed by the natural working of the hot water is a marvel. The water runs over the edges and sides of the terraces in thin, pulsating waves, and from a little distance it is difficult to tell whether there is any water or not, until one becomes familiar with the coloring which the water imparts. Upon ascending the steps and terraces—which is quite a fatiguing climb on a hot day—great numbers of boiling hot springs are found, bursting out of vents at the top of successive terraces. The water is of marvelous clearness, so much so that it hardly seems possible that it should contain any sediment. The deposits take on a great variety of shades of color, from pearly white to cream color, yellow, ashy gray, faint and bright pinks and crimsons. The overflow from the main vents forms pools, the sides of which are formed of the same material, and which take an infinite number of exquisite shapes as well as of colors, a scalloped, shell-like form being quite common. The work of formation appears to be more active at the surface than at the bottom, and the edges usually project over the water, as does ice when forming at the edges of a pool. How many of these terraces there are I cannot say, but they rise to an elevation of several hundred feet above the level of the hotel, and extend back at least two miles. The most notable are the Minerva Terrace, the Jupiter Terrace and the Cleopatra Terrace, and Cupid's Cave underneath what is called Cleopatra's Bowl at the top of this terrace, is the most exquisite in coloring of any. Should Cleopatra ever desire to bathe in this bowl, she would find it constantly supplied with boiling-hot water,[17] which comes out fairly hissing at one side of the formation. The overflow passes into Cupid's Cave underneath, running over a side consisting of fluted columns, four or five feet in length and of great number, before dripping into the cave underneath. It would be an endless task to describe all these various terraces, each of which differs from the others in some respect, but all of which have many things in common. The extent of these living springs can be estimated when it is considered that they cover 170 acres of land. Back of them, and higher up are a great extent of extinct springs, the whole area of calcareous matter embracing no less than three square miles. About a mile and a half back from the hotel I found a beautiful body of tepid water, in a wood, and a [sign]board announced it as "Bath Lake."[18] I took the hint and had a delightful bath. It covers something less than an acre of ground, and on one side the hot water comes in strong, bubbling up a couple of inches above the surface, and on swimming over I found that the heat steadily increased in that direction. The water is quite deep, except about the edges of the lake. I spent a half an hour very pleasantly swimming about and experimenting as to how near one could approach the source of supply.

Notwithstanding the great number of hot springs at this point, there are no active geysers here. Back of Bath Lake there is a mound about twenty feet high, called the Orange Geyser, from its shape and color, I presume, but the water barely bubbles up at the top, [and] I do not think it fairly entitled to the dignity of a geyser. My scientific friend, Mr. Henderson, is authority for the statement that this geyser raises its mound but one foot in a hundred years, and therefore it is now twenty centuries old. There is a mound somewhat smaller on the plateau on which the hotel is situated, slimmer, but fifty feet high. From the peculiarity of its shape it is called the Liberty Cap. It has been extinct ever since the white men came into this section. Another somewhat similar formation is called the Giant's Thumb.[19]

I climbed down a ladder fifty or sixty feet into a cave in the "formation" called "Devil's Kitchen."[20] At the top there is barely room to crawl through, but is gradually widened to fully twenty feet at the bottom. The walls, which were covered with hard globules about the size of a walnut, gave ample evidence that this had once been the interior of a large boiling spring. I went as far laterally in the fissure as the light would permit, but I could not see the end in either direction. The air was exceedingly close, and six or eight feet below the ledge on which I walked I could see water, but I could not tell whether it was cold or not. Two or three bats, disturbed by my presence, flew back and forth about my head in a very careless fashion. On reaching the surface I found the fresh air most welcome.

I have seen hot springs in California and Nevada, but never anything on such a scale as this. I am told, however, that while the formation here is not duplicated elsewhere in the Park, the hot springs will sink into insignificance when we see the geysers, which are situated at Norris Geyser Basin, Lower and Upper Geyser Basins twenty-two, forty and fifty miles south of here, respectively.

The Second Day's Journey

Lower Geyser Basin Hotel
National Park, Wyoming Ty.,
July 15, 1888

[We] Inmates of the Mammoth Hot Springs Hotel were up bright and early this morning, in preparation for the long stage ride to the geysers. A few preferred to remain over one day at the Hot Springs, but a majority were out on the hotel veranda at 8 o'clock, after an excellent breakfast, when the four-horse stages of the National Park Association were driven up. The excellent system of transportation through the Park is one of its most striking features, and is one that must require considerable skill to handle. During the busy season it is said that an average of fifty people per day go into the Park from Mammoth, and if they were all going on the five-day trip there would be 250 people on vehicles all the time. George W. Wakefield,[21] who for thirty years has been a stage man in the mountains, runs the transportation department for the Yellowstone Park Association, and his first lieutenant and executive officer is Adam Deem.[22] It is one of Adam Deem's duties to assign the passengers to their respective coaches, and as they are thrown into each other's society constantly for the five days of the trip, it is of no little consequence to the individual that he be parceled off into an agreeable crowd. I asked Deem how he managed that part of the business.

"Well," he said, "I try to get all the pleasant people together. Then I pick out all the cranks and kickers, and put them all in a carriage by themselves if it is feasible. I have been at this business so long that I can tell a crank as far as I can see him. The minute they go across the floor to register I pick out the cranks and mentally begin to assign them to carriages for the next day. I give the pleasant people to the most accommodating drivers, and to the kickers I give some crusty old frost-bitten driver that will fire it right back at them. In that way everything moves as smooth as glass."

My Fellow-Passengers.

Adam Deem in his wisdom assigned me to the wagon with the two merry Chicago commercial men, the young German traveler and his two German friends, and the lady teacher from the Illinois Normal School, and at my request gave me the outside seat with "Red-Headed Hank," the boss driver of the Park.[23] Owing to a sudden change of plans I have not exactly a tourist's outfit; but clad in a long linen duster, a Harrison plug hat,[24] and an American flag around my throat, I hope to protect myself partially from the sun and frighten away stray bears and other carniverous or omniverous beasts that may be prowling about seeking whom they devour. Hank cracked his whip over the heads of the leaders the moment Deem announced "All set!" and away we went, past "the formation," as the natives call it; the "Capitol," as the United States army headquarters is called, where a private on duty handed us a copy of the "Rules and Regulations" of the Park, as formulated by the Secretary of the Interior. These rules require that nothing in the Park shall be defaced, broken or changed in any way; so that campers shall put out their forest fires so that they may not spread to the forests; that horses shall not be driven or ridden on the "formation," in the Park, and that specimen fiends and vandals generally shall be "set down upon." Parties offending in these particulars will be taken out of the Park under the escort of a file of cavalry, a troop of which is constantly on duty, a captain of cavalry being the government superintendent of the Park. Putting a bar of soap in a geyser, or "soaping" it, as it is called, by reason of which it will go off at the wrong time and permanently affect its working, is attended by a serious penalty.[25]

A Picturesque Route.

The first four miles out of Mammoth involves a stiff climb, in which a raise of 1100 feet is effected, the elevation of the hotel being 6200 feet, and that of the West Gardner Falls 7300.[26] It passes through a dead forest, the trees having been killed by fire some years ago. The trees are small, and I have observed this to be the case throughout the Park, few trees being more than one foot in diameter. Before reaching the end of the big grade we passed through a narrow defile between Mount Bunsen and another high point. The road is carried around a perpendicular cliff, and is fairly suspended in mid-air. We also passed a large extent of extinct geyser formation, known as the Hoodoo Geysers.[27]

The raise placed us on the great tableland of the Park, from which we will not descend until our return four days hence.

The road proved a very delightful one. It traversed forests mainly of white pine, with occasional breaks of mountain meadow and park, and in the near distance mountain ranges and lofty peaks gave character to the scene. Beautiful mountain streams were crossed by means of well-constructed bridges, and lakes of limpid water were frequently passed. The names of all these watercourses are marked on signboards by the government,[28] as, indeed, are all the prominent and interesting objects in the Park. Beaver Lake was divided into two or three parts by beaver dams, but the animals have found it to be too near the road, and have deserted the lake for another point more secluded. After the first ten miles we encountered hot springs very frequently, and also passed a mountain of obsidian, or volcanic glass, of which material the road alongside is constructed. The Park guide books make much of these obsidian bluffs, but I have seen far larger deposits of the same material in California. South of Mono Lake, in Mono and Inyo counties, there is a line of extinct volcanoes, some of which are almost exclusively obsidian, and my time as extensive as these bluffs in the Park. Still, they impart variety to a section that is wonderful in the diversity of its attractions.

The Norris [Geyser] Basin

About noon we drew up at the Norris Basin Hotel, situated in a beautiful valley. Here we met a pleasant party who had made the detour to the Yellowstone Grand Canyon and Falls, twelve mile[s] to the east, as some do, before visiting the Lower and Upper Geyser Basins. Among them were a prominent Oakland physician and his bright and interesting daughter, on her way East to attend school in Massachusetts, and a well-to-do and comfortable Illinois farmer, with a young lady daughter and his son who have been making two month tour of the coast. A splendid hotel building was burned here last year,[29] and a rude board structure has been put up in its place; but it is clean and neat, the dinner was good, and the service, which in the dining room consists of neatly-attired and modest-appearing young women, was excellent.

After dinner we all strolled out to the Norris Geyser Basin, which is about half a mile from the hotel and over a little hill. The first view of the basin whatever may have been his preconceived idea, fills the beholder with astonishment. A valley of considerable extent is covered with hard white sedimentary deposit,[30] which might easily be mistaken for ice, with occasional pools of water and small streams flowing off the lower side. Great quantities of steam arise in every direction, over pools [that] are seen to be boiling and from fountains of hot water, which spring up here and there at brief intervals. Much of the steam contains a strong smell of sulphur, and around some of the springs and vents quantities of sulphur are to be found. In the center of the basin the most prominent object is the "Constant" geyser, which threw up a fountain of hot water to a height of thirty or forty feet every seventeen seconds. The "formation" has a hollow sound, and one [goes] very gingerly about walking on it; but after a little experimenting all our people walked out to the center to make a more intimate acquaintance with the "Constant." All around the hills there were other hot springs in operation, and along the roadside there was one peculiarly loud-mouthed and ferocious vent [that] emitted steam but no water. It is called the "Steamboat,"[31] from the peculiarly regular and characteristic noise it makes. It is very hot and I found it impossible to bear with my hand a few inches from it. The hot pools and springs, of which large and small, there are great numbers about this basin, vary as to color and quality. A great majority are perfectly clear, but others were of the color of soap-suds, some pale drab, others almost inky black, and still others of a thick paint-like consistency, amounting in fact to a fountain of hot mud. The largest geyser in this group is the "Monarch." It has but one eruption a day, when it throws a large stream from 100 to 125 feet high for twenty minutes, through three openings 2 × 12, 2 ½ × 11 and 5 × 6 feet respectively in dimensions. It was seething and sputtering, but did not do the grand act for our benefit. A more accommodating but less grand geyser close by his majesty, and appropriately called "The Minute Man," went off regularly every sixty seconds.

The Afternoon's Ride.

We examined these and various other marvels for an hour, when our conveyance arrived, and "Red-Headed Hank" assured us that this was nothing to what we would see at the Upper Basin. We therefore resumed our places for the afternoon ride. The scenery was very much like that of the morning, but a greater number of hot springs [was] passed, many of which would be deemed very remarkable elsewhere, being with a name here. Hills and mountains of the same calcareous

FIRE HOLE HOTEL—YELLOWSTONE PARK.

FIGURE **8.1.**

The Firehole Hotel—formerly Marshall's Hotel and photographed here in 1885—
was where our chronicler H. Z. Osborne stayed in 1888. Osborne, like Ms. Drake
in 1885, found the hotel rooms a bit primitive, commenting, "I woke up during
the night and heard someone breathing so plainly and so near that I felt sure . . .
that there was one too many in my bed." (Yale Beinecke Library, New Haven.)

deposit, evidently of thermal origin, are to be seen all over the Park.
In some places the springs have died out entirely and in others a few
lingerers give a faint idea of what has been in the centuries past. The
Gibbon Paint Pots,[32] remarkable for their extent and their variegated
color, are a collection of hot mud springs, and the Monument Geysers,[33]
a field of nearly extinct geysers, are passed during this afternoon ride,
which also takes us through a beautiful canyon, the walls on one side
of which rise 800 or 1000 feet above the roadway. The Gibbon Falls,
where the river of the same name passes over a precipice 160 feet high,
is well worth the climb which tourists are compelled to make in order
to obtain a good view of it.[34]

An Evening In The Park

Arriving at this hotel about 6 o'clock,[35] our party, most of them rather
tired after the forty-mile ride and sightseeing, were glad to be assigned
to their various rooms. The main house, and two large cottage buildings

detached, are filled with tourists. Those twenty-four hours ahead of us stop here over night on their way out, and have plenty of information to give us as to the sights which we will see to-morrow. This hotel is situated on the Madison, or "Firehole" river, so named from the fact that it has its rise in this fiery region. It is, in fact the principle of the three branches which go to form the Missouri, and ought to have been called the Missouri. There are no geysers immediately about the hotel, and we have spent the evening strolling around, examining some of the many hot springs and other beautiful and interesting works of nature in this vicinity. The hotel is supplied with hot water from the adjacent spring. The twilight holds on wonderfully, and it is scarcely dark at 9 o'clock. To-morrow we visit the great geysers of the two basins, returning here to-morrow night.

The Great Geysers.

Lower Geyser Basin Hotel
National Park, W.T., July 16, 1888

Sleeping in a hotel where partitions between rooms are so thin that you cannot help hearing everything that is going on around the house is sometimes amusing and sometimes an embarrassing situation. You may hear your own merits and demerits discussed with all the frank familiarity superinduced by a belief in the complete privacy of the conversation. I woke up during the night and heard some one breathing so plainly and so near that I felt sure that a mistake had been made, and that there was one too many in my bed. I prospected the situation, in the dark without result, fortunately, and concluded that my neighbor's bed was alongside mine in the next room.

To-night I am back to the point from which the start was made this morning. It has been a day of wonderful sightseeing. A good early start was made from the hotel a little after 7 o'clock. The road at once crosses the "Firehole," or Madison river,[36] and does not depart far from the course of that stream during the route. Indeed, none of the great geysers are far from its banks, and some are immediately alongside it. The Lower Geyser Basin, I may say by way of premise, covers an area of thirty or forty square miles, and comprises within its boundaries 600 or 700 hot springs and seventeen geysers.[37] It therefore may be assumed as a fact that I did not see all of them, and that my attention was given only to those which presented the most remarkable appearance. I first visited the Thud Group and the Paint Pots. These latter consist of a small lake of boiling mud of about the consistency of mush, and of colors varying from brilliant red to pure white. The great body of it is a creamy color. It bubbles and pops constantly. All about the main body are smaller earthy pots, cauldron shaped, in which a separate boiling is going on. As each of the large bubbles breaks the pasty stuff is thrown back into symmetrical flower-like shapes, often resembling the rose and other similarly shaped blossoms. A young lady tourist inadvertently stepped into one of these smaller paint pots last season and had her foot badly scalded.

The Excelsior Geyser

The Excelsior Geyser is situated about four miles from the hotel on a ridge of "geyserite,"[38] as the formation is called, about fifty feet above the river, toward which there is an abrupt slope. The road runs along on the opposite side of the river. As our carriage approached it an unusually heavy puff of steam and a large overflow of boiling water into the river admonished us that the geyser was about to "go off,"[39] and the inmates of our own and one or two other carriages ran for a little foot-bridge which crosses the river, in order to be close at hand when the event occurred. There proved to be plenty of time, for five or ten minutes elapsed upon our arrival as near the crater as we thought it prudent to remain, before the eruption. This crater, if it may be so termed, presented an awful appearance, and different from that of any other geyser which I subsequently visited. It looks like a small lake, 200 by 350 feet in dimensions, of boiling water, its surface being depressed twenty or thirty feet below that of the observer. Its walls are of the laminated structure peculiar to most of this hot water formation, but instead of having been formed by the Excelsior, were evidently formed long before it had assumed its present violent action, and are now being torn down and enlarged by it. These walls shelve outward, so that if one were to stand close to the edge, in many places he would be over the edges of the hot lake. So dense is the covering of steam over the water that it is only when a sharp puff of wind for the moment clears it away that it can be seen that the center of the lake is an infernal looking boiling cauldron. We had barely time to take in these general points and to receive warning from the party not to go too close to the crater, when, without further premonition, and with a tremendous roar and display of activity the whole lake seemed to be suddenly shot up into the air, while numerous

FIGURE **8.2.**
Excelsior Geyser erupts for a tourist group in 1888 as photographed
by T. W. Ingersoll. Our traveler H. Z. Osborne saw it erupt that same
year, and he displayed nearly as much excitement as the unidentified
tourists in this photo. (Yale Beinecke Library, New Haven.)

fountains, impelled apparently by more direct force, played to a vastly
greater height through the great mass of boiling water. Stones and rocks
were also thrown out with a force that could hardly have been exceeded
had they been thrown by a blast of powder or dynamite. I observed one
stone whirling in the air above the highest jets of water, and, while it is
only guesswork, I should think it was 150 or 200 feet above the surface of
the lake. This indescribable display lasted for one or two minutes, when
the eruption gradually died down and the lake, which is called "Hell's
Half Acre,"[40] renewed its former appearance. I picked up one of the rocks
thrown out by the eruption. It is white, of spongy appearance, and was
full of water and very heavy; but I soon drained it of water and it was quite
light. I shall keep it among my curiosities.[41] The vast quantity of water
thrown out by this geyser may be estimated from the fact that when it is
in eruption it raises the Firehole river several inches, and the river is from
75 to 100 feet wide.

The Excelsior Geyser, which is to-day the largest in the National Park, as it is the largest in the world, was in eruption several years, up to 1882, when it ceased, and until the present year has been merely a boiling lake. This season it commenced to again blow off, and now has an eruption at intervals of action from an hour to an hour and a half. In action it is to me one of the most marvelous spectacles that I have ever witnessed.

Prismatic Springs

Two remarkably beautiful hot water springs, or small lakes, are situated on the same plateau and close to the Excelsior. The largest of these, which is 250 by 350 feet in dimensions, is called the Grand Prismatic Spring, from the marvelous variety and beauty of the colors it presents. At the edges it is shallow with sc[a]lloped, shell-like borders, and its bottom presents stripes and streaks of color from pearly white to crimson. It rapidly deepens toward the center, its shape being something like a morning glory, which shape, indeed, is that of a large number of the springs. The sides of the deeper part of a pearly whiteness, and little globules, not unlike pearls in appearance, are thickly studded along these sides. The water in its deeper part, is torquoise blue in color, and of such wonderful clearness that one can see to an incredible depth. I threw pieces of white rock into the center of the Torquoise [sic] Spring, which is the second one on the plateau, and is 100 by 100 feet in dimensions, and I could keep sight of it as it sunk into the blue depths for what I have no doubt was 75 feet or more. I threw flat pieces of white rock in[to] another similar spring—that at the Castle Geyser[42]—and as they descended they moved from side to side, taking on most wonderful prismatic hues, resembling in movement and color some marvelous sub-aqueous butterfly.

The Upper Geyser Basin

Excepting the Excelsior, all the largest geysers in the Park are in the Upper Geyser Basin. We passed numerous hot springs and geyser cones on the road, and as we come in sight of the hotel, "Old Faithful," which has had an eruption every hour since Lewis and Clark made note of it in 1804,[43] and no one knows how long before that time, until now, threw up a column of water and steam 150 or 200 feet into the air. Our party [was] about a mile away at the time, watching the "Castle" sputter preparatory to an eruption, and each one felt that Old Faithful had hardly done the right thing in going off without our immediate presence. However, we were all promptly on hand [for] the next occasion, and [for] three or four others. The eruption is preceded four or five minutes by a few spasmodic outbursts, the hot water dashing up through the orifice from ten to twenty feet, when suddenly a large column of boiling water rises swiftly and grandly to a height of 150 feet. This discharge lasts four minutes. The form of this wonderful fountain is swayed and changed by the direction and force of the wind which may be blowing at the time. The sediment from the waters of Old Faithful, during the centuries it has doubtless played with no audience until recently save an occasional aborigine, who viewed its action with superstitious wonder, has slowly raised a fitting pedestal for so grand a fountain. The base of the cone is elevated above the plane of the valley immediately surrounding it fifteen or twenty feet, to which it slopes by means of successive terraces not above a few inches in height. Each terrace has its shallow pools of translucent water, received from the last discharge of the geyser. The cone itself rises six or eight feet above the pedestal, and its dimensions are two by six feet on the inside and four by eight on the outside. During the discharge one can approach quite close to the cone on the windward side. I got within ten feet of it. The few drops of water which one encounters are considerably cooled by their long passage up and down in the air above the surface. But when the geyser is receding, and the water runs over the edges of the cone, I found my position unsafe, and retreated to a greater distance. After the eruption ceased, there was a blowing off of steam, lasting several minutes. When this was over, I gave the cone or crater a careful examination outside and inside so far as possible. It is a beautiful white in color with a very faint pink tinge and quite hard. In form it is a combination of large nodules, boulder like, but all joined together into a common and symmetrical mass. These nodules in turn are covered with small white globules, common to hot water formation, a little larger than peas. In composition it gives evidence of lime, magnesia, and a considerable percentage of silica. The coloring and tints of the formation are, upon examination, beautiful beyond description. The prevailing color is an ash of roses, with modifications of various shades of yellow, crimson, and white. The process of formations in some places presents in its initiatory stages the appearance of silk, but upon feeling of them are found to be hard and stone-like. In other places it forms like onyx, with a polished surface and of a pearly white color. I noticed on one of these surfaces a name written in lead pencil, partly obscured.

Upon rubbing it I found that the opaque formation had continued and was steadily covering the name. It was already beneath the surface and I could not rub it out with my fingers.[44]

An Encounter With The Soldiery

The rules of the Park against specimen fiends are very rigid, and the troop of cavalry who patrol the country are remarkably vigilant, as I found out. I had a desire to carry off a bit of the Old Faithful formation, but had conscientious scruples about knocking off a piece—with two United States soldiers in plain sight.[45] I stepped on a beautiful exposed piece real hard, however it broke off. After this accident I had no hesitation in dividing it up among my compatriots, which act of generosity brought them all within the rule of accessories after the fact to any crime that might have been committed. About ten minutes afterward a minion of despotic power, in the person of United States trooper, questioned all of our party, each of whom had a bit of Old Faithful concealed in his or her clothing, as to the identity of the person who had "broken a piece off the formation." A Minneapolis lady, who had so large a piece that she could not get it into her pocket, but was compelled to carry about the evidence of her guilt in a pocket handkerchief, modestly remained behind the cover of a cedar tree while the inquiry was going on. For some reason, the soldier asked me no questions, and I told him no lies, and my fellow tourists had not seen the acted committed. The troopers remained around in our vicinity and followed our meanderings all the afternoon. To such a degree were their attentions directed that I thought it well to have a conference with the enemy. I therefore engaged in conversation with the most bloodthirsty appearing of the cavalrymen; complimented him upon the efficency of the service, and spoke with sarcastic severity of the specimen fiends who rendered their duties so laborious; expressed the opinion that the government should pay far heavier salaries than it did for the services performed by the soldiers in the Park, and parted with him upon terms of mutual respect and esteem.[46]

Other Geysers

I saw the Old Faithful in eruption six times, the Castle twice and the Splendid once. There are thirty or forty others in the same neighborhood, a majority of which I visited, but they were not at the time in active operation. None is precisely like the other, but they all have certain general characteristics, such as I have described. The Castle is so named from the resemblance of its cone to an ancient castle. It is about fifteen or twenty feet high, and its fumes, when not in eruption, are quite sulphurous in character. Some of our party clambered up the sides to take a look down the crater, including our jolly Chicago commercial travelers and our Illinois Normal teacher, when the water gushed up suddenly, and some one shouted, "Look out! She is going to erupt!" One of the Chicago boys made the champion backward jump of the trip. Some said it was like the bound of a panther, and that he cleared forty feet. It was enough, anyway to remove him beyond the reach of danger, except that of broken limbs. But he was not far ahead of the remainder of the party. After the Castle has an eruption it blows off steam like the exhaust of an immense engine for about four hours. The roar can literally be heard for miles. If all the power about these geysers now going to waste could only be transferred to Los Angeles, what a manufacturing boom we would have!

The Splendid is another magnificent geyser, which I saw in eruption, but at a little distance. It throws up water in a magnificent stream 200 feet high. Those who were close by it thought it the finest geyser in the region.

The Bee Hive is another grand geyser, near Old Faithful, but on the opposite side of the Firehole river. Its cone is the shape of an old-fashioned bee hive. I found its orifice to be comparatively small—not more than eighteen inches in diameter, and as straight and smooth, so far as I could see down, as a rifle barrel. It throws a noble stream 200 feet high, at intervals of from ten to thirty hours. This is the geyser into which some vandal threw a bar of soap to force an eruption, about a month ago,[47] with the result that its action has been less frequent and most irregular ever since.

Indicators.

It is a curious fact that nearly all the great geysers have a miniature geyser alongside them, within twenty or thirty feet, which work energetically for some time before their chief has an explosion, but which die down during the eruptions of their powerful brothers.[48]

Laundry Work Extraordinary.

One of the amusements of tourists is to throw handkerchiefs into the crater of Old Faithful, which is said to throw them up on the next eruption, perfectly washed. A gentleman told me that he threw his handkerchief into the "indicator" of Splendid, and that it was passed out of the main crater the following day. In 1882 General Sheridan's men did all their washing by throwing their garments into the craters. The linen and cotton fabrics came out clean and neat (but not ironed); the woolen articles came up in the shape of pulp, or about as the original fleece would have done before it had been woven into cloth.

"The Chinaman."

Haynes, the photographer of the Park, tells a story, for the truth of which I leave him responsible, to the effect that at least one geyser was startled into action by being soaped. A Chinaman went out with a basket of soiled clothes and a bar of soap, to a hot spring, to do a day's washing. He soaped the clothes thoroughly and threw them into the spring. There was an instantaneous explosion, and a column of hot water shot up about forty feet, filling the air, and cov[er]ing the Chinaman with hot water, overalls, undershirts, drawers, and the like. The Chinaman crawled out badly blistered exclaiming: "Chinaman heapee no likee Melican man spling!" Since which time it has been called the Chinaman's geyser.[49]

List Of Principle Geysers.

NAME.	HEIGHT FEET . . .	INTERVAL OF ERUPTION . . .	DURATION . . .
Old Faithful	150	65 minutes	4 minutes
Bee Hive	200	10 to 30 hours	8 "
Giantess	150	14 days	12 hours
Lion	60	24 hours	8 minutes
Lioness	80	Irregular	10 "
Cub	12	Frequent	20 "
Surprise	100	Irregular	2 "
Spasmodic	40	Irregular	20 "
Sawmill	35	Very frequent	30 "
Grand	200	15 to 20 hours	30 "
Turban	40	Fol'w'g Grand	20 "
Riverside	100	8 hours	15 "
Mortar	60	8 hours	6 "
Fan	70	8 hours	10 "

NAME.	HEIGHT FEET . . .	INTERVAL OF ERUPTION . . .	DURATION . . .
Artemecia	150	Irregular	10 "
Automizer	20	Irregular	10 "
Soda	50	5 minutes	1 "
Grotto	30	4 hours	30 "
Giant	250	6 days	90 "
Oblong	30	8 hours	4 "
Splendid	200	3 h. ev'y ot'r d.	10 "
Comet	60	Irregular	5 "
Castle	150	10 hours	25 "
Mud	30	Irregular	5 "
Cliff	100	Irregular	8 "
Lone Star	75	40 minutes	10 "
Chinaman	40	Irregular	2 "

A Theory Of Geysers.

One cannot contemplate these wonderful evidences of the manifold works of nature without speculating as to their cause. What produces the hot water, and whence comes the incalculable force that projects such volumes of it two or three hundred feet into the air? I notice that Prof. Bunsen, in whose honor one of the most prominent mountains in the park is named,[50] is of the opinion that the cause is volcanic. I have a theory of my own in the matter, and I do not know whether it has any scientific backing or not. It is this: The water originally comes from the rains and melting snows in the higher mountains. It follows the fractures and crevices in the rocks, and in this particular region a very considerable quantity collects. The water would naturally rise to the surface if it met underground obstruction, and could find a vent, in the shape of cold springs. In its course, however, it comes in contact with lime-rocks, and probably with other mineral substances, which, upon contact with water and air, develop great heat. In other words, the heat is not volcanic, but is due entirely to chemical transformation in the rocks and substances with which the water comes in contact. Sulphuric acid in water in sufficient quantity will cause [it] to immediately boil, as will the slacking of lime. The work of disintegration of the rocks hollows out chambers, which will hold a certain amount of superheated steam. The steam fills these chambers, and when they can hold no more the work of heating and steam-making is still going on. An outlet must be found, and it is naturally found at the point of least resistance—the vent which the water has followed to the surface. An explosion occurs, and the hot water is thrown upward and into the air, to the astonishment of all dwellers upon the outer surface of the earth. After the water has been discharged, the steam blows off until the chambers are again comparatively empty. The work of refilling them then recommences and goes on until they are again filled, when another explosion occurs. This, is my opinion, accounts for the regularity of the eruptions. The presence of magnesia, lime, sulphur, and silica in the sediment thrown up by the water confirms me in this theory that the geysers are of chemical and not of volcanic origin.[51]

Back To The Lower Geyser Basin.
The ride back to this hotel was made in good time. Upon our return we met our Milwaukee friends, and others whom we had left the day before at Mammoth. The meeting was as cordial and happy as though we had been friends for years, parted for months.

Watching The Beaver.
We made up a party in the evening, to go a mile down the Firehole river, where a colony of beaver have made their home. It is essential that those who desire to see the beaver at work should keep still, as they are a very shy animal. We had in the party a Young Girl, who couldn't keep still, and a Young Lady who wouldn't, and a lady who would wave her handkerchief wildly at new-comers and cry "Sh-h-h!" and a million mosquitoes. But the beaver were most accommodating, and came out all the same. I shall always recollect the scene, partly on account of its novelty and partly on account of the peculiar ferocity of the mosquitoes. Our little pioneer party was followed by many other tourists, several of whom were attired in a marvelous headgear of mosquito netting. Creeping in quietly under the trees along the river bank they presented a ghostly appearance, and I marveled that the beaver would remain in the same country with them. While I was forgetting to fight mosquitoes on my own account, I received a sudden and resounding whack on the ear that fairly made it ring, and was told that if I didn't kill my own mosquitoes they should be killed for me. The beaver had a structure of poles on the opposite side of the stream from beneath which they would

emerge into the river, which was about 100 feet wide, swim up stream 150 or 200 feet, dive down, and bring up grass growing in the bottom, and eat it or carry it back to the dam. After some of our party had left, the industrious animals grew bolder, and crawled out upon the opposite bank of the river and played around for our benefit.[52]

To-morrow we go to the Grand Canyon of the Yellowstone and the Falls.

The Grand Canyon And Falls.

Grand Canyon Hotel,
National Park, W.T.,
July 17, 1888

From the Lower Geyser Basin the return trip to Norris was made very quickly and pleasantly. Having an hour before dinner—the midday meal has been "dinner" ever since I left home—we made up a crowd to pay a fraternal visit to a party of campers, in the timber a quarter mile from the hotel. We found that they were from Bozeman, Montana; that they had been a week on the road, would stay in the park a week, and consume another on the way home; that they were three generations in the party, and that their names were Griffin. "Who are you for for President[?]" inquired Grandpa Griffin, a patriarch of seventy! "What's the matter with [Benjamin] Harrison?" I asked, and the Chicago contingent responded, "He's all right!" After a cordial interchange of compliments and good wishes, and three cheers for Harrison and Morton, we parted in great good humor and with an excellent appetite for dinner.[53]

After the midday meal we parted with our Minneapolis friends, the good Illinois farmer and his family, the amiable and intelligent Oakland physician and his bright daughter, with more regrets than most people feel on parting with casual acquaintances. The almost family life that tourists necessarily lead soon brings out the good and bad qualities of individual character, and warm friendships are formed in a brief period, as they are on sea voyages and on long trips across the continent. The handsome young Chicago man of our particular stage load was greatly depressed for more than half the way from Norris to the Grand Canyon, but recovered his usually excellent spirits late in the afternoon. The road, which runs at right angles to that which we had been traveling, was through much the same character of country—heavily wooded with pine, with occasional parks of mountain meadow, in which the grass was high and green.[54]

At half past three we drew up in front of the Grand Canyon Hotel, which is but a few rods from the Upper Falls of the Yellowstone, and found horses all saddled and ready to take us around the trails to the Lower Falls, Inspiration Point, and other places of interest in the neighborhood, which can only be reached by horseback or afoot.[55] By virtue of my California residence I was the lead of the cavalcade, and after explaining to my German and Eastern friends the peculiarity of the mountain horse, that he is guided by the pressure of the rein upon the neck and not by the bit, we started down the trail in Indian file. A short ride brought us to the brink of

The Grand Canyon Of The Yellowstone.

The first view of this great chasm fills the beholder with wonder and admiration. It is not altogether its great depth, although it has a perpendicular of 1500 feet, that so much attracts the mind, as it is its delightful peculiarities of form, and more than all else, the remarkable brilliancy and variety of the coloring of its rocks, and walls. The pervading color is a bright yellow from which I presume the Yellowstone took its name.[56] Upon this background there are great splashes of various shades of red and brown, and ledges of crimson rock extend from the level of the great plateau into which the vast canyon is sunk, down to the surface of the beautiful river, which, resembling a line of dark green ribbon, runs its furious course in its narrow and rocky bed below. The canyon comes to a point at the bottom like a capital V, and has practically no width. At the top it is perhaps a half-mile wide, but looks much narrower. The sides are not vertical like those of the Yosemite, but many points jut out from the edges of the chasm from which magnificent views can be obtained of the canyon below and above. Such a formation is Inspiration Point, the best place for an observation of the beauties of the Grand Canyon. Climbing out upon a rather narrow ledge of rock, one can drop a stone down a vertical depth of about a thousand feet. Looking up the river, the view is as beautiful as any that I have ever witnessed. It lacks the awful depth and grandeur of many points in the Yosemite, but for charming, entrancing beauty I do not think I have ever seen its equal in nature. To supplement the rich coloring, scores of pinnacles of rock, like the spires of some vast cathedral conceived by a more than human architect, spring up in irregular grandeur from the sides of the canyon. Upon the points of many of these pinnacles the eagles have built their nests, and standing upon Inspiration Point one may watch them sailing about in majestic circles in the depths of the canyon hundreds of feet below.[57] Perhaps the crowning beauty of the scene is to be found in the splendid view of one of the most symmetrical and beautiful waterfalls that I have ever seen—the Lower Falls of the Yellowstone, about two or three miles above Inspiration Point, which we passed on the way down. It is a sheer fall of 360 feet of a body of water 75 feet wide at the surface and of an average depth of from six to ten feet. There is an unobstructed view of the fall from top to bottom. It is impossible to reach the foot of the falls except by being let down by a rope 800 feet. In this way the photographs of the falls from that position were taken. Our young German traveler, who is endeavoring to learn English, in its purity, undefiled by slang, took a good look at the scene, and drawing himself up to his full height, exclaimed, "It ees a dan-dee!" And when the laughter that greeted the honest outburst had died away, he asked in all sincerity, "Ees that slang?"

Looking down the canyon, the view is almost as grand as it is above, but there is not quite the same brilliancy of color. The Grand Canyon extends fully twenty miles in length, but the best part of it is within view of Inspiration Point. Thomas Moran's celebrated painting of the scene, which hangs in the Capitol at Washington, was made from the opposite side of the river.[58]

Upon my return to the hotel I rode my horse down a narrow trail to the head of the falls, notwithstanding [that] I was told that a horse could not go there. He was an immense help in getting back to the top of the canyon again. A splendid view is to be had from the top of the falls. In the mists which rise a hundred feet from the cavern below a perpetual rainbow is to be seen when the sun is shining, if the right point of view be obtained.

I also visited the Upper Falls, which are but 100 yards from the hotel. They would be regarded as magnificent were it not for the more beautiful falls a mile below. They have a fall of 160 feet.[59]

Two English ladies kindly gave me some ammonia to cure mosquito bites, and it took off the skin wherever applied.

Back To Mammoth

Mammoth Hot Springs Hotel,
National Park, W.T.,
July 18, 1888

The trip back to Mammoth was made without notable event. At Norris we met and said goodbye to our charming Milwaukee friends for the last time. They promised to spend next winter in Southern California. One hundred and fifty Iowa editors and their wives are here to make the trip to-morrow, and our pleasant company will part and go their several ways.[60] Already we begin to feel the conservative effects of a return to civilization, and a bath, shave and a change of clothing produces upon me a marked impression that I am a different sort of person from the man who yesterday gave three cheers for Harrison and Morton on the verge of Inspiration Point. The road from here to the *Evening Express* office and 22 West Pico street cannot be short enough, nor can the railroad trains run too fast [for] my pleasure.

H. Z. OSBORNE

Notes

The account is H. Z. Osborne, *A Midsummer Ramble, Being a Descriptive Sketch of the Yellowstone National Park* (no place [Los Angeles]: Los Angeles Evening Express, no date [probably 1889]).

1. *Who Was Who in America* (Chicago: Marquis, 1943), I, 921. See also U.S. Congress, *Biographical Directory of the United States Congress* (Washington, DC: Joint Committee on Printing, 2006); "Henry Z. Osborne Called by Death," *Fresno Bee*, February 9, 1923, 13; and "Congressman Osborne Dies at Home Here," *Los Angeles Times*, February 9, 1923, H1.

2. The Albemarle Hotel was a long-lived and important institution in early Livingston, located at the corner of Park and Main streets, where the Livingston Guest House condominiums are today.

3. This was G. L. Henderson, one of early Yellowstone's most important personalities. His story is told in Lee Whittlesey, *Storytelling in Yellowstone: Horse and Buggy Tour Guides* (Albuquerque: University of New Mexico, 2007), 119–66.

4. For information on the names Henderson gave, see Lee H. Whittlesey, *Yellowstone Place Names* (Gardiner, MT: Wonderland Publishing Company, 2006).

5. Hal K. Rothman (*Devil's Bargains: Tourism in the Twentieth-Century American West* [Lawrence: University Press of Kansas, 1998], 45) says that this branch

was the first railroad in the United States to be run specifically to a tourist designation.

6. Hunter's Hot Springs was then located a few miles northwest of Springdale, Montana (east of Livingston), in deep rural Montana. Almost nothing remains of the resort, which got going in the 1870s.

7. This is as early a mention of amateur photography in Yellowstone as exists in any account. The round-format Kodak cameras first became available this very year. Hence, all photos that show up in this format date from the three years 1888–90. After that, amateur photos were square in shape. We thank Dr. James Brust for pointing this out to us.

8. The stretch of the Absaroka Range extending south from Livingston to Yellowstone National Park is sometimes known today as the Snowy Range, but the official name is Absaroka Range.

9. Maps today show Emigrant Peak's height as 10,921 feet.

10. This is Yankee Jim Canyon, located thirty-seven miles south of Livingston or fifteen miles north of Gardiner.

11. The proper name of the formation on the east slope of Cinnabar Mountain is the Devil's Slide. It was named in 1870 by members of the Washburn expedition. Nathaniel Pitt Langford, *The Discovery of Yellowstone Park: Journal of the Washburn Expedition to the Yellowstone and Firehole Rivers in the Year 1870* (Lincoln: University of Nebraska Press, 1972), 14.

12. He was not alone in this opinion. See the discussion of satanic place-names in Whittlesey, *Yellowstone Place Names*, 13–14. Nevertheless, at least nine such devil-related place-names have survived.

13. The Northern Pacific Railroad did not finish its line to Gardiner until 1903. Lee H. Whittlesey, "'They're Going to Build a Railroad!': Cinnabar, Stephens Creek, and the Game Ranch Addition to Yellowstone National Park," 1997–2005, unpublished manuscript, Yellowstone National Park Library, Yellowstone National Park, 33–36.

14. This spot was today's Boiling River, on Gardner River below the present Mammoth Campground.

15. His reference here is to F. Jay Haynes (1858–1921), official park photographer. The Mammoth Hotel had an orchestra that played there each summer. Apparently the "pretty, black-eyed girl" played in the orchestra as well as working for Haynes. See Freeman Tilden, *Following the Frontier with F. Jay Haynes: Pioneer Photographer of the Old West* (New York: Alfred A. Knopf, 1964), 372–98.

16. This is the hill of the Mammoth Hot Springs proper.

17. None of the Mammoth Hot Springs reaches the temperature of boiling, although some reach up to 170 degrees Fahrenheit.

18. Bath Lake, on the upper terraces north of Ladies' Lake, was used continuously for bathing from 1872 to 1918. Whittlesey, *Yellowstone Place Names*, 44.

19. Osborne is correct here that Orange Spring Mound is not a geyser. It is a flowing hot spring. G. L. Henderson named it "Orange Geyser" or "Orange Spring" in 1883, and his age estimate of twenty centuries is known today to be far too old. Travertine builds up quickly, sometimes up to twenty-two inches per year, so Orange Spring Mound is much younger than 2000 years. Whittlesey, *Yellowstone Place Names*, 195. His "Giant's Thumb" is today's Devil's Thumb.

20. G. L. Henderson placed the ladder into Devil's Kitchen cave in 1884, allowing visitors to explore it. Entering caves in the Mammoth area is today illegal because of potentially poisonous gases. G. L. Henderson, "Down the Terraces," *Helena Daily Herald*, May 10, 1888. See also Whittlesey, *Storytelling in Yellowstone*, 149.

21. George W. Wakefield was the park's first licensed in-park stagecoach operator. He began his operations in 1883 under the auspices of the Yellowstone National Park Improvement Company. His operation, called "Wakefield and Hoffman," lasted until 1892 when his license was revoked. Aubrey L. Haines, *The Yellowstone Story* (1977; rev., Boulder: University of Colorado Press, 1996), II, 44–45.

22. Adam Deem, a mere stage driver in 1885, had risen to "first lieutenant and executive officer" by 1888. See G. L. Henderson, *Yellowstone Park Manual and Guide* (Livingston, MT: Livingston Enterprise, 1885), 1, nos. 8–9.

23. This driver may have been Henry "Society Red" Mallon, who drove in the park nearly to the end of stagecoach days in 1916. If so, it appears that he was called "Red-headed Hank" before he received his later nickname of "Society Red" (because he had red hair and liked to attend the park dances). Haines, *The Yellowstone Story*, II, 107.

24. This is probably a reference to General William Henry Harrison, whose hat was pierced by a bullet at the Battle of Tippecanoe in 1811 (http://rootsweb.com/~usgenweb/ky/tippecanoe/chapter6.html).

25. This is the earliest known reference to any kind of a prohibition on the "soaping" of geysers. No such prohibition can be found in the park regulations of the day, so if such a penalty indeed existed, it must have been a verbal order or perhaps an "order of the day" issued by the park military commandant.

26. "West Gardner Falls" is today's Rustic Falls.

27. The "Hoodoo Geysers" are today's fallen travertine rock formations known as the Hoodoos. "Mount Bunsen" is today known as Bunsen Peak.

28. Signboards were the work of P. W. Norris and subsequent superintendents from 1877 to the present. Whittlesey, *Storytelling in Yellowstone*, 90.

29. This, the first hotel at Norris, was erected in fall 1886 and burned on July 14, 1887, almost before it held visitors. See Lee Whittlesey, "A Post-1872 History of the Norris Area: Cultural Sites Past and Present," unpublished manuscript, September 30, 2005, Yellowstone National Park Library, Yellowstone National Park, 13.

30. The material, silicon dioxide, is igneous rather than sedimentary.

31. "Steamboat Vent" (not Steamboat Geyser) was a fumarole in a location (unknown today) convenient for all to see, as documented by T. W. Ingersoll's 1887 stereo photograph, number 1171B.

32. This area, located five miles south of Norris, is in Gibbon Geyser Basin and is now called Artists' Paint Pots. Whittlesey, *Yellowstone Place Names*, 40.

33. Monument Geyser Basin is located on the side of the old "Mount Schurz," on the south side of Gibbon Meadows. It is accessible by hiking a steep, one-mile trail.

34. Gibbon Falls is only eighty-four feet high, but the road in 1888 was different from today's road. That old road ran on the east side of the river at this point, and seeing the falls thus required a dangerous "climb" down an embankment to overhanging rocks.

35. This was Marshall's Hotel (1880–91), later called Firehole Hotel. Built by George W. Marshall in 1880, it served visitors during the period before the construction of Fountain Hotel. See generally, Lee Whittlesey, "Marshall's Hotel in the National Park," *Montana Magazine of Western History* 30 (Fall 1980): 42–51.

36. The Firehole and the Madison are two different rivers today, but because the Firehole flows into the Madison early travelers sometimes called the Firehole by the name "Upper Madison River."

37. Lower Geyser Basin contains about eighteen square miles and probably more geysers and not springs than Osborne stated. George Marler, *Studies of Geysers* (Mammoth, WY: Yellowstone Library and Museum Association, 1978), 1.

38. Geyserite, also called silicon dioxide, is the hard material of which geysers are formed.

39. Excelsior Geyser's only known eruptions were in 1881, 1882, 1888, 1890, 1891, 1901 (probable), and 1985. See generally, Lee Whittlesey, "Monarch of All These Mighty Wonders: Tourists and Yellowstone's Excelsior Geyser, 1881–1890," *Montana Magazine of Western History* 40 (Spring 1990): 2–15.

40. While the area probably received its name because of Excelsior Geyser, the place-name "Hell's Half Acre" referred during stagecoach days in an encompassing manner to all of Midway Geyser Basin.

41. Specimen collecting was illegal in 1888, but this fact did not deter many specimen collectors. The current punishment for such detaching and collecting is a court appearance and no less than a $200 fine, but depending upon severity, the offense can become a felony with up to a $5,000 fine and jail time.

42. He refers here to Crested Pool, a boiling spring just north of Castle Geyser.

43. He has confused Lewis and Clark with the Washburn party of 1870. Lewis and Clark did not actually enter Yellowstone. They passed within fifty miles of the area. However, John Colter of the team did leave the expedition and

by entering the Upper Yellowstone country in 1807 received credit from most historians as the first white explorer of the park region. See Robert Betts, *Along the Ramparts of the Tetons: The Story of Jackson Hole, Wyoming* (Boulder: Colorado Associated University Press, 1978), chap. 5.

44. This practice of writing names on formations became so widespread that army superintendents got angry about it and often forced violators to march to the spot on foot and scrub out the offending words. Superintendent George S. Anderson noted that it was largely women visitors who chipped off delicate souvenir pieces of geyserite from the hot springs and that it was largely men who wrote their infernal names on geyser formations, only to see them cemented in place by the splashing of thermal waters (*Report of the Superintendent of the Yellowstone National Park to Secretary of the Interior. 1893* [Washington, DC: Government Printing Office, 1893], 8). "Nature fixes the insult indelibly," declared writer Rudyard Kipling (*From Sea to Sea: Letters of Travel* [New York: Scribner's, 1899], II, 283). Superintendent S. B. M. Young reported in 1897:

> The mania for carving names and writing names on guard rails, benches, etc. placed for the safety and convenience of visitors, seems to have increased. . . . It is contemplated to erect a large bulletin board for the convenience of visitors next season affected with this insane passion, with columns for name and address, and a heading, "All fools and idiots required to register here only." (*Report of the Acting Superintendent of the Yellowstone National Park to the Secretary of the Interior* [Washington, DC: Government Printing Office, 1897], 23).

45. The U.S. Army took command of Yellowstone National Park in 1886 to prevent vandalism, poaching, souvenir collecting, and the purposeful setting of forest fires as well as to solve complex administrative difficulties. See generally, H. Duane Hampton, *How the U.S. Cavalry Saved Our National Parks* (Bloomington: Indiana University Press, 1971).

46. This kind of matter-of-fact lying about specimen collecting by even some of the best people is a testimonial to how difficult it was for the army to prevent such collecting.

47. This incident was probably the one involving writer Bob Burdet and two officers of the Northern Pacific Railroad. It is chronicled in Haines, *The Yellowstone Story*, II, 18. Wrote Haines, "The geyser 'went off—grandly. So did the great men—ignobly.'"

48. He exaggerates here. Only a very few geysers have actual "indicators."

49. See this volume, chap. 6, n. 14, for information on "Chinaman Spring."

50. This is Bunsen Peak, located a few miles south of Mammoth Hot Springs.

CHAPTER EIGHT

51. Except for his "chemical" hypothesis, Osborne was remarkably correct on the details of geyser eruptions. However, geyser heat is of volcanic, not chemical, origin. Duncan Foley, *Yellowstone's Geysers: The Story behind the Scenery* (Las Vegas: KC Publications, 2006), 6–15.

52. There are no beaver known on Firehole River today.

53. Benjamin Harrison won the 1888 election against Grover Cleveland but lost in 1892, to Cleveland.

54. This is Hayden Valley, north of Yellowstone Lake.

55. This comment represents one of the earliest known references to the Canyon area concessionaire horseback operations. Whittlesey, *Storytelling in Yellowstone*, 274.

56. He is not correct. The river took its name from unknown yellow rocks far to the northeast, possibly the ones at today's Billings. Whittlesey, *Yellowstone Place Names*, 268–69.

57. These may have been ospreys.

58. Comments like this one added to the long-standing misnomer that Moran's painting was made from the south side of the canyon at Artist Point. The painting was actually made from Moran Point on the canyon's north rim. Lee Whittlesey, "A Brief Look at Moran Point . . . ," *Yellowstone Science* 14 (Fall 2006): 7–12.

59. The actual height of Upper Falls is 109 feet, while that of the Lower Falls is 308 feet.

60. For one account of the Iowa Press Association's trip to Yellowstone, see *Livingston (MT) Enterprise*, July 21, 1888, 2.

NINE

Autumn in the Yellowstone Park

A Midsummer Ramble

"LISPENARD RUTGERS"
(HENRY ERSKINE SMITH)

1893

HENRY ERSKINE SMITH (1842?–1932) WAS AN AMERICAN WRITER of minor renown who sometimes wrote under the pseudonym Lispenard Rutgers. His one-act play "Love's Diplomacy" (1899), his fiction work *Pride of the Rancho* (1910), numerous short stories, and *On and Off the Saddle*, the book from which this Yellowstone account is taken, all left enough of a trail of his life to make certain that he appeared in *A Dictionary of American Authors* and *Who Was Who in America*. Born in New York City, he served in the Civil War and then became a member and treasurer of the Society of American Dramatists in Syracuse. At the time of his death, he left a $60,000 estate to Miss Rene Varicle, a much younger woman, and that served as fodder for a scandal involving an alleged living wife. Referred to as a "playwright," he died at New London, Connecticut, at age ninety.[1]

While Smith did not tell us his motivations for writing about Yellowstone, his account is noteworthy for its recordation of a large forest fire near the park's west entrance in 1893 and for the drama encountered by Smith and his fellow stagecoach travelers as they raced against this danger. His writing style is animated and interesting but sometimes confusing as he shifts tenses and dangles participles.

Four prancing horses—Peanuts, Antelope, Mag, and Grizzly—none of them having more than two feet at a time on terra firma, so anxious were they to be set off; for the morning at Beaver Cañon in northern Idaho,[2] where we had been resting for the night, in a very ancient and airy tent, broke upon us with a crispness that even in autumn brought color to our cheeks and made our very fingers tingle.

All seated in a good spring wagon our guide and driver Jim, famous for having been a cowboy in Montana, and for having "killed his man," one of the necessary qualifications to be respected by his comrades, swung aloft his wicked looking whip, and we were off with a jerk, as though we had been aided by a cannon-ball from the rear.

Our way led over an extended prairie, with sharp mountain peaks visible in the distance; the scene soon changes, and we find ourselves ascending to a high table-land with a beautiful rolling country on either side.[3]

[On] A drive of twenty miles back from the railroad, where the shriek of the locomotive is never heard, we began to see signs of animal life; prairie chickens fly up in front of our horses, alighting fifty feet off, so tame were they, and with our revolvers we secured enough to feed five times our party.

On we plunged, until, when passing over the brow of a hill, we suddenly came upon a herd of antelope, about two hundred in the band. Dumb with amazement at our sudden intrusion, they raised their pretty heads, and, after a moment's pause, with a graceful bound they fly as though swept by the wind, their delicate limbs hardly seeming to touch the ground.

Our shadows begin to lengthen as we sight in the distance Snake River, where a good game dinner awaits us, and a comfortable clean tent stands ready to receive us, as we stretch our limbs after our fifty-mile drive.

A row of nightcaps, respectively red, white, and blue[,] emerged from under as many blankets. Before the rising sun fairly reached the horizon, and after a splash in real ice water, we were ready for food, and then for anything. Our horses, especially Grizzly, seemed quite intoxicated with the exhilarating air, and with a dash we were on our way again.

Plunging into dense forests for many miles, [we found that] the monotony was broken by the occasional sight of a flying fox, some Indian hunters, and frequent shots at coyotes.[4] A little episode illustrative of border life occurred during the morning, which assisted in keeping up the excitement. Rounding a turn in the mountain, in a very secluded spot, down in a kind of basin, [we found that] a strange sight greeted our eyes, quite causing us to forget the dust that had accumulated in them.

A small, rough log hut [was] surrounded by six horsemen, each with his Winchester leveled at it. "After a horse-thief, you bet," says Jim, as he cracked his whip, and sent his horses flying, to get us out of reach of a possible leaden shower. Hardly had the crack of the whip sounded, before, flash, flash, came a volley from the hut, and as quickly each horseman's trigger was touched, the Winchesters belching forth a dozen or more shots; when a yell of truce proceeded from the hut . . . and the battle was over.

All eagerness to see everything, we hastened back to behold, standing in the open doorway the captive, a rough yet handsome fellow, and as cool as, yes, several degrees cooler than, a cucumber, as he sullenly stepped out, saying: "I give up, fellows—got no more lead." Without ceremony they secured his horse, which had been quietly grazing near by during the battle, and securely tying him on the animal with ropes about his body and limbs, leaving his hands free, compelled him to ride about ten feet in front of them . . . all [of us] following in the rear. His captors had been pursuing him for seventy-five miles.

Soon coming to a stream, we all stopped for luncheon, and a sociable time we had—the prisoner telling how he had evaded his pursuers by short cuts through the mountains, covering his tracks, etc. Luncheon over, our course lay in different directions, and with a good-by we parted.

The scenery increases in beauty as we advance, our way being through a series of mountain cuts, beautiful valleys, high table-lands, and . . . swift-running streams. Lake Henry, with its grassy shores, lies three thousand feet below the peaks reflected in it, its islands seeming to float on its surface. Cliff Lake,[5] some miles off, with an unknown depth, the plummet finding no bottom at one thousand three hundred feet, is teeming with fish below and ducks above.

After climbing a very steep mountain which made even Grizzly want to stop for breath, the steaming geysers of the Yellowstone National park burst upon our view, about three hundred feet below us in the valley.[6] A slight shudder at first creeps over us as we descend into the steaming atmosphere, feeling as though we were entering the crater of a volcano; but the shades of evening were already upon us, and with a few words of encouragement from Jim our horses soon landed us at the hotel at Fire Hole Basin, one hundred miles from Beaver Cañon, our starting point.[7]

The pen or brush is equally powerless to describe the wonderful geysers of the Park. One must stand in their awful presence, see [them] with his own eyes, feel [them] with his senses, and contemplate with his mind their immensity, and then in vain will he endeavor to solve the great problem,—whence and by what power are they produced? There are numerous theories, but we will pass on for a closer view.

Here we are approaching them; in all directions we see them puffing like so many colossal engines; you hesitate as your guide urges you to follow him. While gazing in one direction, you are startled by one of the smaller geysers suddenly erupting near by, throwing its boiling contents some twenty feet in[to] the air.

You step about uneasily, threading your way midst hundreds of little geysers, sending their streams about as high as your head. The large geysers erupt at certain and quite frequent intervals, the most regular being "Old Faithful," which spouts every fifty-five minutes, throwing a stream six feet in diameter to the height of one hundred and fifty feet.

Approaching one of the larger geysers just previous to its eruption, [we note that] the earth seems to tremble, as with a rumbling noise, like smothered thunder, it begins to give vent to its pent-up force. First it shoots up a few modest spurts, then with a rattling roar and terrible groans, dense volumes of steam fill the air; up, up the boiling, seething water is hurled, higher and higher, accompanied by a deafening boom and a sound as of mighty breakers dashing against a rocky shore, until a column of water, fifteen feet in diameter and two hundred and fifty feet high, stands before you, as a river hurled upwards like a rocket. For twenty minutes its steaming waters shoot upwards, falling in graceful spray, producing an enchanting effect in the dancing sunbeams.

Space will not permit of a detailed description of the attractions of this locality. "Hell's Half-Acre," a lake fairly boiling and steaming with fury; the "Devil's Punch Bowl," a peculiarly and wonderfully formed

FIGURE 9.1.
Here two ladies and several gentlemen watch Old Faithful Geyser erupt in about
1904 as captured by an unknown photographer of the Underwood stereo company.
(YELL 148304, Yellowstone National Park Archives, Yellowstone National Park.)

bowl some ten feet in diameter perpetually boiling and bubbling up
several feet high; to gaze down the yawning depths some fifty feet into
the "Devil's Well," with its clear, transparent boiling waters, makes the
beholder shrink and say, "I have seen enough."[8]

We paid a farewell visit to "Old Faithful" to see it by moonlight: it is
always on time, and with watch in hand we stood waiting.

The night was calm and beautiful, one of those quiet, restful nights
the memory of which lingers long after; the great pale moon appeared

brighter than usual as it looked down on us through the clear atmosphere while the moments ticked away, when lo! The dismal moan, the nerve-shattering boom announces the time is up, and with a deafening roar a golden lake bounds upwards, sparkling in the moon's rays.

We stood in silence before the entrancing spectacle. Such a sight was worth a lifetime, and it seemed as if nothing of more marvelous beauty could ever greet the human eye.[9]

It has been truly said by those who have seen the Grand Canyon of the Yellowstone that no language can do justice to its wonderful grandeur and beauty.

Behold a mighty gorge, carved by the impetuous waters during countless ages in volcanic rocks, descending gradually until reaching a depth of about two thousand feet.

We were fortunate to have our first view of it on one of those bright, calm days, when, with its own hallowed atmosphere, Heaven seemed to diffuse itself over the earth's face with a solemn smile, no less sweet than solemn.

With each fresh lift on the precipitous terraces the view broadened until the great valley lay unrolled at our feet.

About thirty miles long, the walls, in many cases almost vertical, are eroded into towers, spires, and minarets of colors most brilliant, surpassing all the expectations that were conjured up in our imaginations.

The pure white of the decomposing feldspar, blended with sulphur yellows, intermingled with bright red, [and] colored with iron, the brilliant rainbow hues in rich abundance brought out in strong relief by the dark green pines along the cliffs[,] serve[s] as a background for the warmer colors,—the whole uniting to form a scene of enchanting splendor.

We look over the dizzy precipice far down to where the river is boiling and surging as it plunges on its way, battling with mighty boulders as though protesting against its imprisonment as it lashes the solid walls. Yet all is silence; distance has swallowed up the sound of its mighty roar.

The Great Falls of the Yellowstone leap[s] over a precipice three hundred and fifty feet high. As we approach we hear the suppressed roar resembling distant thunder; it seemed as though the mountain, unable to support its great weight of waters, shook to its foundation—the cataract became a falling river.

Prodigal nature has here outdone herself. As this mighty play of waters plunges amid the rocks, the dense clouds of mist and spray produced by the whirling mass as it dashes with the noise of heavy artillery against the resisting rocks produces a rainbow not only richer in color, but grander and clearer than we had ever seen before. The mountains and valleys caught and emphasized the golden rays which were flooding the scene.

Our four-in-hand dashed up to receive us at 7 A.M.,[10] after a breakfast by candle-light, for our return drive. A hard climb found us at the summit of the mountain near by. In the distance, seemingly fifteen or twenty miles ahead, the view was obscured by smoke, indeed—a prairie fire; not a strange sight to any of us. On we traveled, but the expression and earnest look on Jim's face indicated that it might be something serious.

About noon, as we were emerging from a dark, wild, narrow cañon in cutting our way through the mountains, we were confronted with three prairie wolves, [which] were just entering the cañon we were leaving.[11] They were fleeing with desperate speed, and seeing us they stopped short, gazing about them[selves] with a petrified stare, uncertain as to which course to take, but they quickly dashed by us, within twenty feet, and soon disappeared. "A danger signal," said Jim, as he took an extra grip on his reins and stretched his neck. "A big fire we've got about us."

[This was] True enough, for as we passed out into the open prairie we beheld a sight which sent a thrill of horror through us when we comprehended the situation.

We had been traveling westward, while the fire had been travelling in an easterly direction, and had already passed to the left of us and apparently closed up our rear retreat. The horses sniffed the air excitedly, looking about them[selves] in a wild, uneasy manner, their ears moving to and fro, as they nervously neighed to each other.

Away in the distance, where the prairie met the sky, a heated, quivering line arose, surmounted by a dark, wavering cloud. It was the prairie fire! The wind was blowing almost a gale, directly towards us, and the long dead grass was as dry as tinder; the fire was plainly spreading rapidly, and, with a wild shout to the horses Jim showed the stuff he was made of.

Off to the right we shot at a furious speed, leaving the road and taking to the pathless prairie; a band of antelope, with eyes like fire, came

rushing past us, adding to the excitement and fury of our horses. A
glance to the left showed us that the fire was gaining on us as, with a
horrible crackling sound, we could see the bright flames, twenty feet
high, shooting upwards, and tongues of fire leaping ten yards at a time
before the gale.

The fire was fast overhauling us. The dark rolling smoke soon over-
cast the sky above our heads, seeming to imprison us. Jim muttered
something, and his face grew ashen, as the flecks of foam from our wild
horses flew over his breast. It seem[ed] as if our hour had come.

On we went, the fire momentarily drawing nearer, the billows of
smoke each instant growing denser and the heat more suffocating, at
times seeming as though it would blister our faces. Should we throw

out our guns and traps and lighten the wagon: Not a word [came] from Jim, but his strong arm and steady eye were intent on saving us, as we thundered on at terrific speed.

Shall we ever forget that moment when for an instant the smoke cleared, and we realized we were being literally encircled by the raging fire—caused by contrary and varying winds,—only about a quarter of a mile ahead, there was an opening of several hundred feet for our escape! Could we reach it before the gap closed?

Again the smoke wreaths whirled around us; our eyes were smarting from the heat; the panting of the horses, mad with terror, [could be heard as they] blindly rushed through the darkness, as we yelled words of encouragement to them. Could they hold out? It was a race for life! A few moments and we dashed through the opening, when not one hundred feet wide, [and we] were safe.[12]

We reined up in a short time, after fording a stream, and with deep-drawn sighs of relief, bounded out of the wagon.

Our noble horses, our preservers, were trembling with excitement, reeking with perspiration, and almost white with foam. We all set to work to rub and dry them, while soothing and quieting them with words of praise, for we owed our lives to these four noble fellows.

An hour's rest and rearranging found us ready to resume our journey, with a determination to complete our entire trip of one hundred miles without stopping for the night if it were possible.

We soon left the ugly smoke behind us, and set our eyes and minds to enjoy the loveliness of the scene which lay ahead of us; indeed, we were now more than ever sensible to the charms of nature. The gale soon ceased, leaving only as a remembrance a soft zephyr to fan our cheeks; the sun was bright and nature was all smiles.

Our eyes soon regained their wanted clearness, and as we passed on in our journey, leaving the wild, open prairie for the mountains and valleys where the quivering aspen gave life to the solitude, the whole country about us seemed illuminated with its varied colors, for autumn had come with her magic touch and transformed it into a mammoth bouquet.

Notes

This account is from a chapter in Lispenard Rutgers [Henry Erskine Smith], *On and Off the Saddle: Characteristic Sights and Scenes From the Great Northwest To the Antilles* (New York: G. P. Putnam's Sons, the Knickerbocker Press, 1894), 1–19.

1. *Who Was Who in America* (Chicago: Marquis, 1973), IV: 1969–73, 672; *San Antonio Light*, September 17, 1932, 10-A; *Syracuse (NY) Herald*, May 19, 1918, 60; *Washington Post*, March 10, 1932.

2. Beaver Canyon was today's Spencer, Idaho. In 1893, it was one of the stops on the Utah and Northern Railroad and thus one way that visitors could access Yellowstone. But this route to the west entrance represented a much longer trip to the park than the Northern Pacific's access via the north entrance.

3. This was Centennial Valley, Idaho, the route from Spencer and Monida to Yellowstone National Park.

4. Idaho hunting laws, like Yellowstone's, made no prohibitions on shooting predators.

5. Henry's Lake and Cliff Lake are both located on the Idaho–Montana border along the Madison River and west of Yellowstone National Park.

6. His description of the road descent, view, and distance sounds like Lower Geyser Basin, but his hotel and "Old Faithful" militate in favor of this being Upper Geyser Basin.

7. This was the first Shack Hotel, which burned in 1894 and was replaced in 1895 by a ramshackle structure that was also called the "Shack Hotel." Lee H. Whittlesey, "A History of the Old Faithful Area with Chronology, Maps, and Executive Summary," September 14, 2006, manuscript prepared for the National Park Service, Yellowstone National Park Library, Yellowstone National Park, 21–22.

8. He has the name "Hell's Half Acre" out of trip order, for it referred to Midway Geyser Basin with its Excelsior Geyser. "Devil's Punch Bowl" referred to present Punch Bowl Spring at Upper Geyser Basin. "Devil's Well" referred to present Crested Pool near Castle Geyser.

9. He has essentially lifted this sentence from Dr. F. V. Hayden's 1872 report, *Fifth Annual Report of the U.S. Geological and Geographical Survey of the Territories* (Washington, DC: Government Printing Office, 1872), 96. Hayden wrote: "Such a vision is worth a lifetime, and only one of such marvelous beauty will ever greet human eyes."

10. A "four-in-hand" referred to a stagecoach pulled by four horses, and it received its name from the fact that the driver held four reins in his hand— one for each horse. They apparently stayed at the second Canyon Hotel (1890–1910).

11. *Prairie wolves* was then a common term in usage for coyotes.

12. Five hours after leaving the canyon and heading toward the park's west entrance would have put them about thirty–forty miles from the canyon, so this fire must have been between the canyon and the country near

present West Yellowstone, Montana, a town that was not in existence until 1907. A look at the superintendent's report for 1893 reveals that rainfall was sparse that summer and that a very large fire broke out in the park just north of Norris Hill on July 10. It lasted some twenty days and burned an area northeast from the Norris Soldier Station some seven miles long and two miles wide. Because Henry Smith's trip occurred in "autumn" and because of his mention of it being on the "prairie," it is likely that the fire encountered here was a different one and probably outside of the park to the west. A follow-up report noted that "during the entire summer fires were being started, through the carelessness of camping parties and in other ways [probably by lightning]." See George S. Anderson, *Report of the Superintendent of the Yellowstone National Park to Secretary of the Interior. 1893* (Washington, DC: Government Printing Office, 1893), 7; and *Report of the Superintendent of the Yellowstone National Park to Secretary of the Interior. 1894* (Washington, DC: Government Printing Office, 1894), 6.

TEN

Cycling Through Yellowstone Park

LYMAN B. GLOVER

1896

BICYCLING IN THE UNITED STATES BECAME FASHIONABLE IN the 1880s, so it was only reasonable that cyclists would eventually ride through Yellowstone National Park. W. O. Owen claimed to have been the first such Yellowstone cyclist in 1883,[1] but many others followed, including theater critic Lyman Glover, who pedaled through the park in 1896.

Born in Michigan, Lyman B. Glover (1846–1915) became well known as a "sound and graceful writer," editor, drama critic, actor manager, and theater manager.[2] He founded Chicago's *Saturday Evening Herald* in 1874, and in the 1880s, he was the theater critic for the *Times-Herald.* Later, in Chicago's *Record-Herald,* he became "the dean of Chicago's critics."[3] Interested in theater all of his life, he produced a book in 1898 entitled *The Story of a Theater* detailing the history of one such establishment. Glover's wife was Louise T. Glover, and the death of their daughter Mildred was the tragedy of his life. In 1902, he became the manager for actor Richard Mansfield, who was "an intimate friend of Mildred."[4] He resigned as Manfield's manager in 1904 because "he did not like the road life" and turned to managing a theater. There in 1907, he watched his friend Richard Mansfield die right on stage during a performance. At the time of Glover's death, he was the manager of the Majestic Theater and the Kohl and Castle vaudeville interests. The managers of six other Chicago theaters served as his pallbearers.[5]

Glover seems to have made the Yellowstone trip purely for adventure—perhaps he wanted to escape Chicago for the summer—and at the time he was fifty years old. He must have been in good physical shape to endure the trip's rigors. A bicyclists' promotional pamphlet two years later noted that "wheeling" through the park could best be accomplished by devoting "at least five days to the undertaking" because "there is so much to see; the fishing is so good; the side trips so attractive; the climate so delightful; the atmosphere so invigoratingly crisp; the experience in every way such a notable one, that you might spend a whole month in the Park and not regret it."[6]

Lyman Glover found the park to be the finest place he had ever ridden—an "unequaled preserve"—and he responded eloquently to it:

> The journey is one of never-to-be-forgotten exhilaration. The coast [of the bicycle] down the continental divide to . . . Yellow stone Lake, is worth a century of rides to Elgin or Pullman. . . . The wild sweep of that splendid toboggan . . . forever effaced the glories of all other rides. . . . burn[ing] into the memory living pictures so vivid that every other cycling experience seems tame in the comparison.

He loved the adventure!

———⚬⚬⚬———

All roads lead to Rome, but only one [railroad goes] to the Yellowstone National Park, within whose confines are embowered the grandest scenes and the most wonderful natural phenomena to be found on this continent.

The astonishing sweep of the Northern Pacific Road for 1,000 miles from the head of navigation on the Mississippi at St. Paul to the foothills of the mighty Rockies and the gateway of nature's temples of wonders on the Yellowstone is an inspiration.

Running for a hundred miles along the fast diminishing "father of waters,"[7] doomed as it approaches its source to do plebian duty as a sluiceway down which logs are floated to the greedy mills below, the

FIGURE 10.1.

Traveler E. Burton Holmes took this photo of bicyclists in 1896, the
very year of our chronicler Lyman Glover's trip. These bicyclists were
probably a different party from Glover's, because there are five of them
and there were only two in Glover's party. (E. Burton Holmes, *Burton
Holmes Travelogues*, vol. 12 [Chicago: Travelogue Bureau, 1906], 41.)

road plunges through the famed Red River Valley, with its smiling
wheat fields and perennial thirst, rushes into the bad lands of Dakota
with a shriek and a roar, as if anxious to escape from the hobgoblins
of that uncanny place, pierces the historic Indian battle grounds of the
west, where the savage made almost his last stand against the invader,
and stops, as if for breath, at the gateway of the mountains, through

which, like the star of the empire, it presently takes its way to that west where the thunders of the Pacific are forever heard.[8]

... Hemmed in by the tireless bluffs on either side that stalk along keeping pace with the utmost power of steam, the train drifts for many miles in close companion with the famed Yellowstone River, and at last, more than a thousand miles west of St. Paul halts among the foothills of the Rocky Mountains. In front the grim Gallatin Range seems to say, "Thus far and no farther," and to the south the inspiring Electric Peak fitly marks the entrance to the great Yellowstone National Park.

A cycling trip through the Yellowstone Park! That was the idea that tempted Scorcher and Rambler away from the serene but hackneyed excitement of Chicago and buoyed them up during this splendid rush across the continent,[9] from the resounding shores of Lake Michigan to the pine-clad heights of Wyoming and Montana.

"Better stick to the boulevards and potato hills of Cook County," said the Kind Advisor, speaking in advance of the deed. "The towering peaks of Wyoming are not for Falstaffian men who, short and stout and scant of breath, more fitly become the lowlands."[10]

But Scorcher and Rambler heeded not the sinister warning. With the spirit of "Excelsior" animating their purpose,[11] they even turned a deaf ear when the maiden cried "Try not that pass."

"The road being a long one," remarked Rambler, "a pass is a good thing to try," at which small witticism Scorcher looked sad and replied that if such utterances were to happen along the road he would rather stay at home.

Yet, in spite of all discouragements, a banner with that strange device, "A cycling trip through the Yellowstone," was ready in due time[;] the kind friend who imagined that the park was located somewhere near Colorado Springs and the other dear soul who thought it a national preserve full of statuary, peanut stands and artificial lakes a few doors east of Cheyenne, were duly set right in their geography and the expedition was away.

Alas! Tell it not in Gath,[12] speak it not in the streets of St. Louis, but the average Chicagoan seemed to possess only the most vague and uncertain idea of [Yellowstone,] the great treasure-house of natural phenomena and scenic beauties. To most people the name represented a veritable terra incognita somewhere "out west." Where it was and what it contained they could not tell. The Pons Asinorum of Euclid was an easy problem in comparison,[13] and I could well appreciate the truth of the proposition when a gentleman connected with the park management remarked: "The educated classes of Europe know more about the Yellowstone National Park than the intelligent people in America. Over there its remarkable features are recorded in the text-books to be pondered by students and scientists alike, and among European tourists we find the best posted and most appreciative of our visitors."

As every evidence points to the truth of this assertion, suppose we pause for a moment at the gateway of the park to ascertain, with that famed southern congressman, just "where we are at."

The Northern Pacific Road has carried us through Minnesota, North Dakota and partly across Montana to Livingston, a little frontier town nestling among the foothills of the Rockies. Here a branch line runs due south for fifty miles, through cañons and between towering peaks to Cinnabar, near the northern limits of the park, into whose arcady no vulgar railway tracks are permitted to penetrate.[14] Here the Concord coaches, each drawn by six horses, meet the tourist and carry him toilsomely over the mountain peaks and through the wild exhilaration of the Gardiner Cañon for seven miles to the Mammoth Hot Springs Hotel, which is the point of departure for all expeditions in the park. The altitude above the sea at this point is 6,215 feet, or more than 1,000 feet higher than at Cinnabar, seven miles away, thus furnishing an adequate and convincing reason for not beginning a cycling tour at the latter point.

Coming into the park from the lower altitudes the rarity of the air and the consequent difficulty of breathing are a bar to the exertion of mountain climbing, which rash individuals may realize to their cost. Until the respiratory organs are adjusted to the new conditions it is at once unwise and unsafe to risk the arduous labor of pushing up the mountain sides with a bicycle.

The Mammoth Hot Springs Hotel is located in a basin or travertine plain among the mountains, with Electric Peak, Bunsen Peak and Mount Evarts [sic—Everts] towering aloft in the distance, like tireless sentinels. At the other side of this little plain, less than an eighth of a mile in extent, are grouped the comfortable buildings of Fort Yellowstone, where Captain Anderson, superintendent of the park, and a natty troop of cavalrymen, keep watch and ward, for it must not be forgotten that since 1876 the park has been a national reserve,[15] and the preservation of its natural features is due entirely to the military arm of the government service, which, unhappily, was not introduced until within recent years.[16] Over to the west of the hotel are the terraced hot springs, from which the place borrows its name, covering an extent of nearly 200 acres, with their dazzling calcerous formation and fantastic shapes, over which a cloud of filmy steam hangs in all the beauty of nature's own bridal veil.

But have no fear of guide-book details. It is not altogether from the standpoint of geysers and hot springs that we shall explore the park. Yet any attempt to escape the atmosphere of wonders would be an outrage upon nature in her most eccentric mood, and then we must have our bearings at the outset, and know whence we are to start and whither to go.

Geographically we are in the northwest corner of Wyoming, in which the park is chiefly located, although a slice of Montana on the north and another of Idaho on the west give it a footing in three grand divisions of the union. Topographically the park is an irregular and rugged plateau nearly 8,000 feet above sea level, hemmed in by tremendous mountains and extending to the south for sixty miles, through a country so seamed with cañons, pierced with almost inaccessible peaks, gemmed with delightful valleys, punctured by geysers and hot springs and overlaid with solemn pines, that days of arduous travel will not exhaust the wonders that lie hidden within its apparently narrow limits.

As the crow flies, a square of sixty miles is easily covered, but in the tortuous roads of the Eden primeval, leading through great gashes in the mountains, along the verge of sheer precipices, by the side of tumbling cascades, around dizzy peaks that command enchanting views, down into cool valleys that seem forever shut out from the eager sun, along heart-breaking grades full of sinuous difficulties and headlong terrors, with belching springs and geysers and peaceful cañons lying in the eternal calm of their own mystery—the miles multiply, until it would require almost the area of Illinois to straighten out their complex and bewildering confusion.

Through this wilderness the government has constructed something less than 200 miles of road, so directed that it will embrace within its limits the most important scenic features and phenomena of the park.

Other trails lead hither and thither through the mountains to tempt the horseman or the adventurous pedestrian, but the tourist of the stages and certainly the bicyclist will find the way sufficiently toilsome without plunging into by-paths, most of which only the tireless and patient horses of the westland can conquer.

At intervals along the stage road four hotels have been built, and to see these fine and well appointed buildings standing in the midst of an absolute wilderness is a startling suggestion of nineteenth century possibilities.

The Mammoth Hot Springs Hotel is first on the list, while forty miles away, in the midst of another group of thermal wonders known as the "lower geyser basin," is the Fountain House, so named in honor of the great [F]ountain geyser that spouts nearby. The third station is Lake Hotel, at the outlet of Yellowstone Lake, and the fourth is the Cañon Hotel, planted amid the indescribable grandeurs of the Yellowstone Cañon. These hotels are approximately forty miles apart, but between some of them the roads are so steep and heavy with sand that in the estimation of the bicyclist accustomed to the levels of Illinois and the grades of the Chicago boulevards, that absolute distance might be stated at double that figure. At three intermediate stations the hotel company has established lunch stations. One is at the Norris geyser basin, where the earth is perforated with peculiar steam pots and giddy gushers of the most approved sort. The second is at the upper geyser basin, where "Old Faithful" and a job lot of first-class spouters conspire to make the locality one of the most interesting in the entire thermal belt of the Firehole Valley. The third lunch station is picturesquely located on a point of Yellowstone Lake called the Thumb, than which no name could be more hopelessly inappropriate and unfit. If the lake as a whole resembled a hand, which it does not, this pretty little bay could not be transformed into the resemblance of a thumb without a much more powerful imagination than most men or women possess.

But, questions of taste aside, it will be perceived that, although in the wilderness, the tourist is not likely to suffer from the pangs of hunger unless the stage coach breaks down or his bicycle grows weary. The hotels are conducted under a dispensation from the government, for no business of any kind can be carried on in the park without a permit from the interior department at Washington, under whose general supervision the reservation is. The stage company is licensed in like manner and is a large and well-managed concern, albeit rather unkindly disposed toward bicyclists, whose baggage it refuses to carry as express matter. But this little kink will be taken out of its manners before the world is much older. The park is a national pleasure ground belonging to the people, who have an undoubted right to ride bicycles or walk on their heads if they choose without consulting the wishes of any concessionaire in the park. With a monopoly of the transportation facilities the stage line cannot decently refuse to carry a small valise, as it did in the case of a lady cyclist from Chicago only a few days ago. It need not fear being overburdened with luggage, as cyclists travel with but little impediments, yet when the occasion requires it will profit by a more liberal and sensible policy, or else it must make way for a concern more wisely managed.

It must be apparent after these discursive allusions to the general characteristics of the Yellowstone that it is not a pleasure ground, after the similitude of Lincoln or Jackson parks, but a vast mountain and forest preserve, that must be conquered by hard work. The boulevard cyclist and the pretty bloomer girl of the asphalt territory would find cycling through the Yellowstone Park an impossibility, while to the average rider unused to hard scrambles it would be a demnition grind.[17]

The famous gentleman who undertook an essay on the snakes in Ireland found that he had exhausted his subject in the brief statement that "there are no snakes in Ireland."

In like manner one might be tempted upon the impulse of the moment to declare that there is no cycling in Yellowstone Park. But, happily, the statement would not be true in detail, though in its entirety the park is about as well suited to cycling as the stairways and roof garden of the Masonic Temple. The cycler loves a comparatively level road. Short hills are a luxury, but mountains—aye, there's the rub! The mountain road laid with obsidian sand, filled in with powered geyserite, plowed into impassable furrows by the wheels of the stagecoach and of the hunter's outfit, is a proposition calculated to make the stoutest heart quail. Upon such a footing the cyclist can neither ride up nor down hill. The shifting obsidian sand skews his wheel about and the gaping precipice at the side contents him to walk laboriously up or down the steep incline, happy if a firmer interval of bench land permits the luxury of riding for a little while.

This is not the character of all the roads in the park by any means, but when crossing the ranges and plowing through the geyser basins frequent and sometimes almost continuous examples of this misery may be found. In building the roads the government must fill in with the material at hand, which among these mountains happens to be a quasi-volcanic ash and sand that does not pack and can never be made the substance of good roads until a top dressing of crushed rock and clay is administered. Until this is done these stretches of road, amounting to about twenty-five miles in the entire circuit, can never be less than a trial to those who ride in the stages and a barrier for the cyclist, only to be overcome by exertions not always to be regarded with an unruffled spirit. Perhaps more liberal appropriations by congress will remedy the evil and render the park a mountain Elysium for cyclists, equestrians and those who ride in chaises, and the wheelmen of American can promote this excellent purpose by encouraging members of congress to dig deeper down into the national treasury for the benefit of this great national pleasure ground. Until this is done only cyclists who love a scramble and can endure hard work should undertake an entire circuit of the park. For all such the journey is one of never-to-be-forgotten exhilaration. The coast down the continental divide to the margin of that exquisite gem of the mountains, Yellowstone Lake, is worth a century of rides to Elgin or Pullman, if, forsooth, one escapes without a broken neck. The wild sweep of that splendid toboggan, the first tortuous dive of which is more than a mile long, and the second nearly three miles, forever effaced the glories of all other rides. The tingling sensation of danger as the wheel flew along the narrow ledges and bumped threateningly in unseen ruts, the wild panorama of splendid scenery that seemed to rush by on the wind, the flashing glimpses of blue sky above and of foaming, rushing waters in the deep gorges far below—all of these conspired to burn into the memory living pictures so vivid that every other cycling experience seems tame in the comparison.

Again promising no guide book statistics, no ordinary figures, to show the height of geysers, the depth of cañons or the elevation of mountain[s], no rhapsodies inspired by scenic wonders, let us mount our bicycles and hasten away up through the golden gate that commands all approaches to the wonders beyond.

A heavy hoar frost lies thick upon the ground and glistens upon the deep red roofs of Fort Yellowstone, just across the little plain. The sun announced but now by the pealing sunrise gun of the post and the gay barcarole of the trumpeter, is just peering over a distant peak, as if to spy out a new and better course for his daily run, and the mammoth hot springs send into the frosty air clouds of steam that rise high above the mountain ranges round about. Nothing could be lovelier than the picture of that August morning, but wheels are practical vehicles and we cannot ride in cloud land or upon the dizzy verge of fine scenery.

The first stage in the journey is the four miles from the springs to the golden gate, during which there is a gain in the altitude of more than 1,100 feet, chiefly distributed between the last three miles. Pile three and a half Masonic Temples one upon the other and imagine the difficulty of making the grade to the top of this pile with a sharp and tortuous approach of only three miles. A grade of 366 feet to the mile is one which not even steam has yet been able to conquer, and yet here we are with our bicycles, walking, pushing and occasionally riding a little way. The rarified air does not satisfy lungs accustomed to a moist climate, and we breathe painfully and must stop at frequent intervals. This is the penalty of rushing into high altitudes without becoming acclimated, a penalty that sometimes entails serious consequences. There is a sense of exhaustion as we rise higher and higher, and the steam drops farther below us in the gorge that constantly grows deeper.

Surely four miles were never dragged out to such a weary length before, and in the solemn moments of a necessary rest, when the "mountain dew" in us was not gathered from the adjacent slopes, Scorcher made inquiry of Rambler if he could recall the general appearance of a mile post, a query not so incoherent, as it was seemingly hours since the last example of this useful article been seen.

But perseverance conquers at last, and through the bold and beautiful walls of the golden gate the road tumbles into a broad mountain meadow called Swan Lake Valley, across which the wheels romp for miles so joyously that all the woes of that fateful four miles are forgotten and the world seems to have taken on a roseate hue. Electric Peak nods a good morrow from the north, Swan Lake smiles peacefully at the right, and the big mountains of the Gallatin Range turn their bleakest sides to the valley, as if intending in a friendly spirit to prevent this delightful road from wandering back into the rocky and riotous hills where the wheels could no longer spin merrily along.

A dash through the pine slopes and across low ridges stirs the blood, and we wheel into the Norris Geyser Basin lunch station, just twenty miles from the place of departure. Across a little rivulet is the shack of an army outpost, where five soldiers are stationed, and under the canvas roof of the lunchhouse, Larry, the silent man of this famed geyser basin, busies himself [with] the lunch.[18]

Again awheel, past the geyser beds in which a hundred strange forms grow, we whirl along toward the next stopping place twenty miles away. Escaping for a time from the geyserite with its aggravating white powder in which the wheel can gain no footing, there is a delightful run through the Gibbon meadows, leaving Mount Schurz to the right, and then after an arduous climb we plunge into the Gibbon Cañon, where the road winds hard by the dashing river and huge beetling crags piercing the sky almost shut out the sunlight. Upon the experiences that followed one might draw the veil. The long and agonizing climb out of this valley, with miles of deep, black sand as the only roadway, was the unhappiest experience of the trip. For nearly two hours the agony continued. Each moment the way seemed to grow steeper and the sand deeper. The rarity of the air added to the discomfort. No water was to be had, and finally Scorcher sat down upon a drift of sand and murmured that it was hard to die so far from home.

Rambler wished to play babes in the wood and end the trouble then and there, suggesting, incidentally, that the government could never make this part of the road acceptable to cyclists until elevators were put in on all the bad hills. Scorcher supported the proposition, but thought that nickel in the slot machines, producing cool, refreshing beer be scattered at intervals through this Gehenna.[19] How the expedition finally reached the Fountain House, at the Lower Geyser Basin, just as the shades of night were falling fast, need not be told. The credit was entirely due to the cooling waters of Nez Perces [sic—Perce] Creek flowing near by the southern cantonment of the park military force. Ten miles more of trying, tiresome, toilsome road the next morning led to the Upper Geyser Basin, where Old Faithful stands sentinel, and from this point forward around the circuit the roads were firmer, although here and there the old enemy sand was to be found, and towering ranges had to be climbed afoot.

But the twenty miles from the Upper Geyser Basin to the west arm

FIGURE 10.2.

F. J. Haynes, who became Yellowstone's official photographer in
1884, took this photo of a group of unidentified bicyclists at Old
Faithful Geyser in 1895. (Montana Historical Society, Helena.)

CHAPTER TEN

of the Yellowstone Lake was in the main a charming ride, full of exciting experiences. The scenic glories of the road repaid every effort. Twice the continental divide was passed. At Shoshone point, with Shoshone Lake and the Teton Mountains spread out in the distance, the vision was glorious. The view of Yellowstone Lake lying ensnared in its necklace of mountain peaks, which flashed upon the eye at the end of that long coast down the mountains, of which I have already spoken, was an inspiration unequaled by any other scene in this fairy land of wonders, except the grand cañon of the Yellowstone, which, in its bravery of coloring and splendor of fall, cascade, tarn, minaret and palisade, is the cap sheaf of scenic marvels in America.

Seated on the upper deck of the small steamer that carries passengers across the Yellowstone Lake to the Lake House near the outlet, Scorcher remarked, "There's good wheeling in the Yellowstone after all," and then he looked calmly down to where the propeller of the little boat was churning the blue water into foam, while the passengers who had come by stage smiled knowingly.

And how the trout did bite in the outlet of the lake, a dozen big fellows in a few minutes with only a black fly for bait and no jug of any kind in the little rowboat to pour a libation to Izaak Walton.[20] And then at night, with the dreamy waters of this the highest navigated lake in America bathed in the light of an August moon, and the crisp, pine-laden air blowing gently down from the mountain peaks, how slumber and sweet oblivion fell upon us. The turmoil of the city was forgotten, and one felt that here in the heart of nature is the sweet Elysium of rest.

Think not that I intend to drag this narrative over all the miles traversed by Rambler and Scorcher, describing en route, each hill and vale. The purpose is to give general impressions of the park as a grand preserve of mountain, stream and forest, and to furnish some idea of its possibilities for those who ride the bicycle. But having confessed to some stretches of road so arduous that only the utmost perseverance could conquer them there is only the ordinary spirit of fairness in the desire to paint the other side of the picture when the opportunity occurs. It would therefore be inexcusable neglect to omit mention of the twenty miles of splendid mountain road between Yellowstone Lake and the Grand Cañon. With the river rolling near at hand almost the entire distance, at first sleepy from its nap on the bosom of the lake, and then tossed into foam as it approaches the scene of its mad journey down the Grand

Cañon; with mountains and serene meadows all about and a smooth road that seemed to lend wings to the bicycle, this dash across the southern section of the park was an experience never to be forgotten. Some other time somewhere in this great world it may be possible to match the exhilaration of this ride, but until that time and place be found nothing in bicycle memory will equal this splendid rush through the wilderness that left us spellbound; awestricken and speechless in the presence of the might, majesty, power and beauty combined in that splendid creation of nature, the Grand Cañon and the falls of the Yellowstone.

In leaving the subject of roads, it may be said that with the exception of a few stunning hills, all of the way from the Cañon Hotel back to the Mammoth Springs is rideable and most of it enjoyable for any who can endure hard work and a reasonable amount of fatigue. No others have any business in the park at the present time, but gentlemen, and perhaps some ladies who are accustomed to long country tours will find a trip through the Yellowstone Park the crown of all their cycling experiences. There is nothing like it in the entire category of sport. The teeming wonders and splendid scenes of this wilderness are irresistibly fascinating. A week answers for the circuit of the park, but two weeks is better and three weeks would not at all exhaust the attractions that crowd on every hand.

A serviceable woolen touring suit, with a change of wear to be carried wrapped in a mackintosh and attached to the handle bars, will be sufficient for the trip. Other baggage may be left at the springs, ready for the grand resurrection of "style" that occurs after roughing it for a time. Above all see to it that the bicycle is fitted with a very strong hand brake. Neglect of this precaution and reliance upon worthless foot brakes came very near costing Rambler and Scorcher a few legs and arms if not a neck. Many apparently innocent grades will seize the wheel in a grasp of iron and carry it away with irresistible force utterly regardless of the most frantic backpedaling. With an adequate brake one may ride down many slopes that it would otherwise be suicide to attempt. The horses in the park, most of them half-broken bronchos and cross breeds, look upon the cycle as some strange new animal and in the narrow mountain passes some serious accidents may occur unless the cyclist proves that he is a gentleman by dismounting and keeping out of the way when trouble threatens. Next year the park will be full of wheelmen hurrying to see the sights before the primeval blush of the wilderness is brushed away, and to those who are able to stand the fatigue the trip will be a benediction.

I have purposely avoided making any catalogue of the natural charms and wonders of the park, all of which have been set forth in detail by far more competent observers. All of the world knows in a general way that there is an unexampled array of spouting geysers and hot springs within the confines of the reservation, that the scenery is sublime, the fishing unequaled and the presence of game quite beyond comparison with any other known spot. The remnant of the buffalo species is herded here, if a few scattering animals can be called a herd. Elk, antelope, deer and bear, although away from the traveled road, throng the park by the thousand, and as no shooting is permitted, the reserve promises to become a permanent retreat for all the wild animals of the mountains. Of the thermal wonders too much could not be said. The beautiful formations developed by the great area of boiling springs in the vicinity of the Mammoth Hot Springs are most fascinating, while the remarkable phenomena observed in those three centers of thermal activity, the Norris and the Lower and Upper Geyser basins, cannot be matched in kind and in detail anywhere on earth. In the Firehole valley alone, where the streams run hot, more than 1,000 craters and fissures exist, from which steam and hot water issue. They range from insignificant steam vents to splendid geysers, spouting periodically enormous quantities of water, as the Great Fountain and Old Faithful are accustomed to do. Both of these famous spouters I saw play by the light of an August moon, under a deep blue and star-gemmed sky, and the spectacle was one which carried with it an impression strangely majestic and almost uncanny.

Whence comes this latent power that upheaves so regularly and builds up such fantastic creations in crater, beaded environment and delicate filigree of white and many-tinted marble?

But the crowning glory of this wilderness is the grand cañon of the Yellowstone, upon whose seamed and rugged walls nature has painted a tracery of colors that no artist can imitate. With plunging falls, azure and white cascades, battlements in gray and gold, and all the bravery and beauty that nature in her most generous mood can bestow, this splendid rift in the mountains will surely dominate every other memory of that unequaled preserve, the Yellowstone National Park.

LYMAN B. GLOVER

Notes

This account is from the *Chicago Sunday Times Herald*, September 6, 1896, 30.

1. Richard A. Bartlett, *Yellowstone: A Wilderness Besieged* (Tucson: University of Arizona Press, 1985), 62. Owen's account is reproduced in Paul Schullery, ed., *Old Yellowstone Days* (Boulder: University Press of Colorado, 1979).
2. *Who Was Who in America* (Chicago: Marquis, 1943), I, 462.
3. Wilma Jane Dryden, "Chicago Theatre as Reflected in the Newspapers, 1900 through 1904" (PhD diss., University of Illinois, 1960), 29.
4. *Nebraska State Journal*, April 6, 1902.
5. *Chicago Daily Tribune*, April 9, 1915, 19; Paul Wilstach, *Richard Mansfield: The Man and the Actor* (New York: Charles Scribner's Sons, 1908), 401, 408, 461.
6. Burlington Route [Railroad], *A Trip Worth Taking: Through Yellowstone Park on a Bicycle* (Chicago: Poole Brothers, 1898), [8]–[9].
7. This referred to the Missouri River.
8. Passages are deleted here that have nothing to do with Yellowstone.
9. Presumably one of these men was the author, Lyman B. Glover, but we do not know the identity of his companion.
10. Falstaff was a fat, convivial, roguish character in Shakespeare's *Merry Wives of Windsor* and *Henry IV*.
11. Excelsior is from the Latin meaning "higher; loftier; more elevated; ever upward."
12. Gath was one of the five Philistine city-states established in southwestern Philistia. It was the home city of Goliath. Most archaeologists identify Gath with the current archaeological site of Tel es-Safi (aka Tel Safi). See Wikipedia.
13. This refers to a problem that severely tests the ability of an inexperienced person.
14. Arcady referred to a region of ancient Greece in the Peloponnesus where the inhabitants, relatively isolated from the rest of the known civilized world, proverbially lived a simple, pastoral life.
15. The year should be 1872.
16. The U.S. Army took over control of the park on August 17, 1886.
17. Perhaps he means a "damnation" (very difficult) task.
18. Larry was anything but silent. He became famous over his eighteen years in the park (1887–1904) for his humor and conviviality at four different establishments, each known as Larry's Lunch Station. See generally Lee H. Whittlesey, "'I Haven't Time to Kiss Everybody!': Larry Mathews Entertains in Yellowstone, 1887–1904," *Montana the Magazine of Western History* 57 (Summer 2007): 58–73.
19. *Gehenna* originally referred to a garbage dump in a deep narrow valley right outside the walls of Jerusalem (in modern-day Israel) where fires were kept burning to consume the refuse and keep down the stench. It is also the location where bodies of executed criminals, or individuals denied a proper burial, would be dumped. Today, *Gehenna* is often used as a synonym for Hell.
20. Izaak Walton was the author of *The Compleat Angler* (1653).

ELEVEN

The Yellowstone National Park

W. D. VAN BLARCOM

1897

W. D. VAN BLARCOM REMAINS A BIT OF A MYSTERY. EVEN WITH this unusual last name, he has been difficult to track as a person. He is known to have been living in Alton, Illinois, in 1890, was witness in Yellowstone in 1897 to the stagecoach robbery that year, and was later a resident of Fort Worth, Texas, but so far little else is known about him.[1] Per his opening line, he seems to have been living, or at least visiting, New York City at the time of his trip to Yellowstone.

Whoever he was, Van Blarcom was matter-of-fact about Yellowstone. Although his descriptions were detailed and accurate, he made no sweeping pronouncements about the park's beauty or vastness. But like Lyman Glover, he did manage to refer to one stretch of road with "what a ride!"

We left New York for the Yellowstone on one of its warmest days (and every New Yorker knows what that means), came west from St. Paul, and from there took the Northern Pacific to Livingston, Montana, passing through a most interesting country, and a most marvellous one to an easterner. In Livingston the stop was at a quaint little hotel for a few hours while waiting for the train on the branch line to take us to Cinnabar,[2] which is the last town [on] this [north] side of the park. There a big Concord coach met us, drawn by six fine horses, and with a toot of the horn we were off; our fox terriers, which we had brought with us, running and yelping after the coach with the greatest delight, after their long journey in the baggage car.[3] We had a steady climb up the mountains, of eight miles, before reaching the Mammoth Hot Springs hotel at the entrance of the park. But what a ride! The feeling, as you gaze around the beauties and wonders before you, is one of such absolute newness as to be entrancing in this blasé age.

After climbing the mountains in the stage you suddenly arrive upon a small plateau, upon which stands the hotel, and directly opposite that, Fort Yellowstone, with its soldiers;[4] all of which is startling coming suddenly upon you, as it does; when during your drive up the mountains you have seen little that would indicate the presence of man. The hotel piazza is thronged with people from all parts of the world, the stage coming in amid the tooting of horns, the soldiers having guard mount just across the way, all make the liveliest, most attractive picture, after the stillness of nature through which you have just passed.

After luncheon the guide took us out to see the hot springs, which are within a stone's throw of the hotel. We were not the only ones, a crowd of tourists went [too], people from every corner of the earth's surface. We met a gentleman who knew friends of ours, as is almost always the way no matter where one travels. Well! [F]rom the time we started until we returned we were simply walking exclamation points. Such marvellous formations [we saw], with the boiling hot water welling up in ceaseless bubbles, all colors of the rainbow. The delicate pinks, blues, greens, maroons, purples, all blending in such a manner as to render one speechless in surprise and admiration; and there is not one of these springs, but hundreds.

We tramped, loath to give up seeing until we were tired out, [and] then came back to the hotel just in time to dress for dinner. Afterwards the act of custom was to promenade on the wide piazzas, listening to the military band at the fort opposite, having the noted foreigners and Americans pointed out to us by one who knew them, looking them over, and thinking no one would ever know their greatness if they were not told, and altogether passing such a pleasant evening we would not have cared to retire had it not been for the long ride before us early next morning. For you are called at six thirty, breakfast at seven, and start off in the Concord coaches at eight, to make the tour of the park.

This takes five days if you go straight through, but you can go as leisurely as you please, stopping at the different hotels and exploring the surrounding country on horseback or driving or afoot, just as one prefers.[5]

Apropos of the foreigners, we were told that when Count von Bismarck, Prince von Bismarck's son,[6] was here a few seasons ago, he was touring the park with a friend, and was much surprised that his greatness did not produce more of an impression than it did. He was treated as was every one else, and the manager of the transportation company was "a most remarkable man," and he thought he must be a trifle insane "because he insisted upon collecting the fare of Count von Bismarck's friend in advance." Now, all who do not pay in advance for the trip through the park before they start from the hotel, have their fare collected at every subsequent hotel, this being done as all the tourists do not go the entire distance, and prefer to pay as they go. The Count had paid his fare in advance, as he meant to make the entire journey, his friend with him had not, so it was from him that the manager desired to collect the fare due. He had no money with him, and said that he would pay when he returned to the starting point, but the manager insisted, as those were the rules. So Count von Bismarck offered to go security for him, but that would not do; it was a case of no fare no ride. The Count paid for his friend, much to his disgust, that he, the Count von Bismarck, could not be trusted; but of course the manager had to obey the rules, and a count more or less, was nothing to him. It was very funny to see the Count's wrath. He probably realized then that he was in America, God's free country, where every man is born equal, and it remains with himself alone to make his name famous or otherwise.

While waiting to start on our tour of the park, we conceived the idea of visiting the stables of the transportation company, seeing them in the distance, and being very fond of horses. As a special favor we were taken through. First we saw the horses. There were hundreds of them, for during the season at times over five hundred passengers are carried every day. Such great, big beauties; and six of them are used on each tally-ho. Then we went through the coach stables, and viewed with delight the Concord coaches, made in Concord, New Hampshire, and shipped way out here, in the heart of the Rocky Mountains. Upon inquiry we learned that each coach cost about fifteen hundred dollars to build, so it was with much surprise we gazed at the hundreds of them in the stables, all freshly painted, ready to begin the season of '97.[7]

Leaving the Mammoth Hot Springs hotel promptly at eight o'clock, we were driven twenty miles to the Norris lunch station. En route we passed through Golden Gate [Canyon], four miles from the hotel, and one thousand feet higher. It is one of the most picturesque spots in the park, being a pass through what at one time was solid rock. The rocks on one side [rise] to the height of over three hundred feet, on the other over two thousand feet and [are] most beautifully colored a delicate green, owing to the moss covered rocks, shading to deep olive and brown. On one side of this cut is built a roadway, on beams fastened into the rock, a most difficult piece of road building. And as you cross you gaze into the depths below, while ahead of you are to be seen the Rustic Falls, dashing down sixty feet to the Gardiner River,[8] which flows through this opening below, making the whole most picturesque.

Driving on you cross a flat portion of the country called Swan [Lake] Basin, but gazing off in the distance one sees mountains, snow capped all around the horizon, rising to the height of over eleven thousand feet above sea level. In the winter they say this valley is inhabited by hundreds of elk and deer. But as the warm weather comes they go higher up in the mountains to avoid the mosquitoes and flies. Our dogs started two elk while we were crossing, great beautiful animals, and as fleet as the wind they flew to the cover of the pines nearby, so we had but a passing glimpse of them.

Next we passed an obsidian cliff, of black glass, rising some two hundred and fifty feet above the roadway, glistening beautifully in the sun's rays. An amusing story is told about this cliff of glass. A huntsman was looking for elk one morning near this cliff, when he saw a great, big beauty, right before him. He shot at it, but missed it, then shot again and again, each time at a closer range, but the animal never moved. He was furious, because he was considered an unfailing shot, and could not understand why he could not bring down the game. In turning to reload his gun he saw standing on the hill behind him the animal he had been shooting at, calmly gazing at him. Looking quickly back to the spot he had been shooting at he saw the same animal reflected in the black glass of the obsidian cliff. While he was recovering from his surprise the elk bounded away.[9] This happened before the park had been

FIGURE 11.1.
Park stagecoaches of the Yellowstone Park Transportation
Company lined up for this photo in 1896 and waited for F. Jay
Haynes to "snap" them. (Montana Historical Society, Helena.)

reserved by the government for a National Park. Now no hunting is allowed. The Indians who inhabited this section of the country used to make annual pilgrimages to this cliff, to get the glass from which they made their arrow heads.[10] These were made by hand, perfectly shaped. No white man has ever been able to imitate them, not knowing the secret of carving the brittle glass. Next we came to a lake full of beaver dams, and in which a beaver house is standing. At one time trappers used to take hundreds of beavers from here every year. Now they peacefully build unmolested.

A little f[a]rther on the stage stopped, and the driver asked us if we would not like a drink of ice cold Apolinaris [sic—Apollinaris] water. We were incredulous at first, but upon getting out and following a path in the woods a short distance we beheld a clear, beautiful spring, which upon tasting certainly did rival any Apolinaris [*sic*—Apollinaris] water we ever drank in New York. Again we started on, and before long we could see tops of white tents in the distance. These proved to be the first lunch station, twenty miles from where we started. The tents are immense affairs, everything bright and clean connected with them.

When we arrived a most remarkable man rushed out with a "Well! You're here at last, and glad I am to see ye's. Get right out and come in. Ladies, you can go right up-stairs and take off your hats, and lunch will then be ready." So we all got out, ten coaches full of people. We found that "up-stairs" was another tent where we could smooth our rumpled locks and remove a little dust that had accumulated during the drive. Then we all met at several long tables, about thirty people at each table. Immediately a good hot luncheon was served, while "Larry," the manager of the lunch station,[11] went around from one to the other saying, "Now, phat can I do for yez? Will yez have anything more? Don't be bashful as I am. Speak out if yez want anything yez don't see."

In passing the cakes one gentleman took what is called a kiss. Larry, spying it, said, "Ah, take another, [as] one kiss is never enough. It only gives you an appetite for more." And so he rattled on, saying anything and everything, until the whole tent full of people were in convulsions of laughter. One very dignified old gentleman came in late, and Larry said to him: "Now, I wonder what yez might be? a D.D., or an M.D.?" The gentleman looked at him, and seemed to be reflecting, when Larry quietly added: "One stands for donkey driver, and the other for mule driver." Then he hurried away to the other side of the room amid roars of laughter, while the old gentleman recovered from his surprise as best he could.

No one was spared, but all took the Irishman good naturedly, as "Larry" is one of the curiosities of the park. In going up through the park this lunch station is always called the "Norris Station," but coming back it is always called "Larry's."

After luncheon a number of wagonettes drove up to the tents, and we took our seats in them, and were driven around the Norris Geyser Basin. The first geyser we saw in action was the Congress [Pool], throwing boiling hot water some thirty feet in the air. For some years this geyser was simply a boiling spring of pale blue water, while near by was a steam vent, from which great quantities of steam escaped, and whose rumblings and roaring of escaping steam could be heard for miles. Suddenly one year this ceased, and the new geyser, called the

FIGURE 11.2. Our chronicler W. D. Van Blarcom had lunch at "Larry's Lunch Station" in 1897, probably the year that this photo of Larry Mathews and his employees was taken at Norris Geyser Basin. (Marie Augsperger, *The Yellowstone National Park* [Middletown, OH: Naegele-Aner, 1948], 188.)

Congress, appeared.[12] The first eruptions were of great force, and completely blockaded the road nearby with huge rocks and pieces of formation. Next we saw a little geyser called the "Minute Man," or the Constant, because it plays every sixty seconds, throwing jets of water thirty or forty feet in the air. The "Black Growler" [steam vent] is most impressive, and gives one the feeling that the Devil must be piling on the coals below. It is near the road, in a basin some twenty feet in diameter, with three openings in the side. These openings are black, and from them issues clouds of steam, with a roaring and hissing sound, rising hundreds of feet above, the vibrations shaking the ground. It is estimated that the pressure of escaping steam is equal to forty-five thousand horse-power. Around this basin is any quantity of snow, which never melts.[13] We would not believe it until we had picked some up, and saw that it was really snow. In fact, you hear and see so many seemingly impossible things, that at first you are inclined to be incredulous, but finally end by believing anything and everything, for fear the thing that seems most improbable will be true, and vice versa. We saw geysers innumerable, none being very high, as the highest ones are in the Upper Geyser Basin, but we saw enough. After viewing the different geysers and springs, we again took our places in the coaches and started for another twenty-mile drive, when we would reach the Fountain Hotel and remain there over night.

It was here that we saw the paint pots.[14] These are certainly the oddest, funniest things in the entire park. They are like cauldrons of hot boiling paint, of all colors; the most delicate pink, blue, gray, etc., all bubbling and boiling, throwing up jets of this paint like matter, which assumes all kinds of shapes, some like roses or lilies, and then again such fantastic shapes you can imagine almost anything. It is fascinating to watch them, and you leave them with regret.

The next morning we were up bright and early, and found a delightfully warm and sunny morning awaiting us. We breakfasted at seven, and were seated in the coaches ready to start at seven thirty. We drove nine miles through a wide valley, over which is scattered numerous hot springs. The elevation of this valley is 7,250 feet above the sea level, and the surrounding hills are from four hundred to eight hundred feet higher. The drive runs along the Fire Hole River,[15] so named because of the many hot springs along its margin, and emptying directly into the cool waters of the river. It seems marvellous that this should be so. After driving a few miles we came to what is called Hell's Half Acre,[16] and when you finish looking at it you think it is well named. Here is located the Excelsior geyser, whose crater is two hundred and fifty feet in width, by four hundred feet in length, the largest [geyser] in the park. It has not played for eleven years, but when it did play it threw the immense body of water contained in the crater, two hundred and fifty feet in[to] the air.[17] It is now quiet, but the crater is filled with boiling water to the very brim, and looking down through its delicate blue transparency, you can see the beautiful coral like formation of the sides, to great depths, which make you move cautiously back from the edge, knowing that a misstep over its edge would mean almost instant death. Near the Excelsior is Prismatic Lake.[18] It is two hundred and fifty by three hundred and fifty feet [in size]. In the centre of the lake the waters are of the deepest blue, growing gradually lighter to a delicate green, this shades into yellow, then to brighter reds and purples, shading to lavender, while the very edge of the lake is of orange; these exquisite colors blend and ripple towards you, boiling hot, while you stand and gaze, simply transfixed, by its beauty.

We again climbed into the coaches, and soon were in the most interesting portion of the whole park, that part where all the great geysers are. You cannot convey by descriptions how impressive is the sight of one of these massive columns of hot water going up in the air hundreds of feet, with a weird force from somewhere below, and with a power so great that it makes the earth in its vicinity tremble and vibrate, until you are so thoroughly awed, yet fascinated, you are loath to move from the spot. We saw several of the largest ones erupt, and would have liked to have stayed several days in hopes of seeing the others, but there being no hotel we could not do so.[19] I believe they intend to build one this year.

We hope they will, for it is without doubt the most fascinating spot in the park. This is where the people who camp through have the advantage over the people who go to the hotels. They can pitch their tents near by, and stay as long as they wish to at each interesting spot. There are many charming spots where wood, water and grass for the horses is found in abundance, and many thousand camping parties go through the park every year.

We returned to the Fountain Hotel to remain over night. In the rotunda, where all the tourists congregate, is an immense open fireplace, whose fire is made from huge logs, the size of trees. This blazes up and casts a ruddy glow over the faces of all the travellers who are grouped around it, in a large circle, in comfortable old-fashioned rocking chairs, relating their experiences of the day. We all sat and chatted, becoming almost like old friends in our drowsy, comfortableness, until we were so sleepy we were forced to go to bed, especially as next morning we had to be ready to start at seven o'clock, as we had the longest drive of the trip before us.

We were called at five thirty, breakfasted and were seated in the coaches ready for the bugle, which gives the signal to start at seven promptly. We drove twenty-nine miles before we stopped for luncheon, at a lunch station called the "Thumb" so named because it is situated on the thumb of the Yellowstone Lake. The lake is shaped like an open hand, with a thumb and four fingers. It is a sheet of water as blue as the sky, and over thirty miles in length, surrounded on all sides by heavy timber, with the grand old Tetons rising fourteen thousand feet, snow-capped in the distance; while the body of the lake is dotted with many small, picturesque islands.[20]

We had a good hot lunch at the Thumb, and then all started off to see what there was of interest. We were taken by a guide to the water's edge, where he showed us a cone filled with boiling water.[21] This cone extends into the cold waters of the lake. We all went out upon it, while the guide took his fishing pole, threw his fly far out in the lake and almost before we could speak, had caught a beautiful salmon trout, weighing at least a pound and a half. He played it through the water until quite near, then, with a quick jerk, he landed it in the hot spring, and in just two minutes he drew it out and presented to our astonished vision a boiled trout.

As we stood upon the shore of the lake, we saw in the distance a white speck, which grew larger and larger, until we saw the prettiest little steamer making right for the dock where we stood. As soon as she was fastened alongside, we all went aboard, and explored her. We found a pretty little cabin upholstered in red velvet, cabin boys in uniform, and general appointments to match. The steamer carries one hundred and twenty-five people, is named the "Zillah," commanded by Commodore Watters [sic—Waters].[22] We decided we would sail across the lake instead of taking the long drive of twenty-five miles along the shore. The steamer lands you at the Lake hotel fully two hours before the stages do, so we thought it would be a pleasant change. But others thought they preferred the ride, and the chance of seeing the game along the route. Commodore Watters showed us buffalo in their wild state, besides mountain sheep, elk and the cutest little buffalo calf. We made arrangements to go fishing the next day. So by seven-thirty we were aboard the "Zillah," steaming down the lake. We went thirty miles to the extreme end, where they told us the trout were gamey and better than in other parts of the lake.

We disembarked, and pushed off from the steamer in row boats, with a guide in each boat. We rowed near the shore, and commenced casting our flies. The trout stay along the shore of the lake in the shallow water, and it was but a few minutes before a shout indicated that one of us had a bite; and sure enough, a beautiful speckled beauty was carefully landed after much dashing about and playing. Then the fun commenced, as fish after fish was caught. Some of us had never cast a fly before, but the lake abounds in fish, so even the most inexperienced had the pleasure of landing a trout. We took back to the hotel seventy-five beauties, and had the cook prepare one for each of the party. And no fish ever tasted quite as delicious as those.

Along the road to the Canyon hotel the next morning we came upon the mud geyser, the most fiendish, diabolical thing in the whole park.[23] It stands all by itself, a few yards from the road, at the base of the cliff. The crater is thirty feet deep, and funnel shaped. The mud is ejected from below through a black, cave-like opening. This mass of soft mud is being constantly belched forth with a dull, muffled, sickening sound in a most repulsive yet fascinating manner. As you stand on the brink and look down to the depths below, where this constant belching, boiling, sputtering mud is being thrown up, you are possessed by an absolute, abject fear. No wonder the poor ignorant Indians gave this spot a wide berth. Even we twentieth century people leave it with a weird, uncanny feeling possessing us, glad to get away.

After leaving this spot we drove on to Hayden Valley, where all the large game of the park congregate in winter. While passing through this we saw several beautiful antelope grazing. They stood and watched us for a few moments, then, with the most graceful bounds, they fairly flew across the valley out of sight. But as we drove along the edge of the timber we saw a couple of elk quietly standing in the shade. They took no notice of us except to watch us until we were out of sight.

Here the road winds down to the banks of the Yellowstone River. We drove along this for several miles watching the trout spring into deeper water at the sound of our wagon wheels; passing many fisher-men patiently catching the speckled beauties. The river here grows swifter and swifter, and before you know it you are upon the Upper Falls of the Yellowstone. They drop one hundred and forty feet, and shoot off a quarter of a mile below where they take another leap of three hundred and sixty feet,[24] forming the lower falls, and from this last leap through the Grand Canyon of the Yellowstone, the river flows, looking like a mere ribbon from the heights above, although it is fully seventy-five feet in width. We now began to climb again until we reached the summit of quite a mountain on which stands the Canyon hotel.

After luncheon the first drive was to Point Lookout.[25] From its very edge we beheld the Grand Canyon of the Yellowstone. Before and below us some twenty-five hundred feet was that vast gorge from which rose turrets and pinnacles of all imaginable shapes, as we picture the ruins of by-gone days; these were colored with every color of the rainbow. Some were bright red, then the delicate lavenders, greens, pinks, browns, [and] orange, all harmonizing most wonderfully. At the bottom of this vast chasm rushed the Yellowstone River, looking like a mere thread. On the tops of some of these vast columns rising from the midst of the very depths of this canyon, were perched eagles' nests. And looking down upon them, you could see the old bald-headed eagles sitting there.[26] Going f[a]rther down along the edge of the canyon you come to Inspiration Point. This hangs over the canyon two miles below Point Lookout, and affords the most extensive view. Looking up towards where the great falls take their leap of three hundred and sixty feet, you see before you a sight never to be forgotten. From the depths below rises the mist of the falls, draping in their soft splendor the highly colored walls, and turrets of the canyon, while all about and beyond you are the silent, gloomy depths of that awful chasm. You stand rooted to the spot, fascinated, yet appalled. You leave it finally, but only to go back again. And there you stand, worshipping, yet afraid, feeling smaller than the smallest grain of sand. Thinking what eternal ages it must have taken to make what you see before you, and for the first time in your life perhaps, you realize what eternity must mean.

A trail leads you down the mountainside to the Lower Falls. A rock juts out over them, and there we sat, watching that mighty fall of water, watched the river as it swept onward, to as it seemed, sure destruction. We threw pieces of timber into the water and watched them go over the falls to be lost to sight almost instantly. How treacherous and wicked looked those waters!

We stayed three days, [as] we could not seem to leave that canyon. But finally we found ourselves once more driving merrily along our homeward way to the Mammoth Hot Springs hotel. When we reached there some of us said farewell and went their way, while the others stayed for the season, to go again and again, to see the sights and enjoy the pleasures of this National Wonderland.

CHAPTER ELEVEN

Notes

This piece originally appeared in *National Magazine*, September 1897.

1. A newspaper mentioned his wife: "Mrs. W. D. Van Blarcom of Alton, Illinois was in the city today" (*East St. Louis Journal*, March 1890). Mr. Van Blarcom and the stage robbery are in the John Meldrum materials, Item 35, letter box 19, Folder 2, Yellowstone National Park Archives, Yellowstone National Park. The *Galveston Daily News*, December 5, 1924, lists Van Blarcom as being from Fort Worth.

2. Cinnabar was located three miles west of present Gardiner, Montana. It was the end of the Northern Pacific Railroad spur from Livingston until 1903, when the rails were extended to Gardiner. The town of Cinnabar disappeared shortly after that time, when its businessmen largely moved to Gardiner.

3. According to Judge John Meldrum, who presided at the 1897 trial of Yellowstone stagecoach robbers "Morphine Charley" Reeb and "Little" Gus Smitzer, newspaperman W. D. Van Blarcom took his two fox terriers with him everywhere he traveled. Van Blarcom told the judge that on the night before the stage robbery (which occurred on August 14, 1897, four miles west of Canyon), he was at the Canyon Hotel with the two dogs sitting in his lap, when all of a sudden Reeb and Smitzer passed nearby. The two dogs bounded off his lap, barking furiously at the two men. Van Blarcom apologized to the men, but the incident cemented their likenesses in his mind such that he was able to later recall seeing them for the court. He remembered thinking of Reeb: "That fellow is in the same boat that I am; he suffers with lung trouble." Van Blarcom's testimony was partly responsible for the two robbers being convicted and imprisoned for three years. John W. Meldrum, in Joseph Joffe, "John W. Meldrum [The Grand Old Man of Yellowstone Park]," *Annals of Wyoming* 13 (April 1941): 122.

4. Yellowstone was governed by the U.S. Army from 1886 until 1918, when the National Park Service formally took over its administration and protection. See generally, H. Duane Hampton, *How the U.S. Cavalry Saved Our National Parks* (Bloomington: Indiana University Press, 1971).

5. The standard park tour package was 5 ½ days, but travelers had the option of staying additional nights at any of the hotels and paying the extra nightly rate for room and meals. There was no additional charge from the stage company for this service.

6. Prince von Bismarck was also known as Count Otto von Bismarck. The "Iron Chancellor" founded the German Empire in 1871 and served as its chancellor for nineteen years. Count Wilhelm von Bismarck-Schönhausen was his second son, born in 1852. "Otto, Prince von Bismarck," Encyclopædia Britannica, available at www.britannica.com/EBchecked/topic/66989/Otto-von-Bismarck, accessed July 23, 2006.

7. The park coaches were made by the Abbot-Downing Company of Concord, New Hampshire, whose coaches were widely used in other western places. Over thirty-seven hundred of these coaches were produced between 1827 and 1899, and they were considered the finest stagecoaches built. Ralph Moody, *Stagecoach West* (Lincoln: University of Nebraska Press, 1998), 13–16. Coaches of the Yellowstone Park Transportation Company were painted yellow. The coach garage that they visited was east of the hotel until 1903, when a new building was erected on the site of present Aspen Dormitory. Lee Whittlesey, *A Yellowstone Album* (Boulder: Roberts Rinehart, 1997), 117.

8. Actually the Rustic Falls goes down forty-seven feet.

9. This is a version of one of the "tall tales" incorrectly attributed to Jim Bridger, who trapped in the Yellowstone region in the 1820s and 1830s. Although some writers (notably Stanley Vestal) have attributed a similar story to Bridger, Aubrey Haines's careful research into the Bridger stories makes it clear that this was not one of Jim's tales but, rather, something created later by others. Aubrey L. Haines, *The Yellowstone Story* (1977; rev., Boulder: University of Colorado Press, 1996), I, 53–59.

10. Named a National Historic Landmark in 1996, the volcanic Obsidian Cliff is famous for having provided Native Americans with obsidian to make tools and weapons. Arrowheads located as far away as Ohio have been traced to Obsidian Cliff. Peter Nabokov and Larry Loendorf, *Restoring a Presence: American Indians and Yellowstone National Park* (Norman: University of Oklahoma Press, 2004), 161–62.

11. Larry Mathews was a colorful Irishman who worked in Yellowstone from 1887 through 1904. He managed the Trout Creek Lunch Station near Hayden Valley from 1888 to 1891 and then moved to West Thumb in 1892, to Norris Geyser Basin in 1893, and to Old Faithful in 1902. See generally, Lee Whittlesey, "'I Haven't Time to Kiss Everybody!': Larry Mathews Entertains in Yellowstone, 1887–1904," *Montana the Magazine of Western History* 57 (Summer 2007): 58–73.

12. Notwithstanding what Hiram Chittenden and others have stated about Congress Pool being named for the fifty-third U.S. Congress, it was actually named for the 1891 Geological Congress, which met that summer in Yellowstone and which was led by geologist Arnold Hague. Hague was the namer of this feature, and his personal papers at the National Archives make it clear in three different places that this was the real reason for the name. Lee Whittlesey, *Yellowstone Place Names* (Gardiner, MT: Wonderland Publishing Company, 2006), 73.

13. Van Blarcom was incorrect here. Snow at Norris usually melts by midsummer, and nowhere in Yellowstone is there perpetual snow.

14. This was the Fountain Paint Pot, known in Van Blarcom's day as the "Mammoth Paint Pot."

15. The name Firehole River may have been applied formally to the river in 1850 by a party that included Jim Bridger and Kit Carson. Bridger claimed

that the stream "flowed so fast down the side of the hill that the friction of the water against the rocks, heated the rocks" (Lee Whittlesey, *Wonderland Nomenclature*, 1988, unpublished manuscript, Yellowstone National Park Library, Yellowstone National Park, 320).

16. This is the present Midway Geyser Basin.

17. Excelsior Geyser is known to have erupted in 1881, 1882, 1888, and 1890. Possible eruptions may have occurred in 1891 and 1901. Current figures measure it at 276 feet by 328 feet. Whittlesey, *Wonderland Nomenclature*, 293–95.

18. "Prismatic Lake," now known as Grand Prismatic Spring, is the largest hot spring in Yellowstone and the third largest in the world. It is 370 feet in diameter and more than 120 feet in depth. Whittlesey, *Yellowstone Place Names*, 120–21.

19. Actually the (second) Shack Hotel, a crude wooden building, was operating at Old Faithful that year. It had been rebuilt in 1895 after a fire the previous year and was generally not included on the standard stagecoach tour. The Old Faithful Inn replaced it in 1904, and that establishment then became a regular overnight stop on the tour. Lee Whittlesey, "A History of the Old Faithful Area with Chronology, Maps, and Executive Summary," September 14, 2006, manuscript prepared for the National Park Service, Yellowstone National Park Library, Yellowstone National Park, 27–38.

20. Yellowstone Lake is believed to be the largest natural lake at its altitude (7,731 feet) in the Western Hemisphere. It has 110 miles of shoreline and a maximum depth of over 380 feet.

21. This is known today as Fishing Cone.

22. Ella Collins Waters brought the steamboat *Zillah* to the park in 1889 and managed the Yellowstone Lake Boat Company until 1907. The forty-ton steamship could carry 125 passengers and ferried passengers from the "Thumb" to the Lake Hotel until 1917. The service was not part of the tour package and required an additional fare from the tourists. Waters's "wild animal" zoo was eventually considered a disgrace and health hazard by authorities and was shut down in 1907. Haines, *The Yellowstone Story*, II, 18; Lee Whittlesey, "Byways, Boats, and Buildings: Yellowstone Lake in History (part three)," *Points West* (Buffalo Bill Historical Center, Cody, WY), Summer 2008: 24–27.

23. Mud Geyser was a very active and popular geyser from at least 1870 through 1895 and 1901–5. After that it became quiet. Due to changes in activity, the name Mud Geyser was often mistakenly applied to nearby Mud Volcano, and that is probably what Van Blarcom did. Whittlesey, *Wonderland Nomenclature*, 729–36.

24. The height of Upper Falls is currently listed as 109 feet, while the Lower Falls is 308 feet.

25. This is known today as Lookout Point.

26. These were probably ospreys.

TWELVE

Yellowstone Park in 1898

JOHN H. ATWOOD

1898

⁂

BORN IN MASSACHUSETTS, JOHN HARRISON ATWOOD (1860–1934) migrated to Kansas City, Missouri, where he became well known in Kansas state history as an attorney and political organizer for the Democratic Party. He received his LL.B. from Harvard in 1884 but became infatuated with Kansas through a friend and moved there to spend the rest of his life. He ran unsuccessfully for Congress in 1892 and successfully prosecuted unscrupulous meat packers in 1919.[1] He became successful as an orator, but his law practice made him most renowned for prosecuting the Metman murder case, the Hillman "false body" case, and cases involving patents, freighting, gas interests, and military justice. He was a personal friend of William Jennings Bryan, who ran several times for president.

Atwood first learned of Yellowstone in about 1883 from Professor F. A. Gooch of Yale University, who had studied the place with geologist Arnold Hague and the Hague surveys, but Atwood did not visit the park until summer 1898. Apparently his memories of Yellowstone stuck with him, for twenty years later he privately published a twenty-six-page pamphlet about the trip. That pamphlet, titled "Yellowstone Park in 1898," is reproduced here.

The pamphlet's small press run made it a rare book immediately, and in it Atwood noted that much of nature is too mighty for the pen of men. "So it is with the wonders of the Yellowstone," he gushed. "They are wider than words, mightier than metaphors, sublime beyond similitudes, and too marvelous to be told of withal." But Atwood felt a duty to tell the story and thought that everyone who visited the park should do likewise. This duty "devolves upon everyone," he declared, so "that others may be induced to journey to this northern wonder land, and come to know more of the minuteness and majesty of Nature's creative power."[2] Like others before and after him, he traveled to Yellowstone and wrote about it because he wanted to help spread the word about the new place.

We left Livingston[, Montana,] early in the forenoon, and for something over an hour rode through scenes [that] alone would have paid for the trip. We passed through a two thousand foot cañon into Paradise Valley, a rather extravagant name for a pretty stretch between the mountains [that] rose majestically on either side.[3] We then struck Yankee Jim gorge or cañon, the height of whose cliffs would startle prairie-bred men. To the right is the Devil's slide, a smooth belt of trap rock, reaching in a slant from the foot to the top of the mountain. *Descensus Averni facilis* must have been thought of by Tullius after having a vision of this Beelzebub's toboggan.[4] We then arrived at Cinnabar, the railroad station nearest the park, a little hamlet that takes its name from the mountains near which it stands, which in turn get their names from the mineral, reddish in color, appearing on all sides.

As we stepped upon the platform, up swept a handsome six-in-hand Concord coach,[5] trappings and horses' coats glistening in the sunshine, and into the coach we climbed for a nine-mile uphill drive to Mammoth Hot Springs. The road wound up the mountain beside Gardner River, which boiled and brawled many feet below. The view from any part of the road was inspiring; crags and peaks and snow and purple sky, the rollicking, yelling river, and wide-pinioned eagles sweeping to and fro.[6]

In time for a rather late luncheon we drove up to the Mammoth Hot Springs Hotel, a huge frame building covering considerable ground and four stories high. Here one found accommodations good enough for anyone; the beds are comfortable, and the food and service good. The afternoon is spent in examining hot spring formation. "Formation" is the name given to the results of the building done by the hot waters, bearing in solution of carbonate of lime, which is deposited as the waters cool. Here has been built up by the deposits of these infinitesimal particles a mountain hundreds of feet high. It has been so built as to form a series of terraces ranging from a few feet to many feet in height. On each of the terraces of the new or more recently built part of the mountain—what one might call the live part—is a boiling spring, bubbling up hot and steaming out of unknown depths to flow away to the edge and over it, cool and make its granular deposits. The water is as clear as absolute purity, and yet bears in its clear transparent waves that which builds and tints a mountain. I say tints, for while the prevailing color of the formation is white, parts of it are dyed from salmon pink to *terra cotta*, in the most exquisite shading. All sorts of fantastic shapes are taken by these strangely forming terraces so that they look like white or blushing marble carved by some Arab chiseler, into arabesque surpassing in delicacy and beauty the stone lace work of the Alhambra.

At a distance, the mountain shows pure white, glistening and bright; as one gazes one thinks of the description of the holy city—"like a jewel it shone, like a jasper stone, clear as crystal, while its gates are pearl—even pearl of matchless price."

The upper part of the mountain is dead; it is white, but it is chalky white of something dead with leprosy; its terraces are crumbling. The gleaming, steaming mass below and the saline, sepulchral mass above are the quick and dead of volcanic nature. It is said that those terraces are alone in the world—absolutely unique; now that the formation in new South Wales has been destroyed[,] they are the only structures extant, built by bubbling waters. Near the foot of the terraces stands Liberty Cap, a stone cone about fifty feet high, built by some long since silenced spring, shaped like a Phrygian cap,[7] and hence the name.

We looked into the Devil's Kitchen, but were deterred from investigating Satanic cuisine by a blast of hot and sulphurous air. We drank of the cooling waters of these steaming springs, and found them sweet to the taste. These terraces are all named and very appropriately; some of them I remember, but not all. There is Pulpit Terrace, Minerva, Jupiter and Angel; this last being by many feet the highest; and as we stood at its foot, and looked up the shimmering height with the thin veil of water pouring over it, it looked like a slow moving cascade of moulten [*sic*] glass flowing over a cliff in the marble quarries of Carrara.

Tired by our tramp we returned to the hotel to dine and rest. This last we did within overcoats, seated upon the wide veranda, looking toward a collection of government buildings dignified by the name Fort Yellowstone. This is the headquarters of the United States troop kept always in the Park to protect the game from destruction, and the works of nature from vandalism.[8]

The next morning we were waiting for the wagon at eight o'clock and in getting ready we had to solve the clothing question. And let me now say that the best time to make the trip is late in June or early in July. I was there Fourth of July week; circumstances selected the time of my going, and did it much more wisely than I could have possibly done. At that time of year you may run some risk of encountering cold weather, or perhaps a storm, though this risk is not great, but you avoid the terrible, terrific, and appalling dust that haunts as a demon almost every mile of the road, later in the season. The dust is something terrible as described by all, and as I know from one half day's experience. The coach horses cannot endure to do their work at the dusty season for more than a few weeks, when they are sent to pasture and replaced by fresh ones. But late in June the forces of the frost have been pretty well dispersed and the dust is not yet [there].[9] You should take with you two suits of clothing, and two pairs of shoes; hack suit and heavy shoes,[10] for the walks from the road to see the various sights is hard on footwear, and the dirt of the journey will ruin good clothes. Do not burden yourself with heavy coats; they have for rental at the Mammoth Hot Springs Hotel heavy driver's ulsters [that] protect from the cold more perfectly than most overcoats.[11] A coat such as one would want to carry is too good to be subjected to the treatment the park journey will give an outer wrap. These great coats are worn by ladies as well as men, and while not handsome are preferred by the experienced traveler.

Up come the wagons. They are large, roomy Concord coaches with three seats, and a wide seat for the driver. Each seat can accommodate three persons, but is not required to accommodate but two, and as the seats are cushioned and upholstered with leather, one can travel at ease. Our party comprised two coach loads. In my coach [were] Mrs. Atwood and myself, a native and citizen of Johannesburg, South Africa, very English, named Hay, and his sister, and three others. On leaving the hotel the road winds around the base of Angel terrace, which in the morning sunlight looks more than ever like the crystal mountain of a fairy tale.

After making a little dip we began another long climb passing through the Golden Gate. Why it is so called, I can't guess, unless it is because that is its name.[12] The road for a long way is cut out of the rocky mountain side, and for a mile or more you ride where a mishap to your vehicle would mean being dashed to waters boiling over boulders a thousand feet below. The climb finished, we found ourselves in Swan Lake Valley, a valley seven thousand feet above the level of the sea. Along this basin we bowled until we encountered Apollinaris Spring, a spring that they told me was as good apollinaris water as one can buy in bottles, but as I never drank apollinaris water by itself I did not attempt to judge. Next we encountered Obsidian Cliff or glass mountain. This is a sure enough mountain of glass, nearly black in color, [which] glistens in the sun like black diamonds. Understand this is a mountain of glass— manufactured in the vast manufactory of nature. In making the road it became necessary to remove a spur of this cliff, and instead of blasting, the road makers simply built huge fires about it, and after so heating, threw water on it, and the sudden contracting did the work of blasting powder and dynamite. This mountain of glass was the nucleus of the many strange tales that for years after the Lewis and Clark Expedition [circulated] to the East from this region, about crystal mountains.[13] [There are] also in the park petrified trees, and in a few places the silica-laden water has been drawn, by capillary attraction up into sage brush and other bushes[;] silica-laden water [that] forms on the outside crystal-like drops, gave rise to stories strange indeed. It was reported that acres of sage brush bore on their branches diamonds and all manner of jewels, and that among these jewel-bearing shrubs crouched petrified rabbits, wolves and bears. In a word, the tales that came forth from this land would make the Baron Munchausen seem like a worshiper at the shrine of veracity.[14]

At noon we reach the canvas lunch station known as Norris Geyser Basin or Norris Station. There we were met by Larry, the incomparable and inimitable manager of this cloth-roofed tavern.[15] He was a character indeed, with a different greeting for everybody. "How do you do all? God bless your souls, come in, come in!" was his salutation to us. To my traveling companion from South Africa with his English clothes and accent he said, "Come in, me Lord, come in. How is the Queen and yourself, bedad?" At the table the Englishman got to kicking about something until he was overwhelmed by a speech from Larry, something like this: "Me friend, ye grieve me; you are setting in the very same chair, at the very same place, where two years ago me friend, Chauncey Depew, stood when he said, 'Larry,' he says, 'ye are a blessing to the world; when I came,' he said, 'to this wild and tangled wilderness where the hand of man never set foot,' he says, 'I little thought to find a man of great charity,' he says, 'for,' he says, 'Larry will give you anything he has if ye only give him the price,' he says; 'and a man of nerve and courage is Larry,' he says, 'for he comes up here among the mountain peaks, where the lightning raises the devil, and then puts up his prices beyant the mountain tops, and without putting any lightning rods on them either,' he says; 'why, talk about courage,' he says, 'see the seegars he sells to perfect strangers, not knowing if they be dangerous to men or no; sure Larry is a warm member,' he says; 'them geysers be hot stuff,' he says, 'but they ain't in it with Larry,' he says." "No, me friend," continued Larry, "don't kick at me, please, for I am an angel in disguise; I'm bound to admit the disguise is a pretty good one, but I'm still an angel, or will be when I have a change of life, and, anyway, I am willing to be one when I die," and so on, almost without end.

The Norris Geyser Basin gives the first view of the spouters [geysers]. A walk of about a mile and a half gives an opportunity to see most things to be seen at this point. Climbing a low ridge you look down into what might well be the valley and the shadow. The basin into which you look is pitted with hot spring craters filled with ever-boiling water; several small geysers are here; one is called the Constant or Minute Man, for every minute up shoots a little jet of water thirty or forty feet. The [B]lack [G]rowler is here—a black-throated opening which emits puffs of steam, and a roar that can be heard afar. But the feature of this basin that struck me the most forcibly was the [B]aby geyser, which is only four or five years old. There can still be seen the raw unhealed rent in the earth where this geyser burst through; there are the dead trees, killed at the time, mute monuments of the geyser's destructive heat. The out rush of water at this point is considerable, but the altitude to which it is thrown is not great.[16]

Taking the coach again we proceeded through Gibbon's Cañon; the road gently declines until Gibbon's Fall is reached, which led me to remark that this was Gibbon's Decline and Fall, but nobody noticed the remark, and I subsided.

Sweeping down out of the cañon we sighted and soon arrived at the Fountain Hotel. This is in the Lower Geyser Basin, which contains some of the most wonderful features of the whole park. We had hardly cleansed ourselves from the stains of travel when a cry attracted our attention. We looked from the window to see the famous Fountain Geyser in full play,[17] but so far away that the full effect could not be obtained. When we arrived at the spot we found a great well-like opening nearly thirty feet across, from which presently rushed a great mass of water, not to a great height, not over forty or fifty feet, but spreading out in a fan-like fountain and producing an effect simply indescribable. The whole mass of water seemed disintegrated into drops, and standing as I was with my back to the sun, the whole seemed transformed into a multitude of brilliants; the volume of water is considerable. The controlling impression created was one of surpassing beauty. There are many other hot springs round about and for acres around nothing can be seen but the geyserite or chemically formed rocks.

Near by is what is to my mind one of the most remarkable things to be found in the whole park, and that is what is called the paint pots. Prof. [F. A.] Gooch had told me of them,[18] but I failed to grasp anything like an idea of the reality, and I fear I shall be able to serve you to but little better purpose. They are well named, for nothing in nature or art can more perfectly resemble paint than the substance seen in the basins called the paint pots. There are many of them near Fountain geyser, but the greatest is what is called the Mammoth Paint Pot.[19] Imagine a circular basin some fifty feet in diameter, some fifty feet across, surrounded by a ridge of clay four or five feet high, and perhaps a little more, looking for all the world like the outer rim of a huge circus ring. This rim confines a mass of this paint, liquid and boiling. So perfect is the resemblance to the lead paint of commerce that when a quizzical soldier told me that all the buildings in the park were painted with paint taken from this pot, I bethought me of glass mountains, and apollinaris springs, and never dreamed of doubting the statement until I happened to think that none of [the park] buildings were painted white, and then looked for and saw the twinkle in my informant's eye.[20] This mass is composed of finely granulated clay, fine as the finest flour, and mixed with boiling water to the consistency of that which we see in the house painter's bucket. From a furnace far down in the earth steam is constantly sent up to keep the giant caldron bubbling; from all over its surface little jets of steam are constantly leaping, and in their upward rush they carry little flecks of paint that on falling back on the mass take the most remarkable shapes—roses, lilies, lace work, but more often the shape identical with that of an egg when broken in the skillet for frying. When I say rose, I mean it appears as though you were looking down upon the open blossom of a full blown rose. And to stand and watch this steam modeling in clay suggests thermal possibilities that the ordinary imagination could but imperfectly grasp. Other colors than white are here—red is here, in every shade from blush pink to royal purple. Surrounding the mammoth paint pot are many others with gamuts of color so complete that were a Raphael to here paint the diluvian sunset, with the bow of promise in the sky, he would never find his palette wanting of a single tint. The beauty and strangeness of the paint pots, and the brilliant loveliness of the Fountain geyser made the stay at the lower basin a noteworthy day.

The next morning found us bowling along the banks of the Fire-hole River, whereon, in the course of an hour or so, we came to Excelsior Geyser. It is in the midst of numerous other hot springs of high temperature; and when you look down into the pit from which this geyser springs when in action, remember you are looking into the throat of the greatest geyser in the world. The pit is some 250 or 300 feet in diameter. This immense column of water is, in eruption, raised to the height of 250 feet, and so great is the volume of water shot out by this geyser that the great Fire-hole river is raised several inches at every eruption. If this geyser has played during the last few years it has occurred in the winter and was not observed.[21]

Not far from the Excelsior is Turquoise Spring, typical and representative of hundreds of tinted pools found in the park. They vary in size from a few feet to a hundred feet in diameter. They are nearly all the shape of an inverted bell, starting from a narrow throat at the bottom, and expanding to an extended circle at the top; all of them are warm, and many of them above the boiling point. The waters kept therein show every shade of blue and green. The green of the sea is there, and the green of the new unfolded leaves; the tender green of the grasses of June and the rich virile green of the sabrelike leaves of the corn. This infinity of greens shades into [a] marvelous variety of blues. The blue of the turquoise and the blue of the noon-day cloudless heavens shade into the darker blue of the star-lit midnight sky. We all remember the legend of Cleopatra dissolving pearls in the wine cup. As one looks down upon the blended splendor of emerald and sapphire flashing to the eye from the depths of these gleaming bells, one is almost constrained to believe that Dame Nature has here played the part of Egypt's erratic queen, and filled her steaming beakers with the distillations of gems and jewels.[22]

A few miles farther we came to the Upper Geyser Basin, a space about four miles square, which embraces within its limits more geyser springs than all the rest of the world contains. There are twenty-five or thirty of sufficient magnitude for each to be entitled to pages of description, and did any one of them stand alone it would rank as an eighth wonder of the world. Never is the poverty of language more perfectly manifest than when it is employed in an attempt to convey an impression of one of these gigantic geysers. The first one that I saw was the Bee Hive. Out of a cone, some four feet high, and three feet in diameter on the inner side, shot a column of water of the thickness of the opening, straight up in the air two hundred feet; with a roar like a thousand steam engines, with the rushing sound of a hundred sluice ways, with a power too tremendous for possible calculation, that column of water rushes up into the air to a height equal to the mighty monument that crowns the brow of Bunker Hill. It played, as I remember, for about ten minutes; at the distance of several hundred yards I viewed it, and then running to its side, touched the up-shooting water with my hand and thus grasped some notion of the overwhelming, unconquerable force that made of that mass of upward moving liquid, a crystal tree two hundred feet high. For very like a tree it was with a trunk, smooth and unbroken for one hundred and fifty feet, and then breaking into a spreading top not at all unlike the upper part of some beautiful elm that grows in perfected beauty by the banks of the Connecticut. But while the Bee Hive and the Giant, and the Splendid, and the Grand, may leap to greater heights, the most marvelous of all these geysers is Old Faithful.

Every hour and a little more, every seventy minutes, to be exact, with the regularity and consistency of the sun, Old Faithful sends a column of gleaming water, two and a half feet in diameter, to a height of one hundred and fifty feet. Old Faithful is no misnomer. In the gray of early morning, in the blazing splendor of noon, amid the golden glories of the sunset, and in the silvery sheen woven in the loom of Diana, can be seen gleaming Old Faithful's column of crystal and gems; in the green of the spring time and the russet of autumn, and when the snow pall of winter is drawn over nature's rugged face, this mighty clepsydra, this mighty water clock of the ages, hurls its sparkling pillar to meet the lances of the sun or the onward rush of the cohorts of the storm.[23]

Another notable geyser is the Castle. It sends its water to a height of two hundred fifty feet,[24] but it is not the altitude to which its waters rise that makes it so worthy of observation; it leaps from a great mass of accumulated geyserite not unlike an ancient castle in form, and plays for a period of some twenty minutes, when it is followed by eruptions of steam, without water, with a roar that can be heard far away.

It would be a task that approximates the impossible to describe in detail each of the springs found within this basin. The description of one is bound to be very like the description of another, and while one can wander from geyser cone to geyser cone, and gaze upon the awe-inspiring splendors that ascend from these steaming bowls, such description as I can muster might pall in a little time. The beautiful pools of which I spoke some minutes since are found scattered through this basin among the geysers as well as [in] many other parts of the park. The naming of the springs is in most instances very apt. For instance, there is one called Economic Geyser because, strange to relate, not a drop of water that is upward thrown is lost from the well [from] which it is shot, but drops back into the basin from which it springs, an after the eruption is over, sinks away into the earth again.[25]

On the morning of the fifth, we bade our final farewell to Fountain Valley and quickly arrived at the Upper Geyser Basin where we had spent the day before.[26] It was our good fortune as we swept through this basin to see five geysers play at once, Old Faithful, the Bee Hive, the Castle, the Jewel and the Fan;[27] and as I gazed upon their leaping splendors, I bethought me of the time when in Paris many years before I had gone all the way to Versailles for the express purpose of seeing the Versailles fountains play; and while they were magnificent they sink into insignificance when compared with the aqueous wonders of the Yellowstone.

The larger part of the day is consumed by a not very interesting ride to Yellowstone Lake. One of the interesting thoughts that accompanies one on this ride is that one is passing over the continental divide where the head waters of the Columbia, that empties into the Pacific, part company, as it were, with the head waters of the Yellowstone, that after numberless miles of wandering finally find their way into the hoary arms of the Atlantic.

About half way of the journey [at Shoshone Point] one comes upon a magnificent view of the sentinel peaks of the Teton mountains, fifty miles away, towering seven thousand feet higher than where you stand and fourteen thousand feet above the level of the sea.

A little past noon you arrive at what is known as the thumb of Yellowstone Lake. The whole lake is in its outline not unlike the shape of a man's hand, when outspread, and the part which we approached first was called the thumb. Here we encountered another canvas lunch stand, and found here a series of paint pots as beautiful, if not as large as those we found in Fountain Valley. Pink was the prevailing color and the shading as exquisite. Close by the shore of the lake at this point is one of the scalding springs, its urn lying partly within the lake proper. There are doubtless other places in the park where it can be done, but this was the only point where I actually saw fish caught and cooked without the fisherman moving his tracks.[28] The water of the lake so teem[s] with fish that to catch one is a task without labor, and if one stands close by the scalding bowl when doing his angling, he has only to turn and drop his still wriggling catch into the hot water at his side to have it cooked as perfectly as could be done in any pot that ever swung on crane, or that demonstrated the efficiency of the modern gas stove.

Here it was that we were brought to a complete realization of the actuality of the water's heat, for as we drove to the hotel we encountered another vehicle being driven with such care as to excite comment, when inquiry disclosed that its chief occupant was a poor fellow who had some days before fallen into one of the boiling springs in the neighborhood, and so cooked the flesh from his limbs below the knees, that amputation was deemed a necessity and he was being removed to the Mammoth Hot Springs Hotel for better treatment.

Shortly after lunch you encounter the irrepressible Captain [E. C.] Waters, who is owner and manager and pilot of the only steamboat on Lake Yellowstone.

She is a trim little craft, capable of accommodating a couple of hundred, I suppose, and apparently in perfect repair.[29] You are a little startled when you are informed that in order to test her many qualities you have to give up three dollars, but the average man will think as I did, I suppose, that three dollars can be gotten somehow most any time, but

FIGURE 12.1.

Mr. E. C. Waters, owner of the steamboat *Zillah*, walks to his boat in about 1904 at
the dock in front of Lake Hotel. Our traveler John Atwood met the "irrepressible"
Mr. Waters and claimed that the *Zillah* was "a trim little craft. . . . An experience
such as this was not to be missed." (Montana Historical Society, Helena.)

a ride on the second highest body of water in the world is not an everyday possibility.

This is a sheet of water with an area of one hundred and fifty square
miles and lacking about one hundred feet of being eight thousand feet
above the level of the sea. Only one body of water in the world is higher,
and that is Lake Titicaca in South America. An experience such as this
was not to be missed, and giving up a trinity of dollars we sailed away
over a surface nearly eight thousand feet higher than the waters that lap
the base of the Statue of Liberty in New York Harbor; more than seven
thousand feet higher than the great unsalted seas that bear on their
surface the commerce of Chicago, Detroit, and Buffalo; seven thousand
feet higher than the level on which live and move seventy million of
people who proclaim themselves American citizens.

As we sped over the lake surface, a more perfect idea of the topog-
raphy of the whole park was obtained. It could be there seen that on all

sides of the plateau or basin which is embraced in the park limits tower mountain ranges from ten to fourteen thousands feet in height, making indeed a mountain wall that the hardiest could hardly climb. Away to the east as we sailed could be seen the sleeping giant of the Tetons, for clearly outlined against the skies was the upturned face of a sleeping man.[30] Brow and nose and mouth and chin were there, upturned to the clear and flashing sunlight of this upper region. The mountains whose configuration made this face were fifty to one hundred miles away, and yet no sculptor who wielded mallet in the Valley of the Nile, or wrought his wonders beneath the shadow of the Acropolis, ever more perfectly outlined a man's face than has the unnumbered chisels of the rain, driven by the hand of the storm, carved a human face among these far off mountain tops. There the giant of the peaks has slumbered since the days when the earth was young; when Semiramis ruled in Babylon, when Memnon sang to the morning, when Rameses reared aloft his huge towers of stone in the rainless air of Egypt, the silent slumberer of the Yellowstone still lay with face turned to the sky; there he slept when thrones crumbled beneath the blaze of Napoleonic batteries, and when again these thrones were built anew from ruins of the great Corsican's Empire; and there he rested when Lexington and Yorktown gave to us a country which we pray may be permitted to continue until the final day of dissolution shall dissolve the mountains couch upon which this world-old slumberer has lain so long.

The hotel which stands close by the Lake is like that found at the Fountain and at the Mammoth Hot Springs, excellent in every way, and after a pleasant meal we again boarded the steamer for a run to an island where are gathered the animals that are indigenous to the park.[31] There were the mountain sheep, buffalo and antelope, but the most interesting of all to me were the huge bison, being among the last of those vast hordes that used to wander over the prairies of the West. A moonlight sail across the lake, returning to the hotel, was delightful indeed, although the keen mountain air made all our outer wraps exceedingly comfortable.

The next morning found us again aboard our coach, and after a ride of an hour or so we came upon one of the most peculiar features to be found within the Park. It is called a mud geyser or mud volcano. Climbing up the cone twenty-odd feet high, evidently reared by the action of the geyser, we looked down into the conical pit probably thirty feet in depth, at one side of which was a low cavern-like opening.[32] The bottom of the pit was filled with a slate-colored mud of about the consistency of soft mortar, and every minute or so there would rush from the cavern-like opening a gush of steam and hot air that throws the muddy contents of the basin high upon its sides and even on the top. The odors of this sickening mass are far from pleasant, and yet there is a grewsome [sic] fascination about the place similar to that which is said to have characterized the dark tarn of Auber.[33]

Another curious feature of this place is that within a distance of fifty feet is a spring, possessing all the characteristics that mark the mud geyser, except that the waters are as pure as crystal.[34]

Upon leaving the mud geysers we sweep down into Hayden Valley, the largest and most picturesque valley in the Park reservation.

And now we come to the crowning glory of the Park, aye, of the natural world. As we rode down from the mountain top, the Grand Canyon of the Yellowstone opened to our view.

The Grand Cañon of the Yellowstone! The most stupendous sight that was ever mirrored on human retina! At the upper end is the great fall—a mass of foam three hundred and sixty feet high, as white as hammered platinum, while from its foot, like incense before an altar of silver, rises the mist eternally.[35] Down from the falls the cañon opens; a gorge piled with tower and dome and minaret and castellated wall and ragged arch as though it were a world wrought upon by a giant architect gone mad. Here are unnumbered capitals and columns upholding a might mass the whole of a yellow, as golden as the temples of the Incas whose walls and roofs of beaten gold blazed like mighty jewels in the bosom of the Cordilleras; there gleaming garish in the sunlight that just reaches it, is a pile, white as a whited sepulcher; over beyond is a huge red rock, crimson as an Aztec stone of sacrifice reeking with human blood. And the color of the whole! Every tint known to Tit[i]an's palette is there. The river below bounds the bottom of the picture with a framing of ultramarine; black is there and brown; the pinks and the purples, orange and ochre; and gray and blue; and beside it the opalescent gonfalon of the dying day;[36] while above and over all, at the cliff's edge, the solemn pines wave forever the dark green standard of the Prophet. It is as tho, some titan painter had in a rage hurled his colors against the cañon's walls where innumerable fairy fingers had blent hue with hue into infinitude of shading—into a perfected harmony of color that God alone can call

FIGURE 12.2.

Even though our chronicler John Atwood missed this spectacular view from
the canyon's bottom, he still thought the canyon to be the "most stupendous
sight that was ever mirrored on human retina!" This H. C. White stereo view
depicts a look at Lower Falls that was then more commonly experienced than
today. From about 1898 to 1906, both men and women clambered down to
the bottom of the canyon via ropes, ladders, and eventually a stairway. (YELL
9921, Yellowstone National Park Archives, Yellowstone National Park.)

into being. In such a presence all speech seems as sacrilege and silence
the only homage meet and fitting to be offered up in that faultless fane,
built by nature in her grandest mood as an altar to the Infinite.

All this of course was not seen in a moment; the whole of that afternoon and a good part of the following morning was devoted to an

imperfect study of this wonderful spot. Words cannot describe it; paint-ers can never portray it; as the infinite, is beyond the finite mind, so is this perfection of magnitude and beauty beyond the reach of human powers of presentment. Of such a sight "the hunger of the eye grows by feeding."

Our journey was nearly done and a short ride to Norris Basin to receive Larry's benediction and parting word, a little longer ride to the Mammoth Hot Springs with a couple of hours for rehabilitation, and we were again on the road by brawling Gardner River [b]ound for Cinnabar and civilization.

My parting word to you in connection with this subject is, trust no man's description of this wonderful place; go see it for yourself, for when you have imagined the most indescribable thing that lies within the range of your knowledge, multiply that description by a thousand, and you may approximate in your mind in some remote degree that which is beyond reproduction by tongue or pen or pencil, the might and the marvel of the wondrous Yellowstone Park.

Notes

1. *Who Was Who in America* (Chicago: Marquis, 1943), I, 36.
2. John H. Atwood, "Yellowstone Park in 1898" (no place: John H. Atwood, 1918), 4.
3. The name Paradise Valley dates to the 1870s, as it appeared at that time in issues of the *Bozeman Avant Courier* newspaper.
4. This Latin translates as "the descent of Avernus is easy," referring to Avernus, a deep lake near Pozzuoli and an entrance to the underworld. Hence, "it is easy to slip into moral ruin." Tullius probably refers to Marcus Tullius Cicero (106–43 B.C.). The reference to "Beelzebub's toboggan" is really a reference to Devil's Slide, the natural formation just north of the town of Cinnabar, Montana, and which Atwood had just seen.
5. "Six-in-hand" refers to the number of reins the driver held in his hands to control the team of six horses drawing the coach.
6. The birds were probably ospreys.
7. In antiquity, Phrygia was a kingdom in the west-central part of the Anatol-ian Highland, part of modern Turkey. The Phrygian people settled in the area from circa 1200 B.C. and established a kingdom in the eighth century B.C. The Phrygian cap or liberty cap is a soft conical cap with the top pulled forward, worn by the inhabitants. The name Liberty Cap in Yellowstone actually came from the caps worn during the French Revolution.

8. The U.S. Army served in Yellowstone from 1886 until 1918 to protect the wildlife from poachers and to prevent pieces of the geysers and other features from being carried off as souvenirs.

9. The dust on park roads prior to 1901 was indeed terrible. Park tour guide G. L. Henderson noted in 1885 that

> when the season fairly opens in July, and all the freight wagons and heavy Concord coaches are constantly passing over the roads, deep ruts are made by numberless wheels, [and] vast clouds of dust rise and hang suspended in the air when there are no currents; when the wind blows you either ride in your own dust and in that of the carriages behind you, or, if [there is] a head wind, the dust is driven into your face with a force that blinds and maddens you. ("Rapid Transit in the Park," *Livingston (MT) Post*, March 10, 1900, in Ash Scrapbook, 20, Yellowstone National Park Library, Yellowstone National Park.)

Beginning in 1901, road sprinklers traversed park roads.

10. "Hack suit" probably refers to light but sturdy footwear, comparable to our hiking boots.

11. Ulsters are long, loose overcoats made of heavy material. The coats are of Irish origin and first appeared about 1876.

12. Golden Gate Canyon was named from the gold-colored lichens growing on its canyon walls. Lee Whittlesey, *Yellowstone Place Names* (Gardiner, MT: Wonderland Publishing Company, 2006), 118.

13. The story of the park's "glass mountain" (present Obsidian Cliff) was a very early tall tale told by park storytellers. Lee Whittlesey, *Storytelling in Yellowstone: Horse and Buggy Tour Guides* (Albuquerque: University of New Mexico, 2007), 124.

14. Baron Munchausen's name was corrupted from that of Baron Karl Friedrich Hieronymus von Münchhausen, a German officer in the Russian service who died in 1797. Münchhausen tales were tall tales, and they included stories of petrification in early park days. Aubrey L. Haines, *The Yellowstone Story* (1977; rev., Boulder: University of Colorado Press, 1996), I, 53–59.

15. Larry Mathews managed the Norris Lunch Station 1893–1901 and was known for his Irish wit. See Lee Whittlesey, "'I Haven't Time to Kiss Everybody!': Larry Mathews Entertains in Yellowstone, 1887–1904," *Montana the Magazine of Western History* 57 (Summer 2007): 58–73.

16. The Constant Geyser or "Minute Man" indeed erupted twenty feet high during the 1890s at intervals of about a minute. Black Growler Steam Vent remains the most famous of Norris's many steam vents, and it historically thrilled visitors with its ferocious roaring. "Baby geyser" probably referred to present Steamboat Geyser, which had a huge eruption in 1894 that

ripped new craters for the feature. Whittlesey, *Yellowstone Place Names*, 238. John L. Stoddard (*John L. Stoddard's Lectures*, vol. 10 [Boston: Balch Brothers, 1909], 245) shows a photo of this "Baby Geyser" in 1896, and it is indeed Steamboat Geyser.

17. Fountain Geyser was one of the most famous features of the Lower Geyser Basin at this time. In 1898, it erupted about every five hours to heights of around fifty feet. Whittlesey, *Yellowstone Place Names*, 108; Kitty Walker, "Wild Wonderland," *Livingston (MT) Post*, April 20, 1899.

18. F. A. Gooch was a scientist of that day, who with J. Edward Whitfield coauthored "Analyses of Waters of the Yellowstone National Park," *U.S. Geological Survey, Bulletin* 47 (1888).

19. This was today's Fountain Paint Pot, one of the most famous park mud pots.

20. Actually there is some truth to this tale. See Lee Whittlesey, "Music, Song, and Laughter: Yellowstone National Park's Fountain Hotel, 1891–1916," *Montana the Magazine of Western History* 53 (Winter 2003): 34n41.

21. Excelsior Geyser was the largest geyser in the world in its day when "large" is measured by both height and diameter. It erupted three hundred feet high and three hundred feet wide in its heyday years, which were 1881, 1882, 1888, 1890, and probably 1891 and 1901. Lee Whittlesey, "Monarch of All These Mighty Wonders: Tourists and Yellowstone's Excelsior Geyser, 1881–1890," *Montana Magazine of Western History* 40 (Spring 1990): 2–15.

22. Atwood was not the first to compare this thermal beauty with that of the Egyptian queen Cleopatra. By 1898, "Cleopatra's Bowl" (today's Cupid Spring) at Mammoth Hot Springs had already been so called, as well as Cleopatra Terrace. Whittlesey, *Yellowstone Place Names*, 69, 79.

23. In 1898, Old Faithful erupted about every sixty-five to seventy minutes to (as today) heights of 130 feet with durations of 1 ½ to 5 minutes. While never quite as regular as Atwood claimed, it has exhibited good regularity for an inherently irregular natural feature known as a geyser.

24. Actually the Castle spouts to one hundred feet.

25. In 1898, Economic Geyser erupted about every four to twelve minutes to heights of fifteen to twenty feet with durations of one minute. Lee Whittlesey, *Wonderland Nomenclature*, 1988, unpublished manuscript, Yellowstone National Park Library, Yellowstone National Park, Economic Geyser entry.

26. As was typical of this time, they traveled back north for a second night at Fountain Hotel and then went south to Upper Geyser Basin to view the geysers again.

27. There is no way they could have geographically seen these five geysers erupting simultaneously, although they could certainly have seen Old Faithful, Beehive, and Castle together. Thus he probably listed two that were incorrect here (Jewel and Fan), and it is more likely that he saw two others on nearby Geyser Hill, such as Lion Geyser and Giantess Geyser.

28. This was Fishing Cone, a stone-rimmed hot spring surrounded by the cold waters of Yellowstone Lake.

29. This was the steamboat *Zillah*, which was taken to Yellowstone Lake in 1889 and ran on the lake from 1891 to at least 1907. Richard A. Bartlett, *Yellowstone: A Wilderness Besieged* (Tucson: University of Arizona Press, 1985), 191–93.

30. This formation, called the Sleeping Giant, was named as early as 1895. Whittlesey, *Yellowstone Place Names*, 230. According to one source, it is composed of parts of Castor and Pollux peaks.

31. They sailed from Lake Hotel to Dot Island, where E. C. Waters kept animals in pens, in a kind of zoo.

32. This was Mud Volcano. The nearby Mud Geyser was nearly extinct. Whittlesey, *Wonderland Nomenclature*, Mud Geyser and Mud Volcano entries.

33. The reference is from a poem by Edgar Allan Poe (1809–49), "Ulalume," wherein Poe explored the dark, inner workings of the mind on a dark lake. The relevant part of the poem goes thusly:

> The skies they were ashen and sobre;
> The leaves they were crisped and sere;
> The leaves they were withering and sere;
> It was night in the lonesome October
>   Of my most immemorial year;
> It was hard by the dim lake of Auber,
>   In the misty mid region of Weir:
> It was down by the dank tarn of Auber,
>   In the ghoul-haunted woodland of Weir.

34. This was today's Dragon's Mouth Spring, with its noteworthy tonguelike, lashing action.

35. This was Lower Falls of the Yellowstone River, 308 feet high.

36. *Gonfalon* is a word of medieval origin that means "colorful flag."

THIRTEEN

When I Went West

From the Bad Lands to California

ROBERT D. MCGONNIGLE

1900

⸺⁂⸺

ROBERT D. MCGONNIGLE (1851–1912?) BECAME ONE OF THE LEADING citizens of Pittsburgh as someone interested in Pittsburgh's poor and its charitable institutions—those organizations known as "eleemosynary" ones. He served as clerk to the Poor Board in 1880 and manager of Western Pennsylvania Hospital in 1890. By 1899, he worked his way up to secretary of the Guardians of the Poor of Allegheny County and secretary of the State Association of Directors of the Poor and Charities of Pennsylvania. By 1901, he had moved to the business community, working for the Atlantic Tube Company and the Allegheny County Light Company, and he appeared in the 1905 Pittsburgh *Social Directory* as president of the Pittsburgh Hunt Club. He died before May 20, 1912, for an anniversary publication of the Associated Charities of Pittsburgh listed him as deceased at that time.[1]

McGonnigle's trip to Yellowstone occurred in 1900, and he published it in his obscure 1901 book *When I Went West: From the Badlands to California*.[2] His account is noteworthy, because it is one of a select number that we have from visitors who traveled through the park on the horses of Howard Eaton, Yellowstone's most famous wrangler guide, who guided Yellowstone pack trips from 1885 to 1921.

FIGURE 13.1.
Robert D. McGonnigle traveled to Yellowstone in 1900, electing to camp out
with a Howard Eaton horse party. (Robert D. McGonnigle, *When I Went West:
From the Badlands to California* [Pittsburgh: no publisher, 1901], frontispiece.)

XIV.

Into Yellowstone Park.

No sooner had we settled down again among the familiar scenes of the ranch when the roving spirit once more overcame us, and this time we decided to go into Yellowstone Park.

Mr. Howard Eaton promised to act as our guide this time,[3] and once it was settled that we were able to go, it did not take long to complete the preparations. As the Park Reservation does not begin until beyond Gardner [sic—Gardiner, Montana], which is upwards of six hundred miles west of Medora[, North Dakota],[4] it was decided to go that far by rail. We sent our horses ahead of us in charge of Bill Jones, our old cook, with injunctions to this worthy that he was to await our coming at Cinnabar Station. In the meantime we had telegraphed to Edward Staley, a well-known mountain guide from Henry's Lake, Idaho,[5] to make all necessary arrangements for the mess-wagon and a cook.

Our party left Custer Trail Ranch early in August and took the train at Medora a day after we had sent Jones ahead with the horses.[6]

When we arrived at Cinnabar[, Montana,] we found everything awaiting us and all in ship-shape order.[7] This was very satisfactory and put us in a good humor at the very start. There was Ed. Staley, Jim Lee, the cook, as well as the mess-wagon, and at last our old retainer Bill Jones. I asked the latter how he had been getting along while waiting for us, and he replied in his own inimitable way:

"Fine sir; I was drunk twice and had one fight."

A camping trip through the Yellowstone is a pleasure jaunt from beginning to end. In this respect it differs considerable from journey across the prairie. As is well known, the park reservation is under government supervision, and for the most part the going is very good. These trips have become very fashionable of late years, and during the season we were there we constantly met parties the same as ourselves, going from place to place, seeing the sights and camping out in the open air. At most of the attractive sights in the park large tents are erected, where the visitors are enabled to buy something to eat, and as for drinking water, we never had any lack of that during this trip.

We left Cinnabar in the afternoon. Everybody was in the best of spirits and looking forward with the most pleasurable anticipation to the sight of the many marvels and wonders which nature has so lavishly spread out in this region. We rode along without any particular order, except that Mr. Eaton took the lead, the wagon following him, and the rest of us bringing up the rear any way we pleased.

By a peculiar coincidence we experienced another rainstorm not long after we started. This happened at Gard[i]ner, four miles beyond Cinnabar and just at the edge of the Park Reservation. This compelled us to stop here, but as the severity of the storm abated within an hour we continued our journey and went into camp for the night on Gardner river. As a result of the recent storm the river was running up to its banks, and the ground was soaking wet. This dampness, however, did not interfere with us, and we immediately began making preparations for the night. Soon our Chinese cook had a good supper ready for us, and I observed by the energetic manner in which all of us enjoyed our supper that the rain had not impaired our capacity to eat.

In laying out our "tarps" it was amusing how everybody was hunting for a dry spot to sleep, but as it was pretty wet all over, no one succeeded in getting any the best of his neighbor.

The night was beautiful. Millions and millions of stars studded the sky like myriads of twinkling diamonds. We slept well, and the whole camp was ready for breakfast the next morning as soon as the word was given.

We broke camp at seven o'clock and continued our trip along Gardner river, with high mountains on either side of us. On our left, near the beautiful stream, we passed a very high rock, cone-shaped, and called Eagle's Rock, on the top of which a family of eagles had made their home.[8] When we rode by we noticed a young eaglet peeping over the side and looking down upon us with evident astonishment.

Not long after [that] we came to the dividing line [between] Montana and Wyoming, and at an altitude of five thousand six hundred feet we saw the sign post which marked the border of these two states.

XV.

Mammoth Hot Springs And The Golden Gate.

It was a magnificent morning, the air was dry and the weather delightful, and the scenery surrounding us was one kaleidoscope picture of charm and beauty. Traveling under such conditions as I was then was indeed a rare pleasure, and I enjoyed it to the fullest extent.

Presently we arrived at Fort Yellowstone.

This fort is the military headquarters of the park, and a troop of cavalry is stationed there. It is one of the inflexible rules of the park regulations [that] requires all visitors to register their names at headquarters.[9] If you carry firearms you are requested to surrender them, or else the officer in charge seals them, and as there are a number of military posts distributed throughout the park, it is necessary that you report at each one of these posts to show that the seal is still intact.

Fort Yellowstone is located near the Mammoth Hot Springs, and the most famous hotel by that name is not far off. We stayed in this neighborhood for some time. We saw the old extinct geyser [hot spring], called Liberty Cap, and then wandered through the hotel, making some purchases at the store.

The Hot Spring of course was a very interesting sight to us. The water came rushing out hot and steaming, smelling very strongly of sulphur. It is not at all palatable, and almost too hot for bathing purposes, but it has struck me as remarkable that the government has not established a bathhouse here, because it would undoubtedly form a great attraction for almost every tourist.[10]

Leaving this delightful region of the Mammoth Hot Springs we passed Mount Evarts and Bunson Peak [*sic*—Mount Everts and Bunsen Peak], which are 8,600 feet high, and the fact that they were all covered with snow looked very singular to us in the middle of August. We now followed a winding road for several miles and then we found ourselves just within sight of the "Golden Gate."

The Golden Gate is a mountain composed of a formation of rock, which is of a pinkish color, and winding in and out among crags and crevices are various mosses, vines, ferns and cypresses. The whole covers the pink of the rocks in such a manner that looking at it from a distance actually makes it appear like a golden gate. The gap is so narrow and steep that the government has built a causeway through it for the accommodation of the tourist. On one side the rock rises up perpendicularly to a height of fifty feet, while its dimensions at the base are probably twenty feet square.

Going through the gate we found ourselves in an immense open country, rolling like a great meadow land. By this time evening was drawing near, and when we arrived at the "Dairy" we decided to camp there for the night.[11]

From our camp place standing out against the sky we observed the snow-covered summit of Electric Peak, 12,000 feet high. It was probably a distance of twenty-five miles to the peak, but the atmosphere was so clear that to us it seemed like a short walk only.

At the Dairy we found a trout stream, and as we had several disciples of Izaak Walton among our party,[12] they immediately proposed to go a-fishing. Rod, line and bait were soon produced, but whether it was that the trout would not bite or our fisherman were not experts, at all events they did not catch many fish. However, to do them justice, I must say that we all got a taste for supper.

Thus the first day of our trip in the Yellowstone terminated, and I have never experienced a more delightful time than I did then. Our entire tour was replete with marvelous sights and interesting experiences of all descriptions.

We were awake the next morning before sunrise, and we had breakfast almost immediately, so eager were we to be off again. It did not take us long to catch up to our horses. The air was cool and bracing and it seems to fill one with anxiety to be up and about. In the meantime the sun had come out, and as we looked once more at the snow-capped Electric Peak we thought it the most wonderful sight we had ever beheld.

During the morning we continued our route through the rolling country [that] we had entered at the Golden Gate. We passed Swan Lake, Beaver Lake and Twin Lakes. Then we came to the marvelous "Obsidian Cliff," a cliff of natural glass, which stands up perpendicularly before you, shining and sparkling in the sunlight like a crystal structure.

At the natural spring of Apollonaris [sic —Apollinaris] water we stopped for a considerable time,[13] and all of us took several draughts of this wonderful liquid. It was now nearly noon, and we continued our way until we arrived at the Norris Geyser Basin, where we took lunch.

XVI.

The Cheerful "Larry."

When we came near the Norris Geyser Basin, and some of us noticed the large tent, as well as innumerable tables standing beneath it awaiting the coming guests, it was suggested that for the nonce we desert the culinary productions of our Chinese cook.

Most of the party had already heard of the fame of "Larry,"[14] one of the attach[é]s of the Norris Geyser Basin Lunch Counter, who, by his volubility of praise upon the viands and delicacies which are provided here at so much per head, has gained a reputation among the tourists who frequent the Yellowstone Park. None of us, however, has ever been present at one of his performances, and we promised ourselves some amusement. In this we were not disappointed

We were just comfortably sitting down, anxiously looking forward to the lunch which we had already ordered, when another party of guests arrived. While they were dismounting and others alighting from the stages that had brought them, we were suddenly startled by the following:

"Here comes a fine looking lady and gentleman. Bring them a fine bowl of soup, with plenty of roast beef and potatoes and lots of bread and butter."

The man's loud, shrill voice, his way of speaking, his gestures that accompanied all he said, and then the drollness of this manner, were enough to throw even the densest misanthrope into merriment. We laughed till our tears flowed, while Larry continued:

"This is the place where you must work your jaws as well as your tongues!" But our laughter must have attracted his notice, for he now turned around towards our table and shouted:

"Sure, now, you are getting all you want. Don't be in a hurry. Bring on some pie; we have apple, peach, mince and custard. Don't go away hungry. We have more in the kitchen."

In this way he kept on during the entire time we were there, greeting the newcomers and encouraging those who were already the guests of the restaurant. Our party enjoyed Larry's performance very much, and as the meal he had supplied us was also of an excellent quality, we got up in a very good humor.

When we were leaving, Larry came after us and shook hands with every one in the party, wishing us all a pleasant journey.

The Norris Geyser Basin, we found, was located immediately behind the tent where we had our lunch. It seemed to me that what is now called a basin was at one time an immense meadow, probably a mile or two in length. To-day it is alive with hundreds of spouting geysers, some of them shooting voluminous streams of water to a height of fifty feet. While you looked across into that wilderness of geysers you would always find from ten to twenty in operation. The bottom of the basin is covered with a white crystalline formation, which glistens in the rays of the sun like diamonds. We lingered here for a while enjoying the wondrous spectacle, and then we walked over to the right on the side of the road to gaze upon "Old Growler,"[15] which constantly spouts up clouds of steam accompanied by a roar not unlike the noise that is made by a boiler when one of its plates is broken.

In the meantime our party got ready for the continuation of our trip, which presented to us new and wonderful sights at every step we took. Our route lay through Elk Park and towards evening we reached the Gibbon river.

Here we decided to camp for the night, and this was very welcome news to our fishermen, who immediately got out their rod and tackle. Most of them had good luck, for they secured quite a nice mess of fish.

To amuse ourselves a few of us had gone on a tour of exploration before supper, when, to everybody's delight, we discovered an old shed which had been erected over a hot spring. The interior, we observed, had been crudely arranged as a bath-house. Such an invitation for a hot bath was an opportunity we did not want to let escape, and for the first time in our lives we took a bath in a natural spring of hot water.[16]

One of the most interesting sights of that whole day was, however, yet in store for us. This was the sunset. The sun seemed to be resting upon the horizon like an immense ball of fire, from which appeared to be emanating great shafts of light of various colors and shades. We all stood and looked spellbound with wonderment and admiration. I thought then, and I think so yet, that while I have seen many wonders made by the hand of man's ingenuity, the achievements of the Creator are incomparably superior and more wonderful.

CHAPTER THIRTEEN

XVII.

The Paint Pots.

Our departure was considerably delayed the following morning by the falling of a heavy rain. Indeed, the rain made it impossible for us to have our breakfast "al fresco," as had been the custom with us. Instead we had to crawl into the cook's tent, where, on account of the crowded condition, we had breakfast under some difficulties; but the latter were amply compensated for by the amusing pranks and larks the boys were able to indulge in.

About nine o'clock the rain ceased. Then our belongings were packed with the utmost expedition, and by ten o'clock, after our horses had been caught up, we were in marching order. Our route lay through the Gibbon river valley, and soon we passed the Gibbon Falls, which are two hundred feet high.[17] At this point we found the road along the river very narrow and we had to go in single file in passing tourists coming from the opposite direction. Later we reached the spring of natural soda water.[18] Of course we all had a taste of this beverage, and some of us remarked, if we had the necessary acquisitions to brew "Don't Care," a "Vanilla," or some other favorite drug-store concoction, we might imagine ourselves at home.

Our destination for that day was to be the vicinity of the Fountain Hotel, and our way led us presently to the Fire Hole river, [where] we arrived at noon. We rested here for a short time in the reflections of this beautiful stream, which is clear as crystal and cold as ice. It was a charmingly picturesque spot. On each side of us the high mountains of that peculiar pink color which prevail throughout the park rose up like giant walls,[19] covered with a wealth of flowers, ferns and mosses, that made the scene wildly enchanting.

In maintaining our direction towards the Fountain Hotel we continued along the Fire Hole river until five o'clock in the afternoon, when we entered the Lower Geyser Basin, some two miles from the hotel and within sight of the soldier post. At the latter we all registered. We had been induced to make our camp here on account of the attractive surrounding[s], which consisted of a large, magnificent meadow, on which was spread out, as far as the eye could reach, a richly colored floral carpet. Here we laid out our "tarps," and although we did not sleep that night on the proverbial "bed of roses," we certainly rested on

FIGURE 13.2.

Photographer T. W. Ingersoll titled this photo from about 1887 "Packed
Innocence." While 1870s travelers all trekked through Yellowstone
by horse because there were no park roads yet, horse journeys later
became only one option for travel. (Bob Berry collection, Cody, WY.)

a bed of flowers, which was in so far an advantage that there were no
thorns in it.

Near the soldier's camp was a natural hot water spring, and Uncle
Sam's boys, with an eye to "creature comforts" had erected a bath-house
adjacent to this spring,[20] where we again had an opportunity to enjoy
the luxury of a bath. The water of this spring was so hot, however, that
we had to add some cold before we were able to get into it.

We were so much in love with the location of our camp, and in view of the fact that in the neighborhood were so many wonderful sights worth visiting we decided to remain here for several days, making short excursion into the surrounding district.

The next morning when we woke up we were greeted by a wonderfully clear sky, and all indications promised a very pleasant day. We started at about ten o'clock for a ramble on horseback, leaving the camp in charge of the cook.

Nearly all of this day we spent examining and gazing at the many wonderful geysers with spouting springs which were to be found here in all directions.

But one of the most interesting spectacles we saw was that peculiar, natural phenomenon called the Paint Pots.[21] They covered a space of possibly one hundred and fifty square feet. These paint pots are formed of a mass very much like what we know as potter's clay, but it has [a] tinge of pink through it. In some places the clay is hot and steaming, throwing up large bubbles like soap bubbles, which, however, are of the consistency of white paint. These bubbles burst with a loud "pop." The whole surface of the paint pot area shakes and quivers, as if the entire mass were composed of gelatine. A very strong odor of sulphur pervades the surrounding atmosphere, and the amount of heat [that] is also thrown out by these paint pots makes it quite warm around here.

Towards evening we went to the Fountain Hotel for supper, and afterwards we had an opportunity of seeing the Yellowstone Park bears, of whom everyone has heard, coming back to the hotel for their supper.[22] In the meantime the sun had set, for which we were very sorry, because we would very much have liked to take some snapshots of these bears with our cameras.

This had been a busy day for us, and although we had not been away from the camp for any considerable distance, we had nevertheless covered a great deal of territory and we had seen some wonderful sights.

XVIII.

"Old Faithful."

When we awoke the next morning we found frost all about our camp, but by nine o'clock it had disappeared, and we had every promise for another glorious day.

Our program for that day was an expedition into the "Upper Geyser Basin," where we hoped to go into camp that night. Thus we were not going to cover a greater distance than five miles, but we knew there would be enough to interest us along the road to make the time pass quickly. The traveling was not very good here, either, on account of the dusty conditions of the road, as well as the hot August sun.

All along our route we passed one geyser after another, some of more importance than others. There was the "Castle" and the "Giant," neither of which we found in operation.

But when we got to "Old Faithful" we were just in time to see it spout. This geyser, as is well known, goes into operation every hour, and it is in this respect as reliable as a Waterbury watch. Old Faithful is one of the grandest sights in the whole of Yellowstone Park, and it is safe to say that no tourist ever went through the reservation without paying a visit to this famous geyser.

This geyser, perhaps the most celebrated of them all, has a crater, which is formed like an immense chimney, some twenty-feet high, and having a diameter of probably fifteen feet. When it is not in operation one may go close enough to look into this crater, and there you can see the hot water boiling and swirling at the bottom.

The operation of Old Faithful is at its height every hour, when the boiling, seething mass of water is forced up into the air for a distance of one hundred feet. This lasts perhaps for several minutes, and then it begins slowly to recede. Gradually the column of water becomes smaller until it eventually disappears altogether within the brink of the crater. But lower and lower it sinks even then, and when it reaches the very bottom its operation seems to have ceased. This might be called its suspended agitation, which goes on for the duration of a very few minutes, after which it begins slowly to rise again until its operation once more culminates in the column of water one hundred feet high. So it goes all the time, day and night, as promptly and regularly as if its operation were controlled by some invisible force or some marvelously mysterious machinery. Our entire party stood and wondered at the peculiar spectacle, and so fascinating was it that some of us had difficulty to tear themselves away.

The whole valley appears to be dotted with a network of geysers and springs of all sizes, and the whole basin is covered with a formation somewhat similar to salt, the residuum from the spouting craters.[23] Hundreds of tourists are to be seen here during the season all day long, and judging by the multitude around you, it is not difficult to imagine one's self at a circus or a country fair.

XIX.

At Yellowstone Lake.

The next morning we broke camp very early, knowing that we had a long distance ahead of us before we should take another rest.

On our route we passed several of the geysers we had seen the day before, and we also had another glimpse of Old Faithful, which was spouting at its very height, and some of us remarked that the geyser was putting on these particular airs as a token of farewell by which we might always remember it.

We now traveled along Spring Creek,[24] and we came into one of the most beautiful can[y]ons I have ever seen, the ground as well as the mountainous walls being bedecked with a great profusion of wild flowers, mosses and ferns. The water of the creek was cool and clear, and tumbled and slashed along between its banks in the most riotous fashion.

Soon our journey led us through a long, winding, narrow road, and all the time we were going up hill until about noon, when we reached the "Continental Divide," which is marked by a sign post, one side pointing to the Atlantic and the other to the Pacific Ocean. At one side of the post is a small pond, the surface of which is covered with water lilies and other water plants; and so nicely balanced is this small body of water that a fairly strong breeze either from the west or the East will cause it to flow in whichever direction the wind blows.[25] The Continental Divide is located at an altitude of 8,240 feet, and some of us, especially your humble servant, were affected by the lightness of the atmosphere.

Continuing on our way we rode down hill, and the air was so clear that at a turning in the road we were able to look over an immense range of country; indeed, some of us pointed out "The Tetons," a range of the Rocky Mountains, about seventy-five miles in the distance and rising to a height of 12,000 feet. The panorama [that] spread out before us at this point was very impressive. Besides The Tetons, covered with ice and snow and glistening in the sun like sparkling diamonds, we also caught a glimpse of the "Shoshone Lakes," which are situated in the Yellowstone Park, but they are not accessible.[26]

Yellowstone Lake was reached at about five o'clock in the evening, and as the place here looked rather inviting, we decided to go into camp for the night. Not very far from where we stopped we discovered two springs that formed an interesting phenomenon. One of the springs threw out water just warm enough to make it convenient for us to do our dish washing, while the water in the other spring was so hot that eggs could be boiled in it within ten minutes.[27] This, with the beautiful, clear, soft water of the lake, made a peculiar combination.

Yellowstone Lake is about fifteen miles long and is surrounded by a mountainous country.

Looking across from our camp we saw Mt. Sheridan, which is said to be an extinct volcano.

We left camp the next morning to journey around the lake, when we discovered that three of our horses had strayed away, so we had to dispatch a detail of men on the hunt for them.

Our road along the lake took us through dense woods, in which we saw several deer and elk, while on the lake we observed innumerable ducks, swans and geese. In the evening we arrived near the Lake Hotel, and here we determined to stop for several days, because we promised ourselves much fun and entertainment with fishing and excursions into the neighborhood of the lake region.

XX

A Real Hero.

In looking back over our trip through the Yellowstone, where we saw so many wonderful sights and where I had so many pleasant experiences, the memories that seem to linger with me longer than all others are those of the hours we spent of an evening around the camp fire. In very truth let me assure you, my dear friends, there is nothing more delightful to me than living in a camp with a party of jovial and congenial companions; and if any one of you should ever contemplate a trip through the Western countries, join some outfit like ours and make the journey that way. True enough, you will have to undergo some hardships, suffer inconveniences, but the advantages of that mode of traveling are so manifold there really is no comparison.

Danger? Why, there is none worth speaking of. The Indian is docile, and the wild element, which at one time terrorized the traveler through the West, scarcely exists any longer.

Well, as I was saying, the evening around the campfire was a pleasure we all looked forward to day by day, and it was a great disappointment to us when it rained and we had to crawl beneath our "tarps" without indulging in a review of our day's experiences and listen to the stories which were usually contributed by some to the amusement of others.

One of the most delightful evenings around the campfire we had on that night at Yellowstone Lake. On this occasion we had some visitors from among the soldiers who were stationed at the post nearby. We had also some musical instruments amongst us, and the evening passed away very pleasantly with smoking, singing, talking over the events of the day and listening to the musical entertainment provided for us.

Among these soldiers was Sergeant Edward Norlin,[28] who was in charge of the post. This man Norlin impressed me very much, because he looked to me the real soldier; one who said little, but who had it written upon his face that when it came to action he would be right at home.

How true this first impression was which I had formed of Ed Norlin I had occasion to find out the next day.

I happened to be a visitor at the post, when I noticed a photograph hanging upon the wall, representing a number of soldiers, and underneath I read this inscription: "The Carlin Relief Expedition."

Turning towards one of the soldiers standing beside me, I asked him what the photograph meant. Said he: "I don't know much about it, but Ed."—meaning Sergeant Norlin—"was one of the party; ask him."

This very hesitation on his part, however, made me more curious than ever and by dint of a little persuasion he said at last: "Well, it was this way." And then he told me the following story, which I shall try to narrate in his own simple manner:

"About four or five years ago when I was stationed up North, a hunting party under the leadership of a man named Carlin passed out [of the] post. This party was bound for the Bitter Root Region at the extreme headwaters of the Clearwater river in Idaho. It was already late in the season when they came, and they had not left us many weeks when winter set in with all the fury of such a winter as can be experienced only in that part of this country.

"Of course, we men at the post soon began to talk about the long stay they were making, and after awhile we hoped and looked for them every day to return. But we hoped in vain, and then we knew that unless they were rescued pretty quick every one of these men—and there were six of them—must perish.

"Still no sign of them, and then it was that our lieutenant suggested that some one ought to go to their relief. But who should go? It was as much as anybody's life was worth to brave the elements of that region in the middle of winter; in fact, there was not one who did no know that it almost meant certain death.

"However, when the lieutenant asked for volunteers, seven of us jumped to our feet, and we all said that we were ready to follow him whenever he would ask us to go.

"'Now mind me,' said the lieutenant, 'whoever goes on this journey must be ready and willing to do everything I ask him without asking any questions and without any murmur. Upon absolute discipline alone will depend our success.'

"Of course, we all knew that as well as he could tell us, and so we merely bowed our heads, and smiled. Well, the next day we got ready, bundled our 'chuck' together, took our guns, horses, and ammunition and then departed.

"We had calculated that the hunters would come [illegible copy]. We got that far with our horses, although, owing to the lateness of the season, not without much difficulty and trouble. But when we got to the Clearwater we could take our horses no [farther]; in fact, the dangerous part of the trip was only just about to begin. Our commander, who realized this, then said to us: 'Now, men, is your time to speak, if anyone wants to go back. You know what is ahead of you.' But none of us faltered, and we all went on.

"With considerable difficulty, literally groping our path over snow and ice in the bitter cold, we at last reached the edge of the river. But naturally we could not travel along the banks of the stream, because to attempt it was impossible. So we constructed a raft, upon which we put our effects, and then jumping into the ice cold river, we pulled up stream. Oh, but how cold that water was! Ice and snow all around us and the thermometer always below zero. But we got there. Sometimes in the evening when we rested, after having pulled the raft all day, our clothes would be like one mass of ice, and it took quite a while to dry them even after they were thawed out. Well, I do not remember how many days we were going up the river, [but] anyhow we met the Carlin party coming down. The condition they were in I cannot describe. Their clothes, what few they had left, hung around them in rags. They had been feeding on a dog for the last two days; indeed, they were almost at death's door. Their cook they had been obliged to abandon thirty-five miles higher up the river, and his corpse, frozen stiff, was found next spring. It was the happiest moment of my life when we found them, and we came up just in time to save them."

Here Norlin stopped and he did not seem to care to go on with his story. So I said: ":Well, and what did you do then, Ed.?"

"Oh, we brought them out," and that was all I could get him to say. But I learned afterwards that every one of these brave volunteers who went on that expedition was on the "convalescent list" for months after. The brave lieutenant had to resign from the service, because after those hardships his physical condition incapacitated him forever from the life of a soldier.

And these men did all that without any thought for compensation or hope for any reward; simply because they believed it was their duty.

After all, this world cannot be such a bad place when we consider that such men as the Carlin Relief Expedition lived in it.

XXI.

The Grand Cañon And Falls Of The Yellowstone.

The time we spent around Yellowstone Lake was full of interesting sightseeing incidents, and we were all sorry when we went away. But there was still so much in store for us in this wonderful region in the way of fresh marvels that it would never have done to spend too long in one place, and hence we had to wish good-bye to Yellowstone Lake, as well as [to] the genial soldier boys at the "Post," who had done so much to make our stay pleasant for us.

At the lake the weather was quite cold in the mornings and evenings, and when we got up we usually had to brush the frost off our tarps before we put them away.

From the Yellowstone Lake we continued our journey along the left bank of the Yellowstone river, which is the outlet of the lake. Its water is very clear, and until it reaches the "Upper Falls," it is composed of a regular succession of cascades, falls and riffles, over which the water rushes, rumbles and tumbles with a great noise. Presently we turned away from the course of the river to go through the "Hayden Valley," and at three o'clock in the afternoon having reached the Upper Falls, we went into camp some distance above. Here we had a slight fall of snow in the evening. In the month of August this was a remarkable experience, we thought.

I almost forgot to mention that on our road to the Upper Falls we passed the "Mud Geyser," which is a very interesting spectacle. This geyser forms an immense hole in the side of a hill, the diameter at the opening measuring probably sixty feet. It runs back into the hill in an oblique direction and in the shape of a funnel, the bottom having a diameter of not more that twenty-five feet. The entire funnel is constantly filled with steam, which smells very strongly of sulphur. The discharge of the Mud Geyser, as you will have guessed perhaps, is very muddy, dirty water, and it comes out in a large stream, like three or four Pittsburg[h] fire plugs turned into one. While I was wondering at the amount of mud that came out of the side of this hill, I looked around to see how it was carried away, but I failed to discover even a sign of a channel for this purpose. Expressing my surprise at this extraordinary phenomenon to one of our guides, he said that it was carried off by a subterranean outlet.[29]

We had now been in the Park about ten days, and we had seen some of the most marvelous sights that have been produced by nature in this world, and when we were told now that what we had seen so far was no comparison with the wonderful sight of to-morrow, we shook our heads somewhat incredulously, thinking that our guides were merely exaggerating as a matter of business. What they told us we would see was the Grand Cañon and Falls of the Yellowstone, which is said to be the climax, the "pi[é]ce de r[é]sistance" of everything that is interesting and worth seeing in that whole region.

This announcement naturally threw us all into some excitement, and in the evening around the camp fire we asked some of them who had already been there to give us some description of the place. But they all declined to do this.

"You will have to see the Grand Falls and Cañon yourself to appreciate and realize its grandeur and its beauty," they said; and we had to be satisfied. It had been arranged to leave camp at four o'clock in the morning and of course we were astir long before that time.

We rode in a column two abreast, and in the many varieties of our traveling costumes we presented quite a picturesque calvacade [sic]. On our way we heard the noise of the Upper Falls, but we could not see them. So we dismounted and climbed down a narrow path, which ended at a boardwalk, and this led us on to a very large rock where we had a fine view of the falls. Retracing our steps to the road, we remounted and then continued on our journey. Our route wound around and around along the left bank of the river, and in some places it ran quite close to the edge of the precipice, which leads down to the water's bed. There is a narrow path leading down to the brink, but we concluded to take the route passing "Inspiration Point."

When we arrived there we instinctively halted, and [when] we looked around a panorama opened up before our eyes that left us literally speechless with admiration.

"Inspiration Point," on which we stood, forms a plateau 1,400 feet above the Yellowstone river, and from there the traveler has one of the best views of the cañon. You can see up and down the river for miles.

I should very much like to give you a description of the marvelous view that is here spread out before the observer, but such a feat is far beyond me. It would require the pen of Robert Louis Stevenson or the descriptive genius of the Rider Haggard to do justice to the grandeur of the Great Falls Cañon.

I trust, therefore, that you will take the will for the deed if I give you a f[a]int sketch of the matchless scene which was then before me.

If you were to look upon this panorama spread upon a canvas you would see in the far distance the Great Falls, over which the crystal waters of the Yellowstone rush like a silvery stream down into a chasm 365 feet deep.[30] And as that stream strikes the bottom the waters rebound in monstrous clouds of mist and spray, reflecting the rays of the morning sun in myriads of rainbows. But soon the waters flow on, and now the river takes the form of a silver thread, which winds itself in graceful curves through the walls of the cañon.

Like most of the stone formations of the Yellowstone Park, the walls of the cañon are composed of a soft, chalky substance, containing a certain amount of iron, which lends to the rocks the color of a mellow, golden hue.[31] Between these yellow walls you see the flowing river.

But to relieve this golden glare with a tint of green the sides of the cañon present a thick growth of cypress trees, while over and around the tops of many pillars and pinnacles, which seem to have grown out of the mother rock, you see scores of eagles gracefully flying about.[32]

Towards the top of the cañon its walls appear to be hewn out of rough, cyclopean rocks, but f[a]rther down the stone has crumbled, and in many places it rolls to the water's edge soft and smooth, like the ocean's sandy beach.

As we stood there on that August morning and contemplated the magnificent spectacle before us, we were struck with awe and wonderment at the majesty of nature's handiwork.

The immensity of this picture, the marvelous coloring, the roar of the falls and the rushing of the river filled us with rapture, and not a word was spoken above a whisper.

That sight left a deep impression with all of us, and for days it formed the chief theme of our camp fire conversation.

How long we stayed on Inspiration Point I do not now remember, but I recall very distinctly the fact that when we left there on our way to the Cañon Hotel we caught ourselves several times involuntarily looking back to catch once more one last glimpse of that wonderful place.

Notes

1. Percy Frazer Smith, *Notable Men of Pittsburgh and Vicinity* (Pittsburgh: Pittsburgh Print Company, 1901), 188. See also the *Pennsylvania, Indiana County Gazette*, May 20, 1891, and September 9, 1891.
2. Robert D. McGonnigle, *When I Went West: From the Badlands to California* (Pittsburgh: no publisher, 1901).
3. Howard Eaton spent nearly forty years guiding pack trips through Yellowstone National Park, 1885–1921. After he died the main trail system in the park was named for him, the "Howard Eaton Trail." Today the National Park Service has decided no longer to maintain that trail.
4. Medora was the location of Eaton's first ranch.
5. Henry's Lake is located some fifteen miles west of Yellowstone National Park.
6. Custer Trail Ranch appears on the U.S. Geological Survey map of Chimney Butte, North Dakota, and is located near Medora. It was founded by Alden and Willis Eaton in 1882.
7. Cinnabar was the terminus for the Northern Pacific Railroad at Yellowstone National Park from 1883 to 1903. The line was extended to Gardiner in 1903. Only cellar holes, nails, glass, bricks, and pieces of metal mark the Cinnabar site today.
8. Early travelers constantly mistook the ospreys that lived here for eagles, hence the name of the rock.

9. Actually the army registered visitors at entrance stations and at remote soldier stations, so that wax seals could be placed in tourists' guns to prevent hunting.

10. McGonnigle must have missed them, for there were bathhouses on Yellowstone hot springs from 1871 until World War I.

11. The Dairy was located on Swan Lake Flats and was essentially a cattle ranch kept by the Yellowstone Park Association to provide meat and milk for the park hotels. It appeared on a 1904 U.S. Geological Survey map in the Hague *Atlas* (Arnold Hague, *Atlas to Accompany Monograph XXXII on the Geology of the Yellowstone National Park* [Washington, DC: Julius Bien and Co., 1904]).

12. "Disciples of Izaak Walton" was a term then in use for *fishermen*. The name came from Izaak Walton, an English writer born in 1593, who authored *The Compleat Angler*.

13. Apollinaris Spring, located two miles north of Obsidian Cliff, contains magnesium bicarbonate water (carbonated). Lee Whittlesey, *Yellowstone Place Names* (Gardiner, MT: Wonderland Publishing Company, 2006), 37.

14. Larry Mathews became as much a feature of Yellowstone as the geyser basins, with his Irish brogue and dominating sense of humor. He ran Trout Creek (1888–91) and West Thumb (1892) lunch stations before settling at the Norris Lunch Station (1893–1901), after which he moved on to run the Old Faithful Tent Camp (1902–3) and Old Faithful Inn (1904). See, generally, Lee Whittlesey, "'I Haven't Time to Kiss Everybody!': Larry Mathews Entertains in Yellowstone, 1887–1904," *Montana the Magazine of Western History* 57 (Summer 2007): 58–73.

15. "Old Growler" probably referred to Black Growler Steam Vent. Newer, more northerly vents broke out in 1899 and were continuing to break out in 1900. Lee Whittlesey, *Wonderland Nomenclature*, 1988, unpublished manuscript, Yellowstone National Park Library, Yellowstone National Park, Black Growler entry.

16. The location and circumstances of this apparently crude bathhouse are unknown today, but it appears to have been located in Gibbon Geyser Basin, probably near the present Artists' Paint Pots.

17. His enthusiasm appears to have gotten the better of him, for Gibbon Falls is actually eighty-four feet high.

18. Iron Spring in Gibbon Canyon near Secret Valley Creek was long a drinking stop for thirsty stagecoach travelers. It was a carbonated spring, hence his comments about soda fountain drinks. Whittlesey, *Yellowstone Place Names*, 138.

19. The pinkish purple color of Gibbon Canyon is caused by orthoclase feldspar in the rhyolite.

20. The "soldiers' camp" was probably the encampment near Fountain Soldier Station on the north side of Lower Geyser Basin. The hot spring was

probably Hygeia Spring, which had formerly served the Marshall's Hotel (1880–91) near there. Whittlesey, *Yellowstone Place Names*, 133.

21. The "Paint Pots" are today called Fountain Paint Pot. It was named by early observers who thought the mud springs here looked like a vat of bubbling paint, hence the name. Mud springs or "mud pots" are hot springs whose rising gases change the water into a mild acid that then breaks down the surrounding materials into mud. The heat and gasses continue to rise, resulting in a bubbling-mud hot spring.

22. Bears at the Fountain Hotel's garbage dump had become quite well known by this time. Lee Whittlesey, "Music, Song, and Laughter: Yellowstone National Park's Fountain Hotel, 1891–1916," *Montana the Magazine of Western History* 53 (Winter 2003): 29.

23. This material, of which geysers are made, is silicon dioxide, also known as geyserite.

24. Spring Creek runs from Norris Pass westward to the Firehole River. In 1900, the road from Old Faithful to West Thumb led up it.

25. Isa Lake flows to both oceans backward, due to a peculiar "crook" in the Continental Divide's route. The west side of the lake flows to the Atlantic Ocean, while the east side flows to the Pacific. Whittlesey, *Yellowstone Place Names*, 138.

26. There is only one Shoshone Lake. It is the largest lake in the lower forty-eight states that is not reached by a road. It is accessible by hiking. Whittlesey, *Yellowstone Place Names*, 225–26.

27. They were at West Thumb Geyser Basin. The exact two springs that he referred to are unknown.

28. Nothing much is known about Norlin, except that he was in the park at least in 1899 and 1900, per Superintendent to Sgt. Harvey Smith, October 3, 1909, Army Records, Letters Sent, vol. IX (Item 221), 6, Yellowstone National Park Archives, Yellowstone National Park, and in several other letters in that same volume: 12, 14, 46, 280.

29. Mud Geyser was still active in 1900 but ceased operations by 1906. Whittlesey, *Yellowstone Place Names*, 182.

30. This figure of 365 (sometimes 360) feet was commonly used then as the height of Lower Falls, which is known today to be 308 feet high.

31. The chalky material is altered rhyolite rock, while the yellow color is a hydrous oxide of iron called limonite.

32. These were actually lodgepole pine trees and probably ospreys.

FOURTEEN

From New York to Heaven

MYRA EMMONS

1901

⟞⟡⟝

MYRA EMMONS WAS BORN IN WISCONSIN IN JULY 1861 AND became a writer of articles and fiction stories for magazines such as *Harper's Bazaar, Everybody's Magazine, All-Story Magazine*, and *Munsey's*. She also wrote for the *New York Press* and the *New York Sun*. By 1900, the census stated that she was an assistant editor of *Monthly Magazine*. Emmons was interested in the natural world, for following her Yellowstone trip she wrote about naturalist Ernest Thompson Seton for the September 1901 *Ladies Home Journal*. She seems never to have married and was still alive in 1930.

In 1905, she published "The Summer Outing" and in 1911 at least one other article about traveling and camp life,[1] so perhaps her 1901 trip to Yellowstone influenced her to write in that genre.

Forty years old at the time of her trip to the park, Emmons did not fully identify her friend "Gertrude," with whom she made the trip. Like so many before them, she and Gertrude were constrained to silence at the view of the Grand Canyon of the Yellowstone, and at Yellowstone Lake she was moved to quip poetically that the winds whipping across it "bite and thrill like a first kiss."

⟞⟡⟝

"If you can take but one Western trip in your life let it be through the Yellowstone National Park."

Thus [spoke] Louise, who had just returned from an extended tour of the West; so Gertrude and I, who had been undecided where to spend a precious month, set merrily forth to do the great Park, unattended by gallant knight, unguided by masculine wisdom.

Our first pause was at St. Paul, where we stopped to offer greetings to Mr. Chas. S. Fee, of the Northern Pacific, whose road is the only one leading directly to the Park, and to Mr. F. I. Whitney, of the Great Northern, who cheerfully promised to forgive us for not traveling over his line if we would agree to make amends in future.

Our young minds were unhampered by any knowledge of geography[;] Gertrude had but one guiding passion in visiting the West, a fixed determination to see Pike's Peak. In vain her friends explained that she would not pass within a thousand miles of it. She had heard of the clear atmosphere of the West, and she met all their arguments with an unconvinced and injured gaze. Coquina finally appeased her by telling her that if she would keep quiet while crossing the Missouri river she might hear Pike's Peak; and I forgave Coquina first because I was going away for a long vacation, where I could recuperate, and secondly, because his suggestion offered a hope that I should have at least one period of quiet on the journey.

West of the Twin Cities the prairie lies like a beautiful woman[?] laughing up at her sun lover, her golden hair tossed back in the wind, the velvety gauze of her garments streaming close about her in greens and grays, yellows, browns and burnt reds of rapture. Who can find that ride across the prairie tedious has no soul for color. To eyes that see, it is a riot of joy and glory.

The western cowboy is an old story, and we were prepared to accept him as a matter of course, rather than a novelty, but his first appearance was picturesque. When the broken and jagged tumult of the badlands began to greet our eyes we kept watch for Medora[, North Dakota,] in the hope that a premonition of the joy of seeing us might bring Howard Eaton to the train.[2] What to us were the semi-historic ranches of President Roosevelt and the Marquis di Mores compared with a visit from that genial spirit of the badlands![3] As the train drew into the station 3 flying horsemen, in full cowboy regalia, appeared from nowhere, dashed madly across our line of vision, and with joyous whoops wheeled up in front of our car, all unconscious, oh masculine subtlety! of our entranced gaze. What a group they made against the background of red buttes cutting a ragged line across the sky!

"Those are some of Mr. Eaton's cowboys," said the porter.

"Perhaps, they would take your card to Mr. Eaton," suggested Gertrude.

A more helpless and pathetic picture than a cowboy with a lady's visiting card in his hand is impossible to imagine. Subdued, quelled and dejected, he first tried sticking it in[to] his hat. Then, apparently fearing that might be disrespectful he essayed his belt. That seemed equally hopeless, and not knowing enough about his attire to make suggestions, we saved him further embarrassment by returning to our car. We eventually decided he solved the problem by putting the card down his boot. When the train started all recovered their spirits, and gave us a farewell exhibition of horsemanship West Point can never hope to touch.

Two days and a night took us to Livingston[, Montana], where a stop of 20 minutes gave us a chance to take a much needed walk up and down the platform. At the imperious "All aboard," we sprang up with light and airy tread through the train toward our sleeper in the rear. A porter looked at us curiously.

"Weren't you ladies going to the Park?" he asked with something more than friendly interest in his tone.

"Yes."

"Well, this train goes to Portland. Your car for Cinnabar[, Montana,] was switched off here," he explained kindly, as the "North Coast Limited" sped joyously onward. The shriek that rang through that train might have stopped a bigger engine than the one which was rapidly bearing us away from our baggage and our rightful destination.

"Yes, yes, they'll stop it," said the porter soothing meantime regarding us with watchful eyes, that we should not hurl ourselves from the overland flier. Fancy the Empire State Express having a heart from feminine distress! But the long, heavy train of the Northern Pacific was gallantly brought to a standstill and chances were taken on making up the time. We were helped off and for the first time in our lives we walked the ties. Walked? Rather ran, with an occasional flying leap, which I particularly recommended as a novel banting[?] exercise. Not the least of our distress was that the Cinnabar train was already due to leave us, and as we fled over the cinders we waved frantic signals, which we hoped might be seen and heeded.

Fortunately for us, Major E. W. Bach, Secretary of the Yellowstone Park Transportation Company, was on the Cinnabar train, and, we were later to learn, the traveler who comes under the care of the Transportation Company is safe from all anxiety. The Park train waited; and every resident of Livingston was on the platform to enjoy the situation when we arrived. Breathless? Try running a mile at an altitude of 4,000 feet if your habitat is the sea level. During the subsequent short ride from Livingston to Cinnabar, Gertrude and I were objects of curiosity and interest to all our fellow passengers, who invented many and varied excuses for coming to our car to take a look at "those women who held up 2 trains." We could not help discovering after a time that the sightseers were disappointed in us because we did not furnish a fitting climax by dropping dead of heart disease.

At Cinnabar the picturesque and practical are delightfully mingled for the service of the traveler. As the passengers alight from the train the great comfortable yellow stages of the Transportation Company promptly whirl down to the platform to gather them up. The weather-beaten drivers, in their soft slouch hats and dust-colored clothes, look the incarnate history and romance of the wild West. The company has already been advised by the wire of the exact number of passengers for the Park, and has provided ample stage room. There Gertrude and I dropped all care of tickets, luggage, berths, meals and service on to the broad shoulders of the Transportation Company and gave ourselves up to sight seeing and joy.

It would never be possible to forget the emotions aroused by the drive from Cinnabar to Mammoth Hot Springs Hotel, as the warm dusk of the September evening crept up from the valley of the Gardiner river to wrap at last in its purple folds the towering crags above us. Gertrude and I had mentally all but defied the West to give our frazzled New York nerves a thrill. At the foot of the great hills it came to us and left us without words.

That night we had dinner at the Mammoth Hot Springs Hotel. The trip from there through the Park can be made in 5 days. At each important point of interest commodious hotels and lunch stations have been built, and the drives between are easy distances along a line of varying wonders. The hotels and stages are all under the control of one

FIGURE 14.1.
Johnny McPherson was the driver of this stagecoach, year unknown,
on the road between Gardiner, Montana, and Mammoth Hot Springs.
A "six-horse Tally-ho" coach, it was probably similar to the one
in which our chronicler Myra Emmons rode in 1901. (YELL 20172,
Yellowstone National Park Archives, Yellowstone National Park.)

company.[4] As a matter of convenience to himself the traveler pays his bills for the entire trip in advance, and the company does the rest.

The wise voyager will, however, make no such flying visit. We will tarry long at Mammoth Hot Springs, to clamber about the rainbow-hued terraces, to watch the moon rise behind the giant hills, to fall asleep to the sound of taps from the fort and to waken at the call of reveille. He will linger at the Fountain House to make venturesome plays with the bears that come each night and morning to the hotel garbage heap for food.[5] He will refuse for weeks to depart the Upper Geyser Basin, where he can have the pure joy of living in a tent, while at the same time surrounded by the comforts and luxuries of civilization.

He will move not his feet from the Lake House,[6] where the winds that sweep across the silver lake of Yellowstone bite and thrill like a first kiss. He will leave his happy home to take care of itself while he lives among primeval forces at the Grand Canyon until the early snows drive him forth, a rejuvenated, renerved [sic], buoyant, vigorous being, ready to take up anew any battle of life that may come his way.

The perfect care which the Transportation Company takes of travelers is to me one of the wonders of the Park. They leave the tourist nothing to think of but the scenery; and this is enough.

On one point Gertrude and I were agreed and determined; we did not wish to acquire information. We declined to become an understudy for a guide book. It was vain for Major Bach to draw us neat little maps of the Continental Divide, showing where great rivers part to meet no more, flowing each to its own ocean. In vain to tell us there were no more than 4,000 springs and 100 geysers in the 70 square miles of Park, and that the altitude of the Great Divide was over 8,000 feet. Gertrude would turn on her baby stare, before which no living man could confine his mind to cold facts. We were in search of rest, color and thrills. The Park furnishes all; pre-eminently color.

Standing on the great white and red and yellow and brown plateau of Jupiter terrace we had our first sight of the marvelous boiling springs and pools, and drenched our souls in color, which to Gertrude was turquoise, to me green, and which no man knoweth. From that day on we drove through miles of canyons, gorges, forests, mesas; past peaks and cliffs, lakes and streams; past hug[e] crevasses where giants at play when the world was young had piled boulders and crags in mad confusion; up and up; looking down on the tops of great mountains covered with the slim, spear like firs of the Rockies; all a tumult and riot and joy of color. We were drunk with greens and purples, browns, blues, yellows and greys. Sometimes we stopped and guides convoyed us up and over white terraces, past boiling pools of green and gold and blue, past spouting geysers of silver and crystal and rainbows until we were dazed and dumb with wonder and awe. Why try to describe it: Send to Mr. Chas. S. Fee, St. Paul, for a copy of "Wonderland,"[7] which gives facts and figures and views.

Mr. [Harry] Child, President of the Transportation Company, kindly turned on a full moon in our honor, to crown the wonder of the scenes. He also turned on the Giantess, one of the hugest of the great geysers, which travelers do not always see in action, as the lady only disports herself at intervals of 14 days. We were specially conducted up on to the terraces which surround her and sat there several hours while the moon came up dimly over a mountain behind a veil of mist, and shed a ghostly light on the weird white wra[i]th of roaring water, steam and spray. When the eruption subsided we were led to the edge of the pit and allowed to look down into the ghastly hell where with many roars, bellows, snorts, groans and shrieks the Giantess was churning up water and steam for another demonstration of her unspeakable rage. Gertrude looked around at me over her shoulder with large, apprehensive eyes and said, impressively,

"I'm going to reform."

Someone with a graceful and artistic imagination has had the naming of the geysers, pools, springs and other objects of interest in the Park; as witness Turquoise, Morning Glory, Emerald, Topaz and Electric pools, Rainbow lake, Chrome spring, Orange and Lone Star geysers, Angel terrace, Cleopatra terrace, etc. Picturesque also is the suggestive infernal nomenclature, Hell's Half Acre, the Devil's Ink Pot, the Devil's Frying Pan, his Thumb, his Elbow and other royal appurtenances.[8]

One name I resent. It is Old Faithful; which, by the way is always referred to as "she," while many of the other geysers are mentioned as "it." This sex distinction is unquestionably made because of the constancy of the great geyser; but is the lady wise to be so timely and reliable in her displays of her beauty: Not so. She has received in return only a contemptuous name and she is given far less attention than she really deserves, because she is always there. "Oh, we can go to see Old Faithful any time; she plays every 70 minutes," is the oft-heard comment of guide and tourist. "Let us look at something else first."

Ladies, is the moral clear?

One more memorable day Gertrude and I were granted the privilege much coveted by Park travelers, of sitting beside the driver of the coach. He was introduced to us as Doc Wilson, and we stared at him with respectful awe. He looked as gentle as a *debutant*, but to us he represented a dark and mysterious, perhaps a "bluggy" [buggy?—peculiar] past. We were in doubt how to address him, not daring to venture the familiar "Doc" indulged by his acquaintances, and fearing he might resent with firearms the effete "Mister" of the East. After a hurried secret consultation we decided to skate over the difficulty as lightly as

FIGURE 14.2

A rare lithograph of Giantess Geyser conveys a sense of the enormity of its eruption as mentioned by our traveler Myra Emmons in 1901. This image was numbered 98 in a series called the Dayton (Ohio) Spice Mills Company View Cards used as an advertising promotion for Jersey Coffee. (Lee Whittlesey collection.)

possible, to say "Mr. Wilson" if necessary, and to rely on our youth and innocence to protect us from his possible wrath.

The traveler who sits beside the driver is also perched on the insecure and perilous horns of dilemma. He may ask questions and be guyed in reply, or he may sit silent and discreet. The wise tourist does the former. He has to stand the derisive jesting which the drivers feel it their privilege to bestow, with sarcastic smiles at "all them fool tenderfoot questions"; but he saves himself from being disliked. There is nothing a Park driver resents more than he does the tourist who by failure to exhibit his own imbecility deprives the driver of his rightful joy of guying.[9] Besides, the inquisitive one gains rich and varied Western lore; as witness the story told us by Doc Wilson of the 2 road agents who held up a stage load of government officers; of the driver who robbed his own stage, which was carrying many thousands of dollars of government money but no passengers; and of the 2 desperados, who, one black winter night, compelled 8 vigilantes, out in search of a horse thief, to throw up their hands.

The only wild animals we were so fortunate as to see in the Park were bears and chipmunks, though Gertrude assured me she caught a glimpse of a cottonwood rabbit, and kept an anxious lookout for a side-hill gouger,[10] one of the guides having fired her imagination by his description of the same. Everyone knows the Yellowstone Park grizzlies, and there are said to be about 50,000 elk and many deer in the Park, but with unappreciated modesty they kept behind the range. Spring and early summer are, of course, the best times to see the wild animals, and to get in close touch with them one should spend many weeks in the Park, making headquarters at one of the comfortable hotels and taking short side excursions into the hills.

All other wonders of the Park but lead up to the Grand canyon and falls of the Yellowstone river. We reached them the afternoon of the fourth day, with thick heartbeats of anticipation. There was nothing to say. People do not talk much, looking down on the walls of eternity and the waters that leap from the Throne. We had wanted emotion. The only one of which I was conscious was a wish that my mother might stand beside me just then. What faithless friends are adjectives! We had juggled them all our lives, and they deserted us. A shirt-waist girl said, "Isn't it pretty!" Gertrude and I looked at each other in despair and tacitly admitted that one word would serve as well as another. "She hath done what she could," murmured Gertrude; which relieved the strain on my feelings.

It was a silent party that walked slowly back to the carriages, but in each memory was burned a picture of color and wonder and glory, never to be shared with another unless he also can say, "I, John, saw these things."

Notes

This piece originally appeared as Myra Emmons, "From New York to Heaven," *Recreation* 15 (December 1901): 431–34.

1. Myra Emmons, "The Summer Outing," *The Designer*, June 1905.
2. Howard Eaton spent nearly forty years guiding pack trips through Yellowstone National Park, 1885–1921. After he died the main trail system in the park was named for him, the "Howard Eaton Trail." Today the National Park Service has decided no longer to maintain that trail. Eugene Lee Silliman, "As Kind and Generous a Host as Ever Lived: Howard Eaton and the Birth of Western Dude Ranching," *American West* 16 (July–August 1979): 18–22.
3. She probably referred here to Antoine Amedee Marie Vincent Amat Manca de Vallombrosa, the Marquis de Mores (1858–96), a swashbuckling, wealthy Frenchman who tried to establish a cattle empire in North Dakota in 1883. When that dream failed, he returned to France and entered politics, only to be murdered in Africa a few years later. See http://en.wikipedia.org/wiki/Marquis_de_Mores.
4. While the hotels were indeed under one company, stages were not. There were four different in-park stage companies in 1901 along with numerous independent stage operators.
5. Fountain Hotel was located in the Lower Geyser Basin and operated from 1891 to 1916. Lee H. Whittlesey, "Music, Song, and Laughter: Yellowstone National Park's Fountain Hotel, 1891–1916," *Montana the Magazine of Western History* 53 (Winter 2003): 22–35.
6. The "Lake House" referred to the Lake Hotel, which opened in 1891 and is still in operation today as the park's oldest operating hotel. Barbara H. Dittl and Joanne Mallman, "Plain to Fancy: The Lake Hotel, 1889–1929," *Montana the Magazine of Western History* 34 (Spring 1984): 32–45.
7. *Wonderland* was a publication produced by the Northern Pacific Railroad to promote Yellowstone's wonders and the railroad. It appeared yearly, 1883–1906. During 1905–19, a descendant publication was called *Land of Geysers*. Titles varied from *Indianland and Wonderland* to *Wonderland '97*.
8. *Appurtenances* is a real estate term that refers to anything attached to land.
9. *Guying* meant "kidding" at that time.
10. This is a fearsome imaginary creature.

FIFTEEN

Yellowstone Park

A Land of Enchantment
That Even Caucasian Savages Cannot Spoil

C. M. SKINNER

1901

———∞———

CHARLES MONTGOMERY SKINNER (1852–1907) WAS AN AMERICAN
writer born in Victor, New York, who was serving as editor of the
Brooklyn Daily Eagle at the time of his trip to Yellowstone. The author of
many books, he was particularly interested in myths and legends, and
so he produced *Myths and Legends of Our Own Land* (1896) and several
other myth works, books that went into many subsequent editions. One
writer has noted that Skinner "hoped to combine folklore conventions
with New England transcendentalism to keep alive American traditions
endangered by the industrial age." His writings were wide ranging. To
improve the urban environment, he authored a guide to gardening and
urban beautification. He commented on turn-of-the century America's
turbulent economy in *Workers and the Trusts and American Communes*,
on natural history in *With Feet to the Earth*, and on Walt Whitman in
Atlantic Monthly (November 1903).[1]

Skinner is today known for a "really bad prediction," namely, that
"teeth will disappear in about 75 years from now, because the food of
the future will be concentrated and made directly from chemicals so
that there will be no strain on the digestion or gums."[2] Like others of
his day, Skinner lamented the lack of wildness that seemed to be left in
the American West of 1901. But in Yellowstone, he found "the air so full

FIGURE 15.1.

Charles Skinner's newspaper article in the *Brooklyn Daily Eagle* about his 1901 Yellowstone trip is representative of early-twentieth-century newspaper travel and tourism layouts, with striking images cascading diagonally across the page. (*Brooklyn Daily Eagle*, June 30, 1901.)

of life that you leap and shout like a child." "Let us thank heaven and Congress every day," he enthused, "that this region was set aside for the common American people, and all others, instead of being turned over to speculators and adventurers who could put fences around the geysers and charge a half dollar to climb the terraces of the Mammoth Hot Springs."

Looking over the railroad books that they get up nowadays with their pictures of hotels and fine roads and stages and [the] rest of the outfit, I wonder if there is anything of wildness left in the West. The fisherman has whipped the streams till it seems as if a fish would be an odd fish indeed, unless he were cooked. The gunner has been over the plains and the hills, killing everything in sight—buffaloes, Indians, deer, antelope, cranes, mosquitos—no, not the mosquitos, but most other things—and the trees have been chopped off and the rivers dried thereby, and poor old Fleas-in-his Ear and Kicks-on-his-Back loiter about the station that is nearest to the reservation and hope to be invited.[3]

It is as it was twenty years ago that I best like to think of the West, for there was newness and variety and adventure in it. I know persons who are ordinarily truthful and who say just the same thing, only I remember that they kicked and growled like sinners at the time because the boy wouldn't bring up the hot water for shaving, because there wasn't any boy, nor any water, nor any way to shave. And one man who now gloats over the way the Rocky Mountains looked never speaks of how they felt when he had to sleep on the hard side of them. He would get up with dents in his head and his back and his legs and groan no end and say that he liked that kind of thing first rate, only he wished he could go home nights. That was on a trip three of us were making after leaving our team in the Yellowstone, which had not then got its railroad nor its hotels and we were tramping across country attired in our summer clothes,[4] with the temperature dropping below freezing at night and only a blanket to roll up in and nothing to eat but baked beans—Jiminy! Weren't we tired of them!—and not a spoon or fork or a knife or a cup or a plate or a kettle in the company; nothing but appetites.

They tell me it is different now and to look at the photographs and the railroad guides I should say it was. There is the stretch of road, for example, going into the park. No such road could be found in all the West at that time. We had to dismount when we went through with our wagon, and lift trees out of the way in order to get on. There was one place, I remember, where the road dipped into a canyon and ran along the bed of the river; that is, the bed of the river was the only road.[5] But it was worth all the discomfort, and more, to see the show and to hear the picturesque Objurgations of our friend Toot, who was in charge of the party, and who got his name because he was so sober, sometimes. That chap's capacity for liquor would have made a Kentucky colonel wild with envy; yet, so long as he said he wouldn't feel any effect from it, he wouldn't. A quart or so of a cool morning just kept him warm, that was all. He could always drive and fry fish and catch them and shoot and make a camp and toss flapjacks and tell Indian stories and swear. Valuable man, Toot. If he hasn't taken to drinking water, I warrant he is still rustling out in Montana.[6] He allowed it was beginning to look a little serious around there, however; little too civilized; so he may have gone to the Klondike.

Ah, but it's a wonderful land, [Yellowstone is,] with its snow peaks, its canyon, colored like the sunset; its burning geysers, its seething ponds, its mud volcanoes, its blow holes for steam that smells so like Long Island City, its vast reaches of forest, dark, tangled, lonely, mystic: its rushing rivers, its great lakes, its resounding falls, its white deserts and its fantastic sculpture in the cliffs. Steal out of camp at night and be alone with a geyser, when it shoots at the stars, or ramble along the gorge of the Yellowstone at sunset, when the low red light paints with additional depth of color the resplendent rim of that ravine, and you know a new impression, a new awe. True, the canyon is a little one, as compared with that terrific rent in the earth through which pours the Colorado, yet if it is the first canyon ever seen it will leave its memory with the spectator for the rest of his life, even though he should have chance to go to the moon and explore the depths of Tycho and Aristarchus.[7]

The Yellowstone country is a reversal of common experience. Water flows up into the air, springs are hot instead of cold, rocks so slenderly balance on their pedestals that you half expect to see the long dead buffalo hanging in the air about them,[8] exemplifying the truth of the old frontiersman's remark that here "the laws o' nature are petrified." So there can't be any gravitation. Let us thank heaven and Congress every day that this region was set aside for the common American people, and all others, instead of being turned over to speculators and adventurers who could put fences around the geysers and charge a half dollar to climb the terraces of the Mammoth Hot Springs. Ranching, mining, timbering, manufactures and the real estate business are forbidden, though there are many tourists, even among those who consciously seek the picturesque and beautiful, who see the dollars in a neglected water power before they see the beauty in it. Campers who neglect to put their fires out, and so destroy hundreds of acres of ancient forest, are dreaded by the authorities and their fellow citizens, and so are those curious people who cannot see anything of interest without trying to break a piece from it, whether it be the Venus de Milo or President McKinley's head. These vandals go about with hammers and try to pound the geyser cones to pieces, and hew off stalactites from the front of the spring terraces, and they would do it, too, if it were not for the United States cavalry that has been detailed to keep just such people out of mischief. The efficiency of the soldiers has led government to consider the advisability of placing a lot more of them in places where the savages who collect chunks of stone are wont to depredate, as, among the tombstones of national cemeteries, the collections in museums, the sculptures in the Washington Monument, and the Tammany conventions.

Maps of this country printed before the fifties mark this region as "Colter's Hell,"[9] because Colter, of the Lewis and Clark expedition, went through it on his way home to St. Louis, and when he got to that town he told such tales of wonder as had never been recited, even by the most experienced drinkers. He was set down as a shocking liar, and St. Louis apologized for him, but somehow his name attached to the place and would not be forgotten. In 1863 a company of prospectors wandered into it and startled [the] government into an official investigation.[10] Thomas Moran, the painter, who went with the survey presently made his report in the shape of the picture of Yellowstone Canyon, that hangs in the capitol in Washington,[11] and folks said, "Go to! It is impossible. There is no such place. It is theatrical and overwrought." But curiosity regarding what could inspire so fantastic an improvisation led not a few to explore the district, and presently Congress had a superintendent in there protecting the geysers, and men came from England to criticize the landscape.[12]

The weird and prankish scenery of the Bad Lands is a fit prelude to the bigger wonders of the Yellowstone, and if one has the time he should certainly get off at Little Missouri and go up to the Burning Mountain and see the rattlesnakes basking in the heat that ripples up from the pit of darkness. Don't play with them. They lack a sense of humor, and misinterpret your kindness when you would pat them on the head with a rock. From the buttes you will see a purple and crimson and tawny desolation such as you have never seen before unless it may be in your dreams. "Hell with the fires out," is what the cowboys used to call it. Since the missionaries have been out there I suppose they are not allowed to call it [that] now.

The heights that guard the Yellowstone rise from 8,000 to 11,000 feet above the sea and one of the first of them to attract your attention [as you arrive from the north] is Cinnabar Mountain, a red brown mass with a band of red rock running from top to foot, as smooth as if planed, and edged with basaltic ridges. Legend hath it that the Divvle [devil] slid down the mountain at this point, and the copious animal heat in his system scorched it all the way down.[13] I like these names and legends. They show that the vigor has not run out of the Saxon speech nor the Saxon imagination. There are lots of places out in the Western country that have vigorous names, and if any man attempts to pull them down he should be shot with hot buns on the spot. Hell-Roaring Creek, one of our camping places, is to be named Daisy Rivulet, is it? Hell's Half Acre, where the world's biggest geyser plays and rips up the banks and floods the Firehole for a day, is to be named Lavinia's Washbowl, is it? Devil's Thumb is to be Angelina's Thimble, is it? Stinking Water is to be Mignonette River, is it? Devil's Inkstand is to be Sarah's Spring, is it? Well, not if there's any lynch law left on the farther side of the Missouri. Let the first tenderfoot, with eye glasses and a cotton umbrella and a mutton chin and limp whiskers and a pasteboard hat and a tin collar, that tries to substitute some sissiety feebleness for the good old hell and devil names be promptly tied over the mouth of Carnation geyser—known before his arrival as the Damnation Geyser—and allowed to lie there till he sees what happens.[14]

Instead of weakening the names, a lot of them want toning up. Mammoth Hot Springs is an explanatory title, but it doesn't signify, does it? Call them Jupiter's Throne. [That is] If Jupiter didn't mind sitting in a damp place, or the Hill of Opals, or the Baths of the Titans, or something with meat in it. Most of the geysers have names that you can stand: Giant, Giantess, Beehive, Castle, Grotto, Lion, Lioness, Sawmill, Fan, Turban, Old Faithful, Splendid, and the springs and blowholes are

PHOTOGRAPHED BY T. W. INGERSOLL, ST. PAUL, MINN.

1121.B. DEVILS THUMB AND HOTELS.

YELLOWSTONE NATIONAL PARK.--NEW SERIES.

FIGURE 15.2.

Our traveler Charles Skinner saw the Devil's Thumb, an extinct hot
spring formation at Mammoth Hot Springs that is shown here in a
post 1888 photo by T. W. Ingersoll. (Bob Berry collection, Cody, WY.)

not all bad, either; as witness the Paint Pots, Wash Tub, Black Boiler,
Blue Glass, Brown Sponge, Dishpan, Frill, Hell Pot, Iron Pot, Devil's
Kitchen, Kidney, Little Joker, Locomotive, Perpetual Spouter, Soap
Kettle, Steamboat, Thud and Velvet.

You have to go around among these places with caution, unless
you know your ground. When you hear the crust crack and feel your

heels suddenly growing hot and the panting and groaning of hell sound louder below and around, you almost instinctively go somewhere else—some quieter, cooler, dryer place, where you can think a different set of thoughts. You never know where you are going to be steamed. Vapor, so heated that it is invisible, gushes out at you from a crack in a rock, and peels your knuckles in an instant. They say, of course, that water boils at a lower temperature the higher you get, and some prevaricators have told me that it was impossible to get even warm coffee, because it would boil, up in the mountains, at 90 degrees in the shade. When we heard that yarn we used to sigh and turn away, regretfully, from what should have been the breakfast table, but which was a space of grass, for it meant that breakfast wasn't ready. If you wanted anything hot to drink there was plenty of it, though. Indeed, there were many places where the only drink was hot. It puckered your nose and your innards when you bent over the steaming, sulphurous pools of the Mammoth Hot Springs, but it was [drink] that or a jaunt away down to the bottom of the valley [to the river]. Strange to say, the after taste of the [hot spring] water, instead of being nauseous, was bland and not unlike that of fresh milk. Good place to go swimming, too, only it happened to our party that just as we got out of the water a blizzard came ripping over the snow covered mountains, and the way we danced over the cactus when we came out must have been a pleasant spectacle to any onlookers.[15] There weren't any onlookers. Probably there would be now. From that time I have never danced bare footed in a cactus patch. It isn't right.

The waters of some of the hot springs are so charged with lime and silica and sulphur that they will coat a dish or a bottle with a mineral crust in a week—nearly an eighth of an inch. I found a snake skin cemented into one of the mounds, although they say that reptiles are not found in the park, and one of the members of the survey found a mass of grasshoppers fastened into the crust. Here and there are trees that have been overflowed and killed by the hot water, and half buried in the mineral—gaunt, bleached skeletons, they are, with branches that seem to writhe out of the killing clutch of the stone, appealing to be unburied.

Over against the principal group of hot springs is Mount Everts, named for the man who was lost up there and wandered for thirty-seven days before he was rescued. During this time his food was a frozen bird, a gull's wing, a few minnows, a grasshopper and some thistle roots. He had been frozen, and scalded, and treed by wild beast[s], and had come close to death before he was found wandering wildly over the desert talking to his legs and his stomach, which to his shattered mind had taken human form and were imploring him to stop and rest. The animals that treed him were probably mountain lions, and they would not have hurt him, at least, if he had kicked them real hard.[16] So they say, anyhow. Not having lost any lions, myself, I had no occasion to hunt them up, but their remarks at midnight when the moon was rising across the waste of mountains and lighting their snows were not the sort of lullaby to make you drowsy. You think at first it is the squall of a petulant child, but you know there are no houses within miles and miles, and no children anywhere within telegraphing distance, and then you detect something feral in the yell. So, too, you may hear on a still afternoon the booming voice of an elk down in the hollows, and the cries of the eagles that swing on the winds up and down the canyon give the last touch of sublimity to that spot.[17]

Of course you have heard of the glass cliffs that had to be cracked by fires in order to build a road along their feet.[18] It isn't quite the same as bottle glass. Obsidian is a volcanic product, and more nearly resembles slag from a foundry. It is brown and black, and the Indians used it for spear and arrow heads, though a green variety can be cut into a respectable gem. In Mexico you find, to this day, knives of obsidian that are supposed to have been used for carving up the human sacrifices and they had razors made of it likewise. Just imagine the depredations of a barber armed with a glass chip! The Indians did not get much of their glass in the Yellowstone. That country was "Bad medicine."[19] And you may fancy the effect on the mind of a superstitious savage, who personifies the forces of nature, as the Greeks did, when he came in sight and hearing of the geysers and was confronted with boiling fountains in stretches of whitened, deathly desert, and when he heard the roar and sizzle of "frying pans" and the hiss of solfatari.[20] The earth in the neighborhood of the geysers is covered with gritty nodules of ash, and has spots that are not so thick but that you can hear the rumble and gurgle of the flood below. Many paint pots are here: springs that contain mud [that] has been stewing for centuries, and no longer contain a particle of sand. On rubbing this mud over your fingers the feeling is like that of the finest flour. Pots only a few feet apart have contents that are entirely different in color, and you see white, gray, brown, red, yellow, and slate blue, within an acre. They spatter their contents about the margins and great, slimy bubbles break at the surface, exhaling steam and odors that are not of sanctity. Beautiful crystals of sulfur flower about the mouths of the steam vents, and the hot springs of clear water lie in beds of red, green and blue—stains made by metal salts and oxides. The color of the waters, themselves is exquisite. Nowhere else in the world are deeper, purer, more wonderful greens and blues than in the throats of these springs. You look into them as into a deeper sky of underworld, for hours, without tiring. A deeper sky? Ah, but the sky itself is deeper than any you see here in the East. You are thousands of feet above ocean level, and by so much, nearer to space, which begins to suggest itself in the darker blue overhead. In this pure, thin air the stars blaze at night like lamps, and as you lie in your blanket looking up at them and listen to the distant pour of waters and the lulling symphony of winds sounding through the forest you are far away from men in spirit, and no less in fact.

It was the proper thing to swim in the Firehole River, and may be yet, though if stages are rattling to and fro along the banks I suppose you will need bathing suits, and a bath in a suit is only half a bath. At the debouch of the boiling brook from Hell's Half Acre the water of the Firehole is uncomfortably hot,[21] but you can go down stream a little way and find it just about the right temperature. From tepid it is only a step to cold, in midstream it is frigid, and from there you come to shore with a howl and a covering of gooseflesh. The time you never swim at this point is when Hell's Half Acre is blowing.[22] Its eruptions are announced in bellowings to be heard for miles, and an outpour of steam to be seen in Montana.

Grand Prismatic Spring, a hot lake nearby, has shores rimmed with mineral colors, and is a sapphire set in rainbows. In a direct sunlight you see the colors reflected on the under side of the steam clouds drifting over it: blue, green, orange, red, brown, crimson, purple, white and yellow; so that the steam seems iridescent. These springs have no eruptions, but seethe and flow steadily, whereas the geysers have their times of explosions, from once a minute to once in a couple of years. The smaller [the geyser is,] the oftener [it erupts].[23] Like some tempers. The flow in these geysers varies from a few gallons to the contents of a subterranean lake. The heavy column of water in the stone tube is lifted off when the lower end of it, resting on rocks intensely heated by the interior fires of the earth, is converted into steam which must escape, and, as it can no longer escape fast enough in bubbles, it blows off the whole mass lying upon it. The shooting of Old Faithful, which deserves its name, is one of the spectacles you never need wait for, but take a little more time and see one of the colossi break out. The Grand [Geyser] is one of them. It has torn its cones to pieces—those deposits of mineral from the water that held it in solution,[24] and [it] emerges from a well about four feet by two, and of any depth you like to imagine.

This well is fretted by gray, pearly opal, in coral-like masses, and steam lazily drifts from it during its quiescent hours. At last there are agitations, the steam increases, there are subterranean rumblings, hissings, thunders; the water is swashing angrily in the throat; it begins to spatter; the water is tossed out by bucketfuls; the earth shakes, and now, with a crash and a roar, the white column climbs into the air, not in a rocket-like shoot, but with a slow, majestic ascent that is more powerful, till it reaches the height of 150 feet, and hangs there for a minute, snowy, dazzling in the morning sun, giving off clouds that sweep and whirl skyward a quarter of a mile before they return in rain. Soon the column sinks and plays feebly; then it gathers strength and rises again. I saw eleven successive eruptions on the first morning in the Geyser Basin, while the Beehive, which had been one of the constants, omitted its display for two days. After playing for ten minutes or so, the Grand ends its eruption in a rush of steam, the water drains hoarsely down its tube, and the warm brook made by its outpour seeks the Firehole.

They still tell about the tenderfoot who boiled his clothes in one of the geysers. It shot them out at the appointed time, but they were in smithereens, and were distributed all over the place. [It] Served him right. Yet you have no idea how soon you recover from the awe inspired by the first view of a geyser blast. The geysers are born, have their periods of activity, then die, their apertures closed by the deposit of mineral from the water itself, so that they build their own gravestones, and the cones which vary in size from plums to plumbers' bills (patented), become gaunt monuments, like the Devil's Thumb. While the water of the geysers is as pure as air, that in some of the hot springs is coated with a leathery slime which has been compared to hides in tanners' vats,[25] and is held to be of inorganic origin, as it ought to be, forsooth, since it does not seem possible that any substance holding life should endure such commotion and heat. That mineral does assume most delicate forms we see at the rims of the Mammoth Hot Springs, where the sinter has been deposited in tufts as suggestive of fairy work as the frost on the panes.

The Yellowstone is a good place for "lungers," or consumptives.[26] They have commanding and beautiful scenery, quiet, occupation for their minds, which is a good deal, as Christian Scientists ought to tell you, and especially they have the altitude that insures bright sunshine, clear weather and an air that is not only dry and bracing, but is thin, and that means you need more of it than you do of the air on the coast; so you fill your lungs to the uttermost corner, opening disused parts of them, working off dead tissues, cicatrizing old wounds and oxygenating your blood.[27] At the ocean level we use possibly half of our lungs, but among the Rockies we fill them at every breath. Snow cooled, pine scented, unstained by smoke and gas, there is no finer air than that of our great mountain belt.

Of Yellowstone Lake, a vast sheet of beryl, ringed about with white topped mountains, of its beaches of agate and glass, of the Alpine Tetons, ghostly in ice, thrilling in height, of the grassy, flower strewn parks, of the bears and skunks, of the beautiful minerals to be gathered on the hillsides, there is not room to speak, but whatever else one misses he should not allow himself to leave the park before he has seen the grand canyon of the Yellowstone. We have no such depth and distance here as in the gorge of the Colorado, no such reach along the river, for the Colorado is walled for 200 miles and more; but we have ten miles of the most vivid color, the most startling architecture, the most fearsome declivity and we have a cataract which we miss in the Colorado gorge, for the plunge of the Yellowstone at the beginning of the canyon is twice the height of Niagara.

When, having traversed the vale of mist above that leap, you suddenly reach the end of things, a fear comes on you. Nobody speaks. I was alone when I came to it, and for some moments my impulse was to rush back to the camp, for company. It was as if some new part of the universe had suddenly unfolded itself; as if for the first time, to a man theretofore blind, a sight of the stars had been given. As in all places, the dominant sense is that of human powerlessness. At our feet rolls a flood of green water, the green of beryl shading into emerald, it reaches a straight shelf, rolls smoothly over, and like a huge inverted rocket, smashes itself into a million starts of spray on the rocks more than 300 feet below. Yet that is only a slight descent, for as we look outward a fearful gulf yawns before us, roaring with the echo of the fall, with spray clouds surging through it. This chasm is over a thousand feet in depth, [and] its sloping walls are yellow and studded with crags that lift themselves in semblance of ruined castles, monuments and cathedral towers. Eagles nest upon their tops. Matted woods line the edge of the canyon, and as the river unrolls it dwindles to a green ribbon, streaked with white and seeming to be slightly shaken. The color effect is overwhelming. Ochre is the prevailing tint, but the spires and turrets, which have resisted the avalanches, are red, gray, dull purple and brown of every shade, while there are spots and streaks of snow white, scarlet, sulfur yellow and crimson, and at one point I found a delicate rose. Along the rim of the water is a green of moss as rich as malachite, fed by the spray. The colors of October woods, of summer fields, of frozen streams, streak the sides of a chasm so profound that imagination does not realize its depth even while you bend shuddering over the brink. Its sublimity does not come till after hours of gazing. Yet we measure—on paper—the distances of the stars! Brooks that spray into the depths are lost in as fine a vapor as the Staubbach,[28] and as you walk along the canyon's rim you see, on turning backward, the Great Fall, focus of the view, hung like a green curtain against the yellow precipice, the river streaming outward from a chaos of rock and foam at its foot, far mountains in the background, and all about a pathless wilderness of wood.

No spectacle in the world mere[ly] puzzles, fascinates and entices the beholder. Its brightness stuns in sunlight. As evening shadows gather, its mystery almost appals. More and more its influence grows. The spectator tears himself from it by an effort, or he does not tear himself at all, but sinks on its rim and lets the mighty picture work into his imagination and ingrain itself into his being. It is the sphinx mouth of the eternal hills, opened to deliver a message, and he falls, unconsciously, to watching and listening for the immortal secret.

Yet, perhaps the finer experience is that of watching the night at snow line on Mount Washburn, cut off from human kind, knowing that in the 10,000 square miles of wilderness, lying dim to your sight below, there is not one eye of man that sees the twinkle of your fire, away up there at the sky's edge. Above, below, around [is] silence, though now and again a sound arises that you know to be the roar of the wind in the pines. The sky is your only tent, and never has it seemed so magnificently jeweled, nor has it been so spanned and webbed by meteors. Boreas is mustering his forces in the north,[29] and as his Titan armies pass his shining spears irradiate the heaven. Now the snow fields, just above, begin to shine with pallid phosphorescence, a blue light is growing in the east, the stars in that quarter are less brilliant; [and] then the moon wheels up, its disk of gold outlining the goblin shapes of the Hoodoo Mountains. The fire flickers and dies; the chill is biting; still you are wrapped in the contemplation of the skies. Light rolls from pole to pole; the wind and cataracts begin to speak in human voices; the planets swing nearer to the earth, and their choiring falls through space. Louder and deeper comes the song of the worlds. Its tones arouse you.

Rising with a shiver, you find that you have slept and the world is aflame with the glory of a new day, the air so full of life that you leap and shout like a child. The world is young again and you seem to have lived none but an Arcadian life,[30] yet so old that you have lived in it for centuries.

C. M. SKINNER

Notes

The piece originally appeared in the *Brooklyn Daily Eagle*, June 30, 1901, Sunday edition.

1. *Who Was Who in America* (Chicago: Marquis, 1943), I, 1131.
2. *Brooklyn Daily Eagle*, December 30, 1900.
3. These names are negative insults, made-up epithets for Indians who loitered in train stations. The references are typical of the racism that permeated white America in Skinner's day, but at least Skinner felt sorry for them.
4. Apparently this writer made an earlier trip to Yellowstone, sometime before 1883.
5. He was probably remembering the road through Gibbon Canyon, which, before 1885, required wagons to travel *in* the Gibbon River for the stretch between Beryl Spring and Lone Tree Rock.
6. *Rustling* here means having wild, active adventures, and the term was commonly used in late-nineteenth-century America.
7. Tycho Brahe was a Danish nobleman, well known as an astronomer/ astrologer. A crater on the moon was named after him. Aristarchus (310–ca. 230 B.C.) was a Greek astronomer and mathematician, born in Samos. A bright crater on the Moon was named after him.
8. The reference here to rocks balanced on pedestals is probably to Duck Rock in the Gibbon Cascades, which was also known as "Balance Rocks," "Pivot Rock," "Volcanic Mushroom," and "Wineglass Boulder" in the early days.

9. This incorrect reference ("Colter's Hell" actually did not refer to Yellowstone) is a mistake that continues to plague Yellowstone historians today, often in the shallowly researched columns of journalists. See Merrill D. Mattes, "Behind the Legend of Colter's Hell: The Early Exploration of the Yellowstone National Park," *Mississippi Valley Historical Review* 36 (September 1949): 251–82. According to Mattes and to Jim Bridger's 1851 map, the term "Colter's Hell" actually referred to hot springs at the forks of the Shoshone River, east of the park.

10. This probably refers to the Walter W. De Lacy expedition that explored for gold in the park in August and September 1863. De Lacy compiled the first reasonably accurate map of the park, but he did not publish his findings until 1876 and so failed to receive credit for his discoveries. DeLacy Creek was named for him. Lee Whittlesey, *Yellowstone Place Names* (Gardiner, MT: Wonderland Publishing Company, 2006), 83.

11. Moran accompanied the F. V. Hayden expedition of 1871 that was funded by the U.S. Geological and Geographical Survey of the Territories. He completed his massive painting in 1872, and Congress purchased it for $10,000. Jack E. Haynes, *Haynes Guide Yellowstone National Park* (Bozeman: Haynes Studios, 1966), 133–34.

12. The reference could be to any of a number of travelers from Great Britain—from the Earl of Dunraven to Rudyard Kipling—who criticized Yellowstone in their accounts.

13. See the poem that was so repeated in early Yellowstone days by stage drivers: William Tod Helmuth, *Yellowstone Park and How It Was Named* (Helena: C. B. Lebkicher, n.d. [1893–99]), in Rare Box 15, Yellowstone National Park Library, Yellowstone National Park. This is discussed in Lee Whittlesey, *Storytelling in Yellowstone: Horse and Buggy Tour Guides* (Albuquerque: University of New Mexico, 2007), 253.

14. This quote has been touted by Whittlesey (*Yellowstone Place Names*, 13–14) as an example of the fact that not everyone agreed with geologist Arnold Hague's propensity to get rid of place-names in Yellowstone that contained "Devil" or "Hell" or anything negative in them.

15. Apparently he referred here to the Boiling River, on Gardner River below Mammoth Hot Springs, where cactus grows in the arid climate.

16. For this story of Everts's adventure, see Lee H. Whittlesey, ed., *Lost in the Yellowstone: Truman Everts's Thirty-seven Days of Peril* (Salt Lake City: University of Utah Press, 1995).

17. So-called eagles were probably ospreys.

18. He referred here to Superintendent P. W. Norris's construction of the stage road past Obsidian Cliff in 1878. Aubrey L. Haines, *The Yellowstone Story* (1977; rev., Boulder: University of Colorado Press, 1996), I, 237.

19. He was incorrect here. The old misnomer that Indians feared Yellowstone has long been in disrepute. See Peter Nabokov and Larry Loendorf, *Restoring*

a Presence: American Indians and Yellowstone National Park (Norman: University of Oklahoma Press, 2004), 274–81.

20. "Solfatari" is from *solfatara*, a type of fumarole, the gases of which are characteristically sulfurous.

21. By "Hell's Half Acre" he referred to Midway Geyser Basin.

22. Here, by "Hell's Half Acre" he referred to Excelsior Geyser.

23. Or so it seemed to this observer, although his statement is not always true. See generally, T. Scott Bryan, *The Geysers of Yellowstone* (Boulder: University Press of Colorado, 2008).

24. This was not correct. Grand Geyser never had a cone. Instead it is a "fountain-type" geyser, one of those that erupts from a pool rather than a cone.

25. See, for example, Leather Pool in Whittlesey, *Yellowstone Place Names*, 150–51.

26. This referred to persons with tuberculosis, as *consumption* was the old term for that disease.

27. *Cicatrizing* means healing a wound by forming a skin over it.

28. Staubbach Falls is a waterfall in Switzerland, located just above Lauter-brunnen in the Bernese Oberland. The waterfall drops about three hundred meters (one thousand feet) from a hanging valley that ends in overhanging cliffs above the Lütschine River.

29. In mythology, Boreas was the North Wind, son of Astræus and Aurora.

30. In mythology, Arcadia was a delightful country in the center of Peloponnesus and a favorite place of the gods.

SIXTEEN

Touring the Yellowstone on Horseback

An Unusual and Delightful Method
of Seeing the Wonders of the National Park

THE REV. CORNELIUS H. PATTON, D.D.

1902

THE REV. CORNELIUS HOWARD PATTON (1860–1939) WAS FORTY-ONE years old during the summer of 1902 when he traveled through Yellowstone as a "sagebrusher." Sagebrushers were the first "campers-out" in the national park, and they received that name in the 1870s, because they camped with their own wagons and horses in the sagebrush flats next to park roads. Although Patton's title called this camping method "unusual," it was unusual only in that most visitors arrived by train and patronized the in-park stagecoach companies while staying in park hotels. But there were hundreds of campers like him each year as well.

Born in Chicago, Cornelius Patton migrated to Massachusetts early and ultimately became a Congregationalist minister in Boston, probably being influenced early by the fact that he was born on Christmas day. He received an A.B. from Amherst, a B.D. from Yale, and D.D. degrees from Amherst and Williams College. He was author of at least thirteen books, mostly on religious subjects, but two others were *The Lure of Africa* and *Eight O'clock Chapel: A Study of New England College Life in the Eighties* (1896). He traveled all over the world and was well enough known in his day to later earn a place in *Who Was Who in America*.[1]

Many clergymen generally love religious and other kinds of music, and Patton was no exception. His paternal uncle, Ludlow Patton, was the business manager and a singing member of the well-known Hutchinson Family Singers, who became nationally famous in the mid–nineteenth century as a traveling singing troupe. Ludlow's wife was Abby Hutchinson Patton, another Hutchinson singer. The Hutchinsons "were famous for singing in remarkably close harmony," wrote a modern biographer, "and they were infamous for using their talent and fame to promote causes, such as antislavery, woman suffrage, temperance, and the Lincoln presidential campaign" at a time when these causes were disliked by many. Young Cornelius Patton became close to his Uncle Ludlow and Aunt Abby, and as a result he was greatly influenced through his life by both the music and the many important friends of the singing Hutchinson family—persons such as Susan B. Anthony, Phineas T. Barnum, Horace Greeley, and Frederick Douglass and earlier Charles Dickens and even Abraham Lincoln.

Cornelius Patton's marriage to Pauline Whittlesey of Maine in 1889 brought still more music into his life. She too was in the clergy, graduating from Yale Divinity School in 1886. Members of her family had earlier owned the "Music Vale Seminary" in Salem, Connecticut, the first school in the United States dedicated to the subject of music and a place that had influenced the singing Hutchinsons who so affected her husband's life.[2]

The Reverend Patton may have chosen the sagebrusher way to tour Yellowstone rather than riding the park's commercial stagecoaches so that he could get closer to the land and thus become absorbed in nature's "music." His account here was originally published in the *Congregationalist and Christian World* of July 4, 1903, and was illustrated with his own original photographs.

It was highly amusing to find ourselves greeted by the stage-coach tourists as "hay-seeds."[3] Your ordinary tourist is a very superior person. The people of the region ("natives"), the hotel and transportation officials, and especially fellow travelers who elect some more modest way of seeing things, he regards with undisguised amusement. They are part of the scenery and phenomena to be studied. He enters all they say and do and look [at] in his notebook. Sometimes he makes mistakes; and sometimes the condescension and amusement are on the other side. I know of a colored cook in a White Mountain hotel, who was wiping her sweating brow at the kitchen window when she caught sight of a golfing party climbing a hill to "tee off" for the "home green." As she turned to her kettles and her pots, she remarked to one of her helpers, "I do feel really sorry for these city folks who haven't anything to amuse themselves with, and so have to chase those little balls all over the mountains."

To me the most beneficial thing connected with the Yellowstone Reservation is that it is invaded every summer by thousands of humble folk on the backs of work-horses, in prairie schooners, in closed wagons and all sorts of fantastic rigs—people from the farms, ranches and mines of Montana, Wyoming, and even as far off as southern Colorado. With these people it [the trip] is the event of a lifetime. They leave no one at home, apparently. Parents, grandparents, babies, dogs and all go along. I talked with one mother, carrying a four-week old baby and riding all day on the front seat; and both parties, apparently, were well satisfied with the bargain.

The Government has made excellent provisions for these campers, and I am inclined to think they get more good out of the trip than the swell-folks who make ludicrous remarks about them, as they roll by in the fine coaches of the transportation company. As I said, we were lumped in with them, and took the "howdy's" and "Say, look at these chaps," with considerable regularity and no end of amusement. The fact is, we felt rather superior on our own part; and not for a moment would have changed places with the tender-footed, linen-dustered, blue-goggled crowd in the coaches.[4]

At the same time I want to be just with these superior travelers. I confess there was some reason from their humble estimate of our persons. We carried more things on a horse than was ever dreamed of before; and they stuck out in front, and behind, and on both sides in a rather ridiculous manner. There were the pummel-slickers, of course, and the tether ropes and hobbles.[5] No going without these cowboy accompaniments. But then we had also geological bags, with hammers, and usually a gunnysack dangling from the pummel for extra rocks. Both of us carried cameras with dry plates, field glasses, lunch bags and sundry other articles more useful than ornamental. Then there was the professor's hat! I don't blame any inference that may have been drawn

YELLOWSTONE NATIONAL PARK VIEWS.

FIGURE 16.1.

The Rev. Cornelius Patton chose horse packing through the park
in 1902 as his way to see Yellowstone. Here a T. W. Ingersoll photo
from before 1885 illustrates this mode of travel that incorporated
the use of "pack ponies." (Bob Berry collection, Cody, WY.)

from that hat. And finally the dust, O, the dust! Especially in the more
frequented sections of the park, settling down over everything and
making one look like a refugee from the slopes of Pelee.[6]

We were on a six weeks' trip, in a quasi governmental capacity, collecting minerals for the United States engineer's office, photographing

and sight-seeing all at the same time; and we had to carry a good deal of paraphernalia out of the usual. We went in for dry plates and geological hammers, more than for collars and cuffs. As for tents, blankets, extra clothing, etc., these went ahead in wagons to the Government camps,[7] which were our usual stopping places. The beauty of the arrangement was that we were independent of everybody and almost everything, except of own convenience. If the professor wanted to examine a ledge of rock a thousand feet above the road, he could toss the reins over his horse's head, and the well trained animal would stand for hours. In the meantime, I could capture the finest views in the vicinity, or watch the little conies run in and out with their everlasting hide and seek in the rocks.[8] If a man is going to take pictures successfully, he must often wait for the proper time of day, and the most favorable cloud effects. To attempt to photograph the Yellowstone on a five days' stage trip must be more exasperating than pleasurable. Think of being ordered into your seat at the Upper Basin when you feel morally certain that Grand Geyser will begin to play within ten minutes! Good Christians have been known to use emphatic language at such times. If one expects to photograph and also remain in good and regular standing according to Congregational usage, he would better make the trip on horseback or in a private conveyance.[9]

Naturally one's chief interest is in the geysers; and I recall a sensation of actual excitement when waiting for our first geyser to perform, which happened to be the Lone Star.[10] We reversed the usual order through the geyser region, and almost stumbled upon this solitary spouter in the heart of the great pine forest. The performance was not up to standard, but served as an excellent appetizer for the big fellows farther on. Having set apart a week for the geysers, we saw nearly all of the famous ones in eruption, except the Giant. In vain we waited for this sleeping monster to arouse himself. Nothing rewarded our patience but the fierce boiling of the column of water in the broken crater, and the delightful sense of expectation and uncertainty pervading all those days in the basin.[11]

There may be 200 people at the Upper Basin on a given day when four or five of the big geysers are due to perform. As the geysers do not always run on schedule time, the crowd scatters over the mile and a half of the outlying white silic[e]ous formation, peering into empty craters, listening to the deep rumblings far down in subterranean caverns, studying the remarkable colorings of the quiet pools, and all waiting for something to happen. Suddenly the shout arises on the air and is passed from mouth to mouth, "There goes Castle!" Instantly lines of tourists converge at that point, in coaches, on horseback, on foot. In their haste many of them step into hot pools, some even wade the Firehole River—anything to get to the Castle before it stops. When they arrive it proves to be a false alarm, only a premonitory spurt. So the crowd settles down to wait in strained expectancy, swapping camera gossip and stories about "Larrie," the genial host at the big hotel.[12] But alas for the man who cannot wait! It seems cruel to come so far and miss a sight like the Castle in full play. And the same may be said of The Lion, the Great Fountain, and a dozen others.[13] Fortunately Old Faithful never fails to reward the hurried tourist with his hourly exhibition, equaled by few, if any, in the world. To be both great [tall in height] and frequent is to attain the highest distinction in geyserdom.

To us the formations about the geysers were quite as interesting as the geysers themselves. The soft pinks and grays of the silica deposited by the water, the oddly shaped walls of the pools with their nodules and scallops, together with the lace-like delicacy of the pool bottoms, fascinated us beyond all expression. Next to studying these formations, I would advise the observing tourist to examine minutely the quiet hot pools, which abound on every side. It is not enough to look down into their sapphire depths and admire the strange colorings of their brims. It takes a detailed study to reveal the exquisite beauties of these pools. It was an astonishment to find what a large part in these formations is played by vegetable life. Evidently the algae are responsible for the rock building processes fully as much as are the chemicals held in solution by the heated water. The wonderful coloring, too, of the sides of these pools, is due to these same forms of low plant life.[14] When I think of the whole region I find myself saying "O, for another look at Sapphire Pool!"[15]

The larger part of our trip was devoted to the remote sections of the park, seldom visited by tourists, together with the outlying forest reserve.[16] A week was spent in the region of Mount Washburn and Yancey's, points which are being connected by a fine Government road.[17] Eventually the tourist will return over the top of Mount Washburn, which has been called the observatory of the park. At present the route is lacking in mountain scenery, the ride scarcely varying 500 feet in elevation in a single day; but with Mount Washburn and the Yancey region added to the trip, there will be no lack of such variety.

We spent two Sundays in a Government road camp at the base of Mt. Washburn, and had a good chance to get acquainted with the men, from Mr. Kelly, the boss, a fine type of overseer, to the herder who cared for the forty or more horses at night. They were a rough set, as might be supposed, and horribly profane. But on the whole, they were kind-hearted and courteous. When I told them they swore worse than any men I had ever met, they replied, "O, you ought to hear the fellows cuss who work in the railroad camps. We are not in it along-side of them." This was after a [church] service we had held around the camp-fire on Sunday night, and which resulted in our getting quite close to the men. One of them was taken sick, and on the supposition that ministers know everything, Mr. Kelly, who was greatly worried over the case, asked me to prescribe some remedy. The fellow evidently had a case of malaria, and was horribly homesick at the same time. He was greatly impressed by the row of pill boxes and bottles that I laid upon the blanket, and I think began to mend from that moment. At any rate the case yielded readily to quinine and some good cheer; and in a day or two he was sitting up and asking what kind of minister I was. When I said Congregational, he remarked, "Well, I don't hear much about your kind out this way, but I know that on East you are something way up." The professor said, when I announced the man's recovery, "This is *bona fide* case of divine healing."

One night we had an entertainment. The professor talked about the geology of the region, and questions were fired at him from every side; and about half of the men wanted to show him specimens of supposed valuable ore. Then with the help of two of the surveyors we made up a quartet for some college songs. The Wild Man of Borneo [the professor] seemed particularly to catch the fancy of the crowd.[18] So much so, that a week later when we returned, as soon as our horses' heads appeared over the ridge, a shout went up from the gang at supper, "O, the wild man of Borneo has just come to town." Strange to say, the best behaved, most industrious, and altogether [most] reliable among the common working men at the camp were a group of a dozen Mormons. We inferred from this that any religion is better than no religion at all. The idea occurred to us that our Home Missionary Society might well employ a few general missionaries to work in just such places. There were several such camps in the park, employing fully 500 men. Capt. H. M. Chittenden, the United States engineer in charge, is a Christian man and a Congregationalist, and would undoubtedly co-operate in having religious work carried on. Many a minister would welcome the opportunity to work in these camps for the sake of the outing it would afford him.[19]

We spent some delightful days in the extreme northeast corner of the park, examining the fossil forests (which [are] somewhat disappointing and withal inaccessible except for hardy climbers), studying the beavers [that] abound at Soda Butte and fishing on one of the forks of the Yellowstone River. The trout in the park are abundant, but quite lacking in gaminess. It is hardly worth while to carry a rod on the trip, the guide-books to the contrary, notwithstanding. It is more sport to catch a half-pound trout in the Adirondacks or in the Maine woods, than a two-pound trout in the Yellowstone.[20]

Four days were spent in the heart of the Absaroka Mountains, to the east of Yellowstone Lake. The Government is building at great cost a road 100 miles long up [to] the park from the east.[21] It is a wild country, the peaks rising to 12,000 feet, snow-capped, with heavily wooded valleys abounding in large game. Old trappers['] trails run through the passes and connect the park proper with the forest reserve. O, the joy of picking one's way on horseback along these trails! Of course, one will get lost at times, or at least slightly mixed; but the general course of things is plain and the instinct of these Rocky Mountain horses sure. Between the two, one can count upon getting back to camp at night, and always with a rousing appetite for beans and bacon.

We saved three days for the great Yellowstone Cañon and Falls; and were not a whit disappointed, even though we had read the rhetorical descriptions of the guide-books and had listened to the enthusiastic exclamations of tourists. The Yellowstone Falls are the most beautiful single object I have seen in nature. But the tourist should certainly take an extra day here, and spend it with the old guide connected with the Wiley [sic—Wylie] camp, who alone is allowed to ferry parties across the river above the falls, and to conduct them into the chasm on the farther side.[22] Take that side trip, and it will be a red-letter day in your life.

In this connection it is interesting to recall the fact that in 1879 Henry Drummond spent a Sunday hereabouts concerning which he makes this significant entry in his journal, "Sabbath, 7th- Remained encamped all day, spent the day wandering around the cañon . . . the N.T."[23]

We parted, the professor to visit Jackson Hole and the Grand Teton Mountains, seventy five miles to the south, immortalized now by the thrilling descriptions in *The Virginian*,[24] I to return East. It was a hard trip in some ways, but never have I taken one more rewarding. Happy is the man who can visit this wonderland of America, and thrice happy he who can visit it leisurely on the back of a good horse!

Notes

1. *Who Was Who in America* (Chicago: Marquis, 1943), I, 944. See also "Rev. Dr. C. H. Patton, Minister, Author" (obituary), *New York Times*, August 18, 1939.
2. Alan Lewis, *Heralds of Freedom: The Hutchinson Family Singers*, chap. 21, pt. 1, available at www.geocities.com/unclesamsfarm/hutchinsons.htm; John Wallace Hutchinson, *Story of the Hutchinsons* (1896), available at www.geocities.com/hfsbook/storytofc.htm. See also Dale Cockrell, ed., *Excelsior: Journals of the Hutchinson Family Singers, 1842–1846* (Stuyvesant, NY: Pendragon Press, 1989). Patton's connection to the Whittlesey family, including the senior author of this book, is discussed in Charles Barney Whittlesey, *Genealogy of the Whittlesey-Whittelsey Family* (New York: Whittlesey House, McGraw-Hill Book Company, Inc., 1941), under #2080 Pauline Whittlesey and #969 Eliphalet Whittlesey.
3. "Hay-seeds" was a commonly used term for "country folks," who were sometimes looked down upon by "more sophisticated" city people. Patton was a Doctor of Divinity—well educated and thus probably not a "hayseed."
4. This phrase referred to often inexperienced rich people who wore sunglasses and linen dusters issued by the park stagecoach company to protect their good clothing from dust.
5. "Pummel-slickers" probably referred to heavy rain ponchos used to prevent being "pummeled" by rain or snow. Tether ropes were simply extra ropes with which to tie various items onto packhorses. Hobbles resembled handcuffs and were tied around horses' front hooves at night to prevent them from running away.
6. Mount Pelée on the West Indies island of Martinique is a volcano famous for its May 8, 1902, eruption that killed twenty-nine thousand people and destroyed the city of St. Pierre. As volcanoes often do, it covered many survivors with dust. See this volume, chap. 12, n. 9, for a reference to early Yellowstone's dusty roads.
7. "Government camps" referred to U.S. Army Engineers' "road camps" where road workers were housed all over the park in tents. Patton's party had apparently received special permission to stay at these camps. "Dry plates" were emulsion-coated photographic glass plates for making

negatives, which could be purchased already coated and used dry, as opposed to the earlier wet plate negatives that had to be coated on the spot and then exposed and developed while still wet. "Geological hammers" were small hammers that geologists use to chip off rock specimens—legal then but illegal now in Yellowstone.

8. Unfortunately we do not know the name of this geologist who accompanied Patton and whom he refers to as the "professor." *Conies* refers to pikas or "rock rabbits"—small members of the rabbit family that live around rock slides.

9. Here Patton expressed happiness that he was not one of the regular park stagecoach company passengers, who often did not have enough time in the geyser basin to watch the geysers because stagecoach drivers were on a tight schedule and often would "order them back into their seats" to move on.

10. Lone Star Geyser, located south of the Old Faithful area, required a separate round trip of five miles away from the main road in order to see it. It was not one of the usual attractions on the stage tour, so visitors on park stagecoaches could not usually see it.

11. Giant Geyser, then as now, was a much hoped-for sight. In early park days, it erupted every seven to fourteen days to heights of 200 to 250 feet and lasted for more than an hour. Lee Whittlesey, *Yellowstone Place Names* (Gardiner, MT: Wonderland Publishing Company, 2006), 113.

12. Larry Mathews, formerly of Norris Lunch Station, had moved to Old Faithful to run the tent camp there beginning in 1902. His personality made him nearly as much a park attraction as the geysers. Patton's mention here of the "big hotel" is quite puzzling, because Old Faithful Inn did not come under construction until June 1903. Perhaps Patton merely heard that the hotel was soon to be built. Mathews became its first manager in 1904 but was managing the predecessor tent camp in 1902 and 1903. See generally, Lee Whittlesey, "'I Haven't Time to Kiss Everybody!': Larry Mathews Entertains in Yellowstone, 1887–1904," *Montana the Magazine of Western History* 57 (Summer 2007): 58–73.

13. Lion and Castle geysers are located in the Old Faithful area, but Great Fountain Geyser is located farther north in Lower Geyser Basin.

14. The colorful life in the hot springs was then thought to be primitive plants called algae, but today they are known to be bacteria. These bacteria play no role in the deposition of geyserite formations.

15. The deep blue color of Sapphire Pool, located west of Old Faithful Geyser at Biscuit Basin, made it then as now one of the most beautiful of the quiet hot springs.

16. "Forest reserve" was used to refer to what became the national forests that surround Yellowstone. For example, the Shoshone National Forest, established in 1891, was then known as the "Yellowstone Timberland Reserve."

17. The "fine Government road" was completed in 1905 and opened over Mount Washburn to John Yancey's hotel (1884–1903 in present Pleasant Valley), just in time for John Yancey's heirs to abandon the hotel. John Yancey was still running the hotel in 1902, when Patton heard of it, but Yancey died in 1903. Aubrey L. Haines, *The Yellowstone Story* (1977; repr., Boulder: University of Colorado Press, 1996), II, 242; Kenneth H. Baldwin, *Enchanted Enclosure: The Army Engineers and Yellowstone National Park* (Washington, DC: Government Printing Office, 1976), 109.

18. Apparently, the "wild man of Borneo" was the road workers' name for the geologist.

19. Hiram Martin Chittenden was head of the U.S. Army Engineers, the park road builders, for two tours of duty: 1891–93 and 1900–1906. Baldwin, *Enchanted Enclosure*, 95–111; Haines, *The Yellowstone Story*, II, chap. 17. Had Patton's idea come to fruition, any preacher would no doubt have faced a challenge in ministering to Yellowstone's hardened road workers.

20. Patton appears to have completely "missed the boat" in his assessment of Yellowstone fishing, as it has become one of the most famous trout fisheries on earth. See, generally, John D. Varley and Paul Schullery, *Yellowstone Fishes: Ecology, History, and Angling in the Park* (Mechanicsburg, PA: Stackpole Books, 1998).

21. Hiram M. Chittenden began building the park's east entrance road in 1901 to connect to the newly built Chicago, Burlington, and Quincy Railroad that arrived in Cody, Wyoming, that year. The road opened on July 10, 1903. Baldwin, *Enchanted Enclosure*, 104–6; Haines, *The Yellowstone Story*, II, 244.

22. Patton's "old guide" was H. F. "Uncle Tom" Richardson, who boated tourists across the Yellowstone River here 1898–1902 and took them down into the canyon below Lower Falls before the Melan Arch bridge was completed in 1903. The presence of Uncle Tom here and the apparent lack of a bridge along with the publication date of the magazine in 1903 all militate for the year of Patton's trip to have been 1902. For the bridge, see Haines, *The Yellowstone Story*, II, 243–44. For Uncle Tom, see Lee Whittlesey, *Storytelling in Yellowstone: Horse and Buggy Tour Guides* (Albuquerque: University of New Mexico, 2007), chap. 11.

23. Henry Drummond (1851–97) was a minister, teacher of religion, and student of geology. His account of his 1879 trip to Yellowstone with geologist Archibald Geikie appeared in George Adam Smith, *The Life of Henry Drummond* (New York: McClure Phillips and Company, 1901), 165–89. The quote here is from page 174. Drummond died in 1898, so he could not have been Patton's "professor." "N.T." in Drummond's journal probably refers to the "New Testament."

24. *The Virginian* is a 1902 book by Owen Wister.

SEVENTEEN

Through the Yellowstone on a Coach

STEPHEN M. DALE

1903

STEPHEN M. DALE WAS A JOURNALIST WHO TRAVELED TO YELLOWSTONE in 1903 and published this account of his trip in *Ladies Home Journal*.[1] Whoever he was, his account remains delightful today for its lively, colorful writing and the unusual nature of some of the events he chronicled. Nothing else is known of him. At the end of his piece, Mr. Dale opined lengthily on the camaraderie that so many Yellowstone visitors shared during that era of group travel.

"Sawry to disturb yez, sah! But I knowed youse two gennnelmens didden wanta miss yer brekfusses, un the otha train leaves yeah fo' Gardiner in jes' an hour."

The hour was eight o'clock, and the voice was that of our friend of two days' and nights' acquaintance, the loquacious porter of the sleeping car, which some time through the night had been run on a siding at the Northern Pacific Railroad station, town and junction, Livingston, Montana. His shaking wakened me from a dream in which two tenderfeet were dodging, as pursuers, Indians, cowpunchers and coyotes, who in their turn were chasing prairie-dogs and jack-rabbits around a circle in and out among the queer, weird shadows, whistling winds and shifting sands of the Dakota "Bad Lands," where our train was moving when I fell asleep.

It was a beautiful morning and a beautiful place. It was August, yet the air was as fresh and crisp as in the East it would be in October. The little town is but a hamlet, and the houses stand so close about the depot it looks as though they had come in from all the country roundabout one day to see the train go through, and liked the place so well that they just stayed. This very fact leaves all interrupted a wide view over an unbroken landscape to the tall, bare mountains that surround the plain on every side. These mountains seem only a mile away, but in reality are more than twenty miles; the clear air and rare atmosphere combine so as to deceive the eye that they look near at hand and as clear-cut in outline as would some twenty-mile-distant object if seen through a telescope.

But, breakfast over, the conductor's cheery "All Aboard," called from a train made up across the tracks, reminded us that our real destination lay some forty miles off, due south. At the end of this ride through Gardiner Canyon the train brought up, [all] of a sudden, at the very "Gateway of the Mountains."[2] Even here the engine stopped reluctantly, as though it wanted to get through and roam about at will, and while we climbed down from the train stood stamping and fuming at that most wise regulation [that] has barred forever its entrance in through that archway over which there is inscribed "For the benefit and enjoyment of the people of America."[3]

And, by the way, in my haste to get through that gateway, I forgot to tell where we are going. It leads to the Yellowstone National Park, and that Park is that section of the northwest corner of Wyoming, fifty-five by sixty-five miles square, which in 1872 Congress set apart, because of its peculiar character as a unique volcano geyser region, to be the nation's Wonderland.[4] It embraces an area of thirty-five hundred square miles; has an average altitude of eight thousand feet above sea level, and is both encircled and traversed by ranges of the Rocky Mountains. Inasmuch as the land is Government property, and inasmuch as the roads were built and all improvements made at the nation's expense, the civil authority has since then been vested in a Major of the regular army, who, with three troops of cavalry occupies an army post there.[5] It is the duty of these soldiers to patrol the roads and enforce the regulations.

No railroad, trolley line or other such route may either enter or cross the region, but there is a model wagon-road, built by the Government, which extends from the main entrance through and back to it again over a general route a hundred and forty miles long, connecting five important centres and as many different regions where things of the most interest are found. At each of these points there has been constructed a good hotel, accommodating from a hundred and fifty to two hundred fifty guests apiece, each one being a day's ride by stage from the next one before it on the route.

But there! I must be off, or I shall miss that stage. The company have got their baggage loaded, have scrambled to the top, are talking all at once and shouting, each one trying to be heard above the other. If I shut my eyes, to this day I can see that driver gather up those six reins taut, I can hear him crack his twelve-foot whip and call out: "Down the line, now, Boys! Come down the line!" I can see them come, six big Black Beauties, on a gallop, round that curve, to the accompaniment of the most wonderful driving I have ever seen and—There! I barely caught it—and I'm out of breath.

He who would get an idea of that one hundred-and-forty-mile route over which we drove thus for six days must lay down clearly in his mind a figure of the letter Q inverted. The tail, four miles long, is the road leading from the entrance gateway leading to the first hotel, the one at the Terraces.[6] Then let him stick four pins around the circle to locate the four other hotels in this order: The Fountain, The Upper Geyser Basin,[7] The Lake and the Cañon; scratch three lunch-stations on the three long drives of forty miles each day, and he has it.[8] Nor let him think these drives are long or that the people get tired; the buoyancy of the climate and the exhilaration of such novel sights take care of that. Along this route are a thousand spectacles, any one of which alone would gain a national reputation—and merit it—if it had chanced to be placed in some Eastern state all by itself.

And the most satisfactory feature of this six days' drive as a whole is the order of climax in which the sights along the way succeed each other. The six days of the journey are all differentiated, each one by its special kind of spectacle, to reach [when?] it is made, and each of these is just a little greater than the one before. This happens so because of two most fortunate, though wholly accidental, circumstances: first, the more striking phenomena, although of five different kinds, are grouped roughly, each kind in a district of its own—a district of only a couple miles radius: and these districts, each one removed by just a day's drive from the one before; and second, the order of these groups' succession is an order of progressive excellence. Each day presents not only a new but also a more engaging spectacle than the day before: each morning the sun rises on a scene of fresh grandeur, and in the evening outdoes the setting of the day before in beauty. When the journey is completed one imagines one's self having taken part in the rendition of some mighty overture—one strain after another being taken up and woven in and blended with the one or ones before, the volume swelling all the while until it reaches its dénouement in the roar of the Lower Falls and goes off dying in reverberation down the cañon.

Apart even from the sight of any of those special things the very drive itself would be worth taking. The roads are good, the stages comfortable, and the view, at all points, interesting, at some points is entrancing. In the endless variety there is enough to please all. In fact, the very element of uncertainty as to what would come next, at the turn of a road, or the end of a pass, was part of the pleasure. We passed along the edge of cliffs so high that their sides measured hundreds of feet, and went through gorges so deep and so narrow that the daylight at the top seemed but a narrow band of blue. We crept along pathways cut into mountain sides so narrow that turnouts had been constructed where one team might pass another; and traversed broad, open valleys on whose level floor a whole regiment might deploy. We drove in sight of mountains, some of whose summits were cloud-canopied, their bases glacier-furrowed, and their sides a playground for the clouds; and of others that were stark and bare, their outlines distinct in the clear sunlight, and these outlines those of ramparts and castles. There were those along whose sloping sides boulders lay tumbled in mosaic; there were others where pine trees stood thick as bristles on some great, enormous brush. We made long, steep ascents, and, coming out on summits, looked off at the Tetons, ninety miles away, then turned sharp horseshoe curves and wound down corkscrew trails to pass close by a cavern or a grotto, here a grassy plot or there a placid lake. At one time we would drive through aisles of rock, each of which seemed to end ahead abruptly at the base of some precipitous mile-high cliff, only to turn as suddenly when we had reached that end and open up new and still longer vistas through which we would catch glimpses of other mountains beckoning us on and on.

We entered the park that day at eleven o'clock and drove those first four miles to the first hotel, reaching there in time for luncheon, and spent the afternoon there viewing the "Formation." No guide is needed: the strong smell of sulfur, the sight of steam rising from earth-vents, and the brilliant coloring, all serve to locate the points of importance scattered over a three-mile circuit. The form the [Mammoth] Terraces take is due to the dripping of water over sharp ledges of regularly stratified rock cropping out along the hillside. The color is due to the four minerals held in solution by the hot water—lime, sulfur, magnesia and arsenic.[9] The most important of the Terraces, the name[s] suggesting their form and relative size, are the Angel, Pulpit, Minerva and Jupiter. The last is the largest, covering several acres; the first is the most beautiful, being checked in every color of the rainbow. After dinner there was a dance, as there is each evening, in the hotel, where dress-suits, décolleté gowns, and a full orchestra rendering "Hiawatha" off here in the wilderness, are not the least of the surprises one meets in this strange land of anomalies. But this will be the last appearance of such things. Tonight baggage must be sorted, as only one bag may be carried on the stage trip till we come back here.

At eight o'clock next morning [the] party settled on the hotel portico ready to start, the men all wisely wearing their old clothes, expecting dust; the women dressed in dusters and blue goggles, looking like raccoons. We drove twenty miles, through Silver Pass and Golden Gate, past the Hoodoos and Beaver Lake, to Norris Basin. Here we stopped for luncheon for half an hour, and begrudged even that short time— there was so much to see; then on, past Emerald Pool and Obsidian Cliff. The road at this point was constructed in a novel manner. The use of blasting powder was out of the question, for, the hill being of pure glass, no tools could be devised to drill holes in it. So fires were built along the edge, and when it was expanded in this way water was dashed on it to break into such fragments as could be removed.[10]

At five o'clock we reached the Fountain Hotel, at the centre of the second general region of most interest. All about here are the bubbling springs—in reality, halfway volcanoes. The region looks, and sounds

FIGURE 17.1.

Like the visitors pictured here at Mammoth Hot Springs Hotel,
Stephen Dale's party gathered "on the hotel portico ready to
start, the men all wisely wearing their old clothes, expecting dust;
the women dressed in dusters." (Photo about 1904, YELL 967,
Yellowstone National Park Archives, Yellowstone National Park.)

still more, as if a whole city full of factories had been buried underneath an avalanche of earth, only their smokestacks and their steam-
pipes reaching near the surface. A noise goes on underground like the
sound of a Pittsburg[h] rolling-mill, and the surface is all dotted with
exhaust-pits that remind one of great safety-valves. What we heard was
literally the far-off rumbling of that factory in which the very earth was
made: for the forces at work here under our feet are the same forces that
once tossed high those mountains yonder, carved those slopes with the
plowshares of glaciers, and furrowed those valleys with the blades of
rivers. The feature here is the Mammoth Paint-Pot,[11] a remarkable mud
caldron, fifty feet in diameter, in [the] basin of which is a mass of fluid
substance in a state of constant ebullition. It is composed of oil, lime,

FIGURE 17.2.

A lady tourist stands next to the cone of Giant Geyser in this O. C. Watson
stereo, taken in about 1903. "The Giant is due to play," announced tent camp
manager Larry Mathews to our traveler Stephen Dale that year. (YELL
142420, Yellowstone National Park Archives, Yellowstone National Park.)

clay and water,[12] is a natural product, but so nearly like the calcimine of
commerce that the walls of the hotel dining-room, coated with it seven
years ago, still hold their color perfectly.[13]

The drive next day brought us by noon to the Upper Geyser Basin,
where we stayed that afternoon and night. This is the region of those
things the Indians called "Steamboat Springs": those strange eruptions
of hot water from cones raised above the surface of the ground and
shaped like craters of volcanoes. Normally these holes stand level-full of
boiling water; they explode in tall, straight columns, from fifty feet in
height to two hundred and fifty, at irregular intervals varying from once

an hour, as in the case of that reliable friend of the tourist, Old Faithful, to only once a week, in the case of the Giant, and lasting anywhere from the ten seconds of the Economic to the ten hours of the Giantess.

It was twelve o'clock when the stage brought up with a swing at the Camp here kept by one, Larry a Park Character,[14] Irish at birth and also by brogue, who welcomes each guest severally with a hearty handshake; serves fresh trout, hot muffins, gingerbread and Irish wit, and calls a geyser a "geaser." "Hurry up now, Swallow yer lunch. For more luck's wid ye than I know ye all deserve. The Giant is due to play in less than an hour." And so it did. So did three others through the afternoon. We saw them all—saw sights so fearful also so that if Dante had known of them he might well have added them, as other terrors, in his Inferno.

The Fourth Day's Trip

The fourth day's trip we made only half-way by stage. From "Larry's" to the Thumb Lunch Station—so named from its position on a thumb of land projecting out into the lake—is twenty miles. We covered this distance before noon, crossing on the way the famous Continental Divide, the so-called "Backbone of North America." It is the ridge along which is the junction of the two great watersheds, so sharp that two drops of rain falling from the same cloud scarce a hundred yards apart will find their way eventually, the one to the Columbia River, and thence to the Pacific Ocean, the other to the headwaters of the Missouri, thence to the Mississippi, thence to the Gulf of Mexico, and finally to the Atlantic Ocean.

From the Thumb we crossed the lake by boat,[15] twenty miles, to the Lake Hotel, the stages following around the road to overtake us and be ready there to carry us again next morning. This lake is a beautiful body of water; but no one was thinking of that when we reached it: all were looking for what they had all heard of—the Hot Spring Cone.[16] This hot spring boils so close to the cold water's edge that you can stand on the side of this cone, catch a fish in the cold water, and, without removing it from the hook, swing it on the line back over your head and cook it in the boiling water. And there are fish in the lake; so many, in fact, that a man who lets out boats and hires tackle here does so upon terms of a contract: "No fish, no pay"; so many that even the most bungling angler should not average less than one trout to half a dozen casts; so many that that evening, after ten of us had come in from only two hours of this sport, the porter took the catch up to the hotel in a wheelbarrow; so many that—But there! That last one is a fairly good "fish story," even for the Yellowstone.

Before my credit is gone I must tell a "bear story" also. It illustrates the abundance of game in the Park; and it shows how tame wild animals become where they may not be hunted. Every evening at all the hotels, but more especially at this one, because deepest in the forest, the bears come down to the back yard to feed on what is thrown out from the pantry after dinner. They learn to expect their dinner, and the people learn to expect the bears; and neither one is ever disappointed. That evening we counted twelve, and went close enough to them to take pictures of them.

The next day a short forenoon's drive brought us to the Falls and the Grand Cañon. Here we stayed all day and night. Here is the climax, summit, zenith—every other word that means perfect fulfillment of one's hope—of all one ever hoped to see on this wonderful journey through this land of wonders. Here the word Falls stands for a whole river's plunge over the edge of a precipice three hundred and sixty-five feet,[17] and the word Cañon for a great rent in the earth six miles long, half a mile wide, fifteen hundred feet deep, where the earth seems to have fallen open and disclosed its vari-colored wardrobe and its chest of choicest jewels.

A Scene Beyond Exaggeration

Here is a scene [the Grand Canyon of the Yellowstone] which not even guide-books can exaggerate: something that never has been perfectly described, nor ever will be. The description of it is that bow of Ulysses no writer has ever been able to bend; it is the inspiration and despair at once of all who have approached it with notebook in hand. This thing simply cannot be told about: it must be seen. And it should be seen, too, at all hours and in all lights: in the cool, pearly light of the early dawn; through the glowing intensity of the sunshine of midday; in the soft sheen and brilliant coloring of sunset; and beneath the twinkling sparkle of the stars at night.

The only members of our party to attempt comment next day were two. One was a lady who lamented: "Just to think! I chased away last summer over the ocean to look at that miserable little Tyrol when I might instead have come to the Yellowstone." The other was "Deafy," our driver. Taking a hitch in his belt to brace him for descriptive narrative he drawled: "I tell you that there cañon, it's all right. Now, I've been driving stage for fourteen years, and I've heard people kick: but I hain't never heard nobody kick about that cañon yet."

Besides these major features we passed many minor ones along this route; considered minor here only because of the size of the major ones with which they mingle: the Gibbon Falls, for instance, the bands of whose tossing waters are so radiant that the very sunlight seems imprisoned in them; Kepler Cascade, where one can stand on a point of rock and fairly look off to infinity; Alum Creek, of which the composition of the water justifies the name; Sulphur Mountain, where with an axe one could chop out blocks of pure brimstone; Firehole River, so called because hot springs bubbling through the bottom of its channel raise its temperature; Shoshone Lake, whose surface is so smooth and clear that photographs taken of things above its surface show the reflection in as sharp and perfect outline as the picture of the thing itself; and Buffalo Spring, so named because the whitened skeleton of a mountain buffalo [was] found in it once.

We also saw game in abundance, wild creatures grown strikingly tame feeding by the roadside. The lakes and streams also are full of fish. The fish may be caught, but the game may not be killed. Firearms may not even be carried through unless first taken in hand and sealed by the soldiers at the entrance. We saw twenty bison in one herd; a hundred elk in one band; a colony of beavers at work on a dam; mountain goats poised like statues on the summits of crags; and wild fowl of every sort, from ducks, many hundred in a flock, to solitary eagles who put us to shame, when we thought we were at great altitudes, by soaring through the air half a mile above us.[18]

We did all the customary things, too, without doing which no journey would be thought complete: we got each one a souvenir; an old shoe or hatchet coated with that hard formation where the water flows over the Terraces;[19] we cooked and ate an egg apiece boiled in the Punch Bowl [Spring]; we drank from the Apollinaris Spring, and listened to our names called back from Echo Cañon.[20] We heard all the familiar stories told once at least to each party; heard of "Yankee Jim," variously known as Jim Bridger, the Pioneer of Wonderland and the Daniel Boone of the

Rocky Mountains; heard how he went back east in 1840 from exploring here, and told what he had seen, and was rewarded for his pains by being dubbed: "The Monumental Liar of the North Pacific Slope";[21] of Colonel Heyden [sic—Hayden], the first Government explorer here, and the sad tale of that member of that exploring party who got lost and wandered through the hills, till, terrified by the uncanny sights he saw, and crazed by loneliness, he was found, after twenty-six days, creeping along the steep edge of a cliff on hands and knees gesticulating to the mountain goats and talking Latin to eagles;[22] heard of Electric Peak, which is so highly charged with loadstone that surveyors' instruments will not work there; heard of the Devil's Slide, his Kitchen, his Bathtub, and all the many other things named after him.

Rightly Called a Land of Enchantment

But any mere guide-book enumeration of its parts must fail to give any conception of the special charms of this place. This trip, distinct from every other, has a charm all its own. Nor is that charm a single one, but rather manifold. First of all, there is the climate: it is only the water, or some of it, that is hot; the air is always cool—cool though never cold. Its invigorating freshness is due to the altitude—the average altitude of the Park being higher than the top of Mount Washington.[23] At midday it is as warm and balmy as September, but in the morning one wears a light overcoat, and at night sleeps under blankets—and all this in August. The evenings at the hotels are by no means the least enjoyable part of the day: there is that long summer twilight peculiar to the northern latitude, and all about are lovely paths bordered with shrubbery which leads to porches filled with comfortable chairs, where one may breathe an atmosphere both restful and refreshing.

Nor am I sure that even yet I have quite touched the special charm of this trip. Its unique delight is rather, I think "that ravishing delight of a new sensation," that thing in search of which men tour the globe. It is a "scary" venture also, and a man ventures cannily. He feels at one time that he is standing on the very "edge of things," at another on the very "top of things," and at another as though only the thinnest crust were separating him from the "centre of things." A thrill comes to him he cannot explain. He has heard of this great, tremendous rush of feeling: heard that it comes only once, and here it comes. And when it comes is it welcome? It is like being in love for the first time: a man likes it and he doesn't like it. He wishes the feeling would go away, and at the same time is afraid it will go. It gets into his blood and makes him dizzy. He wants to shut his eyes, and yet is afraid if he does he will miss seeing something.

It is this very strangeness that begets abandon and takes the traveler out of himself. The land has been called "A Land of Enchantment," and rightly so; for a man feels here that he is out of reach of everything and everybody; there are no distracting cares, nothing to annoy; even the daily papers are a week behind. He feels free also: in sight of these scenes of both strength and beauty, loads of care drop from tired shoulders, and the man returned to nature springs erect like one of those tall pines that stand in sight upon the mountainside. There is that in the air this week which helps him to unload the burdens of the weeks before and to laugh at the shadows that the weeks to come will cast. It is a place where one no longer thinks of to-morrow and still less of yesterday; a place where he loses all sense of time; a place where time passes so strangely and brings such confusion that one forgets the very day of the week. This last is literally true. On the third day out one member of the party of ten on our stage asked suddenly that it had not occurred to them to think for several days. Not one of the ten could tell either the day of the week or the date of the month—not even the driver, until he had brought up from the depths of his coat pocket his meal-ticket to see what date had been punched last.[24]

Some Types of Tourists

And who were the people, these tourists, this party? In our party, as, of course, in every other, there were all the usual types. There was the lady traveling alone—for such traveling here is no more unusual and is attended with neither more danger nor inconvenience than a trip alone would be across the ocean. There was the elderly couple, solicitous about each other's health, although there was no cause; the trip is made so comfortably that a centenarian might take it. There was the Russian nobleman, who sat apart on the seat with the driver and talked to no one, so that we thought he was "stuck up," until we learned it was because he could not talk English. There was the enthusiastic Frenchman who went into raptures over everything and was loud in his praise, with only one slight reservation—namely the word "Park" is a misnomer: "it is not fitted up." The fact is, that is its chiefest charm.

It is a surprise to all to note how thoroughly such parties became acquainted, and how early they begin to talk freely to one another. Just as when good spirits prompt one to wave to a passing train, so in such parties sheer enthusiasm prompts to speech: people are so happy they are glad to speak to everyone else. There is no place here for the man who will not talk; he who could stand on his dignity and stand silent in sight of such sights as we saw would be either dead or dumb. And when he has once spoken he is lost; for one cannot gush with a geyser and then climb back to his seat on a stage and sit formerly reticent. The whole party—in our case, one [party] of seventy-five people—continue to travel together all the way round for six days, keeping even the same seats on the same stages. Perhaps it is the view that intoxicates; perhaps it is the rare air; but, whatever it is, people are more sociable and more natural here than they are elsewhere in all their lives in any other place.[25]

Introductions Rarely Necessary

No one [on the stagecoach], so far as I can recall, was ever introduced, nor was any one told anybody else's name; but little things like that did not matter: names could be learned from hotel registers. Sometimes not even this trouble was taken: there was no time: there were too many interesting things to do. So nicknames were applied. There was "That Russian," "The German," "The Woman with the Bundle," "The Baby Elephant," and "The Heavenly Twins"; there were "Sunny Jim" and "Foxy Grandpa," "Everyman" and "That Other Man"; while two young chaps who, because of their good nature and vivacity, because of the way they bandied one another and tossed back and forth good natured raillery, were dubbed sometimes "The Baseball Battery," and sometimes "The End Man and the Interlocutor."[26]

It was only when we got back to the starting point, and there met strangers, that we realized what old friends we had all become. On that last day of the tour parties break up with reluctance. In our party at least friends of only six days' acquaintance separated sorrowing, and every one exchanged cards with his neighbor. I have an idea, although that is a secret, that in the case of "The Yale Man" and "The Lady in the Newport Veil," "The Professor" and "The Girl with the Pretty Shirtwaists,"

"The Doctor" and "That Girl with the Gorgeous Eyes," other things may possibly have been exchanged. But, then, as "Deafy" says, "You can't sometimes most always tell."

It was dark that evening down the platform by the train, and all the rest of us were busy with our baggage. What may have been exchanged since nobody but the postman knows.

Notes

1. Stephen M. Dale, "Through the Yellowstone on a Coach," *Ladies Home Journal* 21 (August 1904): 5–6.
2. They traveled through Yankee Jim Canyon, located fifteen miles north of Yellowstone National Park, and then alongside peaks of the Gallatin Range to present Gardiner, Montana.
3. Although miners at Cooke City, Montana, agitated for around twenty years (1875–95) to get the northern strip of the park "cut off" so that a railroad could be built to their town, Congress continually rejected such attempts. See, for example, "A Standing Menace—Cooke City vs. the National Park," *Forest and Stream* 39 (December 8, 1892): 485–87. A summary of this history is in H. Duane Hampton, *How the U.S. Cavalry Saved Our National Parks* (Bloomington: Indiana University Press, 1971), 113–18.
4. The Organic Act of 1872 established Yellowstone as the world's first national park. See Aubrey L. Haines, *The Yellowstone Story* (1977; rev., Boulder: University of Colorado Press, 1996), II, 471–72.
5. Actually the commandant of Fort Yellowstone was usually a captain, rather than a major.
6. This was the National Hotel, also called the Mammoth Hot Springs Hotel, built in 1883.
7. This was the Shack Hotel lunch station and tent camp, in its last season of operation, 1903.
8. These were Norris Lunch Station between Mammoth and the Fountain Hotel, the Shack Hotel lunch station at Old Faithful, and the Thumb Lunch Station at West Thumb.
9. While sulfur and limestone are present at Mammoth, magnesia and arsenic are generally not.
10. This process is described in Lee Whittlesey, *Yellowstone Place Names* (Gardiner, MT: Wonderland Publishing Company, 2006), 191.
11. This is today known as the Fountain Paint Pot, the name being applied as early as 1914. Whittlesey, *Yellowstone Place Names*, 108–9.
12. He was right about all but oil, which is not present here.
13. He was correct about the calcimining of Fountain Hotel's walls using this material. See Lee Whittlesey, "Music, Song, and Laughter: Yellowstone

National Park's Fountain Hotel, 1891–1916," *Montana the Magazine of Western History* 53 (Winter 2003): 34n41.

14. This was Larry Mathews, manager of the Old Faithful lunch station and tent camp during this 1903 season. Larry would return one more time to manage the new Old Faithful Inn in 1904 before leaving the park. See generally, Lee Whittlesey, "'I Haven't Time to Kiss Everybody!': Larry Mathews Entertains in Yellowstone, 1887–1904," *Montana the Magazine of Western History* 57 (Summer 2007): 58–73.

15. They boarded the *Zillah*, a steamboat run by E. C. Waters, owner of the Yellowstone Lake Boat Company. Tourists had the option of continuing on from Thumb to Lake Hotel by stagecoach or taking the boat across the lake for an extra charge. Waters paid the stagecoach drivers fifty cents for each passenger they convinced to take his boat ride. Haines, *The Yellowstone Story*, II, 126.

16. This hot spring at West Thumb is known today as Fishing Cone. Whittlesey, *Yellowstone Place Names*, 106–7.

17. It is actually 308 feet.

18. Animals in the park, although scarce by 1883 because of a massive, ten-year slaughter by hunters, had returned to visibility by 1903. See, generally, Paul Schullery and Lee Whittlesey, "Documentary Record of Wolves and Related Wildlife Species in the Yellowstone National Park Area Prior to 1882," in *Wolves for Yellowstone?*, vol. 4 (Yellowstone National Park: National Park Service, 1992), 1–173. The "eagles" were probably ospreys.

19. This reference was to Ole Anderson's specimen-coating operation at Mammoth. Visitors would often leave an object with Anderson at the beginning of the trip, and it would be coated and ready for their souvenir cabinet upon their return to Mammoth.

20. He stretched the truth here, for Echo Canyon is located so far into the Yellowstone backcountry that there is no way he could have seen it. Whittlesey, *Yellowstone Place Names*, 96.

21. Here he confused "Yankee Jim" (James George) with the more famous Jim Bridger of fur trade fame. Bridger was one of the pioneer storytellers of early Yellowstone, 1825–80, while "Yankee Jim" was a toll road operator. Haines, *The Yellowstone Story*, I, 53–59; Lee Whittlesey, *Storytelling in Yellowstone: Horse and Buggy Tour Guides* (Albuquerque: University of New Mexico, 2007), 32–36.

22. Here he confused Truman Everts, lost from the 1870 Washburn party, with the Hayden Expedition of 1871. Everts was lost for thirty-seven days, not twenty-six, and the animals he saw were bighorn sheep rather than mountain goats. See generally, Lee H. Whittlesey, ed., *Lost in the Yellowstone: Truman Everts's Thirty-seven Days of Peril* (Salt Lake City: University of Utah Press, 1995).

23. Mount Washington is located in the White Mountains of northern New Hampshire. It is the tallest mountain in the northeastern United States, rising 6,288 feet above sea level.

24. The loss of sense of time in Yellowstone remains true today, according to numerous park employees who have experienced it.

25. Mr. Dale's paean to the joys of traveling in groups is probably understandable to those who have taken and enjoyed group bus tours, but this large-group camaraderie from the days of stagecoach and train travel is little known to many of today's tourists, who now travel through the park in small groups in their own automobiles.

26. These two were characters in minstrel shows. See http://en.wikipedia.org/wiki/Minstrel_show.

EIGHTEEN

Through Yellowstone Park with the American Institute of Banking

FRED W. ELLSWORTH

1912

BORN JUNE 27, 1872, IN BATTLE CREEK, MICHIGAN, FRED W. ELLSWORTH became interested in things financial and moved around the nation to follow his chosen career as a banker. Marrying Rose F. Ellsworth of Iowa, he long served (as secretary and publicity manager) at New York's Guaranty Trust Company, and he retired as president of the Financial Advertisers Association and vice president of the Hibernia Bank and Trust Company of New Orleans. He was still living in 1930, eighteen years after this article was published in the November 1912 issue of *Moody's Magazine*.[1]

Ellsworth's 1912 adventure in Yellowstone occurred as part of a commercial group tour of the park. Such large tours had become common by that year as part of the normal touring business of national parks. Ellsworth characterized the group as a collection of "dignified bankers." His large group traveled with Wylie Camping Company, a company that offered one of the most popular ways to see Yellowstone.

"All aboard!" This brief but significant speech uttered by the train conductor at the Oregon Short Line Railroad station in Salt Lake City, marked the beginning of a most remarkable trip [that] was recently enjoyed by about 125 members of the American Institute of Banking. The Institute had just adjourned its annual convention in Salt Lake City and the delegates, many of them with their wives and families had decided to make the trip through Yellowstone Park before returning to their several homes. A special train was chartered and this left Salt Lake City in the early evening, arriving at Yellowstone Station, Montana, the next morning.[2] The ride until bed time was punctuated by all sorts of impromptu entertainment, including a vaudeville show, a sumptuous banana banquet with sandwich trimmings, [and] with a pajama parade concluding the evening's exercises.

We had been warned that the ride through Yellowstone would probably be rather cold. Those who had profited by this advice were not complaining, but the rash ones, as soon as they alighted from the train, began a still hunt for a heavy underwear emporium. "B.V.D.'s," they explained, "are mighty cold comfort on a fall morning in Yellowstone Park."

Without delay after arrival the entire party piles into thirty or forty "Wylie" coaches and the procession moves over rapidly into the Park where at Riverside Camp everybody immediately gets busy at the breakfast table.[3] Oh my! Oh my! How some of those dignified bankers did shine as knife and fork artists.

When every bit of visible provender is thoroughly disposed of the announcement is made that the coaches are ready for the trip through the Park.[4] As fast as the various parties can be sorted out from the general mob and collected in one spot they are sent off down the road toward the geyser basins. The morning ride is interrupted by very welcome stops at natural springs where everybody eagerly and enthusiastically quenches his thirst, for by this time the sun is high in the heavens and it has turned warm. We skirt the Firehole River all the morning and by a strange but most interesting coincidence reach Gibbon Lunch Station just at lunch time.[5] 125 active, well-organized appetites make 125 wild dashes for the dining hall, and in less time than it takes to tell it 125 pairs of perfectly good jaws are working in union with 125 pairs of very busy arms and hands. It is not reported that anyone held a stop-watch on the crowd, but in less than twenty minutes the tables are cleared.

It will never do, however, to delay here very long as we have a great deal to see and only five or six days in which to see it. So back we pile into the coaches and away we gallop to the Lower Geyser Basin, which

FIGURE 18.1.

A group of tourists with the Wylie Camping Company poses for
photographer Harry Shipler while waiting for their coaches at Wylie's
Sleepy Hollow (Gibbon) lunch station in 1912. Our traveler Fred Ellsworth
stopped here for lunch that very year. (Watry collection, Bozeman.)

we reach in the middle of the afternoon. Here we have our first view
of a real geyser. The Fountain happens to be playing just as we land,
and it indeed is a sight to repay a long journey. In this same basin are
myriads of hot springs boiling away like a company of hot tea kettles,
the more interesting being Turquoise Spring, Prismatic Lake, and the
Fairy Springs.[6]

On the way to the Upper Geyser Basin we pass other strange phenomena similar to those which prevail in the Lower Basin, and as we
round a turn in the road the driver points out Riverside Geyser. This,
he explains, has a crater that is slightly tilted and so spouts out over the
river instead of in a perpendicular column. He tells us that it will probably play just about dinner time, and so we make a mental note to get

back here at that time. We reach the Wylie Camp at the Upper Basin in time to wander around a little before dinner. One of the first spectacles [that] meets our eyes is the Daisy Geyser, which plays every seventy minutes or thereabouts. During its action, which, by the way, met with the hearty endorsement of the crowd, it explodes spasmodically, ejecting an enormous volume of boiling hot water which rises nearly a hundred feet in the air.[7]

After dinner, which proves in every respect quite as popular as the other two meals of the day, the company splits up into parties to inspect the wonders in the various parts of the basin. The largest proportion marches procession-like over to Old Faithful, which is scheduled to play about nine o'clock. As it is Sunday the procession very properly keeps step to such orthodox tunes as "Onward Christian Soldiers," and the "Battle Hymn of the Republic." On the roof of the Old Faithful Inn, which is quite as remarkable a hostelry as we were led to believe from the guide books, there is a large searchlight, which at night is used to enhance the natural beauties of Old Faithful Geyser. This, we are told, is the peer of all the geysers in the park, and receives its name from its absolute reliability. It plays at intervals of sixty-five to seventy minutes and spouts a stream for four or five minutes from 125 to 160 feet in the air. With the colored effects from the searchlight playing through this stream of hot steam the scene is indescribably beautiful.

Well, we can't sit and watch Old Faithful forever, so we step over to Old Faithful Inn and inspect that property. This is indeed a wonderful building, rustic throughout, with a chimney that must be at least fifteen feet square at the base. It runs up through the building and out the roof and has an enormous old-fashioned fireplace on each of the four sides. When we see the log fire sending out its cheerful warmth and glow, and the mammoth pans of hot popcorn passing around, and which we sample generously, it suddenly occurs to us that this is a "pretty happy world" after all.

Right here I am reminded of the ball game that occurred directly in front of Old Faithful Inn the next afternoon. One team was made up from the "dudes" stopping at the Inn and the other from the "dudes" that were going the "Wylie Way." Both teams played good ball in spite of the stiff wind that was blowing, but the Inn "dudes" were a little better than their opponents, the score being somewhere in the neighborhood of 8 to 5. The feature of the game proved to be the first-class, all around rooting of the Wylie drivers who, forty strong, were massed back of third base and cheered every good play made by their men, and kicked at every decision that went against them.[8]

Well, when the popcorn is all gone, we march back to camp. "Curfew tolls the knell of parting day" in the Wylie camps promptly at 10 P.M., and it is only a few minutes after that when everything is quiet except the crashing nasal crescendo from several of the "stag" [male-only] tents. Finally the regularity of this tremendous racket acts as a lullaby and we sink into slumber.

The next morning directly after breakfast the entire party, headed by a Wylie [walking] guide, starts on a tour of the Geyser Basin and visits every natural wonder in the neighborhood. The Giant Geyser, which spouts 250 feet in the air every week or ten days, had very obligingly worked off its spasm the day before we got there.[9] As it costs $5.00 a day [to remain] overtime in the Park, it is spontaneously and unanimously decided not to linger.

The camera fiends are in evidence on every hand and it is a wonder that Old Faithful is not shot full of holes, for at each eruption he was bombarded by a battery of kodaks from all sides except the leeward. (A deluge of hot steam is an exceedingly annoying thing most of the time, especially when you are trying to take a picture.) As a spectacle, Old Faithful is a huge success. A column of boiling water mounting into the air as high as a ten-story building, accompanied by the intermittent explosions in the crater, is a sight that one will not soon forget.

But even Old Faithful cannot hold us long, as there are other interesting sights to be seen. Emerald Pool, which is as green as a beautiful lawn and which gets its name, so it is said, from the fact that an Irishman fell in and was drowned there;[10] Rainbow Lake, the Punch Bowl, and scores of other most remarkable natural curiosities are seen on this wonderful journey around the Basin, and when night comes, after the ball game already mentioned, everybody is mighty glad to get back and shove his feet under the dinner table. In the evening, several of the gentlemen who have more or less histrionic ability, arrange a show in the dance hall. This is pronounced an unqualified success by the audience, which includes everybody within a radius of several miles. This show consists of several vaudeville stunts by well-known bankers and concludes with a farce convention with take-offs on some of the more susceptible features of the Salt Lake City Convention. Kramer's unique

FIGURE 18.2.
Harry Shipler took this photo of the interior of a Wylie Camping
Company sleeping tent in 1911. Our traveler Fred Ellsworth slept
in a similar tent one year later. (Watry collection, Bozeman.)

and picturesque method of drumming up the attendance by playing
gospel hymns "from the old book" in front of the tents on the little
folding camp organ, was one of the most satisfying exhibitions of the
entire trip.[11]

Tuesday morning the procession of coaches starts promptly at
7 o'clock for Yellowstone Lake, where a stop is made at the Thumb
Lunch Station at noon for a very obvious purpose. On this ride we twice
pass over the Continental Divide where the streams run in opposite
directions, those on one side of the "hump" starting on their long journey to the Atlantic and those on the other to the Pacific. On the shore of
Yellowstone Lake we see the famous fishing cone which contains boiling water. The story has it that one can stand on the edge of this cone
and catch fish in the lake and drop them over into the cone and cook

them.[12] This sounds plausible, and certainly the water is hot enough, but none of us saw any fish, although we were solemnly assured that there are plenty in the lake. The ride along the edge of the lake, which consumes all the afternoon, is a pleasant one, and in the evening we landed at Lake Camp, not very far from the Yellowstone River. Here we have our first experience with real live bears. Several of the party encountered a half dozen of them unexpectedly in the middle of the road while out sight-seeing. It was said that the bears were far more scared than the men, but did not run as fast—indeed, the men in question claim that they did a hundred yards in considerably less than seven seconds, which is two or three seconds under the record.

The ride from Lake Camp to Canyon Camp consumes all the next morning. Mud Geyser is passed on this trip. As its name implies this geyser consists of a large crater filled with boiling, bubbling mud, which constantly emits great clouds of steam along with a never-ending contribution of dainty sulphurous fumes that evidently come straight from the infernal regions. Indeed, this odor of concentrated hydro bisulphide is so prevalent in the Park that one is inclined to the belief that here is the great central market for all the eggs in the world that need a baptism in the fountain of youth.[13] The contents of Mud Geyser possess wonderful curative properties. A person suffering from rheumatism or carache or household's knee or anything else, by jumping into this geyser can be sure of an effectual and permanent cure.[14]

The ride of fifteen or eighteen miles in a Concord coach with ten or a dozen alert, wide-awake Americans on board is quite apt to develop, for the sake of passing away the time, a goodly measure of wit and humor. And so it is with practically all of the coaches as they travel the long road from Yellowstone Lake to the Grand Canyon. Everything that is seen is made the subject of a jest and even the occupants of the coaches themselves are not spared. Kidding and joking and horse-play become a sort of continuous program. Whether it was with malice aforethought cannot now be determined, but anyhow the driver of coach 15 suddenly turned out from the road and without any warning whatever drew us up right to the edge of the Grand Canyon. We were not prepared for it. We did not know we were anywhere near it. Suddenly, in the twinkling of an eye, there lies before us the most wonderful and most beautiful sight that any of us have ever seen. An awful chasm, almost bottomless in depth, yawns before us. The walls, riotous in every color of the rainbow, descend almost perpendicularly from where we stand a quarter of a mile to the tiny little ribbon of a river below. We notice that the laughing and the joking stop instantly. Everyone seems to realize that we are in the presence of the handiwork of the Almighty. We simply look and look and look. If there had been any doubts in our minds as to the wonders of Yellowstone Park they are certainly dissipated now. We ride along the edge of the chasm for two or three miles and then leaving the coaches walk out to an ample platform on Inspiration Point. Here is obtained a grand view of the chasm, from the Great Falls, three miles away, to the lower bend, four miles in the other direction. Here is also seen to the best advantage the marvelous rock coloring, from the creams and light yellows at the top down through the various shades to the deep green of the moss at the river edge. My pen is too feeble to attempt any description of this wonderful spectacle, so I will turn over the job to the Rev. Dr. Wayland Hoyt,[15] who writes of it as follows:

> The whole gorge flames. It is as though rainbows had fallen out of the sky and hung themselves there like glorious banners. The underlying color is the clearest yellow; this flushes onward into orange. Down at the base the deepest mosses unroll their draperies of the most vivid green; brown, sweet and soft, do their blending; white rocks stand spectral; turrets of rock shoot up as crimson as though they were drenched through with blood. It is a wilderness of color. It is impossible that even the pencil of an artist can tell it. It is as if the most glorious sunset you ever saw had been caught and held upon that resplendent, awful gorge.

The doctor is right. We can endorse everything that he says and then some. There are many pictures, photographs, and paintings of the Grand Canyon of the Yellowstone, but not one of them that we have ever seen gives any conception of the distances, the colorings, [and] the awful grandeur of this most wonderful natural phenomenon.

We all would like to stay in the Canyon for days, but time passes, and so on Thursday morning we again climb into our coaches and are on our way to Mammoth Hot Springs. Roaring Mountain, which is just what its name indicates and sounds as though it was filled with innumerable freight trains continually switching back and forth, was passed on the Thursday trip. The road skirts the base of Obsidian Cliff, a mountain of melted volcanic glass, which for the most part is opaque and is so hard that blasting powder has absolutely no effect on it. Mammoth Hot Springs and their terraces, beautifully and daintily colored, are quite as wonderful and remarkable as any of the other natural wonders in this most wonderful region. They resemble nothing quite so much as terraced fountains—indeed, each of them might almost be taken for a giant fountain touched by the magic hand of Jack Frost and made fast. Retracing our steps from the Springs we pass through Silver Gate and the Hoodoos,[16] the latter a region of enormous boulders scattered about in a reckless fashion and covering many acres. Then we pass through Golden Gate, part of the way over a Government viaduct made necessary by the narrowness of the trail. The night is spent at Swan Lake Camp and we awake in the morning and look out upon a world covered with as heavy a frost as we have ever seen—and this is August! The thermometer in the night has dropped to twenty-two above and we begin to yearn for the summer weather back east. At this camp several of us have a foot race with a bear cub, the cub winning by several yards.

Here comes the last day of our stay in Yellowstone Park and we are confronted by a long, cold ride from Swan Lake Camp to Yellowstone Station, a distance of about forty-four miles.[17] As we are loping along through the Norris Geyser Basin we suddenly hear piercing shrieks from the coach just ahead of us and upon stretching our neck[s] to see what is the matter we almost have heart disease when we observe a black bear about the size of a barn looming up right in front of our horses. The only things on board in the way of shooting irons are a couple of 2A Brownie Kodaks, but Mr. Bear is unconscious of this, for he moves off into the woods when our driver rudely invites him to "beat it." The bears in Yellowstone Park are the most unorthodox bears you ever saw. They don't seem to have any spunk, at all. They are not a bit like the ferocious bears that inhabit the story books.

Along about noontime our old friend, the Gibbon Lunch Station, looms up in the distance and without even waiting for the coaches to come to a full stop everybody piles out and rushes for the dining hall. After all, these life-saving stations—"gastronomic emporiums," as one chap called them—disposed about the Park in convenient places, are quite as attractive as any of the more extraordinary features of the Park. A stop is made here just long enough to feed the inner man and then away we gallop on the final leg of our trip, landing at the railroad station at Livingston just in time to catch the Short Line train for "Salt Lake City and all points east."[18]

"Now you will write, won't you, when you get home?"

"Yes, and remember that you are to send me some of your pictures when you get them developed."

"All right, old man, we've had a dandy time, haven't we?"

"Yes, and now it's 'back to the mines.'"

"All aboard!" calls the conductor, the cars fill up, the wheels begin to turn, "Good-byes" are shouted back and forth, and Yellowstone Park for the American Institute of Banking has become a memory.

Notes

1. Fred W. Ellsworth, "Through Yellowstone Park with the American Institute of Banking," *Moody's Magazine* 14 (November 1912): 367–75.

2. Prior to 1920, West Yellowstone, Montana, was known simply as Yellowstone, Montana. This caused great confusion, so the town was renamed West Yellowstone in or about 1920.

3. In 1893, W. W. Wylie secured a permit to operate a camping and touring concession that utilized its own stagecoaches and several semipermanent camping sites throughout the park. This camp was located at Riverside, a place about one mile inside the park's west boundary. It served only breakfast and seems not to have provided overnight service.

4. Provender is food.

5. This was the Madison, not Firehole, River and the Wylie lunch station known as Sleepy Hollow, so named by stagecoach drivers for the well-known book *The Legend of Sleepy Hollow* by Washington Irving. Lee Whittlesey, *Yellowstone Place Names* (Gardiner, MT: Wonderland Publishing Company, 2006), 230.

6. Turquoise Spring and "Prismatic Lake" (today's Grand Prismatic Spring) are actually farther south at Midway Geyser Basin. It is strange that he mentions Fairy Springs, as they are located well off the road and into the backcountry at Lower Geyser Basin. Whittlesey, *Yellowstone Place Names*, 102.

7. Daisy Geyser continues today to erupt around one hundred feet high at intervals of 85–110 minutes. T. Scott Bryan, *The Geysers of Yellowstone* (Boulder: University Press of Colorado, 2008), 99.

8. This was an early example of baseball played in the Park. Such games involving Fort Yellowstone soldiers occurred as early as 1896. Formal softball leagues organized by the Cooperative Recreation Division are still the rule today in the park, and every location has its league with park-wide championships played at the end of each season. Bill Whithorn and

Doris Whithorn, *Photo History from Yellowstone Park* (Livingston, MT: Park County News, n.d. [1970]), [15].

9. This seems to be one of the only records (if not *the* only such record) of Giant Geyser erupting in 1912. Lee Whittlesey, *Wonderland Nomenclature*, 1988, unpublished manuscript, Yellowstone National Park Library, Yellowstone National Park, Giant Geyser entry for 1911–12.

10. He was incorrect about this name origin, as the name Emerald Pool was given from the natural green color of the spring's water. Perhaps the Wylie walking guide who told him this was merely making a joke and Mr. Ellsworth failed to "get it." Whittlesey, *Yellowstone Place Names*, 98.

11. "Kramer" was apparently one of their party members, for he is not known to have been a park employee.

12. Fishing Cone, a hot spring that is actually surrounded by the cold waters of Yellowstone Lake, had become very famous by 1912 for this very reason. Whittlesey, *Yellowstone Place Names*, 106–7.

13. The prevalent gas here is hydrogen sulfide or H_2S.

14. *Carache* is an old name for sickle-cell anemia.

15. Dr. Wayland Hoyt, who visited Yellowstone in 1878, was a well-known Baptist preacher from Brooklyn. His flowery descriptions of the Grand Canyon of the Yellowstone were quoted for many years in newspapers and park guidebooks. See, for example, Hoyt in G. P. Brockett, *Our Western Empire* (Philadelphia: Bradley, Garretson, and Company, 1881), 1240–42; in Elbert Hubbard, *Elbert Hubbard's Scrapbook* (New York: Wm. H. Wise and Company, 1923), 29; and the slightly different version in Mary C. Ludwig, "A Summer in the Rockies," n.d. [1895], Scrapbook 4209, 130, Yellowstone National Park Library, Yellowstone National Park. Hoyt's original account is in his "The Far West," *Brooklyn Eagle*, January 21, 1879.

16. The Wylie Company generally took its tourists to Mammoth Hot Springs so that they would not miss those famous features and then was forced to backtrack six miles to its own Swan Lake Camp for the night.

17. They were returning to present West Yellowstone, Montana, a distance of forty-one miles.

18. He was confused. This was [West] Yellowstone, Montana, not Livingston. Livingston was on the Northern Pacific rail line fifty-two miles north of Gardiner, Montana, the north entrance to Yellowstone.

NINETEEN

A Little Journey to the Yellowstone

ELBERT HUBBARD AND ALICE HUBBARD

1914

⟶❀⟵

"DO NOT TAKE LIFE TOO SERIOUSLY. YOU WILL NEVER GET OUT OF it alive anyway," advised popular writer Elbert Green Hubbard (1856–1915). Hubbard was renowned in his day as a novelist, essayist, lecturer, critic, biographer, philosopher, and publisher. In addition to hundreds of magazine articles, his books such as *One Day, No Enemy but Himself, Time and Chance, Life of John Brown, A Message to Garcia*, and *Little Journeys* secured Hubbard's place in history as one of America's most interesting characters and prolific writers.

Originally from Bloomington, Illinois, he was the son of Silas Hubbard, a veteran of the Civil War whose work as a country doctor did not provide a plentiful income for the family. Thus Elbert embarked on his first of many jobs working on a farm at the age of fifteen. After his request for a pay raise was denied, Elbert Hubbard "followed Horace Greeley's advice, and went West."[1] With little formal schooling, he worked as cowpuncher, lumberjack, printer, schoolteacher, reporter, salesman, and actor. But it was his partnership in a soap-making business that offered him the opportunity to attend Harvard College for four years. Marrying Bertha Crawford in 1879 and fathering four children, Hubbard took up residence in East Aurora, New York, located just south of Buffalo. There he founded the Roycroft Arts and Crafts movement community as well as the Roycroft Press in 1895, devoted to making deluxe editions of the classics. The printing shop soon became a meeting place for freethinkers, reformers, and suffragists. Hubbard's Roycroft Press published two magazines: *The Philistine*, full of whimsical satire to awaken the spirit and the mind, and *The Fra*, a "serious-minded contribution to the Intelligencia of America."[2]

Writing in a breezy and sometimes recklessly informal style, Hubbard became well known for his engaging and magnetic personality, and he carefully cultivated a reputation as an eccentric. He rejected the stuffy convention of men's dress, and so "with his wide-brimmed soft hat, luxuriant hair, and flowing tie, he challenged attention wherever he went." So widely was his writing recognized that Tufts College awarded him an honorary Master of Arts degree in 1899.[3]

But according to biographer Felix Shay, Hubbard's "best bid for immortality" lay in his *Little Journeys*.[4] "There are one hundred and seventy *Little Journeys*," professed Hubbard, "a biography in miniature, giving brief facts in the evolution of some great man, who has lived or is now living." "If you know *Little Journeys*," he wrote with more than a little exaggeration, "you know all [of] history."[5]

Just three years after he wrote the poignant story of Ida Straus of Macy's department store fame, who refused to board one of the lifeboats awaiting her after the luxury liner *Titanic* struck an iceberg, Hubbard and his second wife, Alice, met their fate in the same way. On May 7, 1915, a torpedo sank the *Lusitania* off the coast of Ireland, sending Elbert and Alice Hubbard on their final "little journey." Shortly after the alarm went out to all passengers, Mr. and Mrs. Hubbard appeared on deck. Asked what they were going to do, Mrs. Hubbard calmly replied, "There doesn't seem to be anything we can do." Arm in arm they turned, entered their cabin, and closed the door. A telegram to East Aurora announced to disbelieving friends, "Both lost at Sea."

Just one year before their last little journey to watery graves, Elbert and Alice Hubbard took a trip to Yellowstone National Park, described in "A Little Journey to the Yellowstone," in 1914. Elbert Hubbard loved everything about Yellowstone. Impressed by the operation of the seemingly invisible government, the organization of the Yellowstone Transportation Company, and the wondrous splendor of nature, he and wife Alice declared their park trip inspiring, magical, and marvelously "unique in a lifetime's journey."[6]

Elbert Hubbard, founder of the Roycroft Arts and Crafts movement,
renowned philosopher and lecturer, and distinguished magazine publisher,
was one of the nation's most celebrated writers when he traveled through
Yellowstone in 1914. (Elbert Hubbard, *Little Journeys to the Homes of the
Great*, Memorial ed., vol. 1 [East Aurora, NY: Roycofters, 1916].)

The Yellowstone National Park was formerly a part of Wyoming, Montana and Idaho.[7] In Eighteen Hundred Seventy-two Congress declared this portion of the United States to be a National Park for the use of all the people all of the time.[8] The general Government assumed the responsibility of putting this Park in condition so that its wonders might be enjoyed comfortably by any traveler who might wish to enter.

Now it belongs to you and me!

Perhaps one of the greatest wonders of the Park is that the impersonal thing, called the Government, has succeeded in keeping itself out of sight and establishing a spirit in the Park so that every one who enters has a genuine community feeling of ownership.

Throughout our fourteen days' travel we saw not one symptom of vandalism or disrespect of the rights of others. On the contrary, every one wanted to preserve the beauty of the Park, to have a part in the protection of the Park, and also to assist in the building and promotion of the well-being of this natural wonderland.

It was not necessary for Uncle Sam to plant his flag at the entrance to the park. An American eagle has made her aerie high on a crag,[9] which is announcement enough that all around are Uncle Sam's possessions.

Mammoth Hot Springs

There is an ascent of almost a thousand feet in the five-mile drive from Gardiner to Mammoth Hot Springs. It is a good pull for the six horses with a coach-load of thirty to forty people, but the trip is made in all too short a time, for the wonders begin as soon as you enter the Park. The sensation-mad world should make this trip. Here is a place to renew your youth and let the lost days catch up with you.

After three days and four nights of continuous travel on a train, you claim the out-of-doors as a natural right. Add to this, wonders, the like of which you have never dreamed, and even the perfectly appointed Mammoth Hotel with a menu comparable with any city cuisine can not long detain you.

It was evening when we arrived. A guide took us out over chalk-white terraces, interspersed with bubbling springs where the water was boiling hot. We saw an effect the cause of which has kept scientists guessing, for no one has been able to say, "I know why this is."

There is a "Bunsen Theory," which many people accept as the scientific cause.[10]

But this does not interfere with the pleasure of every traveler having his own explanation of why the water perpetually boils and leaves great white cliffs as a deposit. He can dilate at length on his reasons for his wise conclusions: there are great strata of lime away down in the earth. Cold water comes in contact with the lime. Anybody who has whitewashed his henhouse knows that if you pour cold water on unslacked lime you will get a boiling substance that looks exactly like that which you see at Mammoth Hot Springs. The outer edge would naturally harden. A great crater would be built up. If the water were abundant, then it would overflow, and terraces would be formed. We were children in the presence of these wonders, and, like the human race in its childhood, we made explanations to suit ourselves.

The Devil's Kitchen

It was an appalling sensation, however, next morning, when we visited the Jupiter Terrace and saw the great mammoth spring. We picked our way cautiously, stepping only where the guide told us it was safe to go, and took no risks with the fascinating beauty in the hundreds of feet depth of that mammoth spring. Down, down as far as the eye could see, were prismatic colors, varying and changing with the light, and shapes and forms of deposits, the most beautiful that could be conceived. The great Artist and Architect of beauty was there and had control, even in these terrifying surroundings.[11]

"Just come this way," said the guide, "and let me show you the Devil's Kitchen."[12] Down, down, down, we climbed, down the rude ladder made of slender spruce-trees that grew close by. Hotter and hotter it became as we descended, and when we reached the very end of the black hole it was hottest.

"What if—" we all began.

And then there started a scramble for the ladder.

Going Down Into the Devil's Kitchen on Terrace Mountain, Yellowstone National Park, U. S. A.

FIGURE 19.2.

These tourists visited Devil's Kitchen cave near Mammoth Hot Springs in about 1906 with their uniformed tour guide (sitting next to the ladder). Our traveler Elbert Hubbard in 1914 likened his experience here to a descent into hell. (Berry, Kelly, and Chadwick stereo, Bob Berry collection, Cody, WY.)

The descent to Avernus was easy,[13] but to come again into the upper air, "that the labor, that the work." [We smelled the rotten egg gas.]

"H_2S_2,"[14] sniffed the university student, learnedly.

"Let's get out of here," said the Fra.

How blue the sky was, how sweet the air when we came from the Stygian Cave.[15]

In and out among these witches' caldrons we carefully picked our way, over the Jupiter Terrace, down to the Angels.

A Genius of Organization

The Yellowstone Park Transportation Company is as well organized as our best railroads. Their schedule does not vary. Their coaches start as promptly as a railroad-train and they arrive as promptly. Their supervision and inspection are complete.

He is a master who has made this organization, who provides the horses, forage, co-operates with the Government, and can so operate the business, for three months, in the Summer, and economically provide for his horses, vehicles and drivers through the Winter, as to make this service possible. This man is a master.

The very nature of the work makes it a miraculous task. It would be easy to provide beautiful, perfect and complete service for twelve months in the year. But the Park is inaccessible to visitors, on account of the snow, except for three Summer months.

If you need mental exercise, or want to solve a hard problem in economics, just figure on Mr. Child's propositions.[16] Also, when you become interested in the problem, work out the modern hotel proposition which Mr. Child has every year. Bring into your equation the reliability, also the unreliability, of human service, even under the best conditions. Take the above-sea-level difficulties—eight thousand feet into the air. Add to your marketing the hauling of all foods from five to sixty miles over mountainous roads, and you will be appreciative of the work that Mr. Child does and does so gracefully.

Very little foodstuff can be raised in the Yellowstone Park district. But all vegetables come on to the table fresh, crisp and inviting.

In the middle of the day the sun is radiantly warm. At night you need steam-heat in your room. The hotels must be cool in the middle of the day, warm night and morning. It costs much to meet these needs. And yet the price for staying at these hotels is very moderate indeed.

In spite of all difficulties, these hotels have the dignity of being self-sustaining. This means that Mr. Child and his assistants are A students in the subject of economics. They are also psychologists, philosophers, and scientific withal.

Earl the Magician

I can not imagine a better driver than the one provided for us. During the hundred and thirty miles we rode with him, he never spoke to his four horses except in kindly tones. He never struck them. His care of them was perfect. He fed them, watered them and cleaned them. His thought for himself was incidental. Besides being a fine driver and teamster; he was a guide and fisherman.

One midday we had a lunch at [a place where a sign read] "Good Camp, Good Water."

Earl hitched his horses in the most comfortable place. Like a magician he was transformed into a fisherman and went out to the Fire-Hole River to get trout for dinner. While we washed our hands, looked up and down at the scenery and wondered about fish, Earl held up a trout. In a minute he had another. In twenty minutes from the time he left us, he returned with four of the most beautiful rainbow-trout anybody ever saw. Who dressed the fish? Earl, of course. Who cooked them? Fifty–fifty. Who ate them? We, Us & Co. And I am glad to say that in the kingdom of our hearts, those who had best served stood highest.

The Land of Surprises

There was no spot along the way that was not interesting. Of course we were looking for wild animals, the unusual and the wonderful, and we saw it.

Some one said, "Now that we have seen deer, I wish that we could see a bear." And, presto, one walked out from the woods, turned, looked at us, and in good bear language said: "Here I am. Have your wish." Three or four more followed.

Then we saw a camp and realized that the bears were there for other than exhibition purposes, for, be it known, that bears' feeding-grounds are around camps, hotels, and in places where human food is discarded. Honey-cans are their delight. Syrup-tins are lapped to the last perfume of sweets. Cake, bread, meat, anything that is left over from your plate, is excellent food for Bruin. So bears are semi-domesticated animals for three months of the year in the Yellowstone.[17]

Mountain-roads are not usually very smooth. The roads in the Yellowstone are remarkably good. But the Government has no easier problem in economics than has Mr. Child. You can not stretch an appropriation.

Although to the layman the amount of money appropriated for our National Parks seems great, yet it is very little for what has to be done in these parks in order that they may be used by the public at all. Those who expend this money have used it to very excellent advantage in building roads, cutting them through solid rock, sprinkling them, building bridges, viaducts and sluiceways. The engineers have done well. There is a natural course marked out for a road by the stream, but to so plan the highways that visitors may see the wonders of the Park most easily and economically is another great problem well solved in the Yellowstone.[18]

"The nation is buying and preserving scenery," said Mr. Daniels, Superintendent of our National Parks and Forests.[19] "We need grandeur of scenery just as much as we need other sources of inspiration. Our National Parks are set aside, preserved, cared for and promoted for the purpose of supplying this need to a nation, and so the engineers laid out the roads to pass just as many inspiring points as possible."

The Norris Geyser [Basin]

As we drove into the Norris Geyser Basin it seemed to us that some one had gathered together a collection of the most interesting natural wonders possible. The whole mountainside, far and near, was smoking and steaming with what looked like the incense of commerce, but we soon found that this activity was from Nature's underworld workshops.

We had seen hot springs, but no geysers until this time. The difference between a hot spring and a geyser is this: A hot spring boils and bubbles only—[it sometimes] is an old geyser. A geyser is a hot spring which at regular or irregular intervals spasmodically throws off water, steam or stones—whatever is in the spring-basin.

The Norris Geyser Basin gave anything that we asked for, and added a baker's dozen for good measure and then more.

We had drunk from the Apollinaris Spring on the way to Norris, a spring that any drugstore in a city could make a fortune out of. Jumbo had climbed the Obsidian Cliff and brought away trophies.

We had seen the Beaver Lake, the beaver-dams, and the Twin Lakes— the one blue, the other green. We had heard the Roaring Mountain at a distance; had seen the Frying-Pan, where the water gurgles, bubbles and boils.

But we were not prepared for the surprises of the Norris Geyser Basin. We reached there just at sunset. We thought Mrs. Cook, the Manager of the Norris Lunch-Station,[20] had turned on the power for our benefit.

The Opal Springs, Iris, Onyx, Arsenic, Primrose, Congress Pool, were all shimmering and glittering in the sun. And look, look! There is a geyser, the first sure-enough one we have seen.

Twenty feet into the air the water shot, and the steam went ten feet higher. For ten seconds this geyser continued, and then it rested. In thirty seconds again the water sparkled and glistened in the sunlight twenty feet above the crater.[21]

The Whirligig

And just beyond there was another where the water swirled round and round—the Whirligig Geyser. Twenty feet high this water was sent, and the steam and drops of water went as far out in every direction.

The great basin was astir with water, steam and that awesome, subterranean noise. What was that perpetual growl?

Was it a den of bears, lions or what?

"After dinner we will go over there."

We were all hungry. Luncheon at the camp had been hours ago, and now dinner was ready.

What a dainty, abundant and delicious dinner it was!

Outside it was weird and wild. Within everything was refined and the food as delicate as you could have in your own home. This was an unexpected combination.

Brook-trout! There was no question about their being fresh.

This dinner gave us unusual courage, and we braved a close inspection of springs, geysers and that horrible noise. Was this the infernal world Virgil and Dante wrote about?[22] The odors from some of the geysers were certainly suggestive of what Dante described.

The pools of boiling water were fascinating to look into.

The Constant and Whirligig Geysers are close together, and the spreading steam made you walk by faith and stick to the boards which marked the safe passage.[23]

On we went into the very presence of this fearful Growler, past the Mud Geyser bubbling and spouting boiling mud, to where a great hole in the hillside was sending out steam and the most horrible growls imaginable.

We came back to the roadway, took a close look into Congress Pool, Primrose Spring, and Nuphar Lake, and then talked it over on the porch awhile, where the stars and the moon calmly shone down on these unique and terrible wonders.

Early the next morning we swished the August frost from the asters and goldenrod and went out into the woods looking for bear for breakfast. We went down into the geyser basin again and then back to Mrs. Cook's superb breakfast.

The Fountain Hotel

It was a pity to leave such delicious food; it was a pity to eat it. However, one delicacy followed another in quick succession on our plates, and then off we started, out for another day of wonders.

The Black Growler growled as we passed him by. The Steam-Valve sizzled and threatened. We looked into the depths of the Emerald Pool and watched the Minute-Man Geyser. The basin was full of surprises that you could not pass by. They demanded attention.

It was almost noon when we reached the Fountain Hotel where Nature has made another collection of wonders. Here are the Mammoth Paint-Pots, a basin forty by sixty feet with a rim on three sides four or five feet in height, ready for the use of Kipling's artist to dip his comet's hair brush, "And splash at a ten-league canvas."[24]

And there is the Silex Pool close by, where he can get any tint he wants.

Picturesque Nomenclature

Many of the springs, geysers and fountains, as well as places throughout the Park, were named by orthodox people who believed that his Satanic Majesty was far superior in strength and power to the God of good. He was also dramatic, alert and active, and so, naturally, the most interesting places were named as being in the dominion of the god of the underworld.

The guide showed us the Devil's Tea-Kettle. It was a big one, boiling and bubbling ready-for use.

Nearby was Buffalo Spring, into which, many years ago, some misguided buffalo walked, and his bones may be seen therein to this very day.[25]

Just beyond was another bottomless pit into which an Indian girl fell and was never seen again.[26]

The Sulphur Spring was bubbling and sending out tragic odors. The Steady Geyser was perpetually throwing boiling water into the air.[27]

Fire-Hole Lake sent the hot water in shallow streams all about us and the horses walked through this unafraid. On we went through creeks of hot water up to the Great Fountain Geyser, which throws boiling water a hundred feet into the air for a half-hour at a time every eight or twelve hours.

It was a place of terrible wonders. No one had time or inclination to think of himself. It was a wonder world, and we were eager for what should come next.

Excelsior

One of the greatest is the geyser known as the Excelsior, formerly known as "Hell's Half-Acre," a great pit in which the water is very much agitated always and covered with thick clouds of steam, but which has not played since Eighteen Hundred Eighty-eight, at which time it was known to have thrown water and masses of rock several hundred feet into the air.[28] As the children say, what goes up must come down, and tons of rock were dropped into the Fire-Hole River several hundred feet away. The Excelsior Geyser is respected profoundly. Nobody knows what it will do next or when it will do it, and even the unwise are not foolhardy near it.

Turquoise Spring, a hundred feet in diameter, has the most exquisite coloring that the earth knows.

Prismatic Lake, two hundred fifty by four hundred feet, has all the colors from deep blue in the center to green and gold at the margins, outside of which there are red deposits which shade into purple, brown and gray, all on a ground of grayish white, which change as the light changes over the opal surface of the pool.

Sapphire Pool is no less beautiful.

Perhaps the most remarkable in its beauty is the Morning-Glory Spring [Pool,] twenty feet in diameter, beautiful as a dream, terrible in its enticing depths.

We were very fortunate in seeing the Artemisia Geyser active. Earl said he had never seen it active but once before, because it is irregular and plays once every twelve to twenty-four hours.[29]

Old Faithful

And now we are fairly into the land of the geysers, and Old Faithful Inn is in sight.

The Old Faithful Inn is surrounded by the most brilliant activities of the entire Park. Beginning with Artemisia there are geysers on every hand.

The natural beauties of Fire-Hole River are enhanced by the Riverside Geyser, and the Giant which throws the water two hundred fifty feet and has a duration of activity of an hour and a half—the most brilliant geyser in the world.

The Oblong is very near to the river's brink. The Witches' Caldron, the Terra Cotta, the Sprinkler, the Lion, the Lioness and the Giantess are close to the water's edge.

The Beehive, the Grand and the Splendid, when active, throw the water two hundred feet. But these large ones are less frequent and sure than many of the smaller ones.

The Old Faithful is perhaps the one most renowned and most loved—if that word can be applied to so terrible a phenomenon as a geyser. Once every hour, varying only by a few minutes, Old Faithful sends a stream of water and steam a hundred and fifty feet high, for four minutes at a time. It is a wonderful spectacle, no matter at what time you see it.

The first night spent at the Old Faithful Inn, if your rooms are, as were ours, where you can see and hear Old Faithful, you awaken in the night and listen for the "sp-sp-bim-bam-fsch."[30] If the moon is shining you look out of the window and enjoy the spectacle of the moonlight on the cascade.

The last morning at the Old Faithful, we arose early. There was a feeling that we were parting from something very dear, and we wanted to see the Geyser in the sunlight once more. We heard her at four o'clock, and now at five the sun would be coming over the mountains and it was time for Old Faithful, so we watched and watched.

True to the minute, as the sun appeared over the mountain, Old Faithful sent up such a glory of crystals of steam and water that it was a salutation to the dawn well worth while waiting for.

Old Faithful Inn

The Old Faithful Inn gets into your heart, too. There is something so big and splendid about the Inn, something so homelike in the care and attention to details which Mrs. Underwood, the manager of the Inn, gives to the entire place, that you regret leaving the great big fireplace, the cozy corners and the sunny dining-room. Most of all, we disliked to say

FIGURE **19.3.**

Old Faithful Inn and its surrounding area have enchanted park visitors since
it was built in 1903–4. This idyllic photo was taken around 1910. Declared our
traveler Elbert Hubbard, "The Old Faithful Inn gets into your heart." (YELL
129062, Yellowstone National Park Archives, Yellowstone National Park.)

good-by to the woman who makes this complete and good time possible for every guest.[31]

We did not forget the bears, either, who have been terrifyingly fascinating. We remembered how their eyes shone like fires away out in the
woods when the searchlight was turned on in the evening. We remembered how we hated to go and yet wanted to see the bears at their evening meal. They stole out of the woods noiselessly. We saw them so
unexpectedly near that we were afraid, and yet did not go away. We
remembered that we had been told never to run from a black bear; that
he could go faster than a horse could gallop; that we must stay and face
him—especially a mother bear. There was a mother bear with her cubs.
She was coming right toward us. Why did we leave the Inn? Why be so
foolish as to throw away our sweet lives for nothing? She was coming
nearer and nearer. Suddenly her baby slid down the long bare length
of the trunk of a spruce-tree and ran to his mother in a very human,
saucy way and tried to grab a morsel she had in her jaws. She stopped

suddenly, chastised him as he deserved, and he ran whimpering into the woods. She followed him of course and consoled him with a part of her supper.[32]

We laughed. It was so human and so a part of natural life that we forgot our fears and the tragedy, and were back to earth.

Good-by, Old Faithful Inn, and good-by, Old Faithful Geyser! Play on every hour and keep watch until we come again for another inspiration!

The Continental Divide

From the Upper Geyser Basin is a stiff climb to the Continental Divide. Up and up we went until the summit was reached—eight thousand five hundred feet above sea-level. Here is Isa Lake, beautiful, cold water, a two-ocean pond. The water on one side runs into the Atlantic and the other into the Pacific.

Earl's skill as a driver was never more shown than in his management of the horses and coach on the narrow, cork-screw road coming down the mountain.

Not the least surprising wonder of the Park is to be found at an altitude of seven thousand seven hundred forty-one feet—Yellowstone Lake, twenty miles across, of irregular shape, of the purest, coldest, clearest water.

You think this is a dream lake or a mirage, until Admiral Dave comes and insists on your having a ride with him across to the Colonial Hotel.[33]

What a ride it was in the clear, cool air, not a cloud in the sky, and our view uninterrupted on every side for many miles around.

They say there is great fishing in this lake, but we could not prove it, because our fisherman was driving the four-in-hand around along the shore to meet us at the Colonial Hotel.

Of course we saw the bears in their feeding-grounds in the woods back of the Colonial Hotel.

Then we heard the stories concerning these particular bears: how one got into the basement of the kitchen where the stores are kept, and pleaded for something extra on account of an accident to one of his paws.

Then we heard how somebody got perilously near a mother bear with twin cubs. Everybody said "run" and did run away, except the particularly brave youth who defied mother love as well as mother wrath, stood his ground, and found that Old Cinnamon did not consider him worth noticing after all.

The Upper Falls

Now the hills are growing larger on each side of the river. They are almost mountains. Here and there are wooded plateaus—great feeding-grounds for elk and deer. Those fields at the left must be the feeding-grounds for those thirty-five thousand elk which they say remain there throughout the Winter. Perhaps, too, they cross the river and eat the grass on those broad meadows on the opposite side from us.

The banks of the river are growing awesomely high. All along the sides are the wonderful colorings of which we have been told—yellow, red, pink, blue—rainbow colors. The river is now far below us. The road is narrow and hewn out of the mountainside.

We stop for a view of the Upper Falls, where the Yellowstone River falls precipitously one hundred twelve feet.[34]

"Oh, this is nothing!" said Earl. "Wait until you see the big falls."

It has been quite a long journey after all, even for us. We wonder how the once joyous pedestrians are getting along! Do their feet still continue to feel like wings? Is Mercury still vying with Mercury in speed and lightness of motion? We will see! We will see!

The Marvelous Canyon Hotel

Is it possible that that wonderful building in the distance, colored like the walls of the canyon, and seemingly of the same size—is it possible that that is the Canyon Hotel? Here in the mountains, a hotel of five hundred rooms, spacious and generous beyond the dream of any city hotel!

Was ever breakfast so good as the one which we had there at nine o'clock! How beautiful and refined was the polished natural wood of the dining-room, reception-room and assembly-room. What a harmony in form and color! It was all in perfect taste with the magnificent natural surroundings.

Then we stood at the rotunda of the staircase looking into and down upon the largest Lounge-Room in any hotel in the world.

What an auditorium! What a community Reception-Room, where families might find their cozy comers—as large or as small as they wished! "How many acres?" inquired an irrelevant one. "But it can not be measured in feet!" she insisted.

And it can not.

"The room cost a million dollars," persisted the young enthusiast. "Look at those rugs! Beautiful as the weavers' craft can body forth an artist's dream! See the hangings, pictures, chairs and lounges! Everything luxurious, rich, magnificent, and yet simple and beautiful!"[35]

"How about the Turquoise Spring, Fire-Hole River, the Giant Geyser at work!" I asked.

"This room is just as wonderful, just as unique, just as well worth seeing as any other wonder we have seen in the Park," was the warm rejoinder.

And all the young lady said is true. This great room alone is worth making the trip to the Yellowstone to see.

The Eagle's Aerie

We went out to look at the Great Falls, down what seemed like a thousand steps, and stood on a platform, which made us a very part of the canyon.

The awful splendor is indescribable.

The Yellowstone River falls precipitously here three hundred sixty feet.[36] As the sun shines down into the spray of beaten water a rainbow is formed—that promise of peace even in this tempestuous activity.

We climbed back, and then went on to Inspiration Point, where a cliff juts out from which you look down into an abysm a quarter of a mile below. It was so tremendous a sensation that the light of reason was put out. The brain would not work. It was terrifying—awful. We tried to think, but the only ideas that would formulate were, "What if—." The animal instinct to fly from danger was getting possession of us, when we were made sane by that cry, common to all kingdoms in life, wherever there is life—the cry of hunger from the young and the answer of the mother. This time it was three little eagles telling their mother that they were hungry. They wanted their dinner.

"Mother, mother, we are awfully hungry. Can't you hurry along with that fish?"

There they were, two hundred feet below us, on the top of a precipitous tower rock, standing carelessly on the edge of the eagle's nest. There was nothing to break a fall for several hundred feet down.

Still they cried. They were soon answered by their economically independent mother, who was a thousand feet below them getting dinner for the family. She came back and told them they must be patient—she would be there soon, but dinner was not yet quite ready.

We watched her wheel away, down, down, to the very surface of the Yellowstone River. Would she have good luck fishing? Was her bait all right?

All personal fear was forgotten. We were just interested in bird economics.

"By the way, where are we?" we said.

"In the Canyon of the Yellowstone."

"Yes, but where is the Yellowstone Park?"

It was once a part of the Territory of Wyoming—the Territory dear to the heart of every Woman who is working for the practical development of woman, and through her, the human race. [Several paragraphs of irrelevant material omitted here.]

Mount Washburn

From the Grand Canyon of the Yellowstone to Mount Washburn is a drive of ten miles.

Evidently the Government has employed the best engineers in laying out that road, and intelligent supervision has been given its construction and maintenance.

It is an exhilarating experience to drive to an altitude of over ten thousand feet above sea-level.[37] It is not quite so interesting to walk it, although you must walk as well as ride in order to get the greatest possible benefit, for the air is crisp and light, and the walk uphill keeps the blood circulating.

From the tip top of Mount Washburn you can see the world in much of its glory. It is an entrancing view. You are in love with living. You want to do more of it. You plan to do big things when you get down into the world again.

It was a long, happy day of scenery, unlike anything we had ever before seen. We were alert from choice. We did not wish to miss anything, and there was something new constantly—buffalo ranging over the hills; elk, deer, antelope may cross the road at any moment.

Everywhere the signs of intelligence in the care for the safety of the Nation's guests; everywhere beautiful service; everywhere the natural wildness of hundreds of thousands of years ago—history everywhere.

The Fort

What are the red roofs and gray stones in the distance?

Yes, those are the Fort buildings, Colonel Brett's Headquarters, from where he goes to every portion of the Park in his careful supervision.[38]

We just met the forage-master and were saluted by him. We return the salute with gratitude for the order, system and organization of which he is a part.

And that is the brilliantly colored Jupiter Terrace. At the right is the Minerva. And the beautiful coloring is surely the Angel Terrace.

How long it seems since we first saw these wonders! We have lived so much since we left here that the days seem years.

The horses start up without being asked as they approach the Mammoth Hotel. There are the same kindly friends to welcome us back who bade us good-by and a beautiful journey when we left. We are given a suite of rooms with every comfort that we could have in our own home—light, warmth, a refreshing bath, a little sleep, and then the dining-room.

Being Born Again

Is it possible we have gone all those miles in these strange and wonder-ful surroundings, alert every instant of the time, and feel refreshed, sunburned and joyous? It is not only possible but true. We have had a marvelous vacation—unique in a lifetime's journey. Senses have been exercised to their limit and the brain has not been idle. We are refreshed, invigorated, alert, alive, relaxed, but ready for work.

What a trip it is! Why have we never known about it before? Why did not some one tell us that the Yellowstone Park was the place for us?

What hospitality everybody in the Park shows!

We leave deeply regretting that it is the journey's end instead of the journey's beginning.

The trip home is a mere pastime. Our friends—how charming, how dear, how thoughtful and appreciative they are! Our capacity for appreciation has been enlarged. So has our sense of beauty and grandeur. We are greater people than when we went away.

And we resolve that the next time we find ourselves growing weary and need inspiration we will take another trip to THE YELLOWSTONE.

Notes

This piece was originally published as a pamphlet in 1915 by the Roycrofters, East Aurora, NY.

1. Felix Shay, *Elbert Hubbard of East Aurora* (New York: Wm. H. Wise and Co., 1926), 27.
2. Shay, *Elbert Hubbard of East Aurora*, 490.
3. *Dictionary of American Biography* (New York: Charles Scribner's Sons, 1927–36), IX, 323–24; *Who Was Who in America* (Chicago: Marquis, 1943), I, 600; "Elbert Hubbard Aboard," *New York Times*, May 8, 1915, 5.
4. Shay, *Elbert Hubbard of East Aurora*, 488.
5. Shay, *Elbert Hubbard of East Aurora*, 488.
6. Though Alice Hubbard is listed as coauthor of the pamphlet, her voice seems to be largely in the background.
7. These three states were mere territories at the time Yellowstone became a national park. Montana became a state in 1889, while Wyoming and Idaho gained that status in 1890.
8. The Organic Act of 1872 established Yellowstone as a national park.
9. This feature was known then and now as Eagle Nest Rock. Generally it has been occupied by ospreys, but we cannot say that it was *never* occupied by eagles. Lee Whittlesey, *Yellowstone Place Names* (Gardiner, MT: Wonderland Publishing Company, 2006), 94.
10. The main point of Bunsen's theory was that an eruption takes place when the water in the tube reaches the boiling point, and to account for it,

> he supposes that the column in the central tube communicates by a long and sinuous channel with some space, be it what it may, which is subjected to the action of the direct source of subterranean heat. The temperature gets raised above the boiling point, due to the pressure, and a sudden generation of steam is the result. This steam rises in the column of water, which, being cooler, causes it to condense. Gradually the heat of the water is raised until the water of the channel must boil, and the steam therefore cannot condense, but must accumulate and acquire a

gradually increasing tension. The condensation of the bubbles possesses a periodic character, and to this is due the uplifting of the water in what Bunsen calls conical water hills, which are accompanied by the subterranean explosions. (Luella Agnes Owen, *Cave Regions of the Ozarks and Black Hills*, Project Guttenberg e-book [originally published by the Editor Publishing Company, 1898].)

11. From his description, this seems to have been a deep pool rather than a terrace. It was probably either Blue Spring or Main Spring(s). Lee Whittlesey, *Wonderland Nomenclature*, 1988, unpublished manuscript, Yellowstone National Park Library, Yellowstone National Park, 162, 1027.

12. Devil's Kitchen was a cave that in Hubbard's day was open to the public. Whittlesey, *Yellowstone Place Names*, 88.

13. Hubbard was speaking figuratively and symbolically. Lake Avernus is located in southern Italy near Naples and occupies the crater of an extinct volcano. The sulfurous and mephitic vapors that rose from it in ancient times were believed to have killed the birds that flew over it. Because of the forbidding appearance of the lake, ancient Greek and Roman writers believed it to be the entrance to Hades.

14. H_2S is hydrogen sulfide. It is the chemical in Yellowstone hot springs that causes the characteristic "rotten egg" smell.

15. Again Hubbard was speaking symbolically, for they were coming out of the Devil's Kitchen cave. *Stygian* is a word that means gloomy and dark, infernal, hellish, or relating to the river Styx. In John Milton's *L'Allegro* (1633) he wrote: "In Stygian cave forlorn 'Mongst horrid shapes, and shrieks, and sights unholy, Find out some uncouth cell, Where brooding Darkness spreads his jealous wings." While an actual feature known as the Stygian Caves is located in the Mammoth Terraces west of Devil's Kitchen (it has partially caved in and is no longer marked on tourist maps), this was not where Hubbard and his party went. Perhaps G. L. Henderson, who named Stygian Caves in the early 1880s, was familiar with the Milton account quoted here. Whittlesey, *Yellowstone Place Names*, 240–41.

16. Harry Child came to Yellowstone in 1892 to run the company and became part owner of the Yellowstone Park Transportation Company in 1898. By 1912 he also owned the Yellowstone Park Hotel Company and the Yellowstone Park Boat Company. See, generally, Mark Barringer, *Selling Yellowstone: Capitalism and the Construction of Nature* (Lawrence: University Press of Kansas, 2002).

17. For the bears' feeding grounds at Old Faithful, see Lee Whittlesey, "A History of the Old Faithful Area with Chronology, Maps, and Executive Summary," September 14, 2006, manuscript prepared for the National Park Service, Yellowstone National Park Library, Yellowstone National Park, 78–81.

18. The road system in Yellowstone is best discussed in Mary Shivers Culpin, *The History of the Construction of the Road System in Yellowstone National Park, 1872–1966* (no place [Denver]: National Park Service, Rocky Mountain Regional Office, 1994).

19. Mark Daniels was a landscape architect schooled at the University of California at Berkeley. In 1914, he received an appointment as landscape engineer in Yosemite National Park and immediately got the attention of the secretary of the interior, Franklin K. Lane. It is fascinating that Hubbard knew of his activities, for at the time this piece was published, the National Park Service (1916) did not exist. Daniels later was promoted to general superintendent and landscape engineer for the entire National Park Service. See Western Neighborhoods Project, www.outsidelands.org/index.php.

20. This was Mrs. Hart N. Cook, who worked at Norris in 1911 and again in 1914–15. See Lee Whittlesey, "A Post-1872 History of the Norris Area: Cultural Sites Past and Present," September 30, 2005, unpublished manuscript, Yellowstone National Park Library, Yellowstone National Park, 24n68, citing Hart N. Cook and Beth Cook, *My Mother the Chef: A Family History of Early Yosemite and Yellowstone National Parks* (Sacramento: LaserType and Graphics Company, n.d. [1990]).

21. This was probably Constant Geyser, a geyser that erupted very often. In 1914, it erupted fifteen to thirty-five feet high for five- to fifteen-second durations at intervals of twenty to fifty-five seconds. Whittlesey, *Wonderland Nomenclature*, 325, citing Edward Frank Allen.

22. Dante Alighieri composed poetry influenced by classical and Christian tradition. Dante's greatest work was the epic poem *The Divine Comedy*. It includes three sections: the Inferno (Hell), in which the classical poet Virgil leads Dante on a trip through hell; the Purgatorio (Purgatory), in which Virgil leads Dante up the mountain of purification; and the Paradiso (Paradise), in which Dante travels through heaven.

23. "Boards" here referred to planks that were laid down for safety and convenience of walking at Norris as early as 1905.

24. Hubbard here quoted Rudyard Kipling's *The End of the Whole Matter*:

> And those that are good shall be happy. They shall sit in a
>   golden chair,
> And splash at a ten-league canvas, with brushes of comet's
>   hair;
> They shall have real saints to draw from—Silas and Peter
>   and Paul;
> They shall work for a year at a sitting and never get tired at
>   all. (*Talent [OR] News*, September 15, 1893.)

25. Buffalo Spring and Buffalo Pool are hot springs at Lower Geyser Basin (Hubbard could have visited either one), while the "Devil's Tea Kettle" was

an unknown feature there. Whittlesey, *Wonderland Nomenclature*, 193, 196, and the obsolete names section.

26. This story, of doubtful authenticity, sounds like one that had been recently published in Robert Schauffler, *Romantic America* (New York: Century Company, 1913).

27. His "Sulphur Spring" is unknown today, while Steady Geyser is at Hot Lake in Lower Geyser Basin.

28. Excelsior Geyser is known to have erupted in 1881, 1882, 1888, 1890, 1891, and possibly 1901. See generally, Lee Whittlesey, "Monarch of All These Mighty Wonders: Tourists and Yellowstone's Excelsior Geyser, 1881–1890," *Montana Magazine of Western History* 40 (Spring 1990): 2–15.

29. Turquoise and (Grand) Prismatic springs are at Midway Geyser Basin, while Sapphire Pool and Morning Glory Pool are both five miles farther south at Upper Geyser Basin. See Whittlesey, *Yellowstone Place Names*, Turquoise Spring, Grand Prismatic Spring, Sapphire Pool, and Morning Glory Pool entries.

30. This seems to be one of the only instances in Yellowstone's vast literature where a writer attempted to articulate and then write down the sound that Old Faithful Geyser made.

31. For more on the Old Faithful Inn, see, generally, Karen Reinhart and Jeff Henry, *Old Faithful Inn: Crown Jewel of National Park Lodges* (Emigrant, MT: Roche Jaune, 2004).

32. The bear feeding area at Old Faithful is discussed in Whittlesey, "A History of the Old Faithful Area," 78–81. For bears generally, see Paul Schullery, *The Bears of Yellowstone* (Worland, WY: High Plains Publishing Company, Inc., 1992); and Alice Wondrak-Biel, *Do (Not) Feed the Bears: The Fitful History of Wildlife and Tourists in Yellowstone* (Lawrence: University of Kansas Press, 2006).

33. The Yellowstone Park Boat Company operated a ferry that could transport guests from the dock at West Thumb to the Colonial Hotel (Lake Hotel). It was not part of the regular stagecoach transportation service and required an additional charge to its patrons. Yellowstone boating expert Leslie Quinn explains that the *Zillah* steamship never ran after 1907 and that in the summer of 1914, the boats that were running on Yellowstone Lake were the *Jean D*, the *Busha*, the *Etcedecasha*, the *Ocotta*, and several eighteen-foot or smaller boats. One of these boats was the one in which Hubbard and his party rode. Leslie Quinn, Old Faithful, conversation with the editors, October 5, 2006.

34. Upper Falls is currently listed as 109 feet in height.

35. The Canyon Hotel opened in June 1911 at a cost of over $750,000. The lounge measured about one hundred feet by two hundred feet in size. The perimeter of the building itself was commonly reported to be a mile around. Tamsen Emerson Hert, "Luxury in the Wilderness: Yellowstone's Grand Canyon Hotel, 1911–1960," *Yellowstone Science* 13 (Summer 2005): 21–35.

36. The Lower Falls, earlier known as the "Great Falls," has a height of 308 feet.

37. The actual elevation of Mount Washburn is 10,243 feet.

38. Col. L. M. Brett was the acting superintendent of Yellowstone from 1910 to 1916. The U.S. Army had been in charge of the protection and administration of the park since 1886. Fort Yellowstone was established in 1891, and the sandstone fort buildings with the distinctive red roofs were built between 1891 and 1913. See, generally, H. Duane Hampton, *How the U.S. Cavalry Saved Our National Parks* (Bloomington: Indiana University Press, 1971).

INDEX

Page numbers in italic text indicate illustrations.

Absaroka Range, 272
Admiral Dave (boat captain), 317
Alaska, 93, 127
Albemarle Hotel, 125
Alder Gulch, Montana, 10
Allegheny County Light Company, 217
All-Story Magazine, 239
Alpine Club, 90
Alta Mining Company, 60
Alton, Illinois, 183
Alum Bay (England), 89
Alum Creek, 25, 285
American Institute of Banking, 293, 301
American West: taming of, 251
Amherst College, 265
Anderson, George S., 171
Anderson, Mr., 55
Anderson, Ole, 290
Angel Terrace, 200, 202, 245, 280, 321
Anthony, Susan B., 266
Antiquary, The (magazine), 105
Apollinaris Spring, 187, 202, 222, 237, 285, 311
"Apollinaris Spring" (Soda Spring?), 86
Arsenic Geyser, 312
Artemisia Geyser, 145, 314, 315
Arthur, Chester A. (President), 90, 93, 94
Artist Point: painting misnomer, 155
Artists' Paintpots, 136, 237
Aspen Dormitory, 196
Asphing, Charles, 9, 21
Associated Charities of Pittsburgh, 217
Atlantic Monthly (magazine), 249
Atlantic Ocean, 208, 229, 283, 297, 317
Atlantic Tube Company, 217
Atomizer Geyser, 145
Atwood, John Harrison, 198, 199, 209, 212; account by, 198–216
Atwood, Mrs. John Harrison, 201

"Baby Geyser." *See* Steamboat Geyser
Bach, E. W. (Yellowstone Park Transportation Company Secretary), 242, 244
"Bad Lands" (Dakota), 277
Barnum, Phineas T., 266
Baronett, C. J. "Yellowstone Jack," 61, 67, 75
Bath Lake, 131
"Bathtub, The" (Vault Geyser), 19
Battle Creek, Michigan, 292
Beaver Canyon, Idaho, 157, 159, 165
Beaver Lake, 85, 134, 222, 280, 311
Beehive Geyser, 19, 22, 49, 50, 69, 86, 88, 119, 143, 144, 206, 207, 254, 259, 315
Beggruen, Dr. Oskar, 91
Belknap, General W. W., 43, 65
Beryl Spring, 262
Big Horn Mountains (Wyoming), 42, 66
Birdseye, Mrs., 9, 22
Bitterroot Range (Montana and Idaho), 231
Black Boiler Spring, 255
Blackfoot City, Montana, 9, 22
"Black Geyser." *See* Black Growler Steam Vent
Black Growler Steam Vent, 122, 189, 203, 224, 312, 313
Bloomington, Illinois, 303
Blue Glass Spring, 255
Blue Spring(s), 323
Boiling River, 95, 112, 263
Boston, Massachusetts, 83, 265
Boulder, Montana, 60, 65
Boyd, John, 65
Bozeman, Montana, 63, 104, 147
Brett, Col. Lloyd M., 321, 326
Bridge Bay, 4
Bridger, Jim, 196, 285
Brittanic, 94
Brooklyn Daily Eagle (newspaper), 98, 121, 249, *250*

327

Brown Sponge Spring, 255
Bryan, William Jennings, 198
Bucephalus (mining claim), 10
Buffalo, New York, 209, 303
Buffalo Pool, 324
Buffalo Spring, 285, 313, 324
Bunker Hill, 206
Bunsen, Mount. *See* Bunsen Peak
Bunsen Peak, 139, 171, 221
Bunsen, Prof. Robert, 145
"Bunsen's theory" (of geysers), 307, 322
Burdet, Bob, 154

Calfee, Henry Bird (photographer), 61, 71
California, 124, 127, 131, 134, 148, 150
Camp Baker, 22
Camp Ellis (Montana), 63
Canada, 106
Canyon (park location), 4
Canyon Hotel, 2, 148, 154, 173, 180, 193, 195,
    236, 278, 318, 325; concession horseback
    operation, 155
Canyon Lodge, 4
Carlin Relief Expedition, 231, 233
Cascade Creek, 25, 29, 43, 88
Castle Geyser, 17, 19, 21, 48, 69, 86, 88, 119,
    140, 142, 143, 145, 207, 228, 254, 270
"Chemical Basin," 118
Cheyenne, Wyoming, 170
Chicago, Burlington, and Quincy
    Railroad, 4
Chicago, Illinois, 22, 82, 127, 143, 147, 167,
    168, 170, 173, 174, 209, 265
Chicago Evening Journal (newspaper), 1
Child, Harry, 244, 309, 310, 323
Chimney Butte (North Dakota), 236
Chinaman Spring, 110, 111, 144, 145
Chinese Spring, 111
Chittenden, Hiram M., 196, 271, 275
"Chrome Spring," 245
Churchman's Schilling Magazine, 105
Cincinnati, Ohio, 127
Cinnabar, Montana, 2, 106, 107, 110, 121,
    127, 128, 129, 171, 184, 195, 199, 213, 219,
    220, 236, 241, 242
Cinnabar Mountain (Montana), 128, 254
Civil War, 124, 156, 303
Claggett, Horace, 63
Clark, Capt. William, 90
Clark, Mary, 9, 22
Clearwater River (Idaho), 231, 232
"Cleopatra's Bowl," 130, 215
Cleopatra Terrace, 130, 245
Cliff Geyser, 145
Cliff Lake, 158
Cody Road to Yellowstone Park, The (book), 4
"Colonial Hotel." *See* Lake Hotel
Colorado, 267

Colorado River, 129, 252, 260
Colorado Springs, Colorado, 170
Colter, John, 153
Columbia River, 42, 117, 207, 283
Comet Geyser, 119, 145
Coming Empire, The (book), 114
Concord, New Hampshire, 185
Concord stagecoaches, 171, 184, 185, 187,
    196, 199, 201, 298
Conger, Patrick, 122
Congregationalist and Christian World
    (magazine), 266
Congress Pool, 188, 189, 196, 312
Connecticut River, 206
Constant Geyser, 117, 122, 135, 189, 203,
    214, 312, 324
Continental Divide, 317
Cook, Mrs. Hart N., 311, 313, 324
Cook County (Illinois), 170
Cooke City, Montana, 289
Crater Hills, 25
Crawford, Bertha, 303
Crested Pool, 153, 160, 167
Crissman, Joshua (photographer), 37
Crosby, Schuyler (governor), 90
"Cub(s)" Geysers, 69, 144
"Cupid's Cave." *See* Cupid Spring
Cupid Spring, 130, 136
Custer Trail Ranch, 219

Daily Oregonian (newspaper), 1
Daisy Geyser, 295
Dale, Stephen M., 276, 281; account by,
    276–91
Daniels, Mark, 311, 324
Dayton Spice Mills Company, 246
"Deafy" (stagecoach driver), 285, 289
Deem, Adam, 132, 133
Deer Lodge, Montana, 7, 8, 9, 10, 63, 64
De Lacy, Walter W., 106, 112, 263
DeLacy Creek, 263
Delaware, 129
Democratic Party, 198
"Dental Cup, The" (Sponge Geyser), 19
Department of the Interior, 9
Depew, Chauncey, 203
Deseret Evening News (newspaper), 1
Detroit, Michigan, 209
"Devil's Bathtub" (Bathtub Spring), 286
"Devil's Den" (Dragon's Mouth Spring), 44
Devil's Elbow, 245
"Devil's Frying Pan." *See* Frying Pan
    Spring
"Devil's Half Acre." *See* Midway Geyser
    Basin
"Devil's Inkpot." *See* Inkpot Spring
Devil's Kitchen (cave), 131, 200, 255, 286,
    307, 308, 323; ladder into (1884), 152